Advertising on Google: The High Performance Cookbook

Over 120 practical recipes to set up, optimize, and manage profitable AdWords campaigns

Kristina Cutura

[PACKT] PUBLISHING enterprise
professional expertise distilled

BIRMINGHAM - MUMBAI

Advertising on Google: The High Performance Cookbook

First published: June 2013

Production Reference: 1180613

Published by Packt Publishing Ltd.
Livery Place
35 Livery Street
Birmingham B3 2PB, UK.

ISBN 978-1-84968-584-9

www.packtpub.com

Cover Image by Suresh Mogre (suresh.mogre.99@gmail.com)

Credits

Author
Kristina Cutura

Reviewers
Ajay Anand
Ivan Beemster

Acquisition Editor
Kunal Parikh

Lead Technical Editor
Mayur Hule

Technical Editors
Vrinda Nitesh Bhosale
Hardik B. Soni

Project Coordinator
Arshad Sopariwala

Proofreaders
Lawrence A. Herman
Joel T. Johnson

Indexer
Monica Ajmera Mehta

Graphics
Abhinash Sahu

Production Coordinator
Nilesh R. Mohite

Cover Work
Nilesh R. Mohite

About the Author

Kristina Cutura is a pioneer of Google AdWords and currently the owner and founder of a search marketing consulting firm. Starting as a Google employee in 2002, she was one of the founding members of the company's AdWords optimization team, where she developed and tested optimization strategies that are still widely used in the industry. Kristina also created and delivered all optimization-related trainings for internal Google employees, external clients, and agencies that manage AdWords accounts. During her tenure, she trained hundreds of Google employees and dozens of AdWords resellers, and developed online training resources. In addition to running training programs, she managed and optimized Google's highest revenue clients.

After leaving Google in 2009, Kristina started her own consulting company, `KristinaCutura.com`, where she is using the skills she acquired at Google to advise a variety of clients on search engine marketing efforts. Kristina has worked with national and global businesses in a variety of industries and sectors, ranging from multi-million dollar corporations to small, family-owned businesses. In her free time, Kristina enjoys taking walks with her dog Lola and exploring the culinary offerings of San Francisco, where she lives. Kristina holds a BA from UCLA, and shares Google AdWords tips and strategies on her blog, `http://kristinacutura.com/blog/`.

A special thank you to my clients and businesses, who I have been privileged to work with. My knowledge and the material in this book have evolved from these relationships, and the journeys we've been on together, to address their unique business needs.

This book would never have come to fruition without my editors and the publishing team. I am grateful to them for keeping me motivated, organized, and on schedule.

I would like thank my family, especially my sister Jozefina and my mother Liliana. Big thank you to Brian for his love and support. Last but not least, my assistant puppy Lola, who mostly slept on the job near my desk.

About the Reviewers

Ajay Anand is Chief Manager, Online Marketing at Times Internet Limited, India's largest Internet network. Prior to this, he was the Head of search marketing with Web 18.

He is a Google AdWords and Google Analytics Certified Professional with over 9 years of experience in Internet marketing with proficiency in Search Engine Marketing. He has been responsible for search marketing of projects, with The Times of India, The Economic Times, `In.com`, `MoneyControl.com`, `Gaana.com`, `Zigwheels.com`, `Ibnlive.com`, Barclays, Taj Hotels, Kotak Securities, New York Life Insurance, Bharti-Axa Life Insurance, and more. Ajay also has experience in other facets of online marketing such as Web Analytics, Social Media Marketing, Media Buying, and Affiliate Marketing.

Ivan Beemster (born in 1986) studied Business Administration and Philosophy – graduating in the former, still thinking about the latter. For three years, until 2012, Ivan worked for the founders of Dutch design, Droog, in Amsterdam, the Netherlands. At this creative pressure cooker, he looked after online marketing, e-commerce, wholesale distribution, and replacing light bulbs, among other things. In 2012, Ivan founded LijnDiensten (`www.lijndiensten.com`), a one-man band helping SMEs to get their online marketing up to speed.

Previously, Ivan co-authored the book *Strategy at Every Corner! Inspiration for a New Breed of Strategists, Synspire Publishing*.

> If I am to thank anyone, it's Kristina Cutura and Packt Publishing, for having me on this book.

Table of Contents

Preface

AdWords is Google's online advertising product, allowing you to show your ads on search engines and other relevant websites, tablets, and mobile devices. It is a highly effective, accountable, and targeted method of connecting with customers, providing reach at the exact moment of relevance as people are searching for you.

Consumers are spending more time online, especially with the evolution of smartphones, and digital ad revenues have continued to grow at a rapid pace. Increasingly, there has been a need for businesses to have a solid online presence and engage with customers as they move through the research and purchase funnel. Google AdWords helps bridge this gap and build relationships with customers, helping companies create awareness and drive direct sales through the online marketing channel.

Although advertisers can start showing ads through AdWords in minutes, correct setup can help you avoid blowing through your budget without getting the desired results. The proper research, campaign planning, and ongoing management will help you get the most out of your investment, while understanding the available features will enable you to navigate the complexity of AdWords and make it profitable.

What this book covers

Chapter 1, Researching the Market and Competition and Setting Goals, will help you with the basic research you should conduct as you consider advertising with AdWords.

Chapter 2, Setting up Your Account, will help create an AdWords account shell and customizing the various key settings for easier management and navigation.

Chapter 3, Tracking beyond the Click, will cover setting up AdWords conversion tracking and analyzing relevant data in Google Analytics.

Chapter 4, Structuring Your Account, will help you choose where to show your ads and how to target campaigns, including common ways to structure an account.

Chapter 5, Creating Relevant Keywords, will cover choosing keywords relevant to your business, using keyword matching options effectively, and taking advantage of available tools.

Chapter 6, Writing Compelling Ads, will provide tips for researching competitors' ads, writing effective ad text, and testing ad copy elements.

Chapter 7, Budgets and Bidding, will help in setting budgets and bids and adjusting them based on your goals and performance.

Chapter 8, Running Display Ads, will cover various options for setting up display campaigns and how they are presented, as well as features that can help you optimize and improved target display ads.

Chapter 9, Remarketing to Past Visitors, will help in reconnecting with users who previously visited your website as they go on to browse the Display network.

Chapter 10, Reporting and Analysis, will help you in analyzing ad performance, including when and where your clicks are coming from, and other useful reports.

Chapter 11, Optimizing Performance, will provide tips on improving relevance, Quality Scores, and ROI.

Chapter 12, Advanced Strategies and Features, will help in implementing advanced ad formats, experiments, and automation to boost performance.

Chapter 13, Managing AdWords, covers troubleshooting ad issues, reviewing past changes, creating alerts, and using AdWords Editor to streamline account management.

What you need for this book

AdWords is an online interface and requires a computer, an Internet connection, and a browser. You'll also need to download AdWords Editor, Google's free application that helps you manage and update your account offline.

Who this book is for

This book is for AdWords novices who are looking to get started with AdWords as well existing advertisers who need to optimize their campaigns and learn about advanced AdWords features and strategies.

Conventions

In this book, you will find a number of styles of text that distinguish between different kinds of information. Here are some examples of these styles, and an explanation of their meaning.

Code words in text, database table names, folder names, filenames, file extensions, pathnames, dummy URLs, user input, and Twitter handles are shown as follows: "In the following example, we searched Google for `PPC ads` to figure out what websites are coming up in both organic and paid listings."

New terms and **important words** are shown in bold. Words that you see on the screen, in menus or dialog boxes for example, appear in the text like this: "Go to the **Tools and Analysis** tab, and click on **Google Analytics**."

> Warnings or important notes appear in a box like this.

> Tips and tricks appear like this.

Reader feedback

Feedback from our readers is always welcome. Let us know what you think about this book—what you liked or may have disliked. Reader feedback is important for us to develop titles that you really get the most out of.

To send us general feedback, simply send an e-mail to `feedback@packtpub.com`, and mention the book title via the subject of your message.

If there is a topic that you have expertise in and you are interested in either writing or contributing to a book, see our author guide on `www.packtpub.com/authors`.

Customer support

Now that you are the proud owner of a Packt book, we have a number of things to help you to get the most from your purchase.

Errata

Although we have taken every care to ensure the accuracy of our content, mistakes do happen. If you find a mistake in one of our books—maybe a mistake in the text or the code—we would be grateful if you would report this to us. By doing so, you can save other readers from frustration and help us improve subsequent versions of this book. If you find any errata, please report them by visiting `http://www.packtpub.com/submit-errata`, selecting your book, clicking on the **errata submission form** link, and entering the details of your errata. Once your errata are verified, your submission will be accepted and the errata will be uploaded on our website, or added to any list of existing errata, under the Errata section of that title. Any existing errata can be viewed by selecting your title from `http://www.packtpub.com/support`.

Piracy

Piracy of copyright material on the Internet is an ongoing problem across all media. At Packt, we take the protection of our copyright and licenses very seriously. If you come across any illegal copies of our works, in any form, on the Internet, please provide us with the location address or website name immediately so that we can pursue a remedy.

Please contact us at `copyright@packtpub.com` with a link to the suspected pirated material.

We appreciate your help in protecting our authors, and our ability to bring you valuable content.

Questions

You can contact us at `questions@packtpub.com` if you are having a problem with any aspect of the book, and we will do our best to address it.

1

Researching the Market and Competition and Setting Goals

In this chapter, we will cover the following:

- Focusing on relevance
- Identifying your competitors using Google search results
- Using third-party tools to research competitors
- Analyzing budgets and bids to determine market saturation
- Setting advertising goals
- Predicting if AdWords will be profitable and calculating potential returns

Introduction

This chapter covers the basic research we should conduct as we consider advertising with **AdWords**. Before we start competing in an online ad auction, we need to understand how saturated the market is and what our competition is doing in the online ad space. The first recipe explains how to identify our **pay-per-click** (**PPC**) competitors, while the next two recipes will help us analyze how much our competition is spending on AdWords. The final recipes will guide us on how to use this competitive information to set our own spend-and-bid goals and then calculate the potential return.

Focusing on relevance

AdWords is all about relevance and ensuring that Google users see quality ads, which directly relate to what the people are searching for. The system was designed to reward advertisers who create quality campaigns and is monitored through key metrics called **Quality Score** and **clickthrough-rate** (**CTR**). Focusing on relevance will help you pay less and achieve better profits from your ad efforts.

Getting ready

Keep in mind the following basic terms and concepts discussed in this book:

- **Keywords**: These are words or phrases describing your products or services that you can choose to help you to determine when and where your ad can appear
- **Impressions**: These are counted each time your ad is shown
- **Clicks**: This is when someone clicks on your ad
- **Cost-per-click** (**CPC**): This is the cost for each click on your ad
- **Pay-per-click** (**PPC**): This is an online advertising model in which advertisers pay for clicks accrued

How to do it...

As you create your campaigns and plan AdWords strategies, focus on relevance by:

1. **Achieving a high CTR**: The general rule of thumb is to aim for a CTR of 1 percent and above, though CTR varies widely by industry and the type of keywords.
2. **Keeping healthy Quality Scores**: Once you create your AdWords account and start running campaigns, you'll be able to see your Quality Scores at the keyword level. Choose keywords that are relevant and have good Quality Scores and then refine those that do not.

How it works...

Clickthrough-rate (CTR) is the number of clicks divided by the number of impressions.

CTR (expressed as %) = Clicks / Impressions

Each of your ads and keywords have their own CTRs, indicating how compelling users are finding your ads and keywords. CTR helps you gauge the success of your marketing efforts and it factors into Quality Score.

Quality Score is a measure of how relevant your keywords are to your ads and to your landing pages. It is calculated at the keyword level every time someone does a search for one of your keywords, and ranges from 1 (lowest) to 10 (highest). Quality Score affects your ad position as well as how much you'll pay for clicks. Advertisers with higher Quality Scores are rewarded with lower CPCs and better ad positions.

See also

- The *Improving relevance and Quality Score* recipe in *Chapter 11, Optimizing Performance*

Identifying your competitors using Google search results

Advertisers considering PPC ads need to understand which similar websites and businesses are already using AdWords, and also how they are positioning themselves in the online search market. This competitive information can be used to research keywords, which the competition is taking advantage of and identify our own unique advantages.

Getting ready

You likely already have a list of businesses that you consider your key competitors in a particular market. However, they may not all be advertising on AdWords. Armed with a list of websites you consider your competition, you can begin researching their online ad presence.

How to do it...

Start with a search on Google using terms that you consider your main keywords or ways that customers look for your products or services. In the following example, we searched Google for `PPC ads` to figure out which websites are coming up in both organic and paid listings.

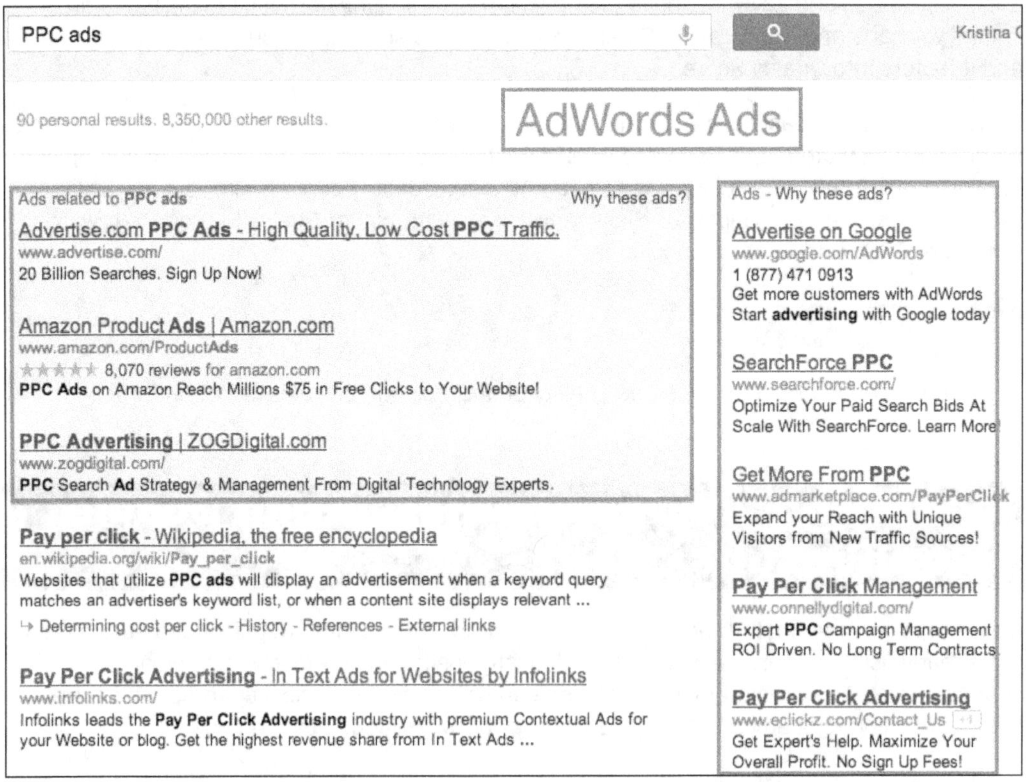

Organic, or natural listings, are on the left below the search query, while the paid ads are to the right and potentially above the organic listings.

Take note of paid ads coming up for your key searches, including how many ads are appearing. Scroll to the next page of search results to see additional pages and websites that come up after the first page of Google's search results. The more ads there are, the greater the competition and the more saturated the market is for those keywords.

The paid ads that we see may not be the same businesses we identified as our competition prior to doing the search. Our competitors may not be advertising with AdWords or our search query may not be triggering their ads at the time of our research. You may also find new businesses that you were not previously aware of that you will be competing against.

It's also possible that your keywords are applicable to different industries and areas of focus. In any case, the ads that consistently come up for your most important keywords in your target locations will be your competition in the online ad auction, and you'll need to better understand their strategies to make your own campaigns successful.

There's more...

Perform the Google search, as previously explained, multiple times a day and on different days. Each auction is in real time and we'll likely see different results every time we search on Google. Your competitors' ads may or may not show when we perform a search based on their campaign settings, including during what days and times of the day they have set their campaigns to show, or what locations they have chosen to target via their campaigns.

See also

- The *Using third-party tools to research competitors* recipe

Using third-party tools to research competitors

There are a variety of tools other than Google that can help us get more information about websites whose online marketing efforts we are interested in researching further. Such tools scan the search results pages and extrapolate keywords and ads for various domains. They'll provide data such as keywords used, daily budgets, how much our competitors are spending on individual keywords, and history of budget and ad changes.

Getting ready

The following are a couple of popular PPC spy tools that will allow us to do basic domain and keyword research for free:

- `http://www.spyfu.com/`
- `http://www.keywordspy.com/`

For a more thorough list of keywords and ads that the various domains are using, you will need to purchase a subscription. However, you can do some basic research through the free look ups using one of the previously listed tools.

How to do it...

Use tools such as KeywordSpy and SpyFu to research competition as follows:

1. Search for your keywords of interest. Following is an example of results for a keyword search on KeywordSpy and the free information the tool provides. For example, you can see how many advertisers are showing for a particular query and average CPCs:

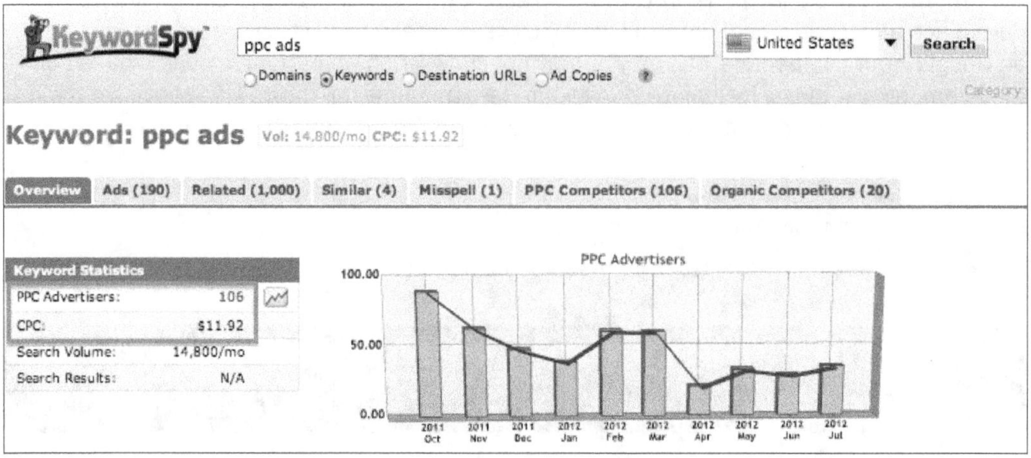

2. Search your competitors' URL to see if they are advertising through AdWords and learn more about their budgets, clicks per day, average ad position, and average cost-per-click (CPC). You'll also learn how many ad copies and keywords a domain is coming up for, which can help you better understand how comprehensive a particular domain's PPC program is.
3. Note budget trends over time, which can help you determine seasonality or changes in a particular business's strategy and marketing budget. You'll also be able to see some of the top keywords and ads for a domain, as well as related PPC competitors who are using overlapping keywords on AdWords:

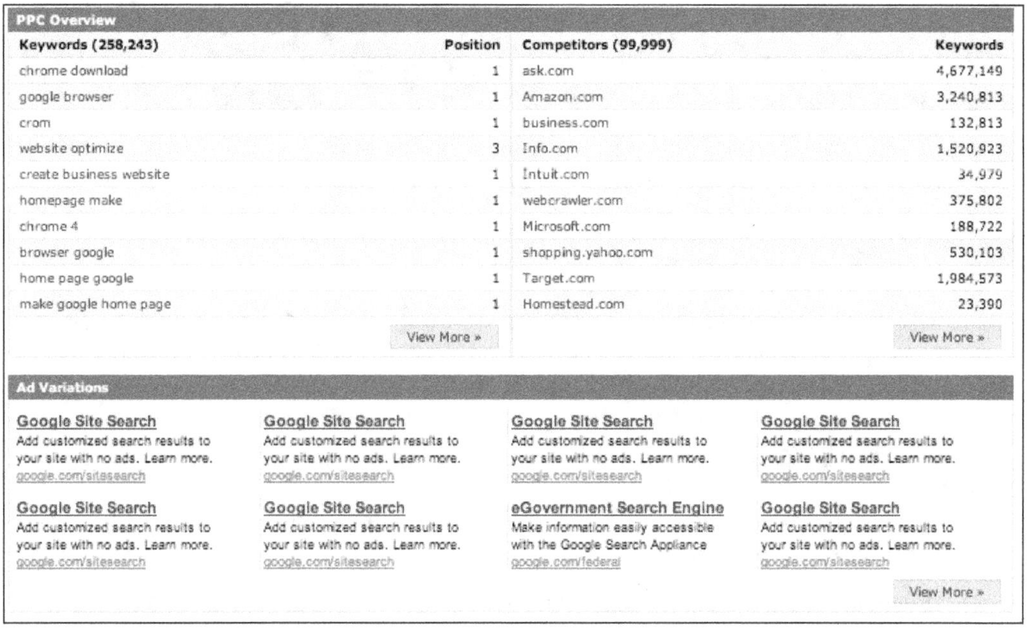

How it works...

Third-party keyword spy tools analyze a domain's behavior over time on various search engines, including what keywords and ads websites are appearing on. Spend data is estimated based on assumptions that take into account ad position and how often ads are appearing for the various keywords. Data may not be available for all countries.

There's more...

It's important to note that PPC keyword spy tools do not actually have access to other advertisers' accounts, and as such they are not 100 percent accurate. You can use them as a starting point in understanding your competition, but ultimately you should do your own keyword testing to determine what works best with your goals and budgets.

Analyzing budgets and bids to determine market saturation

Understanding how competitive the online search ads' market for your industry is, will help you determine your own marketing budgets and how much you may want to bid on your keywords.

Getting ready

Decide which tool you would like to use. You can start with one of the free basic PPC keyword spy tools, such as KeywordSpy (`www.keywordspy.com`), for basic budget and average CPC look-ups.

How to do it...

1. Enter a domain URL into `keywordspy.com` to get daily AdWords spend and average CPC estimates for a particular business.
2. Repeat this search for multiple businesses of various sizes to better understand the different spend ranges.
3. You can also use a tool like `keywordspy.com` to figure out average CPCs for keywords of interest and how many advertisers are showing ads on a particular keyword. Generally, the higher the average CPCs, the more competitive the industry. The more advertisers that show up in the auction, the more saturated the search ads' market is for a particular term. In some industries, advertisers are also more willing to pay for each click, driving up average CPCs, since a single lead can be very valuable. For example, in the legal industry, one ad click can result in a multi-million dollar settlement, making many legal terms competitive and expensive.

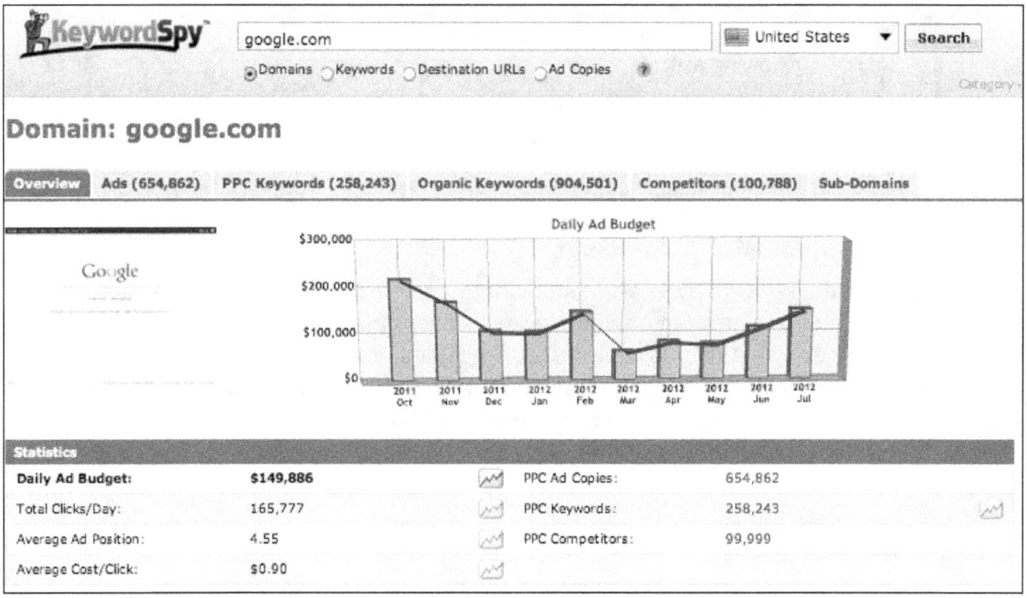

4. Another tool you can use to figure out how high the CPCs are for your keywords is the free AdWords keyword tool. Go to `https://adwords.google.com/o/KeywordTool` and enter a keyword of interest to see search volumes and competition denoted from low to high for keywords related to your search:

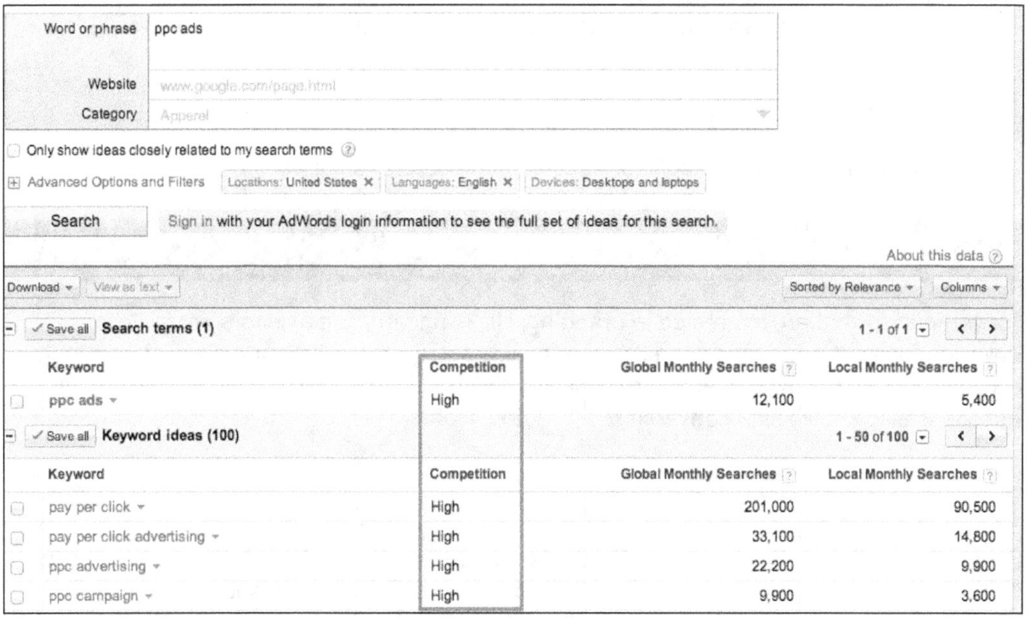

> Check out the most expensive AdWords keywords in the following article:
>
> `http://www.wordstream.com/blog/ws/2011/07/18/most-expensive-google-adwords-keywords`

How it works...

The Google AdWords keyword tool uses historic data and provides estimates only, not exact numbers. Once you have an AdWords account and are logged in, you'll see additional information in the Google AdWords keyword tool, including average CPCs and local search trends, which provide a sense of seasonality and traffic volumes throughout the year. While logged into your AdWords account, you can import the keywords you are researching in the keyword tool directly into your campaigns.

There's more...

Keep in mind that results will vary for different websites and that budgets should be consistent with your marketing goals. High spend advertisers typically have more comprehensive ad campaigns and are likely seeing a positive **return on investment** (**ROI**) from AdWords. However, low spend does not necessarily mean that AdWords is not profitable. A business could simply have budget constraints unrelated to AdWords' performance. Also, just because a competitor is investing a lot into AdWords does not mean that you will not be able to compete without a large budget. I recommend starting with conservative spend as you figure out what works for you and test the various options that AdWords has to offer.

See also

- The *Using third-party tools to research competitors* recipe

Setting advertising goals

For companies that are interested in branding, clicks and engaged visitors are sufficient. However, for most businesses, the ultimate goal is not simply a click, or a website visit, but a sale or a lead. This type of action that we want website visitors to ultimately take on our website is also known as a **conversion**.

Getting ready

Before you start spending money on AdWords, you will want to determine what you'd like your visitors to do once they come to your website. It's important to understand your end goal so you can properly track and measure results of your ad campaigns.

How to do it...

Think about what you would like your visitors to do once they come to your website. The following are some common conversion goals advertisers have:

- Sales
- Registrations
- Leads
- Downloads (whitepapers and apps)
- Sign-ups
- Visits to a particular page, such as the contact page

The goal of online ads is to get as many visitors as possible to take the actions you previously identified. In essence, you'll try to maximize clicks that result in conversions and optimize the ad to increase your conversion rate.

There's more...

Conversion rate is the number of conversions (sales, leads, and so on) divided by the number of clicks received during a set time period. For example, if you received 5 online leads (conversions) out of 100 clicks from AdWords, your conversion rate would be 5 percent.

Conversion rate = Conversions / Clicks x 100

Conversion rates vary based on a variety of factors, including a website's look and feel and how easy or difficult it is for visitors to get through the conversion process. You can get an idea of how your website converts and how many visitors are completing your desired actions in your Google Analytics account, or through other web analytics programs you may be using.

Simplicity is key, and you should aim to minimize distractions and website features that would complicate or hinder the conversion process. For example, "Buy Now" buttons should be prominent and easy to spot, contact options displayed prominently on the website, and lead and registration forms as simple as possible.

I have heard industry experts throw around 2 percent as an AdWords average conversion rate across different industries. Typically, websites with a higher level of commitment required on a user's part (such as e-commerce) will have lower conversion rates than websites with lower levels of commitment required (such as lead generation). The Fireclick Index, `http://index.fireclick.com/`, can help provide some additional guidance on online conversion rates by industry.

The simpler conversion goals such as lead generation or e-mail collection will usually convert closer to 3 percent but can go as high as 5 to 15 percent. For lead generation, conversion rates can be all over the place since the marketing offers, the value of the product, and costs vary so widely.

See also

- The *Predicting if AdWords will be profitable and calculating potential returns* recipe

Predicting if AdWords will be profitable and calculating potential returns

Use simple math to figure out how many clicks you can get with your target AdWords budget by reviewing average CPCs for your industry. You can take this information a step further by taking into consideration your current conversion rates to figure out what types of returns you can expect from AdWords.

Getting ready

First, understand average CPCs for your target keywords by following the steps outlined in the *Analyzing budgets and bids to determine market saturation* recipe.

How to do it...

1. Once you know the average CPCs for your keywords, pick a budget that you're considering testing AdWords with. Next, you can calculate potential returns using some assumptions about conversion rates across different industries, or even better, using conversion rates from other online marketing efforts you may have tried.
2. If you've done some advertising online and have an idea of how your website converts, you can use that number to make some initial assumptions about potential AdWords returns. However, keep in mind that different sources of traffic do tend to convert differently as well. For example, you'll likely see higher conversion rates from repeat visitors who are returning to your website after bookmarking it than you would from first-time visitors who are researching a product.
3. If you are not sure how many of your visitors tend to convert, you can use more general and conservative assumptions. Start with 2 percent until you gather some data specific to your industry or specific to your website.
4. Let's now try to calculate potential return from AdWords. Let's say our average CPC is $1 and we have a budget of $100 with which we'll get 100 clicks. With an assumed conversion rate of 2 percent, we'll get 2 conversions for each $100 spent on AdWords with each conversion costing us $50.

5. Even if we are not sure what your conversion rates will be like, you can use average CPCs to figure out if AdWords is a viable way to advertise online. If average CPCs for your industry are high, say $10, and you are only willing to pay $20 for each conversion, then AdWords is most likely not going to bring the returns you expect, since you would need a 50 percent conversion rate for the math to work in your favor, and such conversion rates are very unlikely.
6. The next important question is how much each conversion is worth to you. If you are paying $50 for each conversion, but make $1,000 from each conversion, then AdWords is obviously profitable. However, if it costs you $50 to convert a visitor but that visitors buys a $10 product and tends to never to come back to your site again, you are likely losing money with a 2 percent conversion rate on AdWords.

One of the most important metrics you'll want to set for yourself is how much you are willing to pay for each conversion and then optimize AdWords campaigns with that goal in mind.

How it works...

The cost-per-conversion is often referred to in the PPC world as your CPA.

Cost-per-action (CPA) = Total Cost / Conversions

> CPA as cost-per-action usually corresponds to pay-per-lead, while CPA as cost-per-acquisition usually corresponds to pay-per-sale.

There is no such thing as high or low CPA that we can generalize across all advertisers. CPA is relative and different business models will have different CPA thresholds. For example, a lawyer could pay $400 for an AdWords lead but that lead could result in a case that brings the firm millions of dollars, in which scenario a CPA of $400 would be a bargain.

Your returns will vary based on a variety of factors, including your website, how compelling your products and services are, pricing, and special offers to name just a few. Your conversion rates will also vary based on how you stack up in all of these considerations against similar businesses online.

There's more...

I've had clients who said that one of their conversions could pay for a month of their advertising costs due to the nature of their business, and I've had clients who were only willing to pay a few dollars for each conversion, as the average value of each converted user was much lower. How much you should pay for each conversion will be unique to your business model, goals, and objectives.

See also

- The *Analyzing budgets and bids to determine market saturation* recipe

2

Setting up Your Account

In this chapter, we will cover the following:

- Creating an AdWords account
- Determining the right billing option for your needs
- Inviting other users to access your account
- Changing user access levels or removing users
- Enabling auto-tagging at the account level
- Changing your notification settings

Introduction

This chapter covers the basics of creating an AdWords account and customizing the various key settings for easier management and navigation. You'll learn how to choose the right billing option for you, invite others to access your account, change access levels, and personalize views and notifications so that you can see the data you care about.

Creating an AdWords account

You can create an AdWords account and start showing your advertisements in minutes. The AdWords interface is very user friendly and will walk you through the necessary steps as you move through the signup process.

Getting ready

AdWords is managed through an online interface, and to sign up and manage it you'll need an Internet connection. You also need an e-mail address, which will be associated with your account. If you do not have a Google account already, you'll need to sign up for one first.

How to do it...

1. To get started, go to `http://www.adwords.google.com/` and click on the signup prompt.
2. On the next screen, you will have the option to either use a Google account you already have or to set up a new one. You can only use one e-mail address per AdWords account, so if your e-mail address is already related to an AdWords account you will need to use a different e-mail ID.

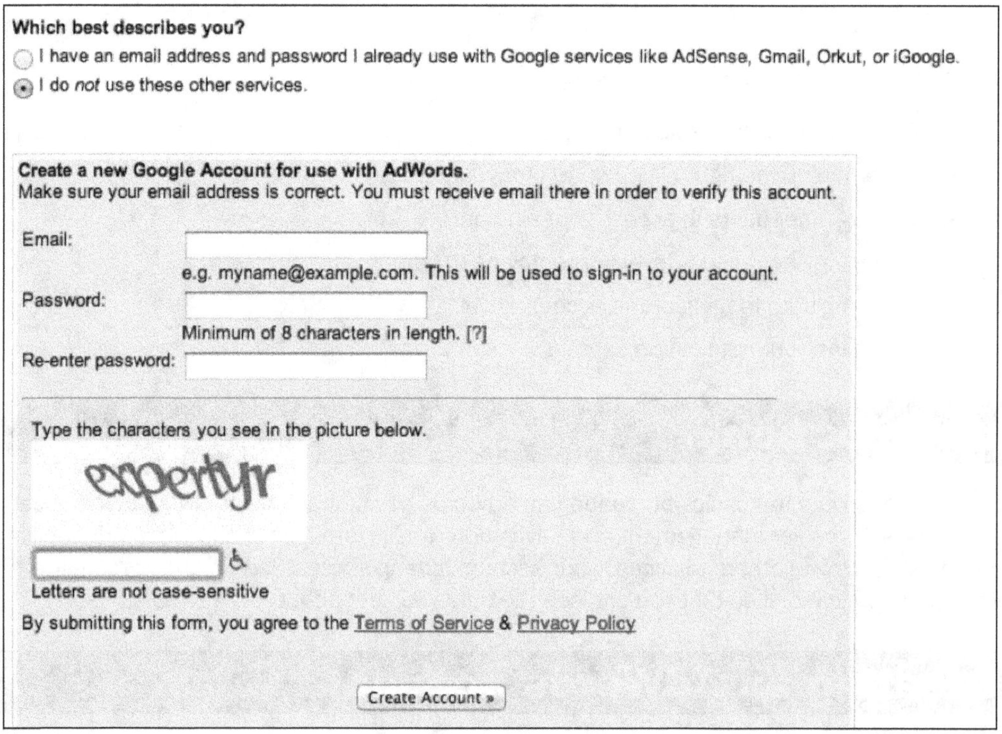

3. Select your time zone and choose a currency for your account. You will not be able to change this information after you create your account; so review your choices carefully before proceeding.

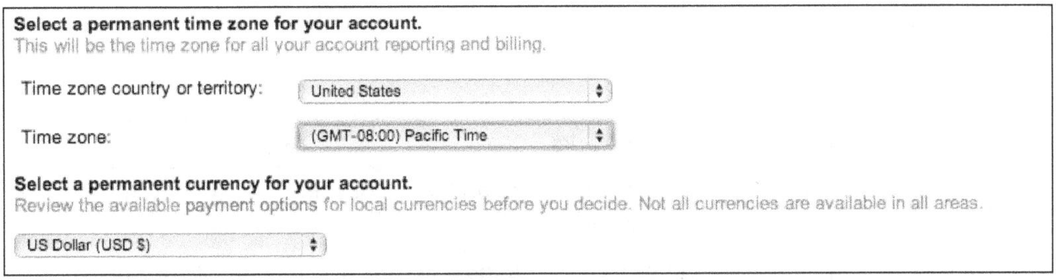

> Choose a time zone that's in sync with your business hours of operation. That way, you'll be able to schedule and adjust when your campaigns should run more easily.

There's more...

After entering your billing information, you will be ready to start setting up your first campaign. If you are daunted by the prospect of choosing keywords and writing ads, AdWords does offer support for new advertisers. AdWords customer reps can answer any questions you may have and can even offer free campaign setup support. Find the phone number for your country at `https://support.google.com/adwords/answer/8206?hl=en` and call AdWords for additional help, or go to `http://www.google.com/ads/new/`.

See also

- The *Determining the right billing option for your needs* recipe

Determining the right billing option for your needs

AdWords offers three main options to pay for ads. Advertisers can choose to pay before ads run (manual payments) or after clicks are accrued (automatic payments). Advertisers can also apply for invoicing to get a line of credit from Google—an option typically used by large advertisers.

Getting ready

The following table explains the three payment options in more detail and for whom each option is most appropriate:

How you pay

Billing option	How it works
Manual payments	Advertisers prepay and add funds manually to AdWords before ads run.
Automatic payments	AdWords charges you after ads run. You are billed either 30 days after your last payment or when you reach your next billing threshold.
Monthly invoicing	Google provides a line of credit and advertisers pay via check or wire transfer after ads run. To be eligible, businesses have to be registered for a minimum of one year, and meet country-specific spending requirements. AdWords will review your credit history and will send you an e-mail with their payment terms and credit line offer.

What you pay with

Once you decide which payment setting is most appropriate for your needs, you'll be able to pick from various methods of payment, including direct debit, credit card, and money transfer. Payment methods vary by country and you'll need to check what options you'll have by going to the billing page in your AdWords account or reviewing country-specific options at `http://support.google.com/adwords/bin/answer.py?hl=en&answer=2375433&topic=1714069&ctx=topic#US`.

How to do it...

Once you have created your AdWords account, you will need to go through the billing preferences pages to complete the account setup.

1. On your billing page, choose your country, or where your billing address is located:

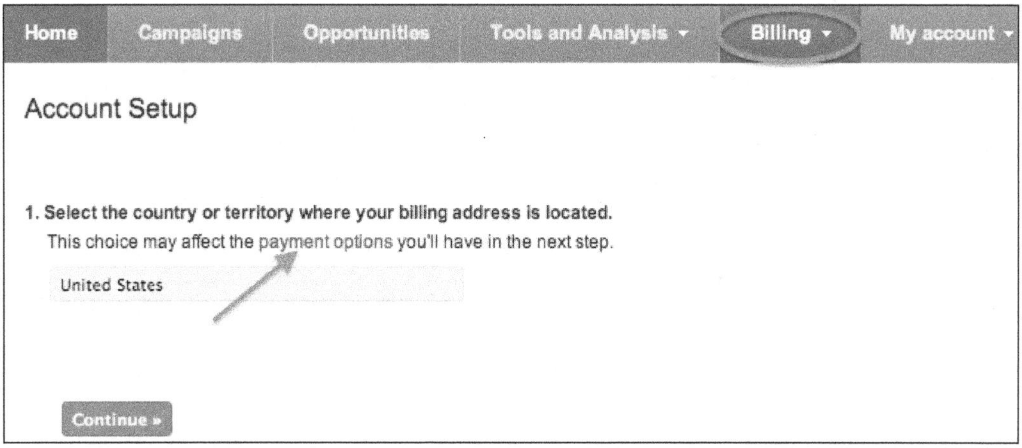

2. Clicking on **payment options** on this screen will bring up another page, which will provide the option to select your currency and will highlight forms of payment available to you.

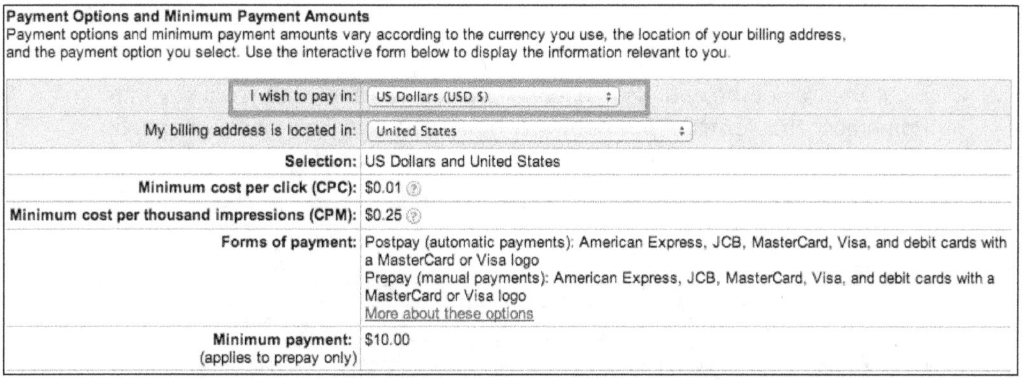

Payment Options and Minimum Payment Amounts
Payment options and minimum payment amounts vary according to the currency you use, the location of your billing address, and the payment option you select. Use the interactive form below to display the information relevant to you.

I wish to pay in:	US Dollars (USD $)
My billing address is located in:	United States
Selection:	US Dollars and United States
Minimum cost per click (CPC):	$0.01
Minimum cost per thousand impressions (CPM):	$0.25
Forms of payment:	Postpay (automatic payments): American Express, JCB, MasterCard, Visa, and debit cards with a MasterCard or Visa logo Prepay (manual payments): American Express, JCB, MasterCard, Visa, and debit cards with a MasterCard or Visa logo More about these options
Minimum payment: (applies to prepay only)	$10.00

3. Next, fill in your business name and contact information.

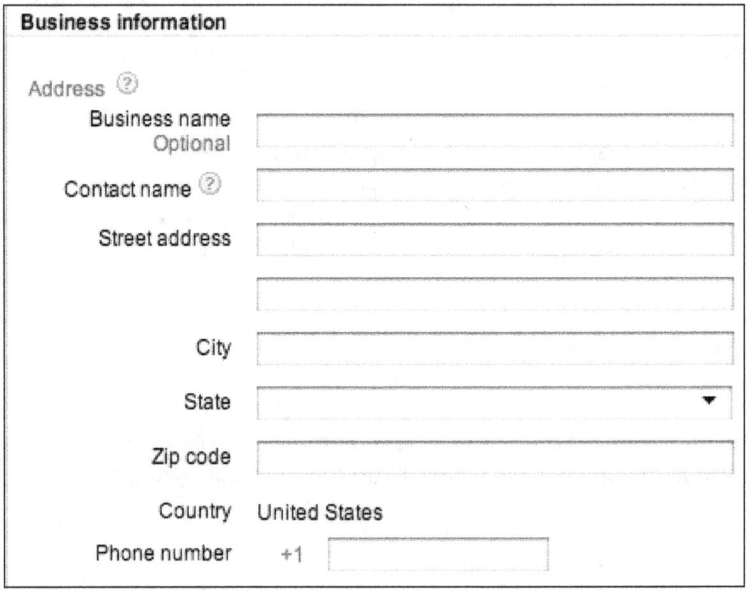

4. Finally, you'll get the options to choose how you pay and what you'll pay with. Remember that forms of payment vary by country and your payment options might look different depending on where you are located.

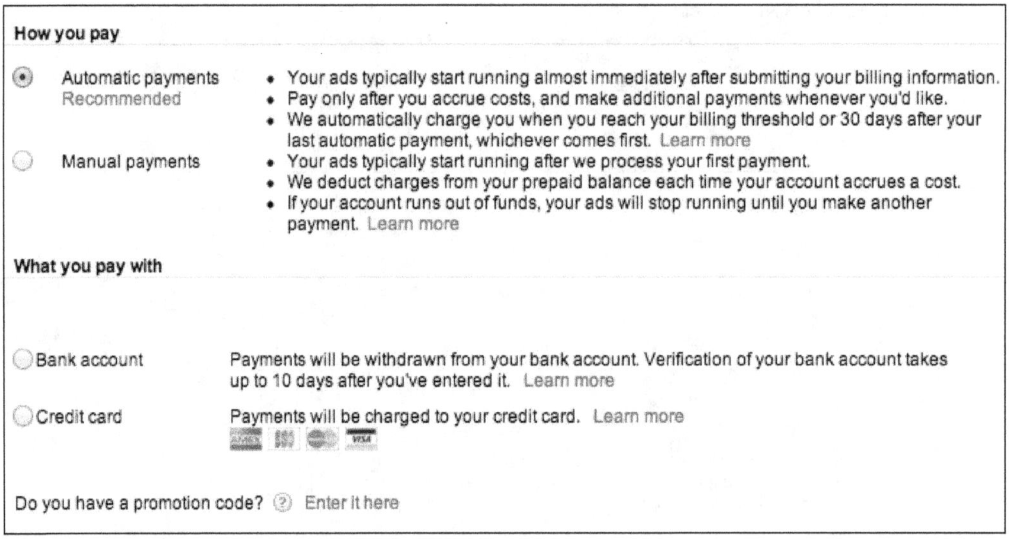

> AdWords distributes coupons to new advertisers that you can use towards free advertising. You may get a promotional credit in the e-mail, through your hosting provider, such as GoDaddy, or you can search on Google.com for AdWords coupons. Make sure to apply the coupon code to your billing page and enjoy the free clicks.

There's more...

It is recommended to choose automatic payments rather than manual, since with manual payments you'll need to remember to add funds to your account each time you run out. Most advertisers will forget to add manual funds occasionally, resulting in your ads being down and a loss of traffic. You can always switch from one payment setting to another (from manual to automatic, for example), but you cannot change the account currency you select.

See also

- The *Creating an AdWords account* recipe

Inviting other users to access your account

As you continue to manage AdWords, you may need to invite other users, such as your associates or employees, to access your account. Depending on the level of access you grant other users, they may be able to review reports or help you make changes to campaigns.

Getting ready

Decide who you'd like to invite and what level of access they should have. For example, should this person be able to make changes to your campaigns or just receive reports?

How to do it...

To invite other users to your AdWords account:

1. Go to the **My account** tab.
2. Select **Account access**.

3. Click on **Invite other users**.

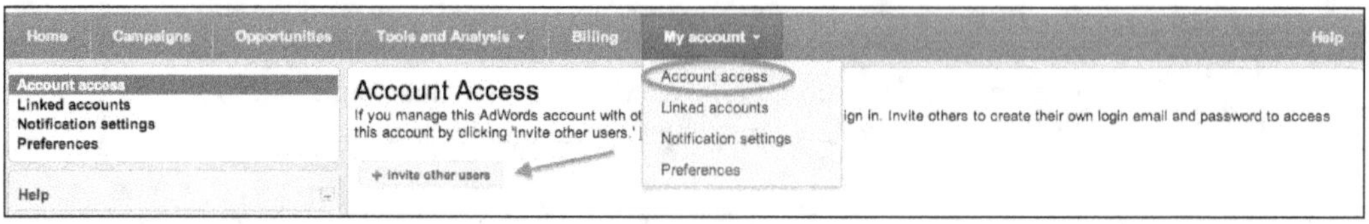

4. Enter the e-mail address of the user you'd like to invite.
5. Choose new user's access level and click on **Send invitation**.

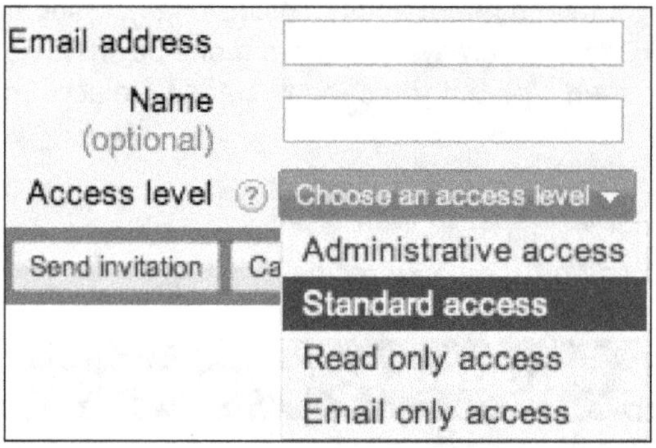

6. After the new user accepts your invitation, you'll receive an e-mail from AdWords. You will need to review and confirm the request under your **Account Access** section in AdWords. You'll see **Pending invitations** on your account access page where you'll be able to take the appropriate action.
7. Click on **Grant access** to confirm and allow the invited user to access your account.

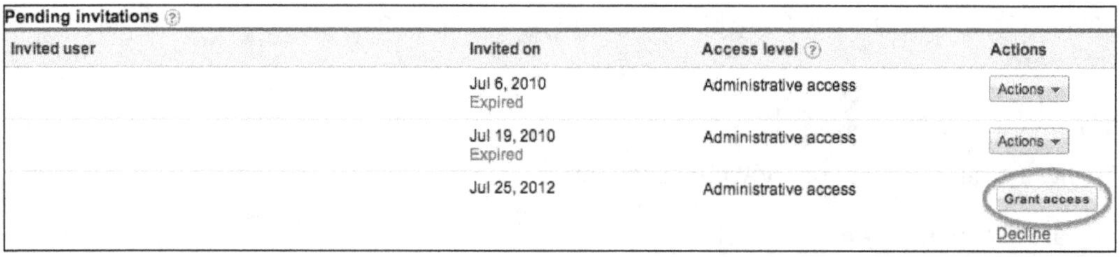

How it works...

There are four different levels of access you'll need to choose from:

- **E-mail only**: Users can receive e-mail notifications and reports, but will not be able to sign in to AdWords, or make any changes to the account or campaigns.
- **Read only**: Users can log in to the account, view and run reports, and review the campaigns, but are not able to make any changes to the account or campaigns.
- **Standard access**: Users can make changes to the account and have most of the privileges of account admins. However, standard access users cannot invite, change, or disable access levels. An exception here is that standard users can add e-mail only users.
- **Administrative access**: Users can make changes to the account and campaigns, add, and remove users or change user access levels.

There's more...

Note that account access invitations do expire, and you will need to resend them if they have not been accepted in time. You can revoke a previously sent invite or re-send expired invitations, which will be listed under your **Pending invitations**.

If you'd like to invite an AdWords agency to connect to your account, you will likely need to follow different steps since agencies typically manage AdWords through a single login AdWords interface called **My Client Center** (**MCC**). If your agency uses an MCC, you will need to provide them with your 10-digit AdWords customer ID, which you can find at the top-right corner of your AdWords screen.

Next, the agency will request access to your account via your customer ID. You'll still need to follow the same steps to accept a client manager request under your account access page. You'll see a client manager access request right below the standard **Users with account access** section.

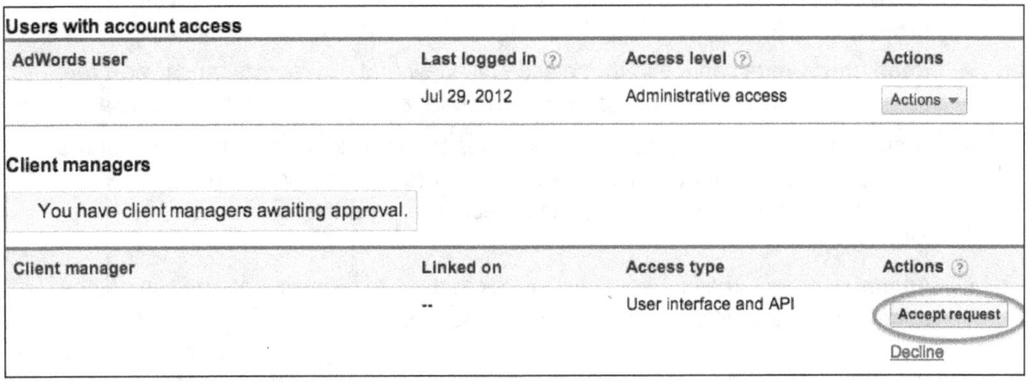

See also

- The *Changing user access levels or removing users* recipe

Changing user access levels or removing users

If you are an administrator on your AdWords account, you will be able to change access levels or remove other users from being able to access your account.

How to do it..

To change user access levels or remove users, follow these steps:

1. Go to **My account**.
2. Select **Account access** where you'll be able to see all of the current users along with their access levels.
3. Click on the **Actions** button next to the e-mail address whose access level you'd like to change and click **Terminate access**.

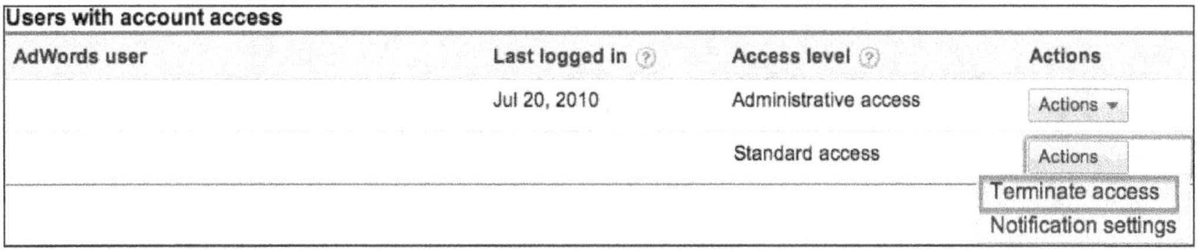

If you'd like to change access level rather than terminate account access completely, you will need to invite this user again with a different access level assigned.

There's more...

Once you terminate a user's access to your account, AdWords will notify the user via e-mail that the account access has been disabled.

See also

- The *Inviting other users to access your account* recipe

Enabling auto tagging at the account level

You are likely already using or planning to use a web analytics program to analyze your website statistics. In order to get AdWords data properly fed into your web analytics program, you should make sure to enable **Auto-tagging** in AdWords.

How to do it..

To enable **Auto-tagging**, follow these steps:

1. Navigate to the **My account** tab.
2. Choose the **Preferences** sub tab.
3. Make sure that the **Auto-tagging** checkbox is selected.

4. Click on **Save changes**.

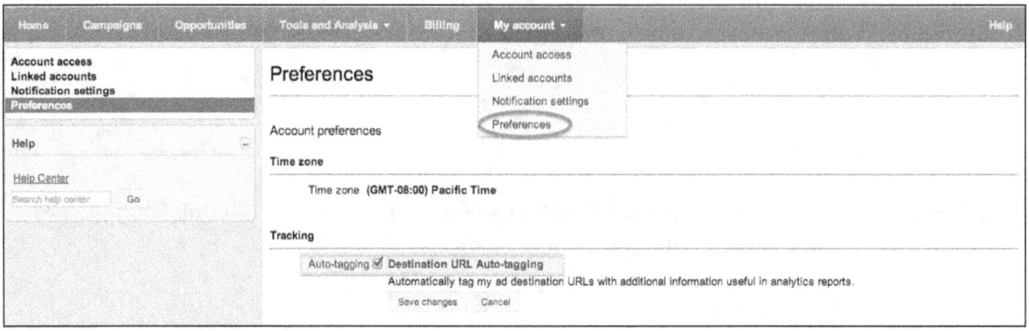

How it works...

Auto-tagging is a feature that helps you analyze performance in other analytics tracking programs, such as Google Analytics, by adding extra parameters to your URLs. For example, you'll be able to see in Google Analytics which campaigns, keywords, and ads led to visits, as well as the associated cost data.

There's more...

You can also choose to tag your keywords and ads manually by adding URL parameters that are compatible with your analytics tracking tool. You'll need to make sure to tag all of your ads and keywords in order to track properly. As this can be a time consuming process, auto-tagging is the preferred method.

See also

- The *Linking AdWords to Google Analytics* recipe in *Chapter 3, Tracking beyond the Click*

Changing your notification settings

Worried about missing out on important communication about your AdWords account? Review and customize your notification settings to ensure you get all of the relevant e-mails from Google.

Getting ready

Think about what information is most relevant to the various users that have access to your AdWords account. For example, you may wish to limit e-mails that are sent out about any disapproved ads to only go out to those that manage the campaigns.

How to do it...

To change your notification settings:

1. Click on the **Campaigns** tab.
2. Go to the **My account** tab.
3. Select **Notification settings**.
4. Select the user whose notification settings you'd like to change.
5. You will see a list of all notifications a user currently receives. Click in the **Email** column to change the notification for each particular alert and choose the appropriate e-mail preference.

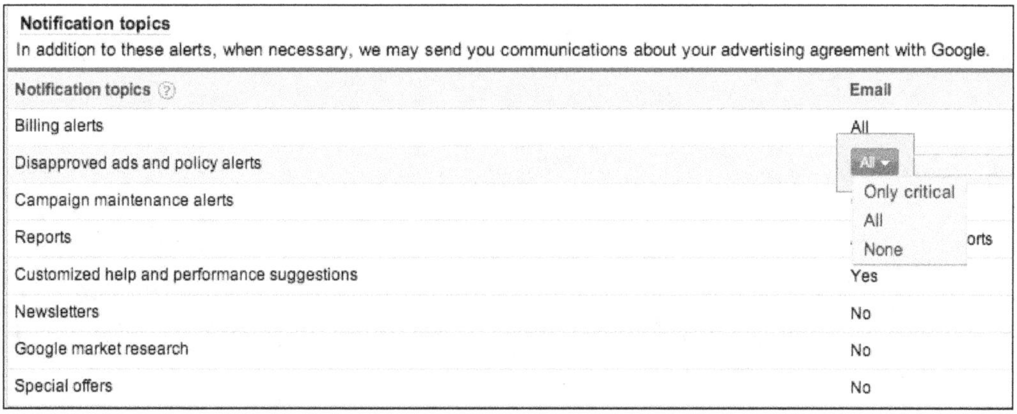

How it works...

AdWords allows you to customize what notifications you and other users that have access to your account receive. You can change these settings any time to reduce unnecessary e-mail or to ensure you are not missing any critical updates or opportunities.

There's more...

If there are certain associates that should be receiving account updates but currently are not, you may want to add them as users. Also, if you do not wish certain users to be able to access all of the information in your account, you may wish to change their access levels.

See also

- The *Inviting other users to access your account* recipe
- The *Changing user access levels or removing users* recipe
- The *Running and scheduling reports* recipe in *Chapter 10, Reporting and Analysis*

3
Tracking beyond the Click

In this chapter, we will cover the following:

- Linking AdWords to Google Analytics
- Creating a conversion goal in AdWords to track leads or sales
- Importing goals from Google Analytics into AdWords
- Verifying that conversion tracking is working
- Analyzing how long it takes to convert customers
- Analyzing assist clicks and impressions
- Analyzing AdWords data in Google Analytics
- Analyzing time on site data and bounce rates

Introduction

This chapter discusses how to set up your account to track past the click, in order to truly understand the returns you are getting from your advertising efforts. For most of you, simply bringing visitors to your website will not be the end goal. You'll likely want those visitors to purchase a product, fill out your lead form, sign up for a trial, or view a key page of your website. AdWords allows you to track these actions via AdWords' **conversion tracking** and Google Analytics. Setting up your account to incorporate the visitor behavior you care about will be the key to optimizing AdWords for the maximum performance.

Linking AdWords to Google Analytics

Linking AdWords and your Google Analytics accounts will help you better evaluate the results of your ad efforts and will arm you with the necessary information to maximize ROI. You'll be able to see how many pages are visited by the people who click on your AdWords ads, how long they stay on your website, how many leave immediately, what pages they browse, and a wealth of other useful information that will help you fine tune your ad campaigns.

After you link AdWords and Google Analytics, you will also be able to compare AdWords results to traffic from other sources. For example, you might want to compare how long visitors from AdWords and Bing Ads stay on your website.

Getting ready

In order to link your AdWords and Google Analytics accounts, you will need to be listed as an administrator on both accounts. You should also have the Google Analytics tracking code installed on your website. Make sure that the same e-mail address that you are using to log in to AdWords is also an administrator user in your Google Analytics.

Of course, you'll also need a Google Analytics account. If you do not have one already, you can create it at `http://www.google.com/analytics/`.

How to do it...

To link your AdWords account to Google Analytics, perform the following steps:

1. Sign in to your AdWords account. You will not be able to link AdWords and Google Analytics unless you sign in to AdWords first.
2. Go to the **Tools and Analysis** tab, and click on **Google Analytics**.
3. Click on the **Admin** link at the top-right corner of the screen:

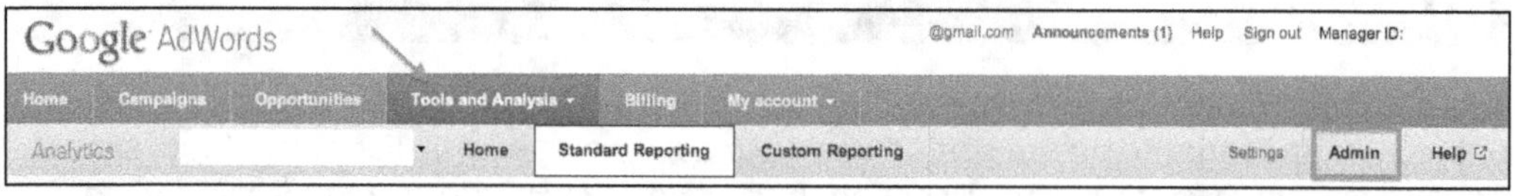

4. Select the profile name that you'd like to link. If you are listed as a user on multiple domains, you might see multiple accounts:

5. Click on the **Data Sources** tab. If you do not see **Data Sources**, you might need to navigate to the profile name right after the **Account list** heading.

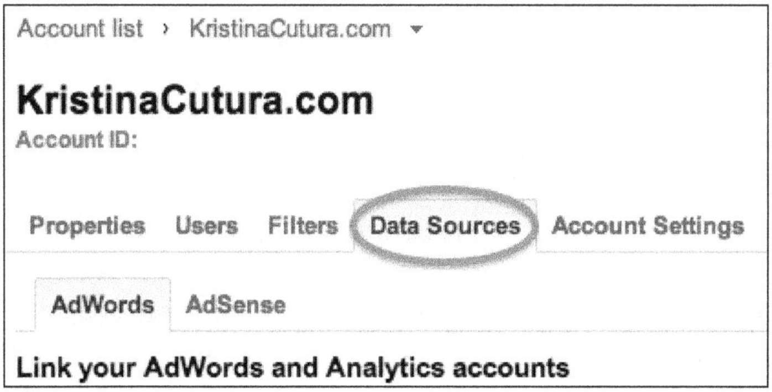

6. Follow the link account prompts.
7. Select the profile(s) you'll want to link and save:

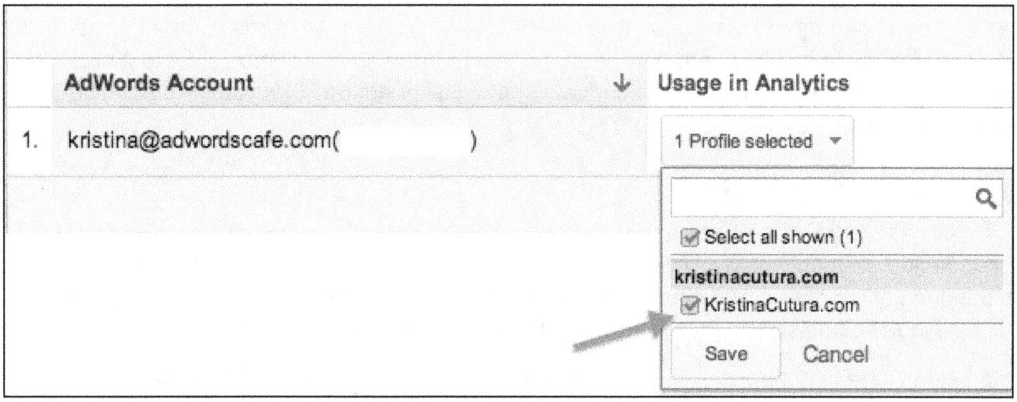

How it works...

Once you link AdWords to Google Analytics, the two will communicate, and your Google Analytics account will reflect AdWords data in the Google Analytics interface. What's more, you'll be able to customize data views in AdWords to include Google Analytics metrics directly in your AdWords account, so there's less need for back-and-forth navigation. In order to see Google Analytics data in your AdWords reports, go to **My Account** and click on **Linked accounts**. Choose the **View details** option in your Google Analytics section and follow the prompts to add your property.

> Make sure that you have enabled auto tagging in your AdWords account in order to see all of your AdWords data in your Google Analytics reports.

There's more...

You and other users listed on your account will receive an e-mail confirmation that you have linked your Google Analytics profile to AdWords.

See also

- The *Enabling auto tagging at the account level* recipe in *Chapter 2, Setting up Your Account*
- The *Customizing columns to personalize data views* recipe in *Chapter 10, Reporting and Analysis*

Creating a conversion goal in AdWords to track leads or sales

I recommend setting up conversion tracking before you run any AdWords campaigns so that you can properly measure them right from the start. Rather than optimizing for just clicks, you should optimize your campaigns for conversions or visitor actions that you care about, such as sales or leads.

Getting ready

First, decide what actions you'd like to track on your website. For many online businesses, sales is the end goal. However, you could track a variety of other behaviors that signify engagement, such as lead submissions, whitepaper downloads, sign ups, and views of key pages.

You can also track multiple conversions in AdWords by creating separate conversion actions in your account.

How to do it...

To create a conversion in AdWords and generate the code, perform the following steps:

1. Navigate to the **Tools and Analysis** tab and click on **Conversions**.
2. Click on **New Conversion** and name your conversion:

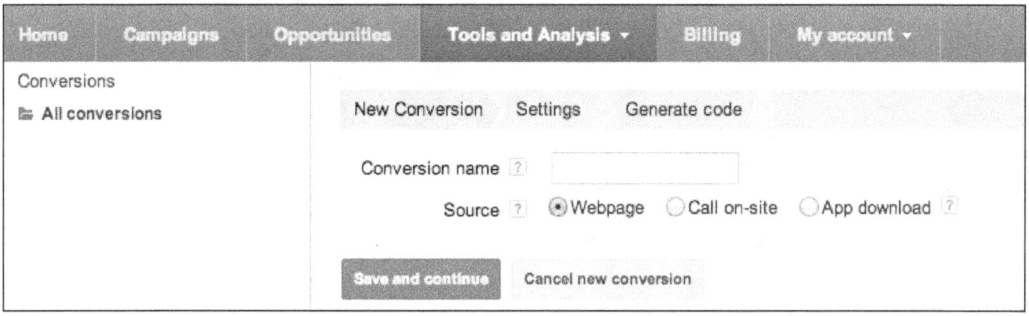

3. Choose from the following three conversion location options:
    - **Webpage** (most common)
    - **Call on-site**
    - **App download**
4. Click on **Save and continue**. In the next step you will be able to choose your settings.
5. Choose your **Conversion category** from one of the following:
    - **Other**
    - **Purchase/sale**
    - **Signup**
    - **Lead**
    - **View of a key page**
6. Choose your **Markup Language**. In most cases, you'll choose **HTML**.
7. **Conversion value** is optional. If a conversion is worth a certain amount to you, say $20, you can assign that value to the conversion.

8. You have the option to show or not to show **Tracking indicator** on your website. If you choose to show it, a Google site stats notification will appear when someone completes a conversion. You have the option to customize what this notification will look like on your website. If you omit the Google site stats notification, be very clear in you privacy policy that you track users' surfing behavior, especially in the EU because of the "cookie law".
9. Click on **Save and continue**.

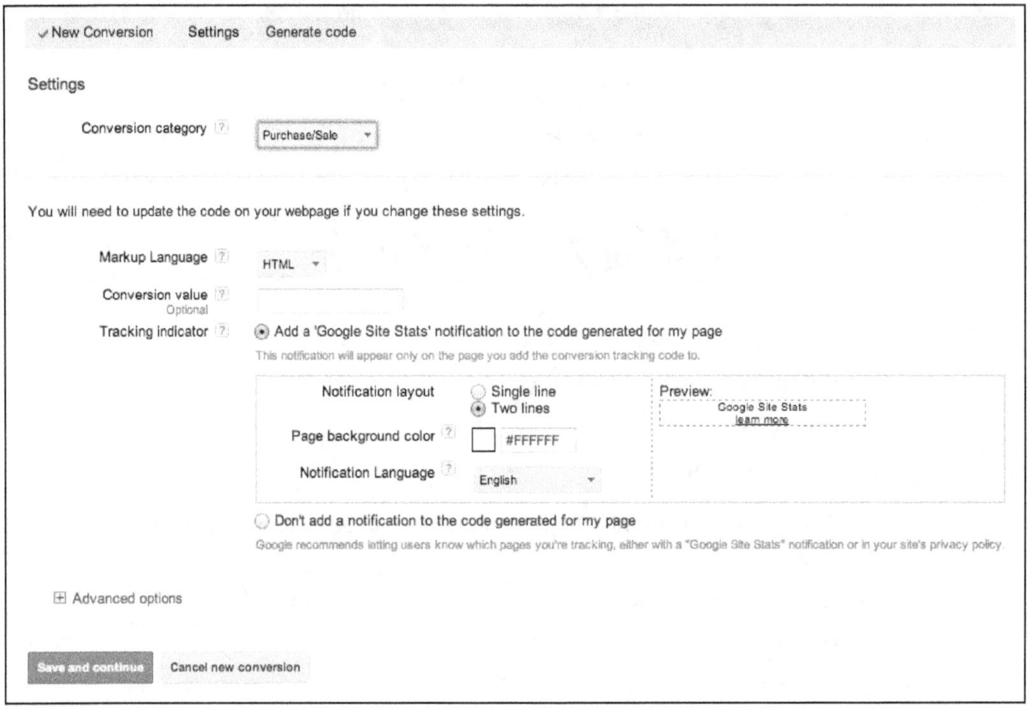

If someone else will be placing the code on your website, you have the option to e-mail them the code through AdWords. Or, if you make changes to your website's code, click the appropriate button to get the code.

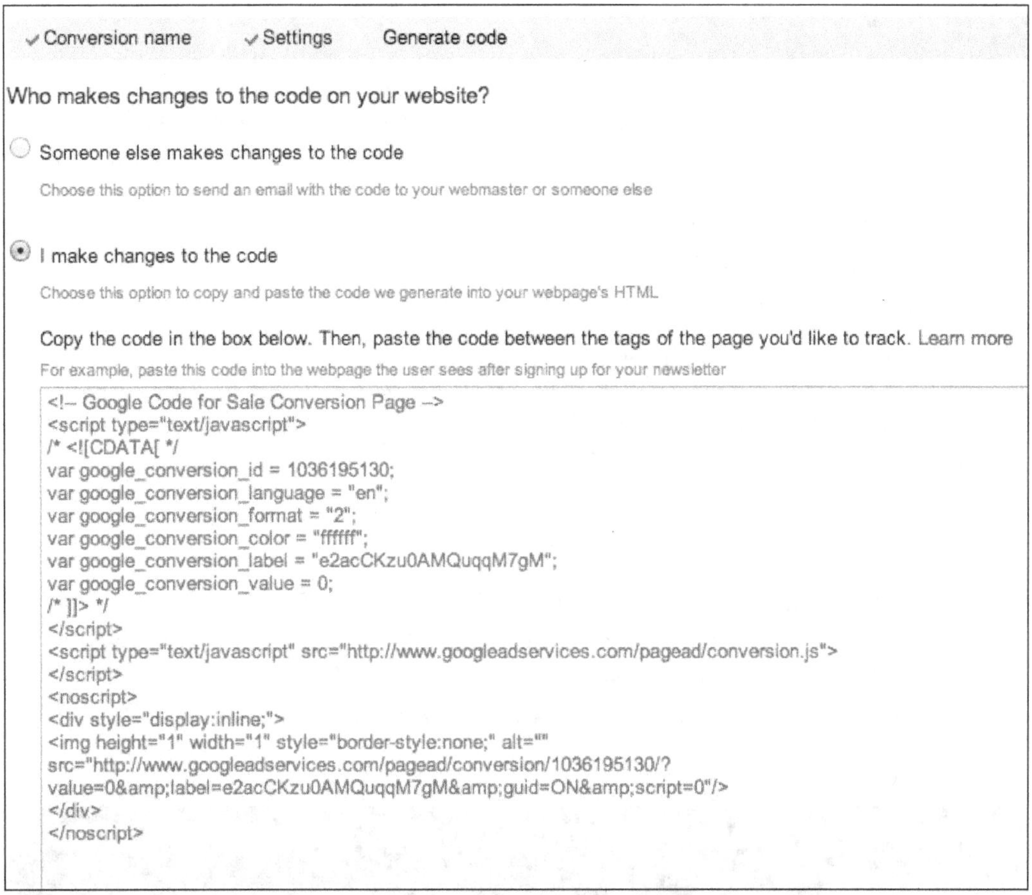

Copy and paste the code between the tags of the pages you will be tracking (between the body tags of the page). The tracking pixel needs to show on your conversion confirmation page when a user reaches that page, in order for conversions to be recorded.

How it works...

It can take up to 24 hours before conversions appear in your AdWords account, so do not worry if you do not see conversion data right away. Once you have enabled conversion tracking and have added the code to your website, AdWords will start to attribute conversions to individual campaigns, keywords, and ads.

> If you make any changes to the conversion **Settings** page, make sure that you update the tracking code on your website as well. Otherwise, conversions might no longer be tracked properly.

There's more...

You might need to customize your data views in your AdWords **Campaign Management** page to ensure you are seeing conversion data. I typically select the following conversion columns:

- **Conv. (1-per-click)**
- **Cost/conv.(1-per-click)**
- **Conv. rate (1-per-click)**
- **View-through Conv.**

Conversions (1-per-click) will count only one conversion per ad click. If more than one conversion occurs after a click, only the first one will be counted. Conversions (many-per-click) will count multiple conversions per click. View-through conversions are counted when someone views an ad and converts without clicking on that ad.

See also

- The *Importing goals from Google Analytics into AdWords* recipe
- The *Setting advertising goals* recipe in *Chapter 1, Researching the Market and Competition and Setting Goals*
- The *Customizing columns to personalize data views* recipe in *Chapter 10, Reporting and Analysis*

Importing goals from Google Analytics into AdWords

Goals in Google Analytics are similar to conversions in AdWords, in that they can help you track specific behaviors on your website, such as sign ups or sales. If you already have a goal (or multiple goals) created in your Google Analytics account, you can import them into AdWords as conversions. This will enable you to see how your ad efforts relate to specific goals you already decided to track via Google Analytics, without needing to set up AdWords' conversion tracking and add an additional pixel to your website.

Getting ready

In order to be able to import Analytics' goals into your AdWords account, your AdWords and Google Analytics accounts will need to be linked first. You will need to enable auto tagging in AdWords, and be opted into data sharing settings in your Google Analytics account under the **Account settings** page in your Admin section. Finally, your AdWords ads will need to have resulted in a goal completion.

How to do it...

To import goals you created in Google Analytics to AdWords, perform the following steps:

1. Sign in to your AdWords account.
2. Go to **Tools and Analysis** and select **Conversions**.
3. If your conversions are eligible to import from Google Analytics, you will see the following message:

4. Click on **Import from Google Analytics** and select the goals you'd like to track via AdWords:

5. Choose your tracking purpose and click on **Import** when you're done.

How it works...

AdWords conversion tracking and Google Analytics are calculated differently, so do not be surprised if you see some discrepancies between AdWords conversion tracking data and goal completions in Google Analytics. The following are the three main reasons for the discrepancies you might notice:

- **Attribution**: AdWords conversion tracking attributes the conversion to the last AdWords click, while Google Analytics will attribute the conversion to the source of the last visit. For example, if a visitor clicked on your AdWords ad, but did not convert, and instead converted after finding your website via Google organic search the next day, Analytics will attribute this conversion to organic. AdWords, on the other hand, would still attribute this conversion to the appropriate AdWords keyword and ad, if you have conversion tracking enabled.
- **Cookie length**: AdWords cookies expire after 30 days while Google Analytics cookies last 6 months. This means that if a visitor converted 30 days after clicking on your AdWords ad, AdWords conversion tracking would not count it but Google Analytics would.
- **Date of conversion**: AdWords reports the conversion for the day the click that led to the conversion happened, rather than when the conversion occurred. Analytics, on the other hand, reports the conversion the day it actually occurred. For example, if a visitor clicked on your ad on October 15th but did not convert until October 17th, AdWords would report this conversion under October 15th and Google Analytics under October 17th.

There's more...

You can set up both AdWords conversion tracking and import goals from Google Analytics. If you choose to do that, your **Conv. (1-per-click)** column in the reporting dashboard will de-duplicate any of the same conversions and only count one conversion. However, your **Conv. (many-per-click)** column will report both AdWords conversions and imported Google Analytics goals. To see individual conversion metrics broken out further, go to **Segment** and choose conversion action name from the **Conversions** segment.

See also

- The *Enabling auto-tagging at the account level* recipe in *Chapter 2, Setting up Your Account*
- The *Creating a conversion goal in AdWords to track leads or sales* recipe
- The *Importing goals from Google Analytics into AdWords* recipe

Verifying that conversion tracking is working

After setting up AdWords conversion tracking, I recommend making sure that it's working properly so you can start acting on your data as soon as possible.

Getting ready

You will need access to your AdWords account, your conversion actions in AdWords, as well as the URL for your confirmation page.

How to do it...

There are a few steps you can take to verify conversions are being tracked.

Check the source code

First, I recommend checking that the code is indeed on the appropriate page and that the code matches the tracking code in your AdWords account:

1. In your browser, go to your confirmation page URL, such as `yourwebsite.com/thank_you`.
2. Click to view the source code. The following table entails the view page source shortcuts for the Chrome and Firefox:

Command	Windows	Mac
Chrome	*Ctrl + U*	*Command + Option + U*
Firefox	*Ctrl + U*	*Command + U*

3. In your AdWords account, go to **Tools and Analysis** and select **Conversions**.
4. Click on the conversion action you created and go to the **Code** tab. Choose the **I make changes to the code** option to view the code you created.
5. Look for `var google_conversion_id` in your code and search for the value you see in your account on your confirmation page's source code.
6. If you do not see it, the code was not added to the right page and will need to be installed.

Wait for conversions to occur

Once you are confident that the conversion tracking code is on the proper pages, you can simply wait for conversions to occur. I recommend checking back 24 hours after implementing conversion tracking to see if any conversions have been attributed to your campaigns.

You should see them in your **Campaign Management** tab next to other performance data. If you do not see any conversion columns in your AdWords **Campaign Management** page, you may need to customize your views and columns to show conversion data.

Another place where you should see conversions in AdWords is under **Conversions** in **Tools and Analysis**:

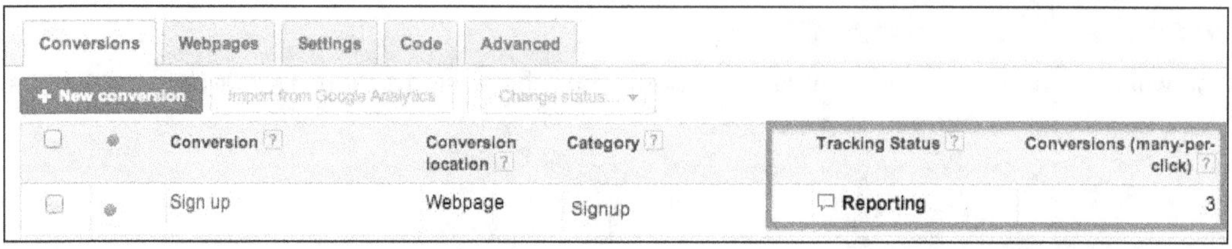

Complete a test conversion

If you prefer testing conversion tracking on your end, you can do so by clicking on your own ad and completing a fake conversion, as follows:

1. Do a Google search for one of your keywords.
2. Click on your ad. You will need to click on your AdWords own ad to do this.
3. Complete a test conversion.
4. Check your AdWords account to see if it's reporting conversions. Allow up to 24 hours for a conversion to appear in your AdWords account.

How it works...

Please note that AdWords reporting is not real time and is delayed by at least a few hours. It can take up to 24 hours for AdWords to reflect a conversion in your account, so make sure to allow for some time for reporting to sync.

If you are importing your goals from Google Analytics into AdWords, it can take up to 48 hours to see the conversion data in the AdWords interface. However, you can still see Google Analytics goals in the Analytics interface, even though they may take longer to sync to AdWords.

There's more...

One common mistake when it comes to conversion tracking includes the code being pasted on the wrong pages, such as on the landing page instead of on the confirmation page. A good hint that you may have made this mistake is if you see an over-inflated number of conversions in your AdWords account. In such an instance, you would be counting each visit as a conversion and you would need to move the code from your landing page to your confirmation page.

Conversions are also not tracked properly if the tracking code is modified in any way, such as with an extra space. To confirm that the code has been pasted exactly as it appears in your AdWords account, copy the entire block of code in AdWords and search for it on your confirmation page.

See also

- The *Creating a conversion goal in AdWords to track leads or sales* recipe
- The *Importing goals from Google Analytics into AdWords* recipe
- The *Customizing columns to personalize data views* recipe in *Chapter 10, Reporting and Analysis*

Analyzing how long it takes to convert customers

Have you ever wondered how long it takes for your typical customer to convert after clicking on your ad and browsing through your website? You likely have assumptions about this process, but luckily AdWords has hard data that can help you better understand the time lag between a click and a conversion.

Getting ready

You will need to have AdWords conversions enabled and tracking in your account. If you do, AdWords automatically tracks the time lag for you, and you just need to dig up the data.

How to do it...

To see how users convert and analyze conversion paths, perform the following steps:

1. Click on **Conversions** under the **Tools and Analysis** tab.
2. Click on **Search Funnels** to see how users convert. The main screen summary will show you total conversions, as well as the average number of days it takes to convert:

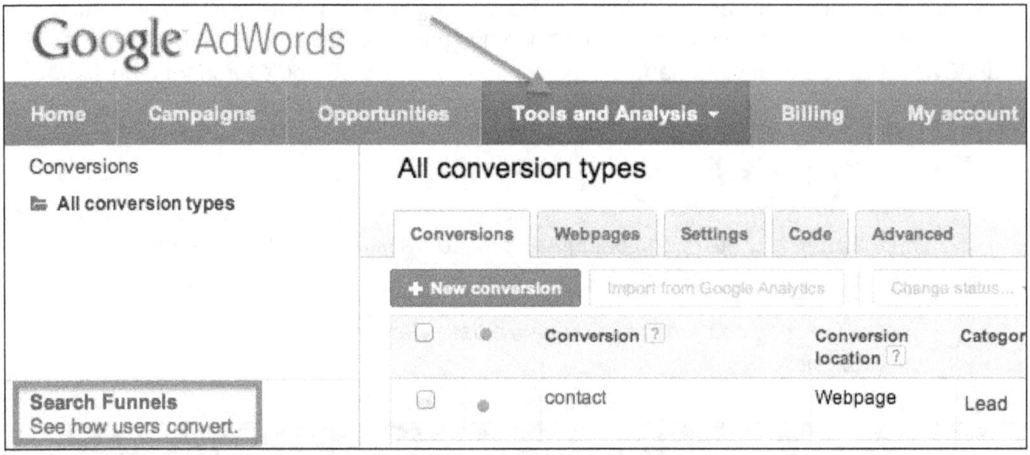

3. Click on **Time Lag** to see additional details, including conversions and percentage of conversions completed by day:

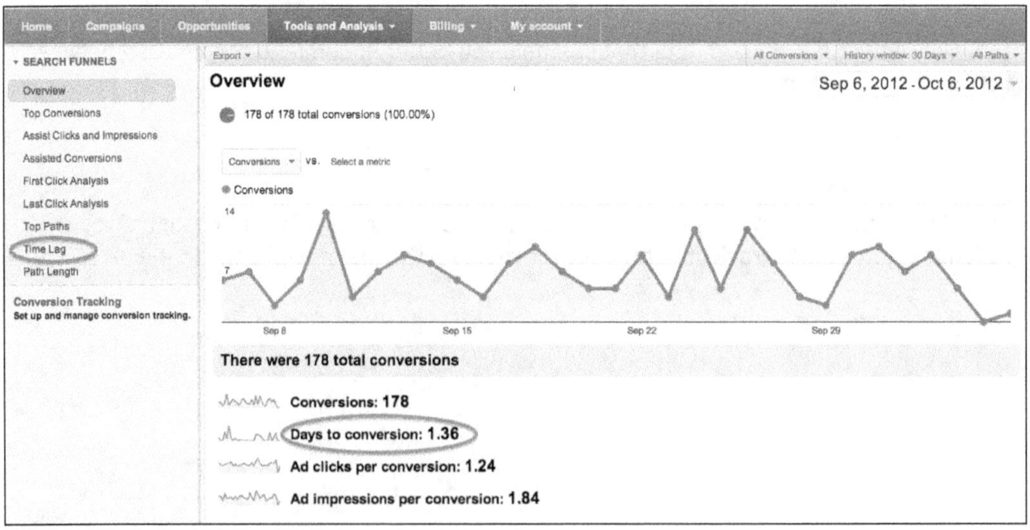

4. Choose from **Days to conversion** or **Hours to conversion** to see the percentage of total conversions completed by day or by hour:

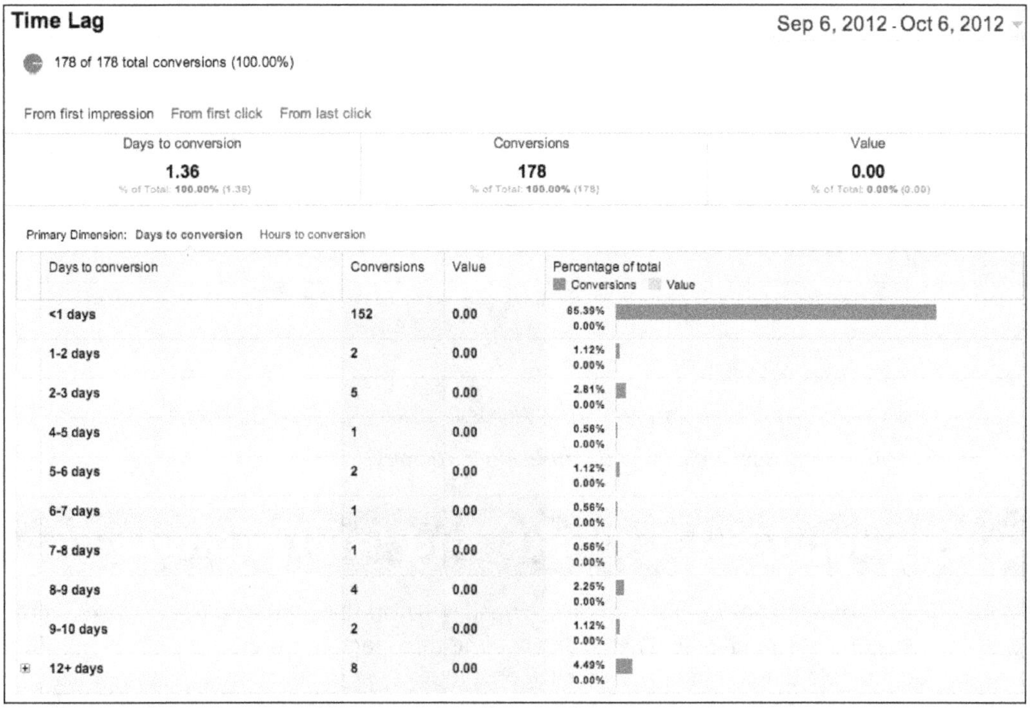

How it works...

AdWords analyzes impressions, clicks, and conversions your ads accrue over time and aggregates this data for a snapshot of a search path. In addition to finding out how many days your customers take to convert, you can also analyze average impressions and clicks before a conversion. In other words, you'll learn how many times users will see your ads and how many times they will click on it before finally taking the desired action.

There's more...

The default history window in **Search Funnels** is 30 days. You have the option to change this to 60 or 90 days at the top-right corner of the **Search Funnels** screen.

You can also choose to analyze time lag from one of the following options:

- **From first impression**
- **From first click**
- **From last click**

If you have multiple conversions, you can analyze them separately by selecting the conversion of interest from the **All Conversions** drop-down menu at the top-right corner of your **Search Funnels** screen:

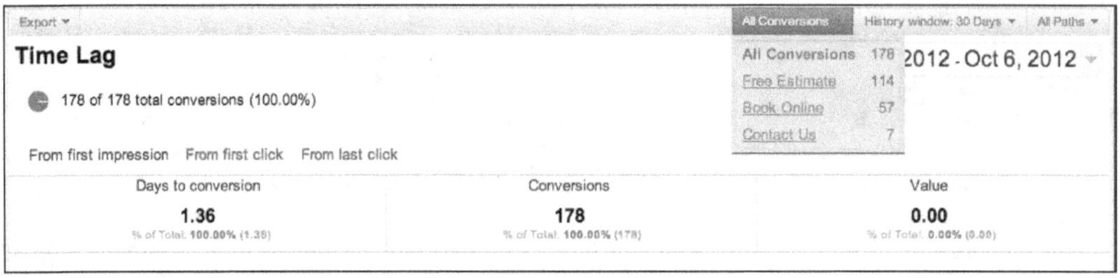

See also

- The *Creating a conversion goal in AdWords to track leads or sales* recipe
- The *Analyzing assist clicks and impressions* recipe

Analyzing assist clicks and impressions

Most of your customers will do a bit of research online before they finally settle on a product they'd like to purchase or choose a service to commit to. In fact, many of your visitors will likely see your ad multiple times and may even click on it more than once before finally converting, and they'll probably use slightly different keywords to research during this process. **Search Funnels** in AdWords, including assist click and impression reports help you analyze this search path that leads up to a conversion.

Getting ready

You will need to have conversion tracking enabled in your account, and your campaigns will need to have generated some conversions.

How to do it...

To analyze which keywords help guide your customers toward a conversion, perform the following steps:

1. Log in to your AdWords account. If you prefer the Google Analytics interface, **Multi Channel Funnels** in your Google Analytics account will provide similar data.
2. In AdWords, select **Conversions** from the **Tools and Analysis** tab.
3. Click on **Search Funnels**.

4. Take a look at the following reports:
   - **SEARCH FUNNELS | Top Paths | Keyword Path**
   - **SEARCH FUNNELS | Top Paths | Query Path**
   - **SEARCH FUNNELS | First Click Analysis**
   - **SEARCH FUNNELS | Assist Clicks and Impressions**

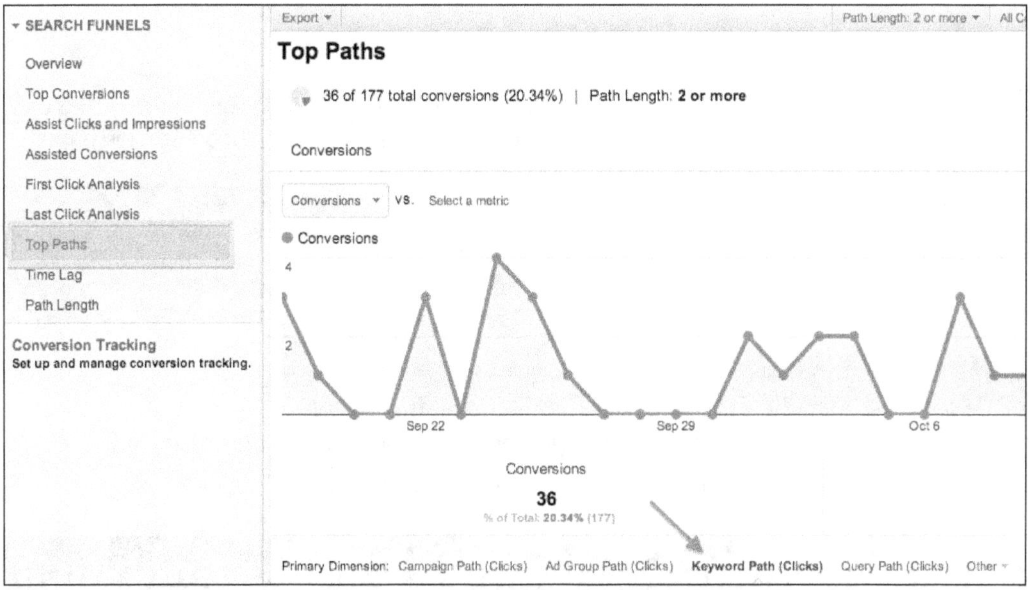

5. Sort by **Assist Clicks and Impressions** or **Last Click Analysis**. The larger the number, the more often this campaign, ad group, or keyword contributes as an assist. If the number is less than 1, then it's mostly a last click contributor.

How it works...

AdWords relies on last click data to attribute conversions. This means that when someone converts via AdWords, the conversion will be attributed to the keyword, which generated the last click, even though that person may have originally clicked on your ad via a completely different keyword. Here is an example:

Mary searches Google for `contact lenses` on Tuesday and clicks on your ad. She does not convert.

Mary searches Google again on Wednesday, but this time types in `buy contacts online` and converts via your ad.

Keyword `buy contacts online` is attributed a conversion in AdWords. You might conclude that keyword `contact lenses` is too costly and does not convert, but you are not taking into consideration that keyword `contact lenses` is in fact a team player keyword, which helps generate sales through assist impressions and clicks.

This information can help you understand which keywords are *good team players*, and while they may not show conversions, are worth advertising on.

There's more...

You can adjust your history window up to 90 days to include more data in your analysis. You can also choose to analyze by path by a specific conversion or the length of your conversion path:

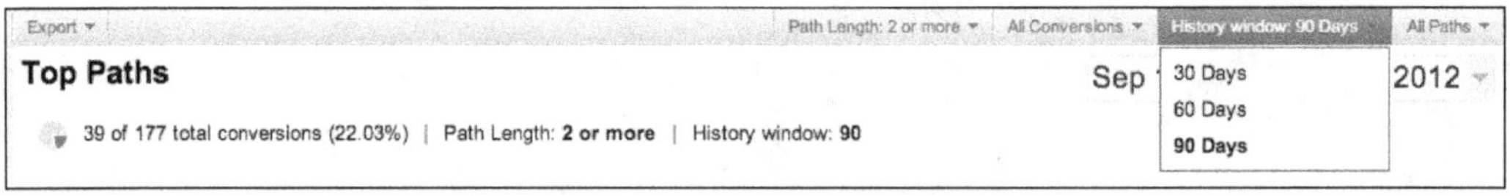

See also

- The *Creating a conversion goal in AdWords to track leads or sales* recipe
- The *Analyzing how long it takes to convert customers* recipe

Analyzing AdWords data in Google Analytics

Once you link your AdWords and Google Analytics accounts, you'll be able to easily analyze AdWords data in your Analytics reports. For example, you'll be able to compare bounce rates (percentage of visitors who view only a single page) or time spent on site by campaign. This will help you better optimize your ad efforts based on user engagement.

Getting ready

The following are a few key Google Analytics definitions you'll need to know as you analyze reports:

- **Visits**: The number of visits to your website.
- **Pages / Visit**: The average number of pages a user visits per session.
- **Avg. Visit Duration**: This specifies the length of time a visitor stays on your website.
- **% New Visits**: The percentage of visits from the first-time visitors who have never been to your website before.

- **Bounce Rate**: The percentage of visitors who view only a single page. For example, a visitor who clicks on your ad and leaves after a few seconds without viewing any other page but the landing page.

> Please note that a visit is not the same as a click in AdWords and you will likely see some discrepancies between the two metrics. Clicks in AdWords are counted when a user clicks on your ad, even if that person doesn't reach your site, such as if they bounce and change their mind or if your site is temporarily down. Visits in Analytics indicates the number of *unique* sessions initiated by your visitors. For example, if a user clicks on your ad twice, Google Analytics will count that as one visit. For a detailed breakdown of the key differences between clicks and visits, refer to the following article:
>
> `http://support.google.com/analytics/bin/answer.py?hl=en&answer=1257084`

How to do it...

To view AdWords reports in your Google Analytics account, perform the following steps:

1. Go to **Tools and Analysis** and click on the **Google Analytics** tab.
2. Click on your website profile.
3. Click to expand **Traffic Sources**.
4. Go to the **Advertising** section, and then click on **AdWords**:

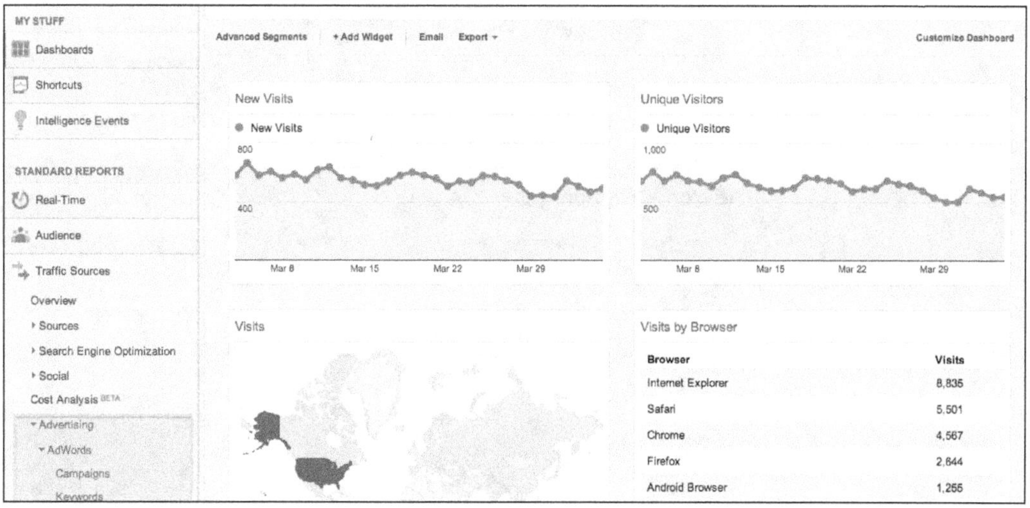

5. Here you will see a list of the numerous options you'll be able to drill down and analyze further. I recommend starting with the **Campaigns** tab, which will give you a summary of all your AdWords efforts combined:

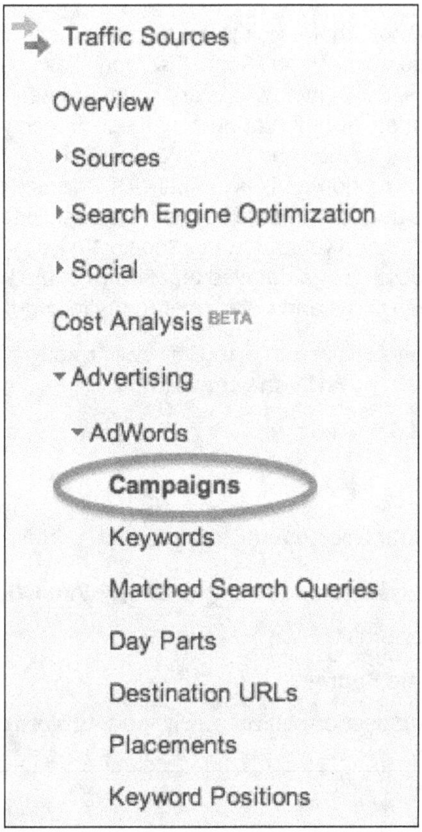

6. Make sure to see if and how the data differs based on what device visitors use:

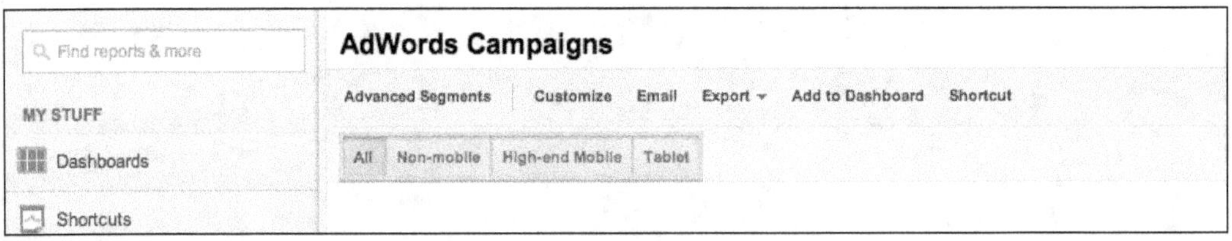

7. Browse through the various AdWords options to see other levels of information available to you, such as **Keywords**, **Placements**, or **Destination URLs**.
8. Go to the **Conversions** section and click on **Multi-Channel Funnels** to review how paid search contributes to your total conversions. Click further into **Top Conversion Paths** to explore how the various traffic channels interact together along a conversion path.
9. Adjust the date range to note trends over time and note the various graph options that Analytics provides based on your selection:

How it works...

Google Analytics imports click and cost data from your AdWords account and displays it in Google Analytics reports, layering on additional information about visitor behavior. For example, you can see how long AdWords visitors stay on your website, how many pages they visit, and what pages they go on to peruse on your website among other useful statistics.

There's more...

In addition to analyzing AdWords data, research where the rest of your traffic is coming from and how the various sources of traffic compare. To check out the top drivers of traffic to your website, go to tab **Traffic Sources** and click on **All Traffic** within **Sources**:

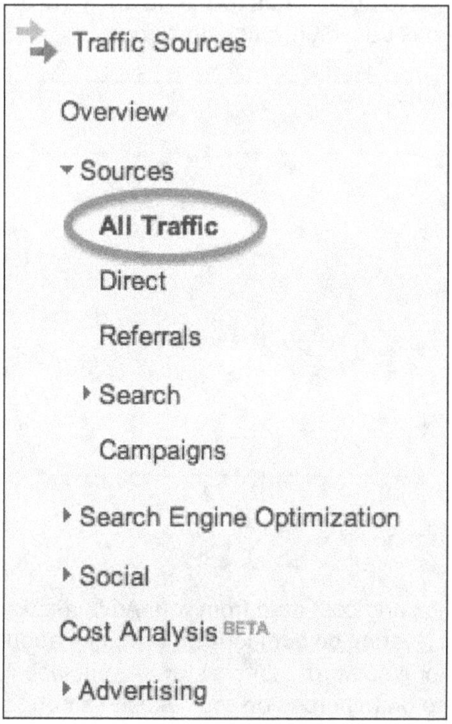

Your top 10 traffic sources will appear in this view, though you can choose to show additional rows. Make sure to find `google / cpc` to understand how much of your total traffic comes from AdWords and how it compares to other sources of traffic, such as organic, which is web traffic that comes from unpaid search listings.

See also

- The *Linking AdWords to Google Analytics* recipe
- The *Analyzing time on site data and bounce rates* recipe

Analyzing time on site data and bounce rates

Understanding how visitors who have clicked on your ads interact with your products and services is vital to optimizing to your marketing campaigns. Some of your campaigns might generate low quality visits and bring users that immediately leave your site. You have an opportunity to analyze this behavior and optimize to ensure that you are focusing your spend on visitors that are interested in your website.

Getting ready

You can analyze AdWords visitor engagement either in Google Analytics directly, or by customizing your column views in AdWords to include Google Analytics data. In order to see AdWords data in Google Analytics, you will need to have first linked your accounts.

How to do it...

To analyze time on site data and bounce rates:

1. Log in to your Google Analytics account.
2. Navigate to the **Advertising** section.
3. Click on **AdWords**.

Start by reviewing campaign-level data first. I recommend initially analyzing the following pieces of information:

- **Bounce Rates**
- **Avg. Visit Duration**
- **Pages / Visit**
- **Goal Completions** (if you set up goals)

Are you seeing differences in user engagement by campaign? If some of your campaigns are bringing visitors who spend a lot less time on your website and are more likely to bounce, you might want to revisit and optimize these campaigns. Similarly, if some of your campaigns are showing really low bounce rates and engaged visitors, you might want to focus more of your budget there.

Keep in mind that high bounce rates are not necessarily always a negative. Perhaps a visitor is comparing shopping options and will return to your website after exploring other options. Before turning off high bounce rate keywords or lowering your budgets and bids, review the conversion data to ensure you are not de-prioritizing high bounce rate campaigns that are actually converting.

In the following example, **Campaign Example 6** is showing higher bounce rates and less time on site than other campaigns and should be further investigated:

	Campaign	Visits ↓	Pages / Visit	Avg. Visit Duration	% New Visits	Bounce Rate
1.	Campaign Example 1	**8,137**	4.00	00:01:28	87.22%	53.93%
2.	Campaign Example 2	**6,515**	6.03	00:02:05	73.42%	32.13%
3.	Campaign Example 3	**3,616**	6.56	00:02:32	88.94%	42.42%
4.	Campaign Example 4	**2,968**	5.06	00:01:40	81.57%	36.56%
5.	Campaign Example 5	**2,228**	5.72	00:01:50	82.81%	36.09%
6.	Campaign Example 6	**789**	2.81	00:00:53	85.93%	60.84%

Clicking on any of your campaigns will take you to the ad group level view, so you can pin-point any particular problem ad groups.

There's more...

Within the **AdWords** tab in Google Analytics, you can analyze user engagement by the following levels of detail:

- **Campaigns**
- **Keywords**
- **Matched Search Queries**
- **Day Parts**
- **Destination URL**
- **Placements**
- **Keyword Positions**

You can also drill down further and analyze additional dimensions within each category. The idea is to identify your low performers, so you can eliminate or optimize them and focus your budget on your top performers.

See also

- The *Linking AdWords to Google Analytics* recipe
- The *Customizing columns to personalize data views* recipe in *Chapter 10, Reporting and Analysis*

4
Structuring Your Account

In this chapter, we will cover the following:

- Planning account structure
- Common ways to structure campaigns
- Deciding where to show your ads
- Device targeting options
- Choosing which locations to target
- Excluding locations from seeing your ads
- Selecting target languages
- Creating themed ad groups
- Renaming campaigns and ad groups

Introduction

Account structure is the fundamental basis of being able to write relevant ads, track and optimize your campaigns, and keep your budget manageable. Poor account structure is one of the most common reasons why advertisers fail, and it can make or break the success of your account. Taking some time to properly plan out your campaigns can save you time and money down the road.

Planning account structure

Proper account structure will help you lay a solid foundation for your ad campaigns and will simplify account management and reporting. Although there are many different ways to structure an account, there are some best practices that have proven to work. Your account structure will depend on your unique business and your goals, and it will likely change over time as you optimize.

Getting ready

Before you start adding in keywords and ads you'd like to advertise on, think about the following:

- What products or services would you like to advertise?
- Are some of your product lines or services of greater priority?
- Where are your potential customers? What locations and regions would you like to target?
- Do you have different budgets for your various products and services?

How to do it...

Before you start creating a campaign, consider the AdWords account hierarchy and how you can best organize your offerings within that structure. An AdWords account has the following major components:

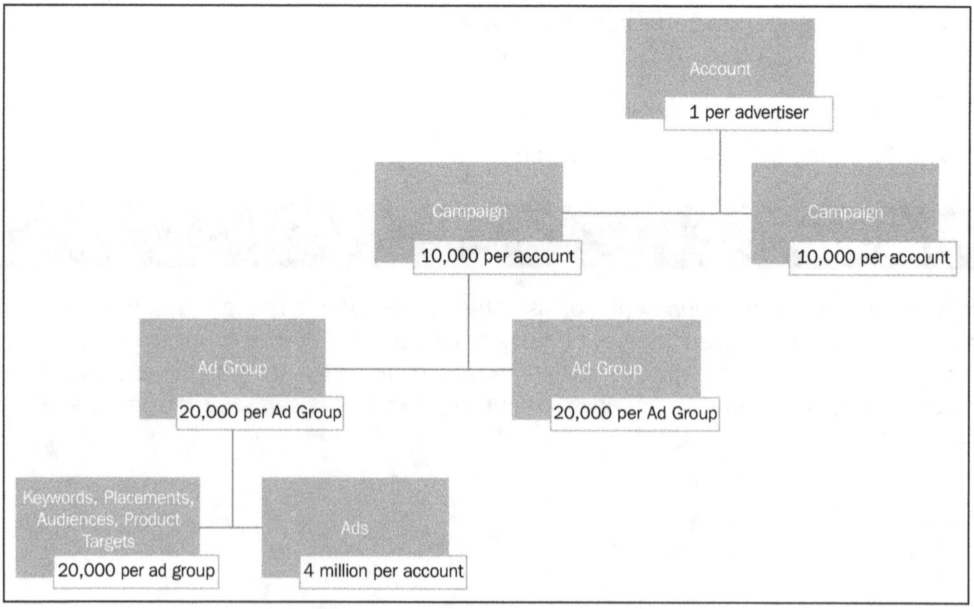

An advertiser typically has one AdWords account with multiple campaigns. Each campaign should have themed ad groups to further group keywords, placements, and other targets. In addition to keywords and other targets, an ad group also contains ads that should reflect each ad group's theme.

As you plan your structure, keep in mind the following best practices:

1. Organize your campaigns by themes. Create separate campaigns for different products or services to take advantage of settings that you choose at the campaign level. For example, as a retailer, you might want to create separate campaigns for the different types of products you sell.
2. Split up your campaigns by Search and Display. Create separate campaigns for the different networks, as they require different strategies.
3. Organize by spend. Create unique campaigns for sets of products that have separate budgets. This will allow you to allocate and control ad spend for each category.
4. An AdWords account has a limit of 5 million targeting items per account, which could include targets such as keywords or placements.

The following are some example campaigns a website that sells furniture might want to start with:

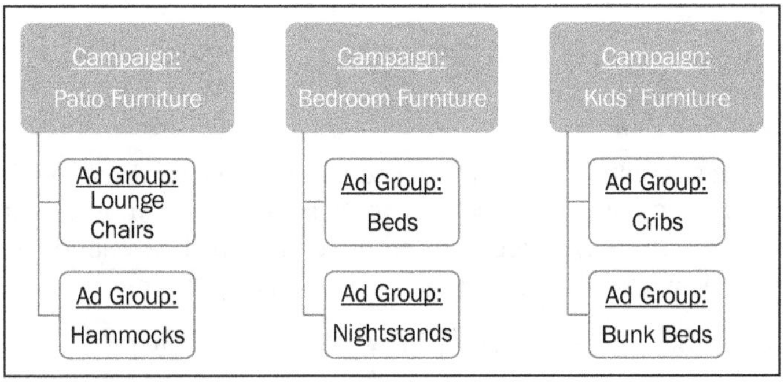

How it works...

You are not forever locked into the account structure that you choose when you first set up your account. You can continue to restructure and refine your campaigns as you go and test. The campaigns you'll develop over time will likely be structured differently than what you start out with.

There's more...

I recommend most advertisers start their initial campaigns by advertising on search only, and to avoid display at first, while you learn more about AdWords and what will work for your business. Once you have a solid understanding of the interface and the various options, I recommend testing display with a smaller budget via a campaign separate from your search campaigns. This way display ads do not dominate your overall spend.

See also

- The *Common ways to structure campaigns* recipe
- The *Creating themed ad groups* recipe

Common ways to structure campaigns

There is no one right or wrong way to structure an account. Each business is unique with different advertising goals, budgets, and priorities. An account structure that works for one advertiser may not work for another. Ultimately, proper account structure with intuitively labeled campaigns will simplify account management and analysis, and will help you to properly test and optimize.

Getting ready

Review your website's sitemap to determine if you can re-use it for AdWords. Many advertisers choose to structure their campaigns according to their website's layout. You have probably structured your website carefully by topics or product, and you'll have landing pages to reflect these categories that you can use for your campaigns and ad groups.

Decide if you'd like to advertise on search, display, or on both networks.

How to do it...

The following are some common ways and best practices to structure your campaigns:

- **By network**: Always keep search and display networks separate. Create different campaigns for search and display strategies so you can customize settings and use different budgets.
    - Halloween costumes - Search
    - Halloween costumes - Display

- **By location**: If your business operates in different locations, you might want to consider creating different campaigns targeting these locations so you can better customize keywords and ads for each region. For example, if you sell Halloween costumes in the United States and the United Kingdom, you could create separate campaigns for each country, customizing ads within each campaign with country specific offers, such as shipping.
    - Halloween costumes - US
    - Halloween costumes - UK
- **By types of products or services**: You can create separate campaigns for sets of products or similar services. For example, if you sell shoes, you can create the following campaigns:
    - Women's shoes
    - Kid's shoes
    - Men's shoes
- **By brand**: Many businesses, especially retailers and e-commerce websites, sell a variety of brands that can each have their own campaigns.
    - Samsung
    - Apple
    - Nokia
- **By priority or ROI**: If some of your products or services are higher priority than others you may wish to keep them in their own campaigns. This will allow you to use a higher budget for that strategic set of keywords. For example, you can have two campaigns:
    - High priority keywords with a bigger chunk of your budget
    - Low priority keywords with a smaller budget
- **By language**: If your target audience speaks multiple languages, you can choose to segment campaigns by language. For example:
    - Kid's shoes - English
    - Kid's shoes - Spanish

> Name your campaigns to reflect the keywords and settings you are choosing, so you can easily analyze the data. You can rename your campaigns and ad groups at any time. However, if you rename a campaign in AdWords, it will be tracked as a brand new campaign in your Google Analytics reports.

How it works...

Keeping campaigns separate is important because you can allocate different budgets for each campaign. It also helps you better analyze returns, prioritize ad budgets and spending on what's working, and act based on changes to business inventory, priorities, or customer demand.

For example, if you had separate campaigns for two different brands of shoes, you could turn off the brand that is currently out of stock and increase the budget on a brand that came out with a popular new model.

If you simply lumped all of your keywords into one campaign, the highest search volume keywords which may not even be converting for you might end up dominating your spend and might prevent your important keywords from showing up.

There's more...

You will likely start with a more simple account structure that will develop and change as you learn what works for you. You can always move keywords and ads from one campaign to another and split up one campaign into multiple campaigns to a more precise target. If you choose to re-organize your campaigns, your new campaigns will start out with fresh statistics, but you will be able to access past reports and data at any time.

See also

- The *Planning account structure* recipe
- The *Creating themed ad groups* recipe
- The *Renaming campaigns and ad groups* recipe

Deciding where to show your ads

As you are setting up your AdWords campaigns, you have the option to choose your targeting preferences more broadly to maximize your ad reach, or to restrict targeting to ensure ads are only showing to your very specific audience. Who will end up seeing your ads will depend on the campaign settings you choose as you create your campaigns.

Getting ready

The first setting you'll need to consider when creating your campaigns will be which networks you'd like to show ads on. Google has two main networks through which ads are served:

- Search network
  - Includes `Google.com`, Google properties such as Google Maps, and search partners, such as `AOL.com`.
  - Ads are text based.
- Display network
  - Includes Gmail, YouTube, and millions of partner websites, such as `nytimes.com`, where your potential customers could be reading the news or articles related to your products.
  - Ad formats include: text, image, video, and rich media.

How to do it...

If you are new to AdWords, I recommend you start with a search only campaign while you learn the platform. If you'd still like to test display from the start, I recommend keeping it separate from your search campaign:

1. Click on the **Campaigns** tab and click on the prompt to create a new campaign.
2. Choose either **Search Network only** or **Display Network only**. I do not recommend choosing **Search & Display Networks** from within one campaign.
3. If you'd like to target both search and display, create two separate campaigns, choosing one network within each campaign.

4. If you already have an AdWords campaign running, you can check which networks you have opted to show on in your campaign **Settings** page under the **Networks** section:

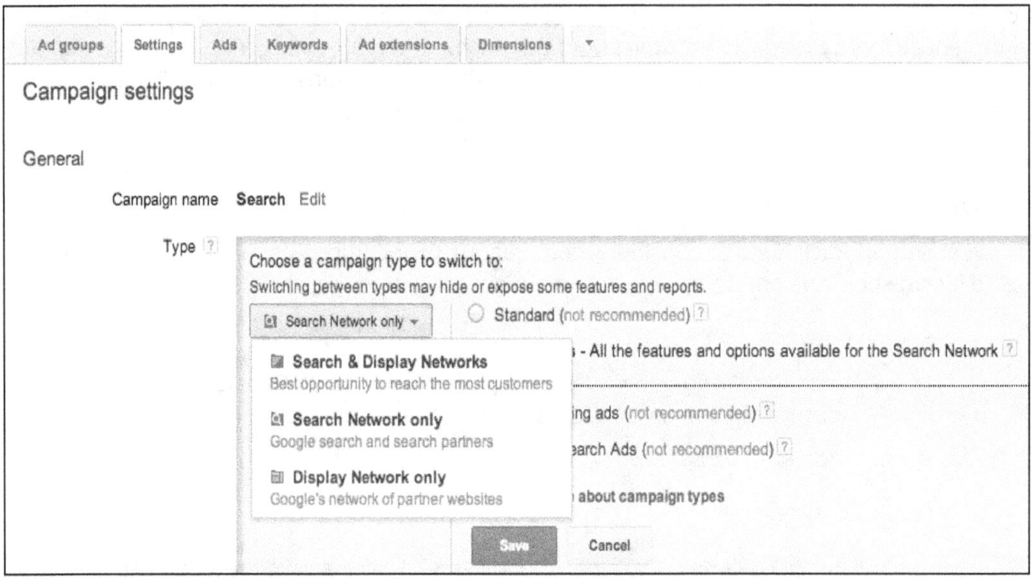

How it works...

On the **Search Network only** option, AdWords ads are served based on a user's search query. Users search for specific information and do so via keywords they type in to a search box. The ads that are shown are driven by search queries, hence **Search Network only**.

On the **Display Network only** option, AdWords ads can be served based on the websites' content or user interests. Users browse online information, such as news articles, and AdWords ads appear alongside this content, which the AdWords system deems relevant based on the keywords and themes you have chosen for your campaign. Advertiser can also choose to target specific websites that they know are browsed by their target audience.

There's more...

Users who are seeing your ads via the Google Search network or through the Display network will tend to be in very different phases of the buying or decision cycle, and you should consider this as you plan out your advertising strategies.

The Google Search network will generally bring you visitors who are more ready to purchase, and they are searching for specific products and services.

On the Google Display network, users are browsing online for content and may not be looking for your product or service at that moment. They are often not as likely to convert as visitors who find you via search ads.

However, through Display, you can show your ads to users who are browsing websites that are highly targeted to what you are offering or websites that are specific to your target demographic. The Display network is a great way to boost traffic and reach those who may not be even aware that they need your products.

For example, a country club in California looking to sell golf club memberships can show an image ad with a beautiful golf course to a user who is reading an article about the latest golf clubs.

For most businesses, the Search network will convert a bit better than the Display network. However, this is not the case for all advertisers. In fact, for some, Display outperforms Search, especially because the former has become quite saturated and competitive for many industries. I recommend you test both networks to find how your audience responds.

See also

- The *Planning account structure* recipe
- The *Common ways to structure campaigns* recipe

Device targeting options

Your customers are increasingly searching for you not just from their computers, but from high-end mobile devices, such as smartphones and tablets. This rapid growth of mobile necessitates custom strategies for the different ways users behave, depending on what device they use. For example, people searching from their computer desks tend to use longer search phrases than those searching on their smartphones. While you cannot opt out of tablet devices, you can adjust mobile bids through each campaign and ad group. Savvy marketers track ROI from each device and create tailored strategies to maximize the potential of each user base.

Getting ready

By default, each campaign is designed to be displayed on all devices. However, before you spend money advertising on mobile phones, make sure that your website is mobile friendly. Many advertisers invest in creating a mobile friendly version of their website, optimized for the mobile browsing experience. Many visitors will not be willing to fill out a long contact form or complete a transaction on their smartphones, so make sure you take that into consideration.

> To check out what your website looks like on a mobile device and to make it more mobile friendly, go to `http://www.howtogomo.com`.

How to do it...

To choose and modify mobile device targeting, perform the following steps:

1. If your website loads properly on smartphones, target all devices to start with and then adjust mobile bids based on performance.
2. Your default device targeting is preset so ads are shown on all devices as you create your campaign:

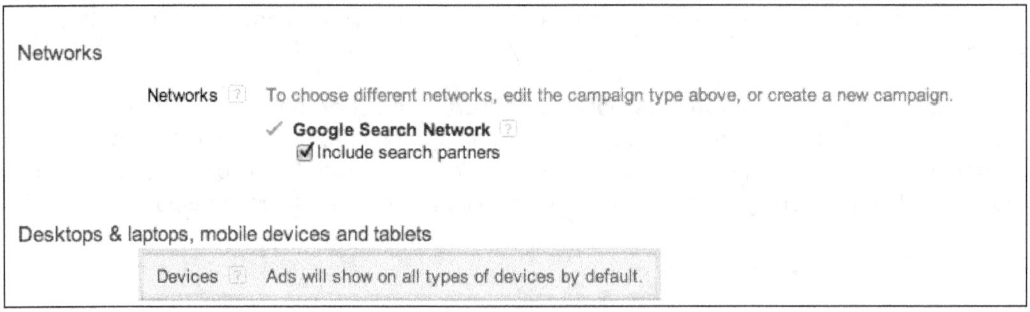

3. After you create your campaign, you can adjust mobile bids in your campaign's **Settings** page. To opt out of mobile completely, use a **-100%** bid adjustment:

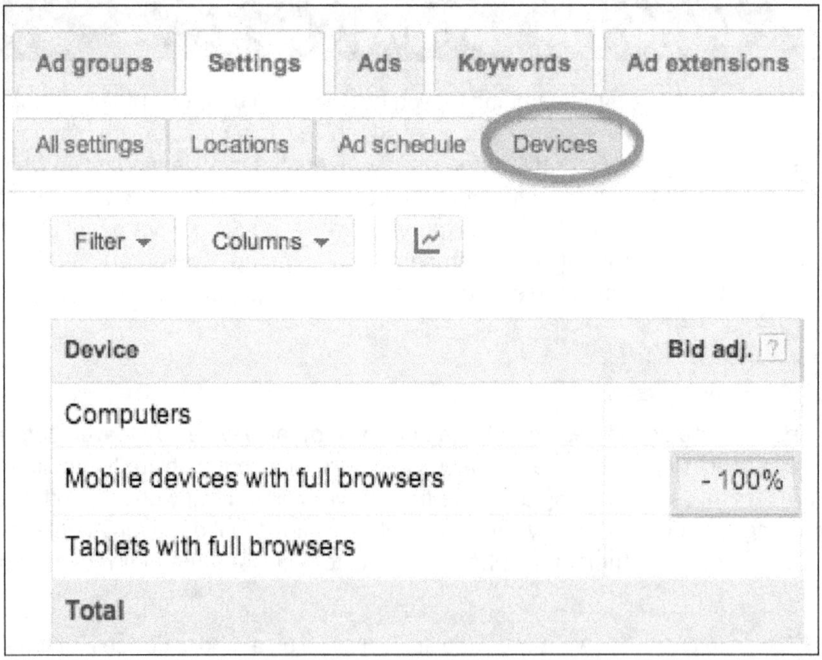

4. Mobile bids are adjusted at the campaign or at the ad group level, and you'll need to repeat this process for each of your campaigns.

5. Your device settings page does not provide the option to opt out of computers or tablets. However, you can set very low default ad group bids (for example, $0.01) and use aggressive mobile bid adjustments (for example, increase by 500 percent) to virtually opt a campaign out of computers and tablets and run mostly on mobile. You may still get some traffic from computers and tablets, but with very low default bids, such clicks should be minimal.

How it works...

To help you better segment how your customers are finding you, AdWords offers the following device targeting options:

- Desktop and laptop computers
- Mobile devices with full browsers
- Tablets with full browsers

Advertisers cannot opt campaigns out of computers or tablets, but you can adjust this by increasing or decreasing mobile bids.

You can see each campaign's traffic segmented by device in your AdWords **Campaign Management** page. Simply click on **Segment** and choose **Device** to see device-specific performance breakdowns by campaign:

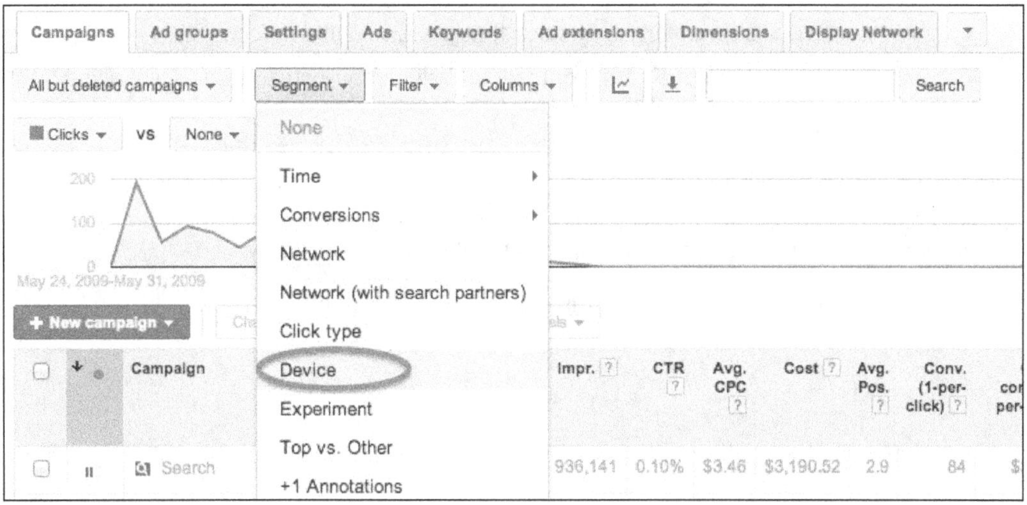

See also

- The *Planning account structure* recipe
- The *Creating themed ad groups* recipe

Choosing which locations to target

Precise location targeting is one of the biggest selling points of AdWords, offering advertisers the flexibility to reach their customers wherever they might be and to customize messaging based on location. You can target as broadly as worldwide, or get as granular as targeting a specific city or a predefined radius.

Your ads will appear to people you are targeting, avoiding irrelevant clicks and helping you to zero in on the most targeted audience, but please note that location targeting may not always be 100 percent accurate.

Getting ready

Think about where your target customers are located and who you'd like to see your ads. Ask yourself the following questions:

- Do you ship products internationally or work with customers outside of your country?
- If you are a local business, how far of a radius are your customers willing to travel from, or how far are you willing to travel to reach your customers?
- Are there specific metro areas or cities that you would like to focus on?
- Do you have multiple business locations that will require customized messaging?

How to do it...

You will choose your location targeting preferences as you set up each campaign. You can also edit any location preferences you may have set up already:

1. Navigate from the campaign setting page to the **Locations** section.

2. If you are a business that services worldwide clients, choose **All countries and territories**:

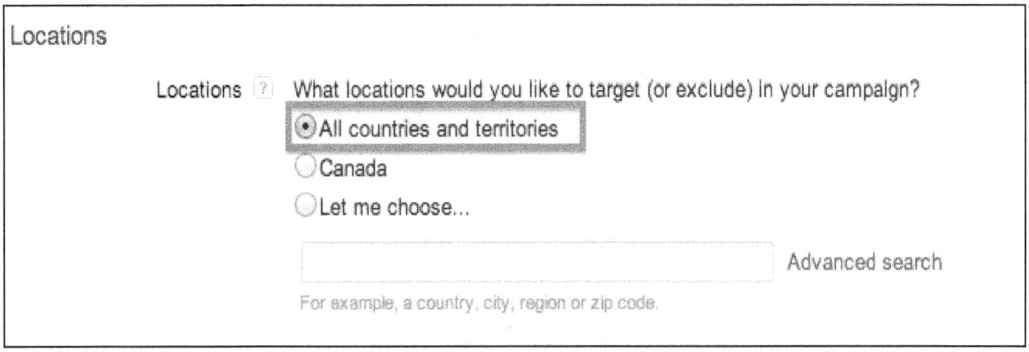

3. If your target audience is in a specific country, state, or metro area, type in your search into the **Let me choose...** box to narrow down your focus. AdWords will start to populate related available targets based on what you are typing in:

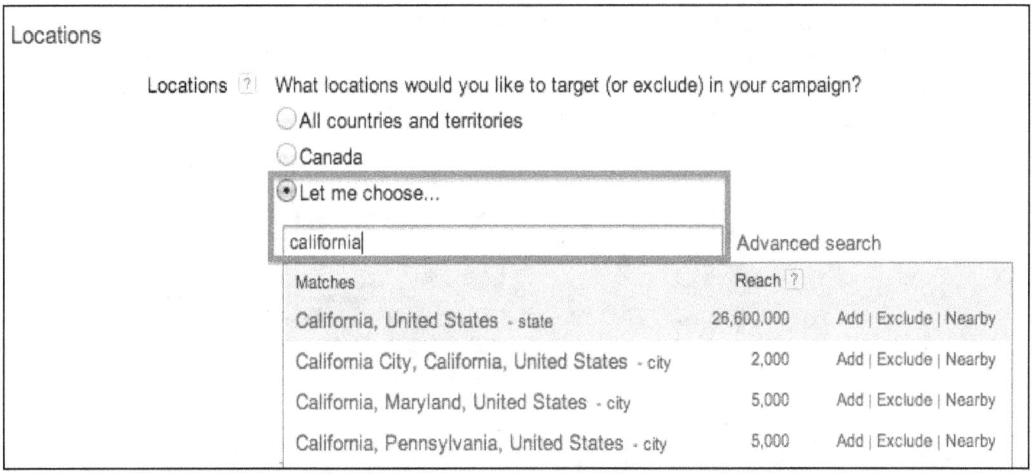

4. Click on **Add** to add a specific location option from your search.

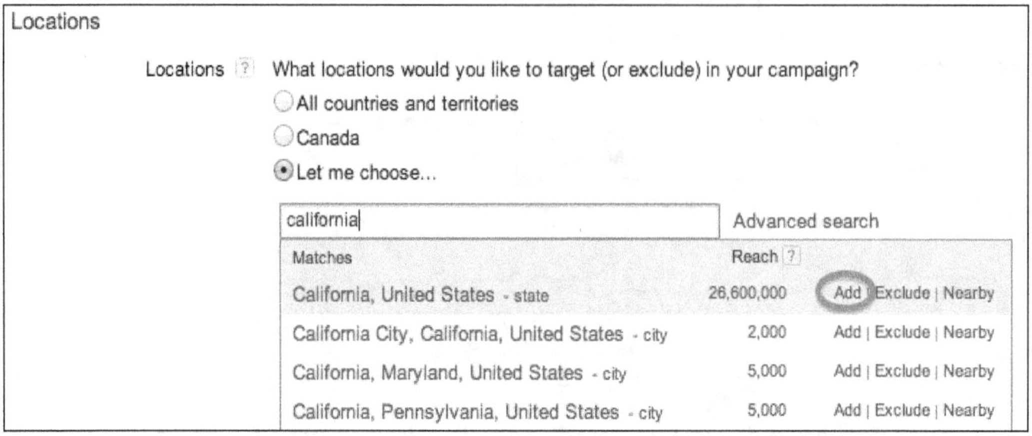

5. Click on **Nearby** if you'd like to see other options that are close to your search. A new box will pop up with additional nearby options that you can choose to target.
6. To target around a radius, type into the search box your zip code, then click on **Nearby**. Another screen will pop up that will allow you to choose a range in miles around a specific radius. Click to add your chosen location, pick the number of miles to target around, and save your selection:

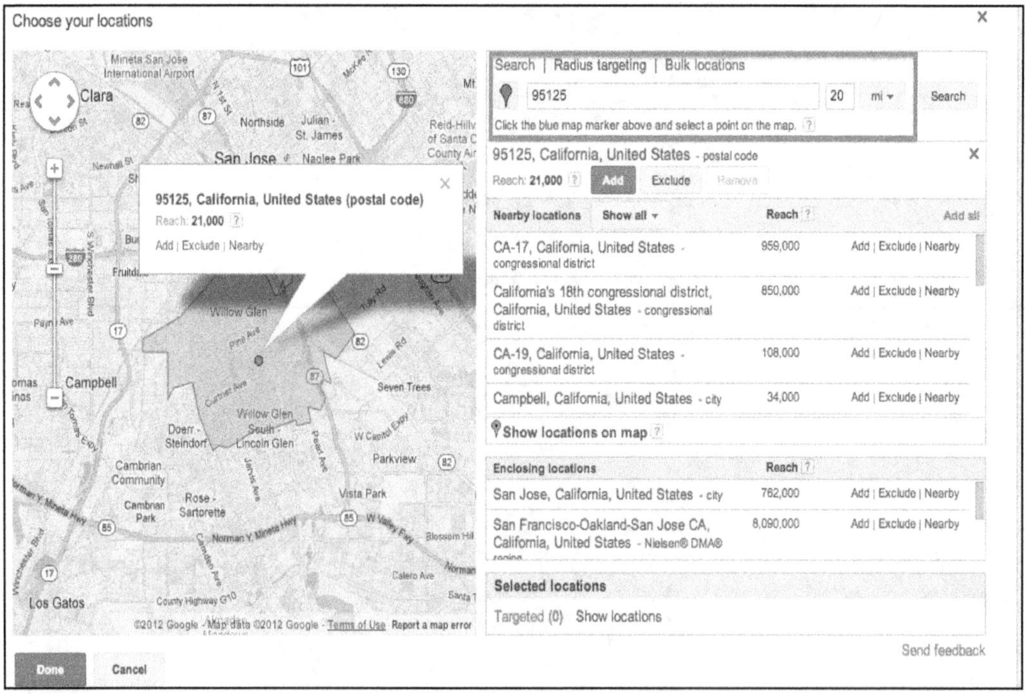

How it works...

AdWords figures out a user's location and serves ads based on one of following factors:

- **Physical location (IP address)**: AdWords determines someone's physical location based on their computer location, which is determined via an Internet protocol (IP) address. An IP address is a unique number assigned by Internet service providers (ISP) to each computer. Please note that some ISPs mask their users' IP addresses, so IP address targeting is not 100 percent accurate.
- **Search intent**: AdWords serves ads based on interest in geographic areas indicated through searches. A user may indicate interest in a specific location via a search query, even though that user could be located outside the target location. For example, Mary from San Francisco is looking for a spa in New York. Even though Mary is physically located in San Francisco, AdWords recognizes that she is interested in a spa outside of her current physical location, because of her `spa in new york` search query, and an AdWords ad targeting the New York area pops up.
- **Google domain**: Each country has a unique URL that helps Google determine where a user is located. For example, someone searching Google from France might be on `google.fr`.
- **Mobile device location**: If a user is searching from a high-end mobile device, AdWords may be able to detect device location and serve relevant ads.

See also

- The *Excluding locations from seeing your ads* recipe

Excluding locations from seeing your ads

AdWords offers the ability to restrict whom your ads are shown to and exclude locations you do not do business with, or cities and zip codes that are not profitable for you. By showing ads only to locations you are interested in working with, you can improve your results and ROI.

Getting ready

The following is a list of who will benefit from excluding locations:

- Business that do not ship to certain states or regions
- Businesses that want to avoid working in specific cities or zip codes
- Companies that may not be licensed to operate in all states

How to do it...

To exclude locations within individual campaigns, perform the following steps:

1. Go to the **Campaigns** tab, click on the campaign you'd like to edit, and choose **Settings**.
2. Choose the **Locations** sub-tab and click on **Edit locations**.
3. Type the location you'd like to exclude in the search box and click on **Exclude**:

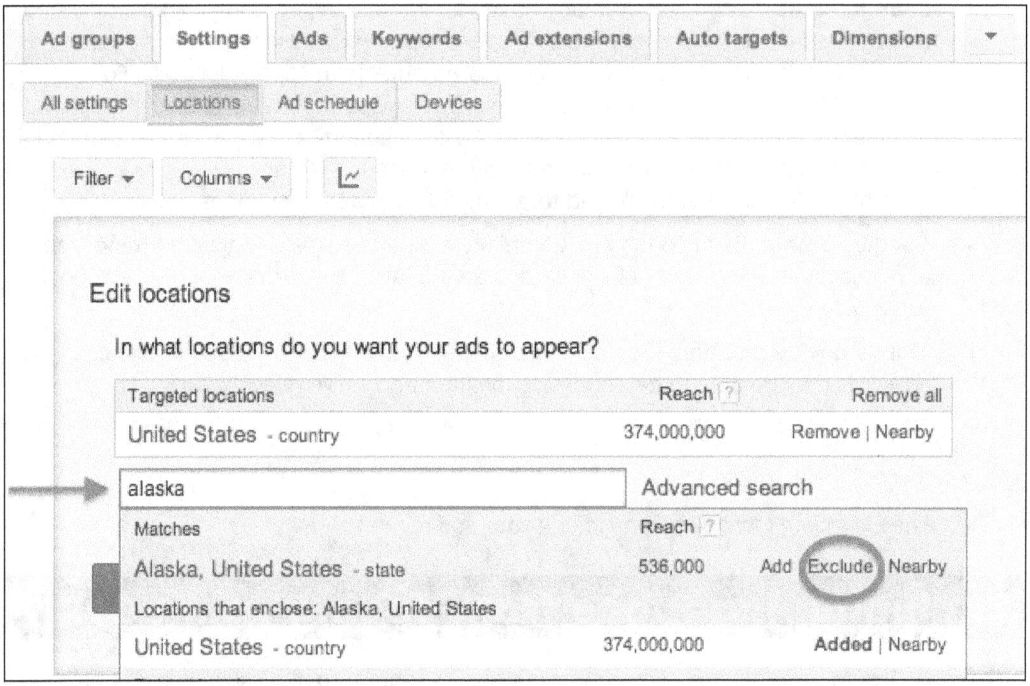

4. Save your selection.

How it works...

Location exclusion ensures that your ads are not shown to people in cities or regions you select. You can exclude a specific zip code, city, metro area, state, or entire country. Once you add a location to exclude, AdWords will not serve your ads within that region.

See also

- The *Choosing which locations to target* recipe

Selecting target languages

AdWords lets you choose the languages of the websites that your ads appear on. You can choose to target specific languages or all available languages for greatest reach.

Getting ready

To determine if you should target multiple languages, consider the following:

- What languages do your customers speak or what languages are spoken in the areas you'll target?
- Is your website available in multiple languages?
- Is your business, such as your customer support and sales teams, equipped to handle inquiries from multiple languages?

How to do it...

To edit your campaign language preferences:

1. Go to the **Campaigns** tab, click on the campaign you'd like to edit, and choose **Settings**. You should be in the **All settings** sub-tab.
2. Scroll down to **Languages** and click on **Edit**.
3. Choose applicable languages and click on **Save**:

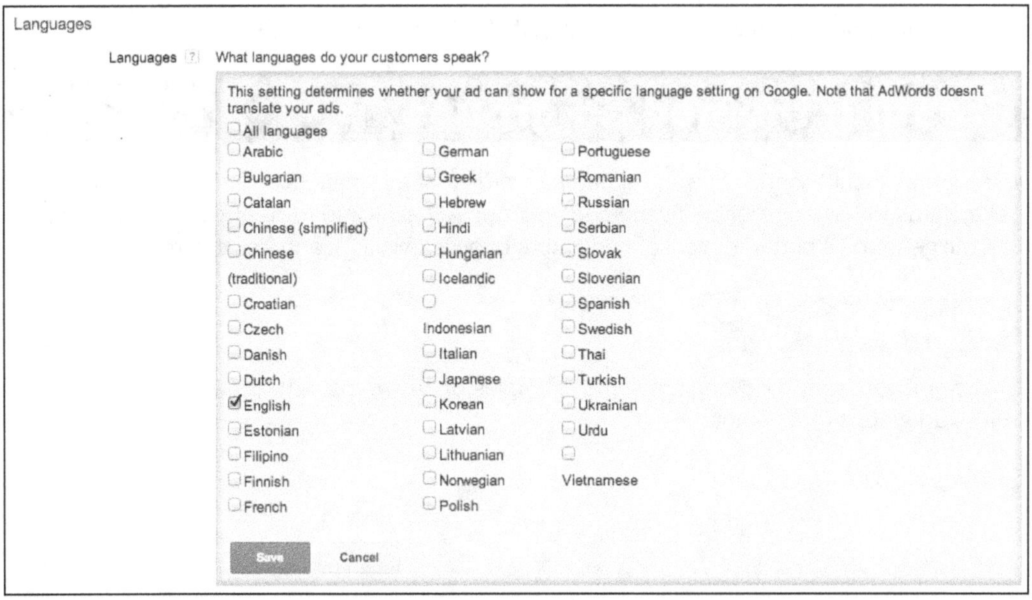

How it works...

AdWords decides where to show ads based on one of the following:

- Google language setting. Each Google domain has a default (for example, `Google.it` defaults to Italian), but you can change your language settings via `http://www.google.com/preferences`.
- Language of a user's search query, or in what language is the user searching on Google.
- The language of the currently viewed page or recently viewed pages on Google's Display network. For example, if a person is reading news in Italian, AdWords will show ads targeted to Italian speakers.

There's more...

Language targeting is chosen at the campaign level. You may wish to create separate campaigns for different language targets, especially if you are considering using keywords in different languages and have a website that's translated into multiple languages. For example, you may wish to have the following campaigns:

- Campaign #1 - English
- Campaign #2 - Spanish

See also

- The *Choosing which locations to target* recipe

Creating themed ad groups

An ad group should contain closely related keywords that all speak to a similar theme. Keeping all keywords within a single, tightly themed ad group will allow you to create more targeted ads that will generate a better response, bring more qualified visitors, and improve returns.

Getting ready

To help you get ready, following are some examples of ad groups that follow best practices as well as ad groups that do not.

Recommended ad group structure

The following three ad groups each have small, closely themed keyword lists, which will allow us to write specific ad text for each group of keywords:

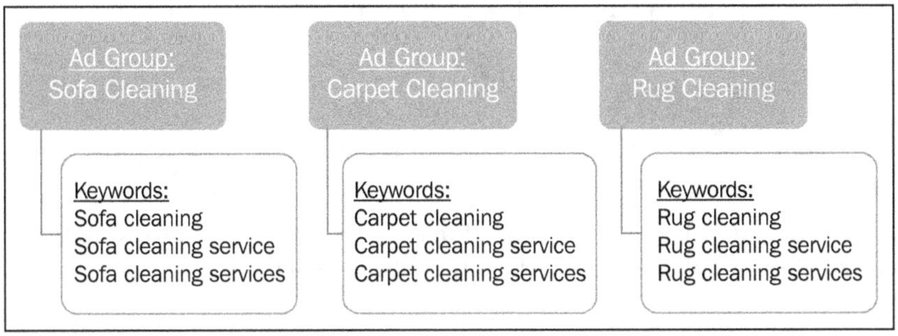

Poor ad group structure

If an ad group has several keywords, all with different themes, your ads are less likely to be effectively targeted. The following is an example of a poorly themed ad group with only keywords within that ad group loosely related:

A good test to double check if your themes are tight enough is to ask yourself if each keyword within your ad group has been reflected in your ad text. Make sure you find a balance between relevant groupings and being too specific. Creating a separate ad group for each individual keyword is likely not the best use of your time!

How to do it...

To create a new ad group within an AdWords campaign, perform the following steps:

1. Go to the **Campaigns** tab, and click on the campaign you'd like to create ad groups for.
2. Click on **+ New ad group**.
3. Name your ad group. Choose a name descriptive of the keywords that you will be adding to this ad group.
4. Write a text ad. Your ads should point out what makes your business unique and include some of your keywords, ideally in your headline:

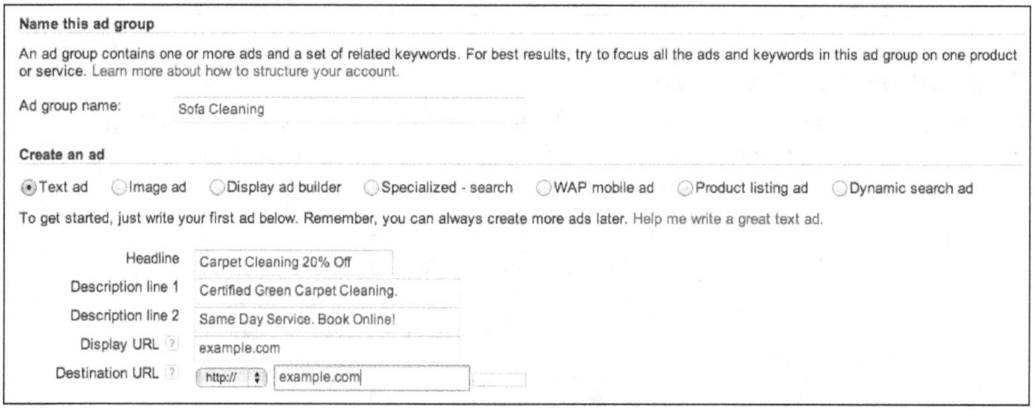

5. Enter your keywords. Start with small, targeted lists of 5 to 10 keywords.
6. Choose a default bid that will apply to this ad group. Refer to *Chapter 1, Researching the Market and Competition and Setting Goals*, and research competitors to get bid ideas.
7. Click on **Save ad group**:

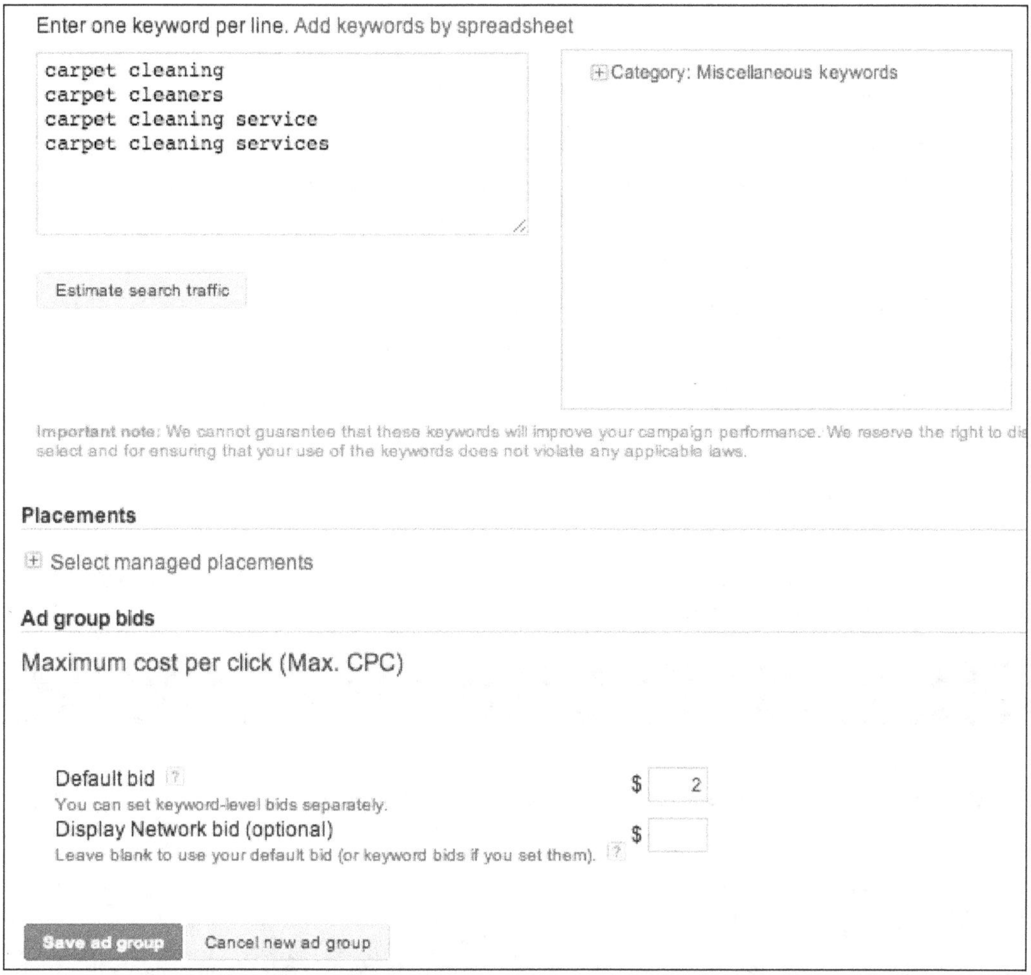

How it works...

An ad group is a set of similar keywords and ads with a default bid. Within each campaign, you can have multiple ad groups. Each campaign can house up to 20,000 ad groups.

There's more...

The following are some common themes to create ad groups around:

- Different products or services (such as carpet cleaning and furniture cleaning)
- Different ways to describe the same product or service (such as carpet cleaning and rug cleaning)
- Multiple locations (such as San Jose carpet cleaning and Santa Clara carpet cleaning)
- Separate ad groups for each landing page, product, or service
- Separate ad groups for special offers or holiday promotions

See also

- The *Planning account structure* recipe
- The *Creating themed ad groups* recipe
- The *Using third-party tools to research competitors* recipe in *Chapter 1, Researching the Market and Competition and Setting Goals*

Renaming campaigns and ad groups

After you set up your campaigns and ad groups, you may wish to rename them to better reflect the theme or promotion you are running. You can rename AdWords campaigns and ad groups at any time.

Getting ready

Plan out your new naming convention. It's usually helpful to describe the campaign's theme as well as the network you are targeting.

How to do it...

1. Click on the **Campaigns** tab, hover next to the campaign or ad group you wish to rename until you see a pencil icon, then click on it.
2. Enter the new name and click on **Save**:

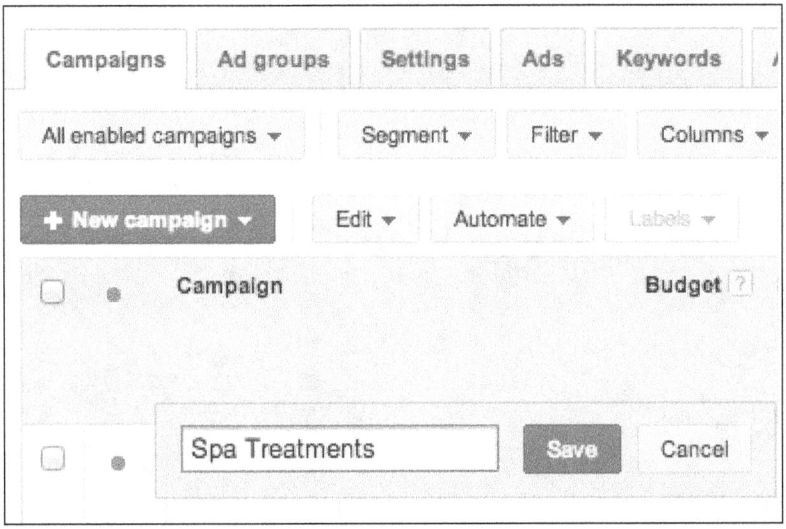

There's more...

You may wish to name your campaigns to reflect the products and services you are promoting, which regions they target, or to indicate what networks you are running ads on. For example, you could have a campaign named `Printing Supplies - Search - USA`. If you decide to rename a campaign, keep in mind that it will start showing as a new campaign in your Google Analytics reports, so try to avoid frequently changing campaign names.

See also

- The *Planning account structure* recipe

5 Creating Relevant Keywords

In this chapter, we will cover the following:

- Using keyword matching options effectively
- Finding relevant keywords
- Analyzing competitor keywords from spyfu.com and similar tools
- Generating negative keywords
- Identifying keyword duplicates
- Multiplying keyword phrases
- Changing broad keywords to broad match modifier
- Adding new keywords to an existing ad group
- Editing, pausing, or deleting keywords

Introduction

Keywords are the backbone of your account, setting the stage for those who see your ads, as well as those who do not. They're a powerful method to connect to potential customers at the moment they are searching for you. Advertisers choose their own keywords in AdWords, and this process of choosing relevant keywords is vital to marketing success.

Many advertisers think that adding as many keywords as possible will boost traffic and generate more sales. However, that's not necessarily the case for AdWords, where adding too many irrelevant keywords can actually hurt you in the long run.

Keep in mind that some keywords are more relevant to your website than others and also have different conversion potential. If you choose to run ads on irrelevant keywords you might end up spending money on clicks that are unlikely to convert.

What's more, adding keywords in AdWords that are too general and irrelevant to your website will likely lead to low Quality Scores and might hurt your chances of being profitable on even the more specific keywords. AdWords punishes advertisers who historically choose low quality keywords, in order to protect the user experience and ensure relevant ads are shown on Google.

I recommend starting with smaller, targeted keywords lists, and adding to them as you learn what works to build your Quality Scores.

Using keyword matching options effectively

Keyword matching options allow you to control who sees your ads by broadening or restricting what searches your ads appear in. They range from broad to specific. The broader match types are designed to generate more traffic and show your ads on related searches that you may not have thought to add to your campaigns. The more specific match types restrict the queries that your ads show on and typically bring fewer impressions, but potentially more targeted traffic.

How to do it...

To add keywords in different match types, perform the following steps:

1. Click on the **Campaigns** tab, go into a specific campaign and ad group where you wish to add keywords.
2. Navigate to the **Keywords** tab and click on **+ Add keywords**.
3. Add keywords according to the parameters outlined in the following table. For example, if you wish to use exact match, add brackets around each keyword, such as `[red roses]`.
4. Click on **Save**.

The following is an example of how to enter the example keyword `red roses` in each of the match types to your AdWords account:

Keyword match type	How to use it
Broad	red roses
Broad match modifier	+red +roses
Phrase	"red roses"
Exact	[red roses]
Negative	-pictures

How it works...

The following table explains how the different AdWords match types work, examples of how they might trigger your ads, and recommended use cases:

Matching Option	How it works	Ads may show on	Best used when...
Broad: red roses	Ads will show on synonyms, related searches, and other variations AdWords finds relevant that you may not have added to your account.	red flowers cheap roses	You want to maximize traffic and do not have time to generate extensive lists of keywords.
Broad match modifier: +red +roses	Ads will show on close variations but not synonyms or related searches.	find red roses red beautiful roses	Broad match is showing your ads on irrelevant queries and you need to restrict traffic. Broad match modifier is a great in-between option when broad is too general but phrase too restrictive.
Phrase: "red roses"	Word order is preserved and the phrase with its close variants will trigger your ads. Words used before and after the phrase you entered might be eligible for the auction.	buy red roses redrozes red roses for sale	When you'd like to preserve the word order and take the keywords out of the broad match expansion.
Exact: [red roses]	The exact keyword and its close variants will trigger your ads. Your ads will not show on synonyms and other variations.	red roses redrozes	When you'd like to limit traffic to only the specific search term you are entering and do not want your ads showing on any other variations.
Negative: -pictures	Prevent irrelevant searches from triggering your ads.		You are getting irrelevant traffic and need to improve ROI.

The default match type in AdWords is broad, and broad is what most advertisers use throughout their accounts. However, you might find that you get better ROI from some of the more specific match types, such as phrase and exact. If you are using broader keyword match types, you can see what other queries your ads are appearing on by running a search terms report.

> I recommend most advertisers start with mostly broad match combined with negative keywords. Over time, you can refine and optimize your campaigns based on results and search query reports.

There's more...

I recommend using your most important keywords, as well as your highest traffic generating keyword in various match types, so you can adjust bids based on performance. For example, you might find that your exact match version of a particular keyword converts at a more profitable CPA than broad match, and you can then increase the bid on that exact match keyword.

By default, AdWords will include plurals, misspellings, and other close variants of your phrase and exact match keywords. However, you have the option to opt out of this in your campaign **Settings** page, under **Advanced settings** for **Keyword matching options**. I do not recommend excluding close variants, since the additional traffic will be very close to the keywords you have chosen.

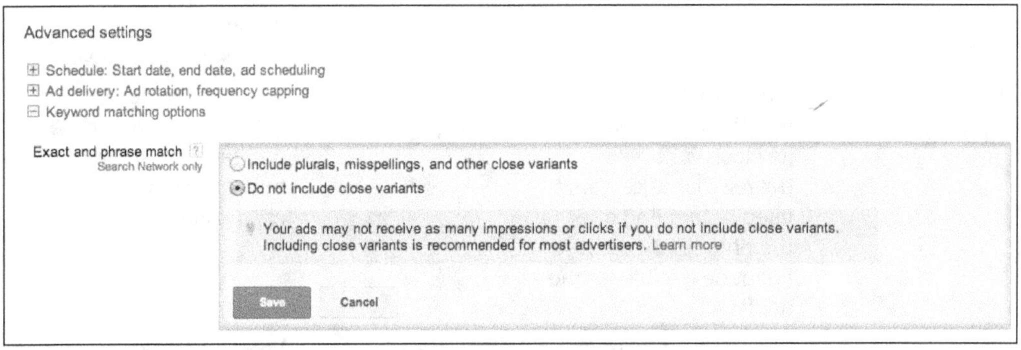

See also

- The *Finding relevant keywords* recipe
- The *Running search term reports to optimize keywords* recipe in *Chapter 11, Optimizing Performance*

Finding relevant keywords

Choosing the right keywords to show your ads can make or break the success of your AdWords account. The keywords you select, if properly researched and are relevant to your website, can bring highly interested visitors to your website, or if too general, can cost you a lot without generating any sales.

Getting ready

Ask your customers what terms they use on `Google.com` to find you. Note down the top phrases that are used consistently and save them for future research and keyword development.

Also, brainstorm key terms, which you think describe your business. Do not worry at this step if they are too general or specific enough for AdWords. Simply note the general keyword ideas.

How to do it...

Once you have brainstormed a list of potential keywords, research and develop them further with Google's keyword tool. The tool is free and is available to all advertisers within their AdWords account.

If you do not yet have an AdWords account, you can access the keyword tool by visiting `https://adwords.google.com/o/KeywordTool`. To access the tool via your AdWords account, go to **Tools and Analysis** and choose the **Keyword Tool** option.

You can research keywords you brainstormed earlier via Google's **Keyword Tool** to find out potential traffic, costs, and the level of competition:

1. Type in the keyword you're considering using in your account in the **Word or phrase** box in the **Keyword Tool** window.
2. Choose your location under **Advanced Options and Filters**.
3. Select the **Keyword ideas** tab in **Keyword Tool**.
4. Click on **Search** to get data on your original search term and additional keyword ideas. The keyword tool will provide you with additional phrases related to your original search that can serve as ideas for new keywords to add to your campaigns.

5. If many of the related keywords suggested by the tool are not relevant to you, your original search query may be too general. Instead, use some of the other, more relevant suggestions from the keyword tool.

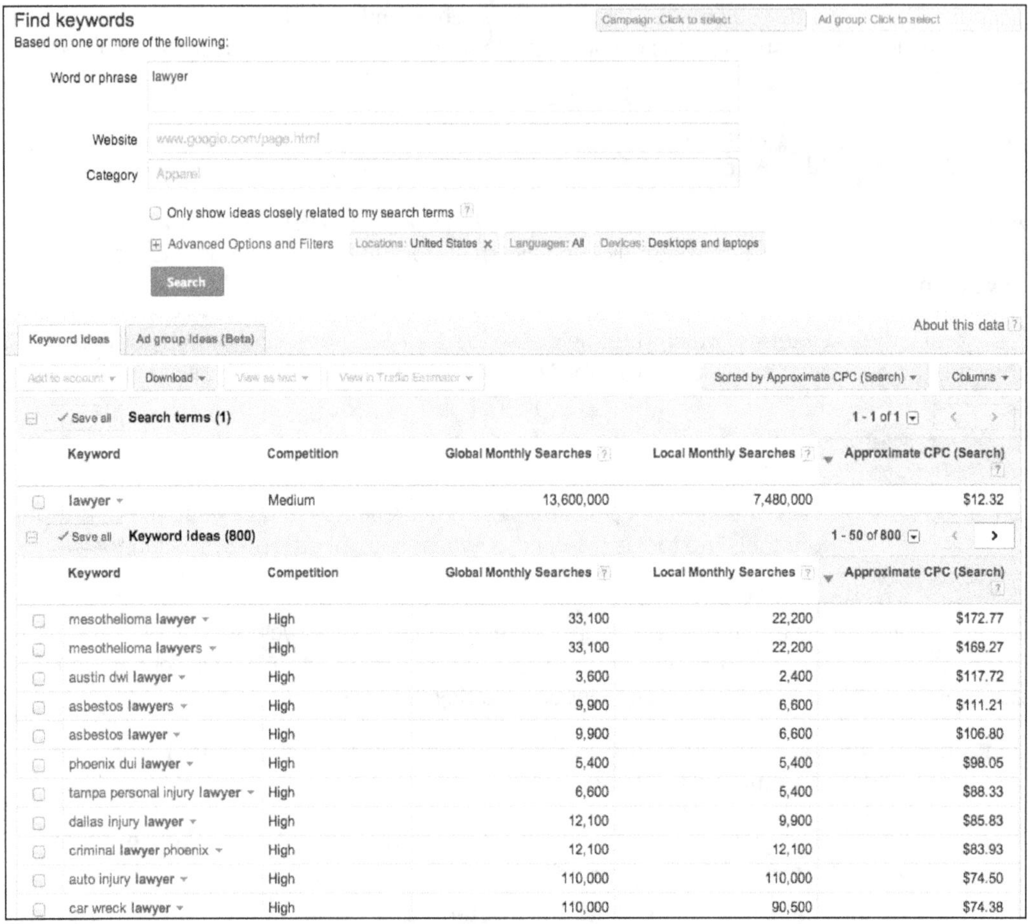

6. In the previous example, a family lawyer looking for new customers is considering running on keyword `lawyer`. When we review the related keyword ideas in the keyword tool, we can see them most of the related searches are not relevant to a family lawyer. So, the keyword `lawyer` is not the best choice for an attorney specializing in family matters.

7. Next, we can refine our search by entering a more specific query, such as `family lawyer`. The keyword tool provides additional suggestions, including keywords with location pre-qualifiers and other ways of saying `family lawyer`, such as `divorce attorney`. The list in the following screenshot is looking more relevant to a family attorney and has some specific keyword options we can work with.

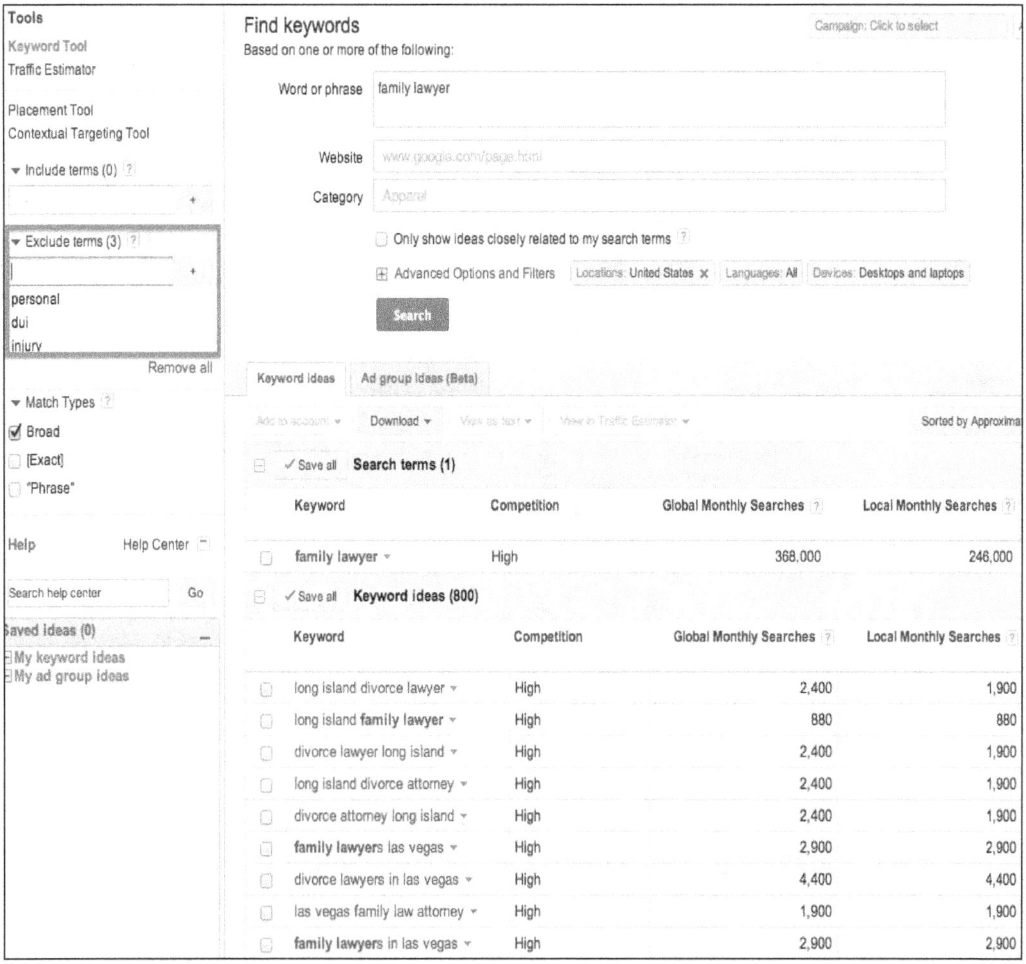

8. We can further pre-qualify our search by excluding terms from the keyword analysis. Enter any words not applicable to your business in the **Exclude terms** box to leave them out from the keyword ideas results.
9. Review the monthly search data and competition columns to get data on how many people are searching related terms, and whether the competition on your keywords will be **Low**, **Medium**, or **High**. If competition is high, there are a lot of other advertisers bidding on those keywords.
10. The **Approximate CPC (Search)** column will give you an idea of how much each keyword costs, or how much advertisers on average pay for each click. Keep in mind that these are rough estimates and actual CPCs will vary greatly.
11. Sort by **Global Monthly Searches** or **Local Monthly Searches** to review the highest traffic search terms first.

12. Check the box next to the keywords you like to save them to **My keyword ideas**.

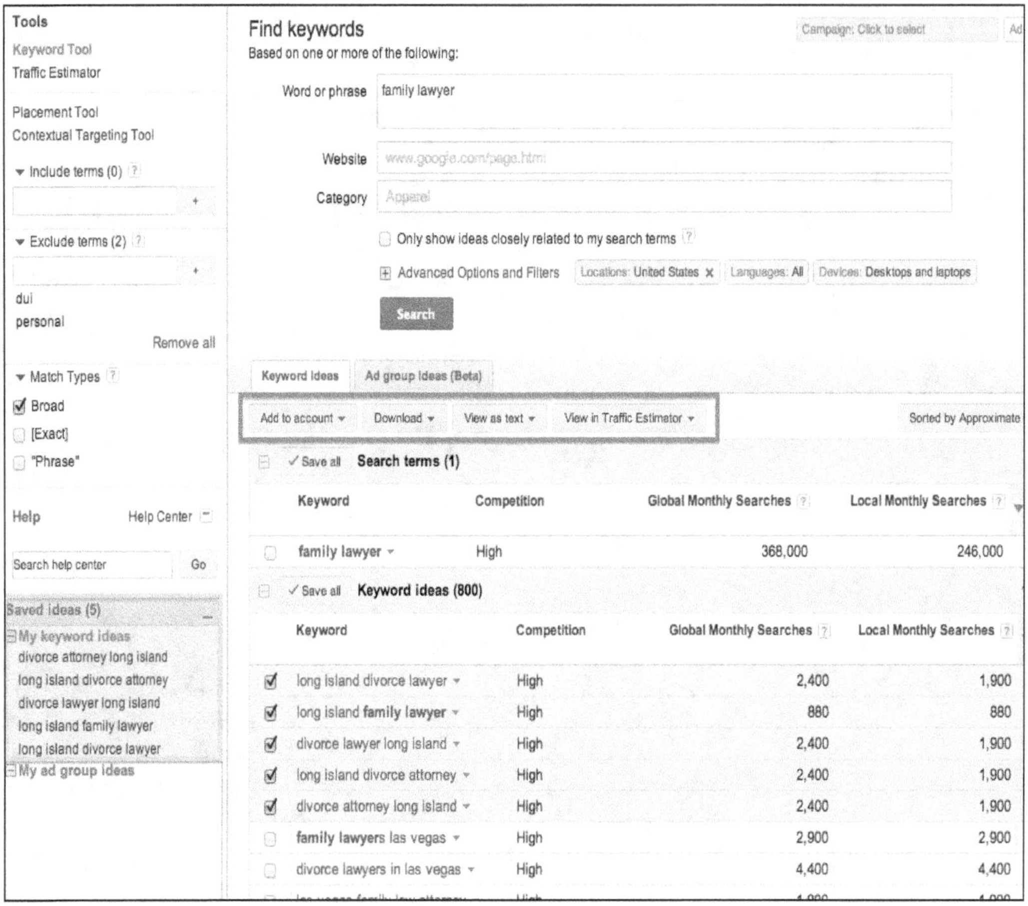

13. Once you have a list of keywords in your saved keyword ideas, you can add them to your account directly, download them, view as text, or view in **Traffic Estimator**.

For those of you who are not sure where to start, the keyword tool will also provide keyword suggestions based on the content of your website. Here is how to use this feature:

1. Type in your website's URL in the **Website** box in Google' **Keyword Tool**.
2. Click on **Search**.

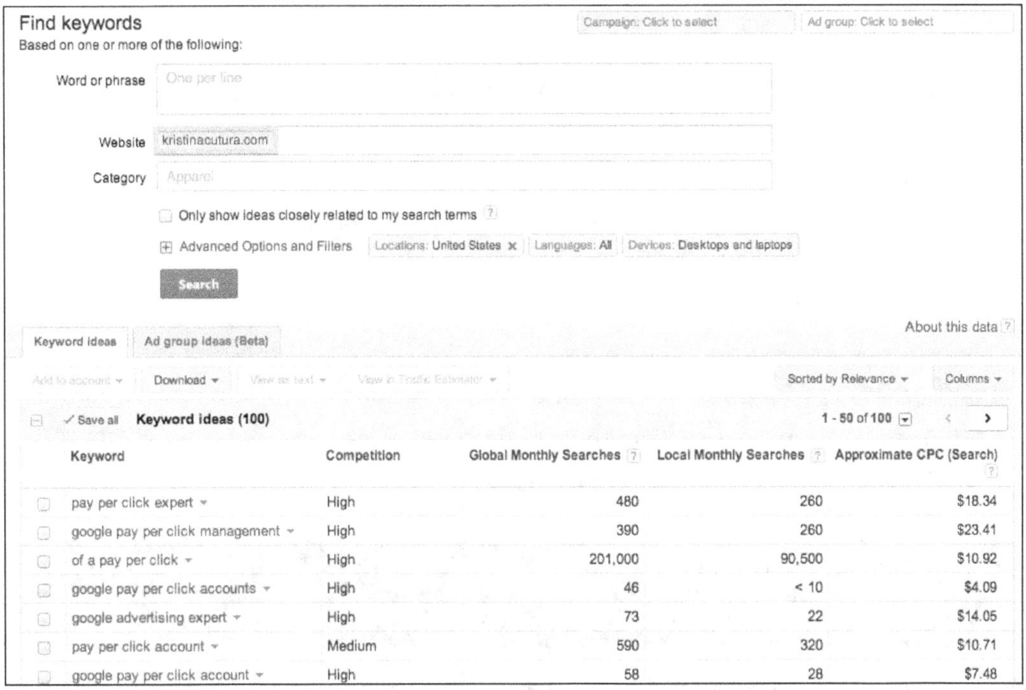

Not all keywords suggested by the system will necessarily be right for your business. You should still review them carefully and only add phrases that are relevant.

How it works...

In general, one-word keywords tend to be too general, as we can often not be sure what the users typing them in are actually searching for. For example, someone searching for `accountant` on `Google.com` could be an actual accountant who is looking for salary information or a new job. Or, it could also be a business that's looking for an accountant to hire.

The more general keywords will tend to have lower Quality Scores, they can be more competitive with more advertisers eligible for the auction, and they will potentially cost more than the specific keywords.

Two to three word keywords are generally a better choice for AdWords. They pre-qualify your users better, tend to get better Quality Scores in AdWords, and may be less competitive with fewer advertisers bidding on those terms.

> If you'd like to use one-word and more general keywords, start by entering them in exact match to restrict any additional expansions to irrelevant variations.

There's more...

There are a number of tools outside of Google that help you research and develop keyword lists. Following are a few options:

- **WordStream** – `http://www.wordstream.com/keywords`
- **Bing Ads Intelligence** – `http://advertise.bingads.microsoft.com/en-us/bingads-downloads/bingads-intelligence`
- **Wordtracker** – `https://freekeywords.wordtracker.com/`

See also

- The *Using keyword matching options effectively* recipe
- The *Generating negative keywords* recipe

Analyzing competitor keywords from spyfu.com and similar tools

AdWords does not provide information on what keywords your competitors are bidding on. However, there are a number of tools outside of Google that can help you analyze who's ranking on specific terms, as well as what keywords individual domains are showing up for.

Getting ready

Several competitor keyword tools provide free basic searches but do require monthly subscriptions to access the full data. You'll need to sign up for the free trial, if available, or purchase a subscription to download all of the keyword data.

The following are some competitor keyword tool options you may wish to consider:

- **AdGooroo** – `http://www.adgooroo.com/`
- **Compete** – `http://www.compete.com/`
- **KeywordSpy** – `http://www.keywordspy.com/`
- **SEMrush** – `http://www.semrush.com/`
- **SpyFu** – `http://www.spyfu.com/`

Not all of these tools will work well outside the US, so consult a few to find one that works for your region.

How to do it...

We shall use SpyFu's SEM keyword tool to demonstrate how to access and review a list of keywords for a specific domain.

1. Go to `http://www.spyfu.com/`.
2. Enter a domain's URL into the **Classic** search box and click on **SEARCH** to see keywords a specific domain's ads are showing up for.

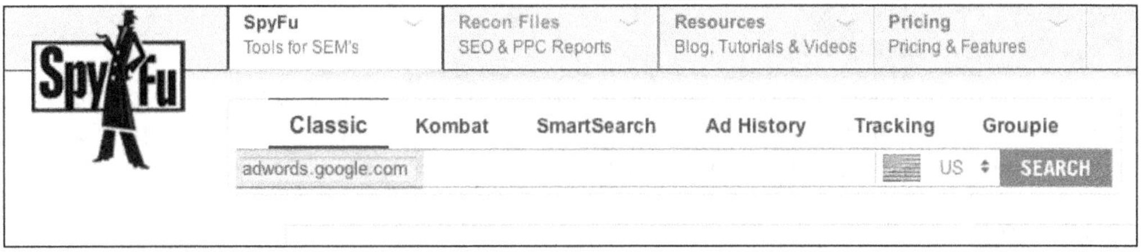

3. You'll get a general pay-per-click (PPC) summary with spend trends, as well as organic and paid keywords this domain is showing up on.

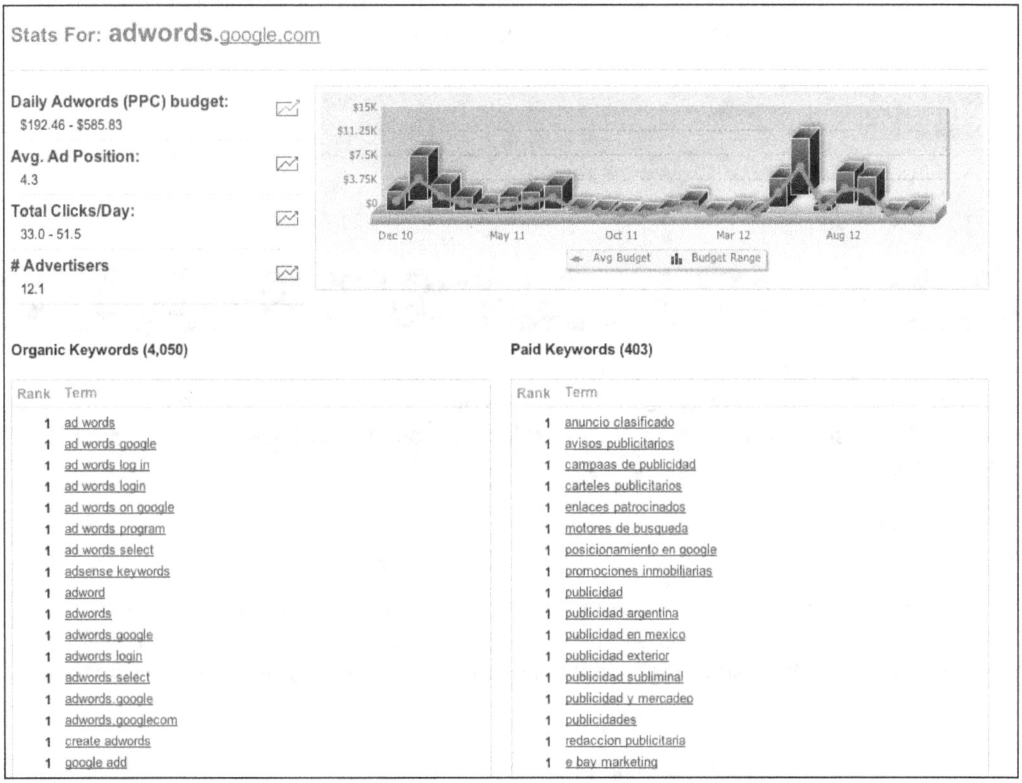

4. Choose to **Export** CSV at the bottom of the paid keywords list.
5. If you purchased a subscription, you'll be able to download a full list of keywords a domain ran on.
6. You can sort this keyword list by clicks or cost per day to figure out a domain's best keywords.
7. Not all of the keywords from these reports will necessarily make sense for you. Make sure you scrub the list and only add the terms most applicable to our business.

How it works...

Competitor keyword tools do not access private AdWords accounts, and individual domains are certainly not sharing this data. Tools such as SpyFu gather public information provided by Google based on what's showing up on their search results pages.

There's more...

Remember that tools such as SpyFu do not have access to your competitors' accounts and that their keyword reports may not be 100 percent accurate. If a competitor is using a lot of broad match in their keyword list, keyword spy tools will pick up domain activity on keywords that are not necessarily in your competitor's AdWords campaigns.

See also

- The *Finding relevant keywords* recipe
- The *Adding new keywords to an existing ad group* recipe

Generating negative keywords

Adding negative keywords to your account is one of the best methods you have at your disposal to improve your Quality Scores and weed out irrelevant clicks. A good list of negative keywords will ensure you are not paying for traffic that you already know will not convert to sales and leads.

Getting ready

You'll need to do some research to generate a thorough list of negative keywords. Part of this process is using your common sense and thinking of potential related queries that will not be relevant. Aside from brainstorming potential negatives, you can also use the following tools:

- **Google's keyword tool**: Type in the most general keywords you'll be running in your campaigns to see other related terms that people are typing in. Anything that does not apply to you is a good potential negative keyword.

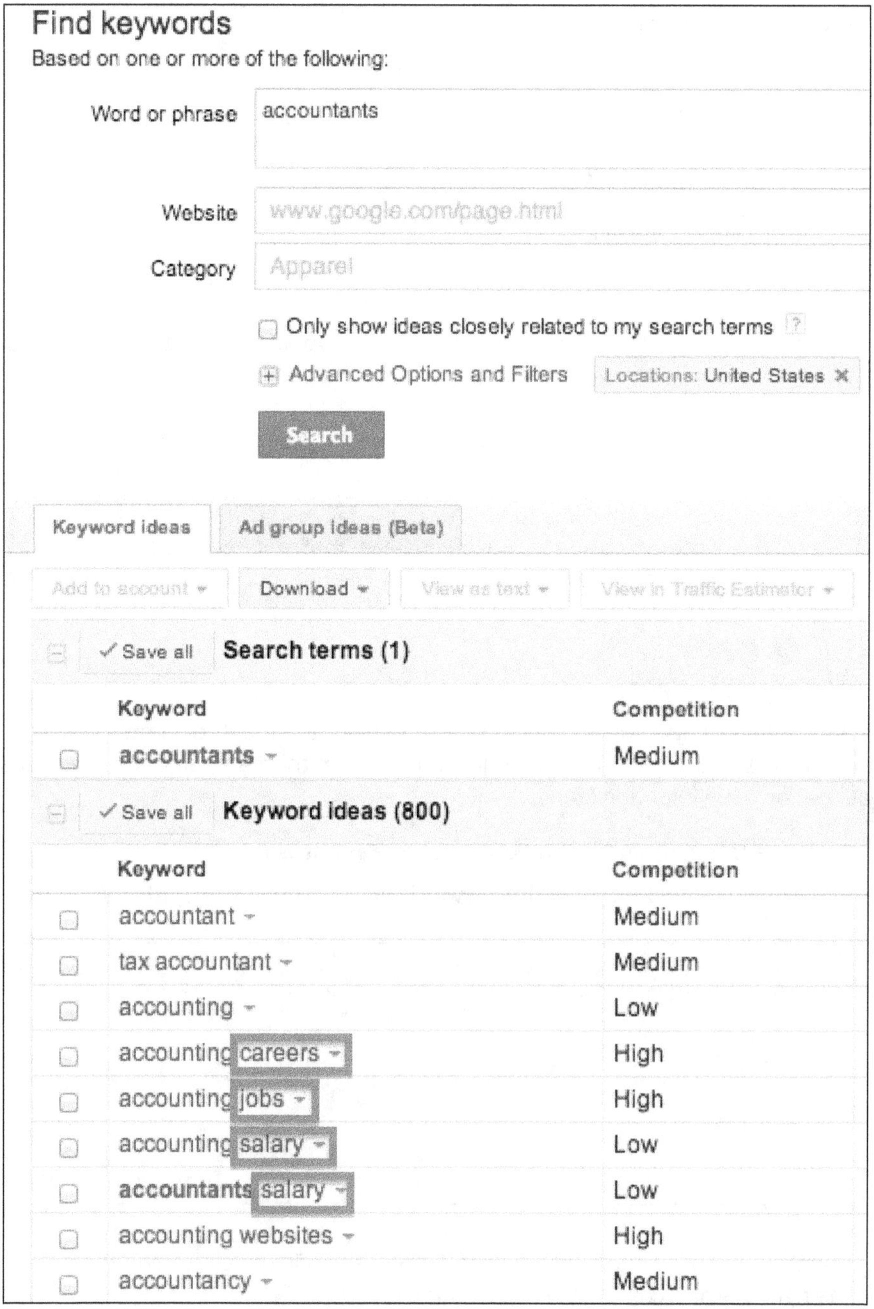

- `Google.com`: Search your most general keywords and pay attention to both ads and search results. Are some of the ads and search results that come up related to products and services that are different from what you offer? Also, pay attention to the search box as you type in your keywords. Are some of the suggested searches irrelevant?

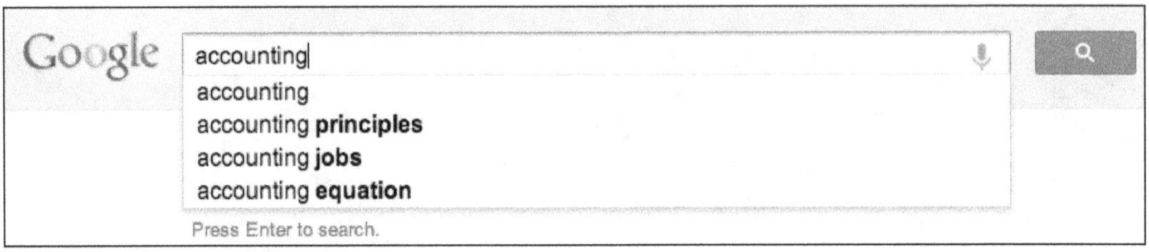

- **Search term reports**: Once your campaigns are up and running, you can run search term reports in AdWords to see actual search queries that triggered your ads. This will be a great source of ongoing negative keyword ideas that directly relate to your campaigns and keywords you have chosen.

> Run search query reports once a week to identify new negative keywords to add to your campaigns. You'll get negative keyword ideas from actual searches that triggered your ads.

How to do it...

You can add negative keywords to individual ad groups or to an entire campaign, if the negative terms are applicable to all of the keywords within this campaign. To add negative keywords, perform the following steps:

1. Go to the **Campaigns** tab, and click on the **Keywords** tab.
2. Scroll down to the bottom of the keyword list until you see **Negative keywords**.

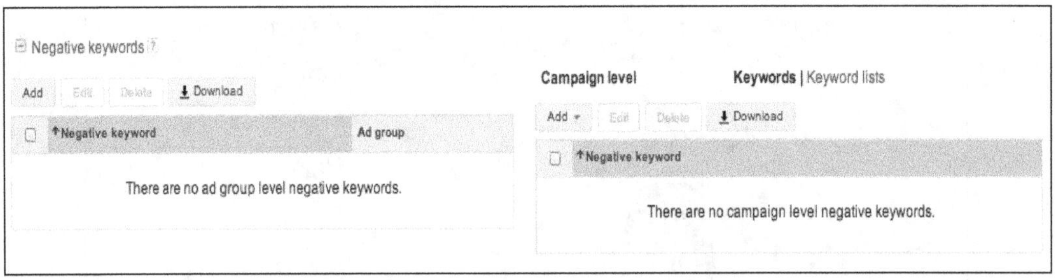

3. Use the column on the left to enter ad group specific negatives and the column on the right to enter campaign level negatives.

4. If you are choosing to add negative keywords at the ad group level, clicking on **Add** will prompt you to choose an ad group.
5. If you are adding negative keywords to an entire campaign, click on **Add** and choose **Add keywords**.
6. Enter one negative keyword per line.
7. Click on **Save** when you are finished.

If you would like to exclude all related `job` searches from seeing your ads, make sure that you enter that word alone, rather than combined with your actual keyword, which may not exclude all possible variations of the negative you are using.

Correct	**Incorrect**
-job	-accounting jobs
-jobs	-accountant jobs

How it works...

Negative keywords are phrases that prevent your ads from showing on certain search queries. For example, if you add a negative keyword `free` to your campaign, any search that contains the word `free` will not trigger your ad.

Negative keyword lists should be thorough and include all possible variations, since AdWords does not include any variations of a negative phrase you add to your account. Expand your initial list of negative keywords to include singulars and plurals, synonyms and similar words. For example, if you decide that you would like to add the negative keyword `jobs`, you can add the following additional negatives:

- Job
- Jobs
- Career
- Careers
- Employment
- Resume
- Resumes

There's more...

You'll likely be able to utilize some of the negative keywords you generate across your campaigns (such as `free`, `images`, and `reviews`). To automate the negative keyword generation process, you can create campaign negative lists to add to your account's shared library. You can then easily access these campaign negatives when you are creating new campaigns. In your AdWords account, go to **Shared library** and click to view **Campaign negative keywords**. Here, you can name your new negative keyword list and enter the specific terms that should be excluded.

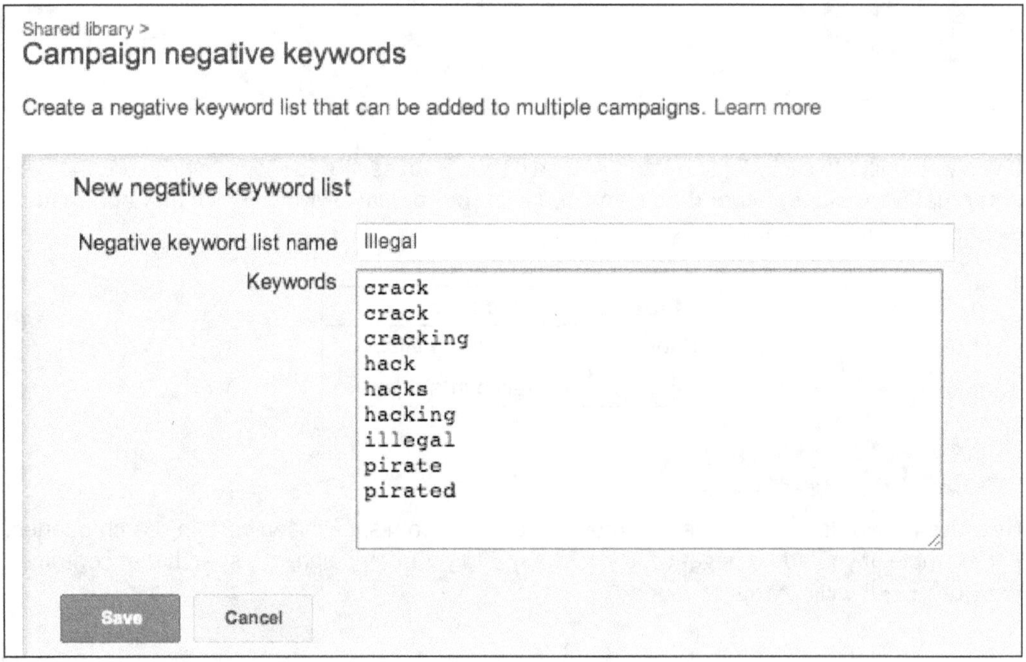

See also

- The *Using keyword matching options effectively* recipe
- The *Running search term reports to optimize keywords* recipe in *Chapter 11, Optimizing Performance*

Identifying keyword duplicates

Having duplicate keywords in your AdWords account is generally not recommended, as they compete against each other and make account management and analysis more difficult. I recommend going through your account periodically to identify duplicates, clean up, and get rid of any low performers to maximize performance.

Getting ready

The easiest way to identify if you have duplicate keywords in your account is by downloading your account to AdWords Editor. AdWords Editor allows advertisers to easily manage campaigns, keywords, and ads in bulk. You can do all of the work offline and typically much faster than through the AdWords interface. You can download AdWords Editor by visiting `http://www.google.nl/intl/en/adwordseditor/`.

How to do it...

To identify keyword duplicates:

1. Open up AdWords Editor and sign in to your account by entering your AdWords customer login and password.
2. Make sure to get recent changes before you proceed to download the latest version of your account. You can choose the **Basic (faster)** option. The download tends to be pretty fast, so the basic option may not be necessary.
3. When you get the option to select which parts of the account to download, select **All campaigns** and click on **OK**.

4. Go to **Tools** and select **Find duplicate keywords**.

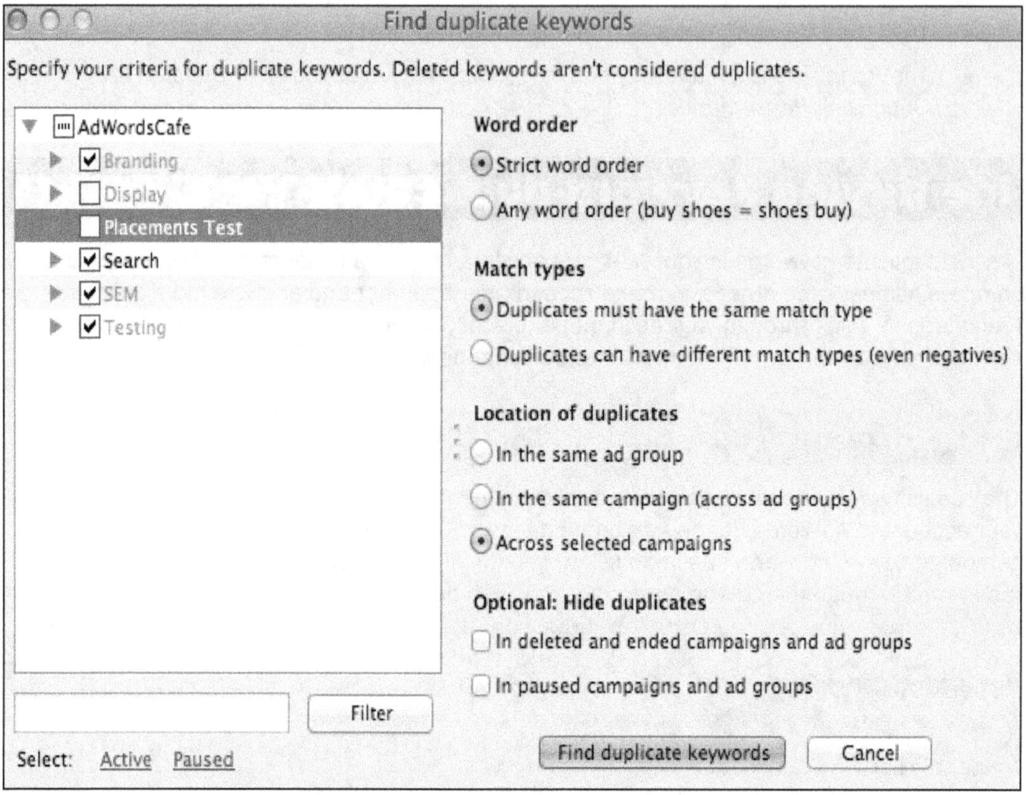

5. Choose the campaigns that you'd like to compare.
6. Decide if you'd like to preserve the Word order. It usually makes sense to choose **Strict word order**.
7. Under **Match types**, select if you'd like to compare keywords with the same match type or different match types.
8. Under **Location of duplicates**, choose if you'd like to analyze the same ad group, the same campaign, or across selected campaigns. In most cases, you'll want to choose **Across selected campaigns**.
9. Under **Optional: Hide duplicates**, you can choose to hide the deleted, paused, and ended campaigns and ad groups. This will ensure any old campaigns or ad groups that you decided to pause are ignored by the analysis.

10. On the next screen, you'll see all of your duplicates filtered out by campaign and ad group. The **Select duplicates by** tool will allow you to select and delete duplicates based on your chosen criteria, such as low CTR or average position. If you have duplicate keywords and one is getting a better CTR, keep the better performing instance.

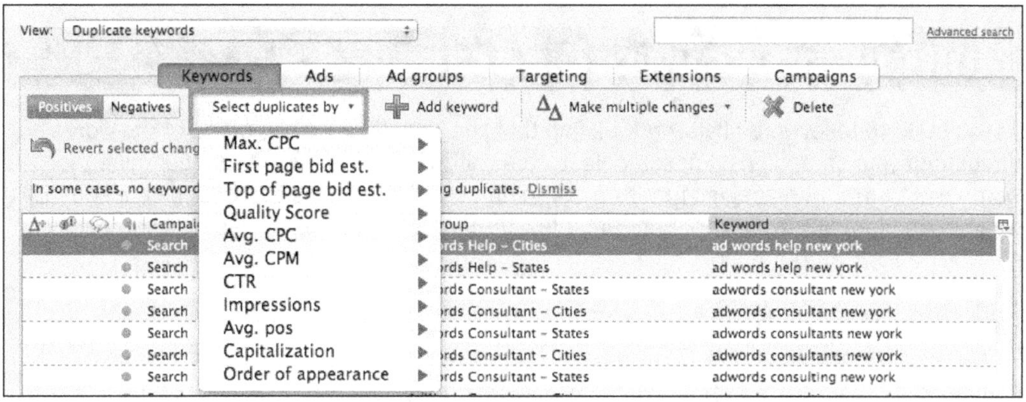

11. You'll likely see some differences in performance between the duplicates in your account, and you will want to go through this list and pause or delete lower CTR or lower converting duplicates, so the better performing instances of your keywords get more exposure.

How it works...

AdWords discourages advertisers from using duplicate keywords across campaigns and ad groups. Only one keyword can trigger an ad per search in the auction. Identical keywords compete with each other, and the keyword with the higher ad rank will show and trigger the ads it is associated with.

There's more...

In some cases, it might make sense to have the same keyword in multiple campaigns, such as if you have different campaigns targeting desktops and mobile devices, or different campaigns for different location targets.

However, if the duplicate keyword is not on purpose and needs to be consolidated, use performance data when deciding which instance of the keyword to keep or remove.

See also

- The *Getting started with AdWords Editor* recipe in *Chapter 13, Managing AdWords*
- The *Making changes to campaign settings via AdWords Editor* recipe in *Chapter 13, Managing AdWords*

Multiplying keyword phrases

As you build your keywords lists, you will find that you'll continue to use some of the words throughout your campaigns. For example, as a furniture business, you might combine the word `furniture` with specific furniture brand names. This process can be time consuming when done manually; however, there are a few free tools outside of Google that can help you streamline keyword expansion.

Getting ready

Build out your core terms and modifiers that you'll want to combine. I usually do this in Excel or Notepad, noting the structure, or what campaigns and ad groups the keywords should be added to.

Following is an example of core terms and modifiers for a legal practice specializing in bankruptcy:

Core Terms	Modifiers
Bankruptcy	Lawyer
Debt	Lawyers
	Attorney
	Attorneys
	Law firm

How to do it...

To multiply keywords:

1. Access one of the multiplier tools in your browser. For the purposes of this example, I will use `http://www.searchcommander.com/seo-tools/keyword-list-mashup/`.
2. Copy and paste your primary keyword phrases and desired words to multiply by.
3. The tool in the following example also allows you to select phrase and exact match variations. Leave them checked, if you'd like the additional keyword match types created, or uncheck if you'd like broad match only.

4. Click on **Create List of Keywords** when done.

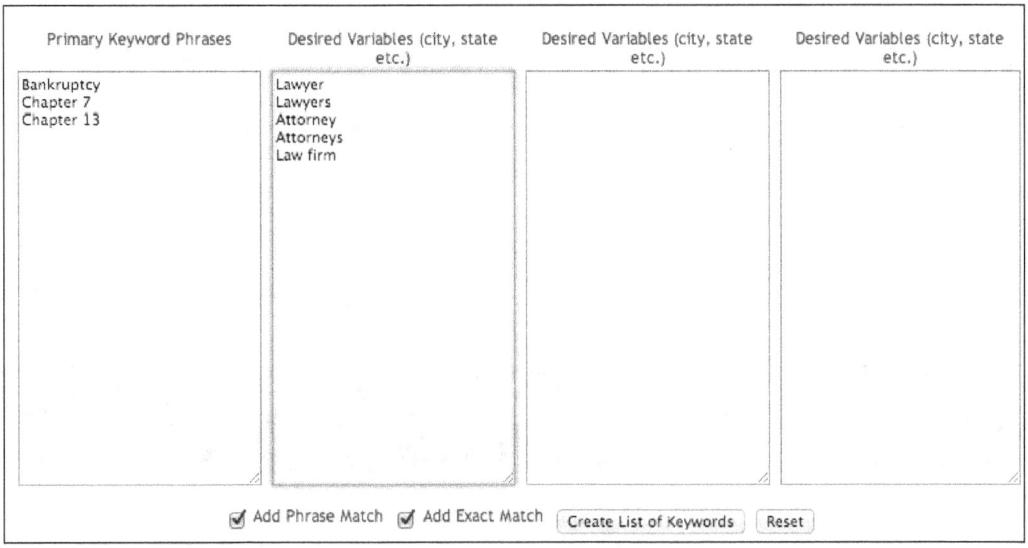

5. Copy and paste the newly created keywords into the desired campaigns and ad groups in AdWords.

How it works...

There are multiple free tools outside of Google that can help you multiply search terms with a click of a button and will help you create hundreds of relevant keywords. Here are a few options you can explore:

- **Keyword Multiplier Tool** - `http://www.searchcommander.com/seo-tools/keyword-list-mashup/`
- **Search Phrase Builder** - `http://kw.tre.sk/`
- **Keyword List Generator** - `http://tools.seobook.com/keyword-list/generator.php`
- **Keyword Deduper and Multiplier Tool** - `http://ppcwarehouse.com/login.html`
- **The Keyword Combinations tool** - `http://www.ranks.nl/tools/keyword_combinations.html`
- **Combine Keywords** - `http://www.searchenginepromotionhelp.com/m/keywords-combiner/word-combinations.php`
- **Keyword Lizard** - `http://www.keywordlizard.com/`

Some of these tools may require you to create an account, while others do not even require a log in and can be used instantly from within your browser.

There's more...

Before you create hundreds or thousands of keywords using all the possible variations, make sure that you are not spending time adding keywords that people are not likely to search for. Make sure that the phrases you are combining make sense when put together. You can also check traffic patterns and if they will receive impressions using Google's keyword tool.

See also

- The *Finding relevant keywords* recipe
- The *Adding new keywords to an existing ad group* recipe

Changing broad keywords to broad match modifiers

Broad match modifier may be the right match type for customers who are seeing poor ROI from their broad match keywords. It's also a good option for those who are mainly using phrase and exact match and are not receiving enough traffic, but are wary of using broad match.

Getting ready

As a first step, I recommend running a search term report to see what actual queries your ads are appearing on. In your **Keywords** tab, go to **Details** and select **All** from the **SEARCH TERMS** drop-down menu. If the report shows a large percentage of irrelevant queries that are triggering your ads, broad match modifier may me the right keyword option for you.

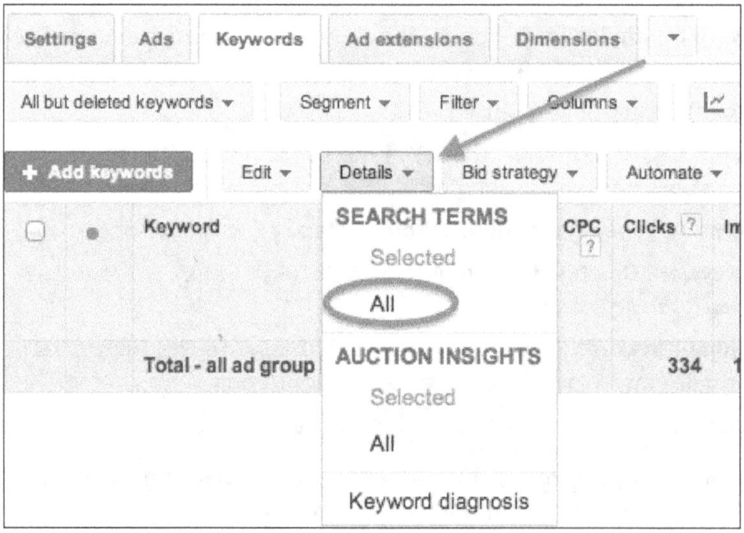

How to do it...

To enter keywords in broad match modifier:

1. Add + before each word within your keyword string.
2. Make sure you do not enter in any extra spaces after the + sign; however, do add a space after each word within a keyword phrase.

The following are examples of *correctly* broad match modified keywords:

- +buy +halloween +costumes
- +halloween +costumes

The following are examples of *incorrectly* broad match modified keywords:

- + halloween + costumes (extra spaces should not be used)
- Halloween+ costumes ("+" should be used before each word you'd like to preserve, not after)
- +halloween+costumes (you need to use a space between each word)

> You can change keywords to broad match modifier in bulk by using Acquisio's free tool, available at the following link:
>
> `http://www.acquisio.com/ppc/google-adwords-modified-broad-match-keyword-tool/`
>
> Paste the keywords you wish to modify and generate modified broad keywords with a click of a button.

How it works...

Broad match modifier is a match type in AdWords that gives you more control than the default broad match, but is still less restrictive than phrase match. It will show your ads on very close variations of your keywords, such as singulars, plurals, misspellings, abbreviations, and acronyms. Synonyms are not considered close variants. For each word that you put a + sign before, the user will have to type in a close variant in order to see your ad.

There's more...

Changing your keyword match type from broad to broad match modifier could potentially cut down on some valuable relevant traffic, since broad match places you in auctions on keywords you did not think to add to your account, and broad match modifier restricts this expanded matching. To test the effects of implementing broad match modifier, you may want to run two identical ad groups, one with broad match keywords and another with the same list of keywords in broad match modifier. You can run both of these ad groups at the same time. Make sure that they have the same bids and ads, so that you are not introducing other variables into this test aside from the match type. Compare the two ad groups and review your key success metrics, such as conversion rates and CPA, before you change all of your broad keywords to broad match modifier. You can also test different match types with AdWords experiments.

See also

- The *Using keyword matching options effectively* recipe
- The *Running search term reports to optimize keywords* recipe in *Chapter 11, Optimizing Performance*

Adding new keywords to an existing ad group

After you've set up an ad group, you may want to add additional keywords to boost clicks and improve performance. Adding new keywords can help you generate more traffic from your top performing ad groups, or it can help you boost clicks on ad groups that are not getting enough traffic.

Getting ready

Prepare the list of keywords you'd like to add to your campaign, if you have specific terms in mind. If not, AdWords will automatically suggest some new keyword options based on your existing keywords.

How to do it...

If you already have a list of keywords you'd like to add to an existing ad group:

1. Click on the **Campaigns** tab, and select the campaign that you're looking to add keywords to.
2. Click on the ad group you'd like to edit.

3. Click on **+ Add keywords**.

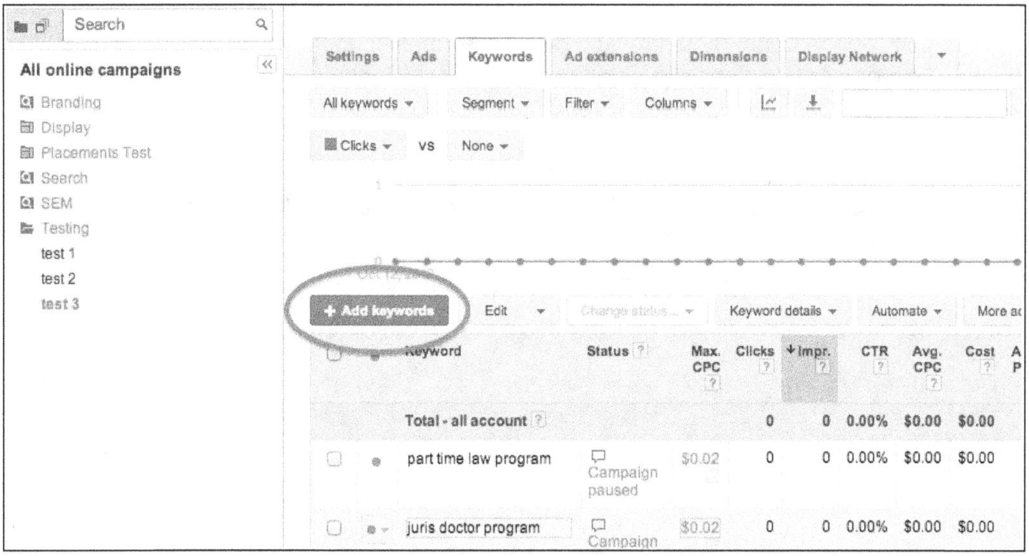

4. Type in the new keywords or copy and paste the keywords you developed.

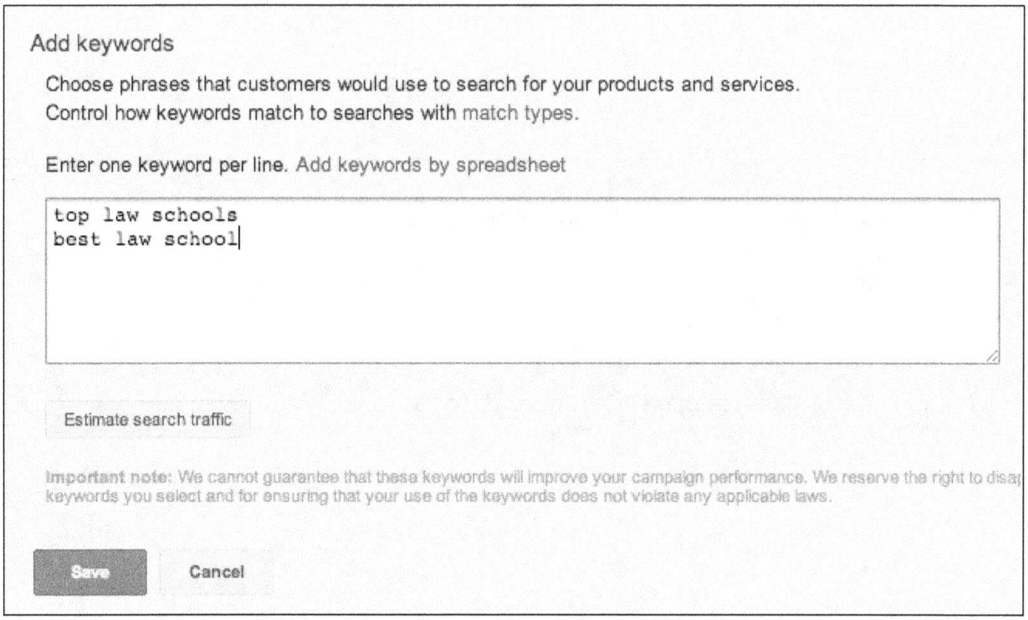

5. Click on **Save** to save your new keywords.

If you'd like to add new keywords to an ad group but are not sure what terms to add, AdWords will provide suggestions based on the keywords that are already within your ad group.

1. Click on the **Campaigns** tab, and select the campaign that you're looking to add keywords to.
2. Click on the ad group you'd like to edit.
3. Click on **Add keywords**.
4. On the right-hand side of the keyword box, you will see additional relevant keywords that are similar to your current list.
5. Click on **Add** to add a keyword you like to your ad group.

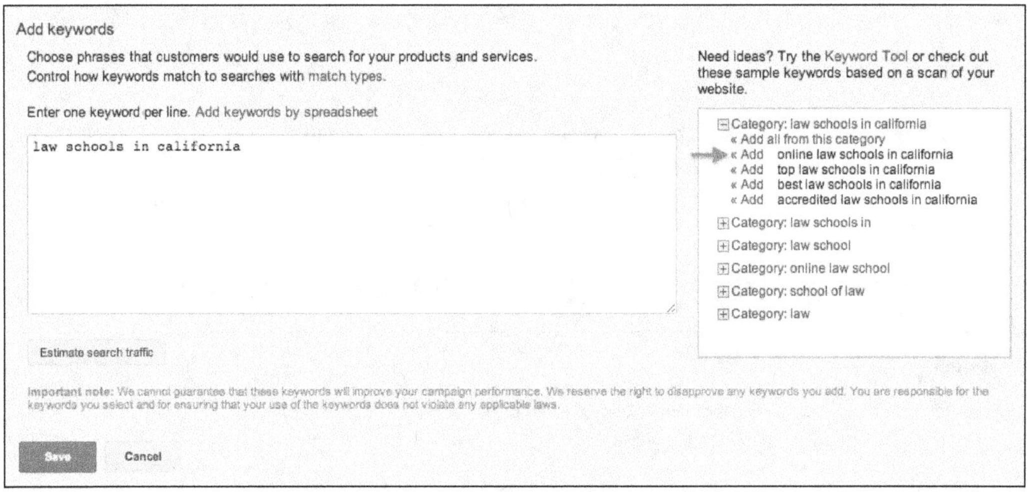

6. Click on **Save** to save your selections when done.

See also

- The *Finding relevant keywords* recipe
- The *Editing, pausing, or deleting keywords* recipe

Editing, pausing, or deleting keywords

After you've been running your keywords for some time and have accumulated impressions on individual keywords, you may wish to pause or delete the low performing terms. You can also edit your poor performers to make them more specific, such as by changing their match type or by refining the search term with additional phrases.

Getting ready

First, analyze the current list of keywords to determine which keywords you may want to remove or edit. Following are the keywords to pay special attention to:

- Keywords with low CTR. Low CTR means that users are not finding your ads relevant to the search.
- Low Quality Score keywords. You'll need to add this column to your reports through the **Customize columns** button in your **Keywords** tab. Optimize keywords that have Quality Scores below 4.
- Keywords that are costing a lot but are not generating any sales.
- Keywords that have a high cost per conversion.

How to do it...

To pause or delete a keyword:

1. Click on the **Campaigns** tab, and go to your **Keywords** tab.
2. Mark the checkbox next to the keywords you'd like to pause or delete.

3. Go to **Change status** and select pause or delete.

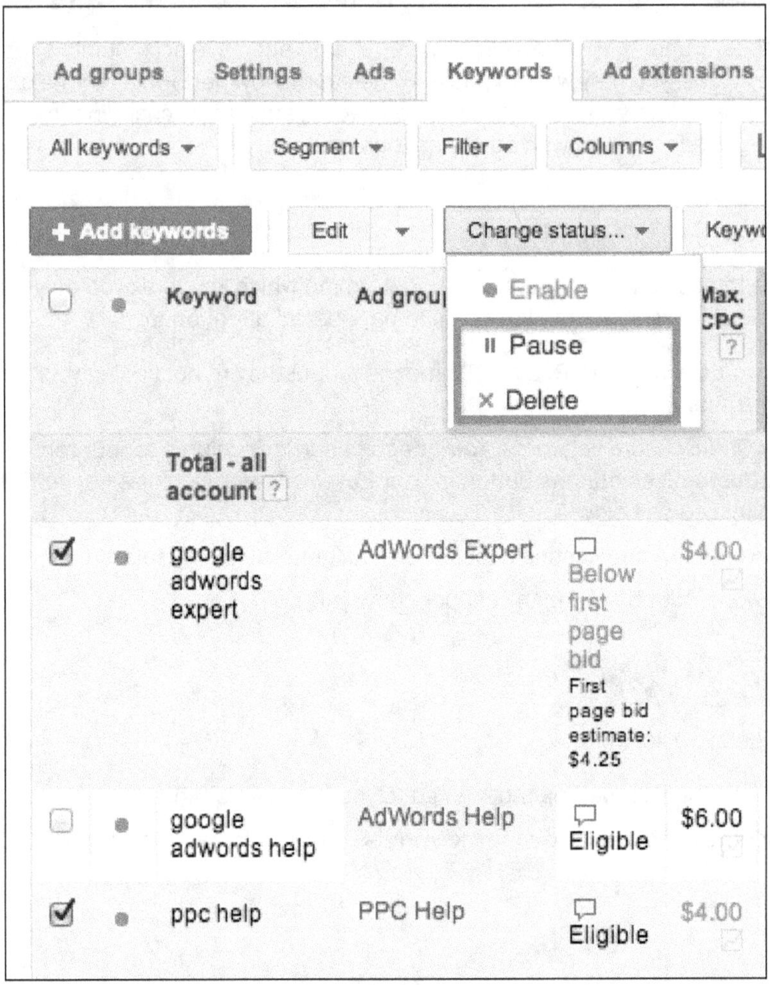

4. You can also pause a keyword by clicking on the green button and selecting the **Paused** status.

To edit a keyword:

1. Click on the **Campaigns** tab, and go to your **Keywords** tab.
2. Mark the checkbox next to the keywords you'd like to edit.
3. From the **Edit** menu, select **Edit in table** or **Edit in spreadsheet**.

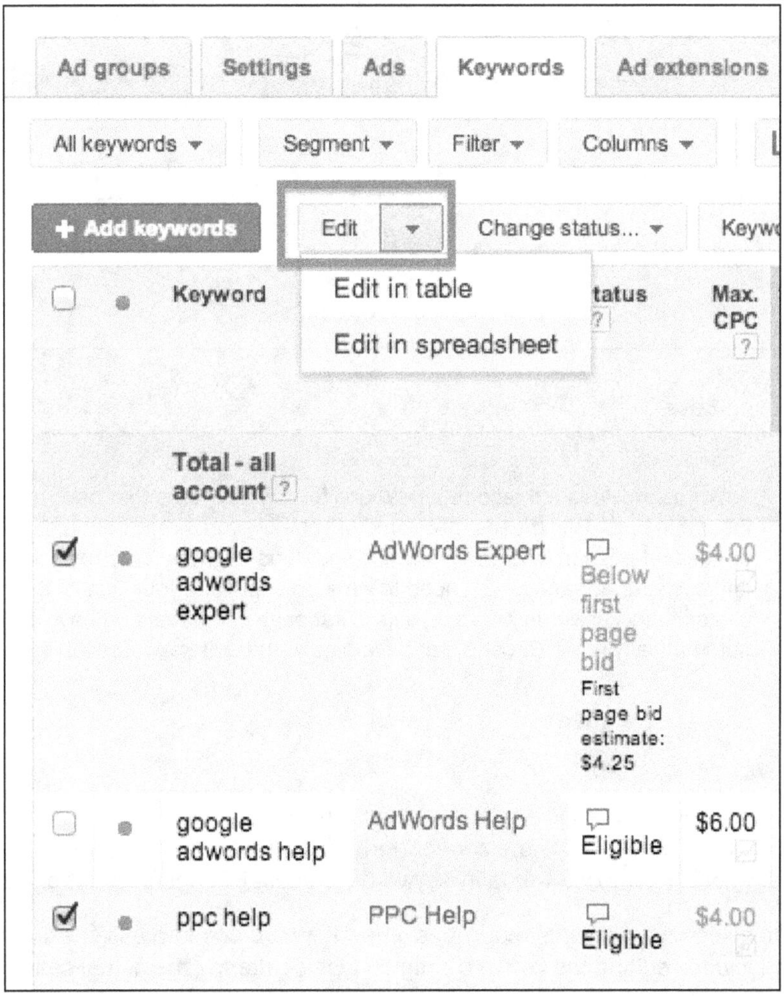

4. Next, make changes to the actual search phrase, match type, or bids.

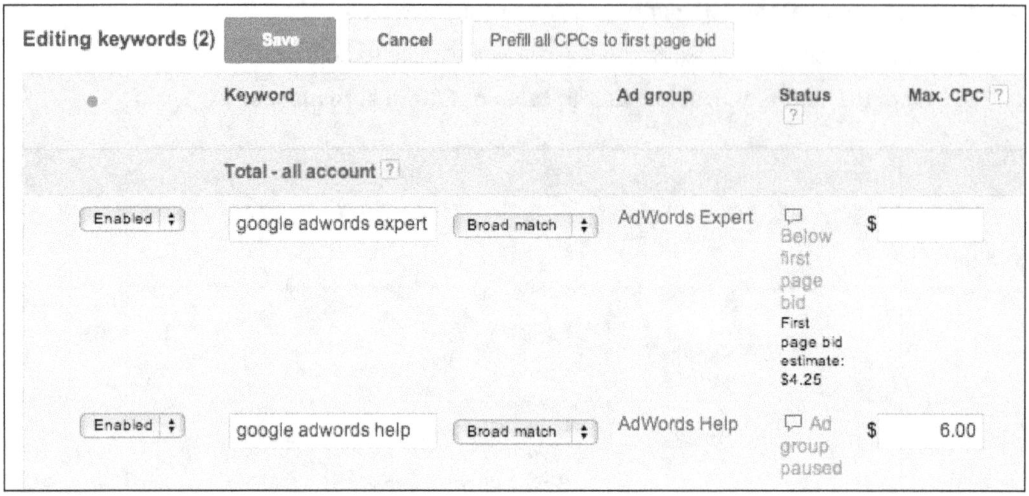

5. Click on **Save**.

> AdWords provides bid recommendations for any keywords that have below first page bids. This means that some of your keywords may not be showing on the first page of `Google.com` and your bids might need to be increased to improve your ad rank or you need to work on improving your Quality Score. You can edit any keywords with bids below first page estimates and have AdWords automatically prefill CPCs to first page bids in the edit keywords table.

How it works...

Pausing or deleting keywords will ensure that your ads are not showing for terms that did not work for you. You can pause or delete poor performers, such as costly keywords that are not generating any conversions or low-quality keywords to boost ROI and account performance.

After you edit a keyword, AdWords reads it as a new keyword and impressions are reset back to zero. This includes editing the keyword's match type or altering the actual search phrase.

If you choose to delete a keyword, you will not be able to restore it if you wish to run it again, and you'll need to re-add it as a new keyword, starting with a fresh history. Pausing a keyword has the benefit of being able to restore it again, resuming its history.

If you move a poorly performing keyword to a new campaign or a new ad group with a unique ad, you can boost Quality Score by achieving a better CTR with more targeted ad copy.

See also

- The *Optimizing keywords to improve ROI* recipe in *Chapter 11, Optimizing Performance*
- The *Improving relevance and Quality Score* recipe in *Chapter 11, Optimizing Performance*

6

Writing Compelling Ads

In this chapter, we will cover the following:

- Researching competitors' ads
- Setting campaign ad rotation
- Creating effective ads
- Choosing landing pages
- Implementing dynamic keyword insertion in ads
- Avoiding common ad copy mistakes
- Split testing ad copy
- Editing your ad text
- Pausing or deleting ads

Introduction

Ads are your opportunity to describe your business to potential customers and entice them to click through to your website. Since AdWords' ad character limits do not provide much space, you must convey your message concisely and choose carefully what to communicate. The most effective marketers test various messages and special offers to find the most effective ad copy that attracts visitors most likely to convert.

Researching competitors' ads

You likely already have some phrases and special terms in mind that you'd like to promote in your ad text. However, I would advise you to research what your competition is highlighting in their ad copy before you write your ads. If the specials and pricing you are considering are not as compelling as what's offered by your competitors, you might want to pick other areas of focus to make your ads stand apart.

Getting ready

Prepare a list of your most important keywords to research. Choose high-traffic keywords that show the highest impression volumes to start with.

How to do it...

Perform the following steps for researching competition on Google:

1. Visit `https://www.google.com/` in your web browser.
2. Search your most important keywords and review the paid ads that show up.
3. Note the special offers, pricing, and calls-to-action that are being used in AdWords ads.

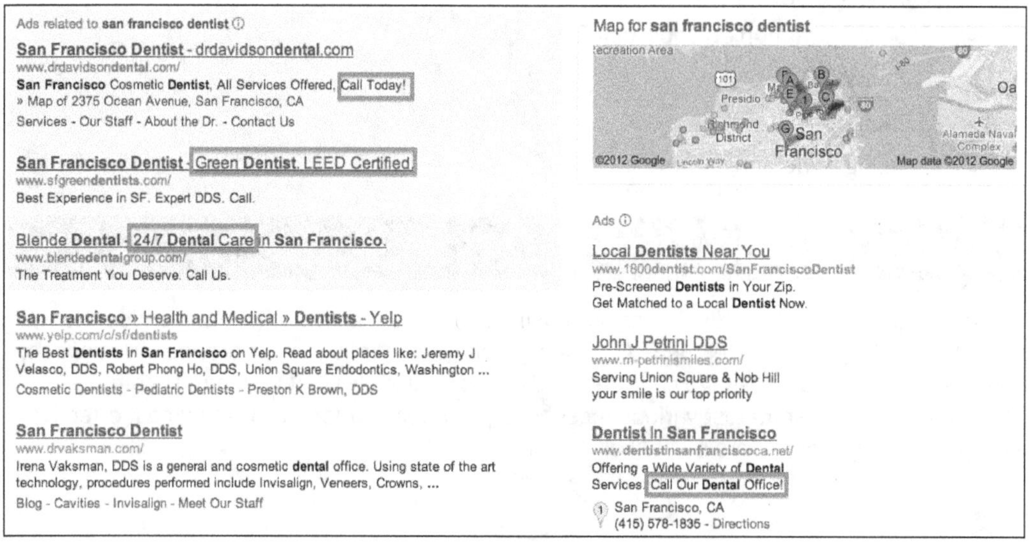

Research competition on third-party tools, such as KeywordSpy or SpyFu.

1. Visit `http://www.keywordspy.com/` or `http://www.spyfu.com/` in your web browser.
2. Enter a keyword of interest into the search box and click on **Search**. For example, search for `San Francisco dentist` to see what competitors are showing ads on that term.
3. Scroll down to the **Ad Overview** list.

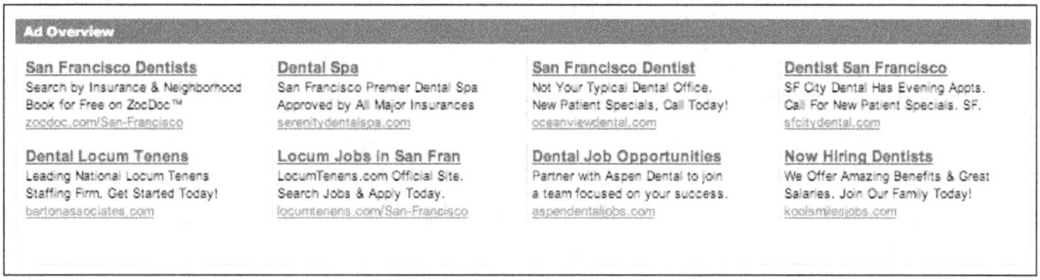

4. Note the special offers, pricing, and calls-to-action that are being used.

How it works...

Each ad auction on `Google.com` is real time and the ads that you see might change as you search on different days or from different locations. Your competitors are also continuing to adjust and refine their ads, so the results you see on one day may be different from ads a month later. I recommend regularly monitoring other advertisers in your industry to ensure your ads are competitive.

There's more...

Avoid looking up your own ad on `Google.com`, since you will accumulate unnecessary impressions and lower your own Quality Scores, which are Google's measure of relevance. Use the **Ad Preview and Diagnosis** tool in your AdWords account instead.

See also

- The *Creating effective ads* recipe
- The *Using third-party tools to research competitors* recipe in *Chapter 1, Researching the Market and Competition and Setting Goals*
- The *Troubleshooting why your ads are not showing* recipe in *Chapter 13, Managing AdWords*

Setting campaign ad rotation

Each ad group can have multiple ads that will trigger the keywords within that ad group. The ads will rotate and either be displayed evenly or start to be preferred and optimized by AdWords, according to the settings you choose.

Getting ready

Here is what you'll need to consider when choosing ad rotation settings:

- If you are not tracking conversions and would like to maximize clicks, choose the **Optimize for clicks** option. This is the default option when you create a new campaign.
- If you are tracking conversions and your goal is to maximize conversions within a campaign, your best bet is to choose **Optimize for conversions.**
- Are you A/B split testing ads within this campaign? If so, you should choose either **Rotate evenly** or **Rotate indefinitely**. A/B testing allows you to experiment and test the impact of using different ad elements, requiring an even number of impressions delivered to each ad.

How to do it...

To edit a campaign's ad rotation settings, perform the following steps:

1. Go to the **Campaigns** tab, and choose a specific campaign you'd like to edit.
2. Click on the **Settings** tab and stay in the **All settings** sub-tab.
3. Scroll down to the **Advanced** settings.
4. Under **Ad delivery: Ad rotation, frequency capping**, choose to edit **Ad rotation.**
5. After you select your ad rotation option, click on **Save**.

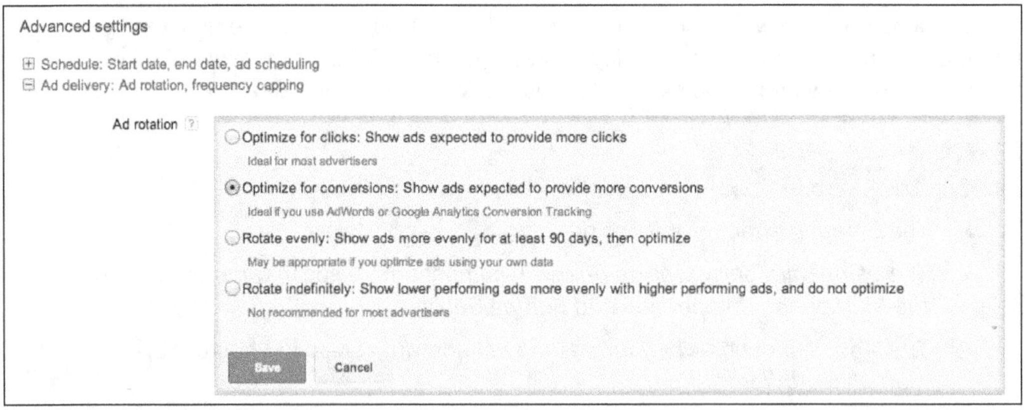

How it works...

In ad groups that have multiple ads, AdWords rotates ads at first evenly, and then eventually the more successful ads start to be preferred and will show more often. You have the option to choose how AdWords optimizes and rotates ads from the following options:

- **Optimize for clicks**: This option shows ads that are expected to provide more clicks
- **Optimize for conversions**: This option shows ads that are expected to provide more conversions
- **Rotate evenly**: This option shows ads evenly for at least 90 days, then optimizes them
- **Rotate indefinitely**: This option shows low performing ads more evenly with high performing ads, and does not optimize

When you first create a campaign, your ad rotation will by default be set to **Optimize for clicks**, and you'll need to change this setting if you prefer to rotate ads evenly or optimize them for conversions.

> If you are tracking conversions, I recommend you change the default AdWords setting to optimize ad rotation for conversions across all of your campaigns. Ads that get the most clicks are not necessarily ads that convert the best, yet they may monopolize your budget and not allow the better converting ads to show if you are using the optimize for clicks ad rotation setting.

There's more...

Ad rotation is set at the campaign level, rather than the account or ad group level. This means that the ad rotation you choose will apply to all ad groups within a given campaign. AdWords does not offer the option to change ad rotation within a single ad group.

See also

- The *Split testing ad copy* recipe

Creating effective ads

Your ad text is the only part of your account that users see. It is your opportunity to convey what you offer and why your website is worth taking a look at. However, the amount of space available for you to write your message in AdWords is limited, so you need to be careful in choosing what to communicate.

Getting ready

First, research your competition to understand how your pricing and special offers compare. Next, make a list of all of your most compelling product or service features you'd like to highlight.

Keep in mind the following five ad copy best practices:

- Use your keywords in your ad text, ideally in your headline. When you use keywords in your ad text, they are made bold by Google, making the ad stand out more.
- Prequalify your products or services, so your visitors know what to expect when they click on your ads. While attracting new visitors is important, you also do not want to pay for clicks that will not convert. Here are some ways you can ensure the right people are clicking:
    - **Display your prices**: This will help you attract visitors who are already OK with your price range.
    - **Explain who should not click on your ads**: This might eliminate some clicks but will help improve your ROI. For example, a mortgage lender can say `For loans over $100,000` to weed out anyone looking for a loan of a lower amount.
- Mention any discounts or special offers, first making sure that these offers are compelling in the industry and that your competitors are not offering more enticing deals. Examples include:
    - 20% off
    - Free shipping
    - Free consultation
    - 24 hour service
    - Free trial
- Instill confidence in your website with industry certifications, awards, accreditations, and years in business. Here are some ideas for example:
    - Serving San Francisco since 1951
    - BBB rating A+
    - Certified partner

- Include calls-to-action that will communicate to your visitors what they need to do once they visit your website.
  - Download free whitepaper
  - Call for a free consultation
  - Get 20% for a limited time
  - Sign up today
  - Try it for free

How to do it...

To write an ad, perform the following steps:

1. Go to the **Campaigns** tab, and navigate to the **Ads** tab or first choose a specific campaign and ad group you'd like to edit.

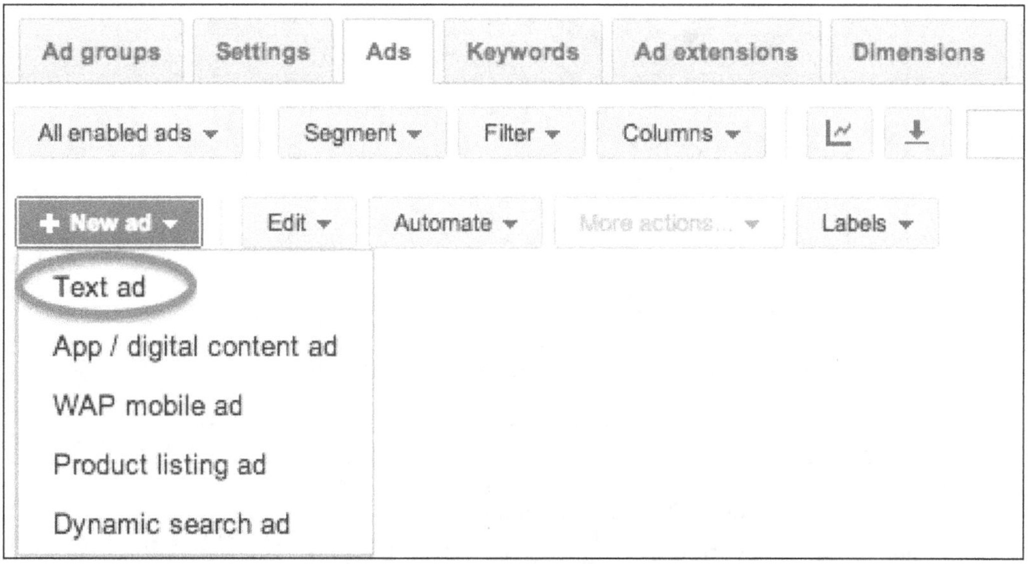

2. Click on the **New ad** button and choose **Text ad** from the list of possible ad formats.
3. If you did not choose a campaign and ad group already, you'll be able to do it on the next screen.
4. Write a headline in the **Headline** field. Ideally, your headline should contain some of your keywords.
5. Describe your product or service in **Description line 1** and **Description line 2**. Mention any special offers and use a call-to-action. I generally describe the product and special offers in the first line and reserve the second line for a strong call-to-action.

6. Enter your URL in the **Display URL** ad text field.
7. Enter the address of your website where users will be redirected after they click on your ad in the **Destination URL** field.
8. If you would like an ad to be given preference on a mobile device check the **Device preference** box. For example, you may want to promote your local store or office with a mobile-preferred ad, which can be shown on desktops when there aren't any normal ads defined. Also, the mobile-preferred ads are only preferred over normal text ads—other kinds of ads (dynamic, image) may still show on mobile.
9. Click on **Save ad**.

How it works...

An AdWords text ad contains the following components:

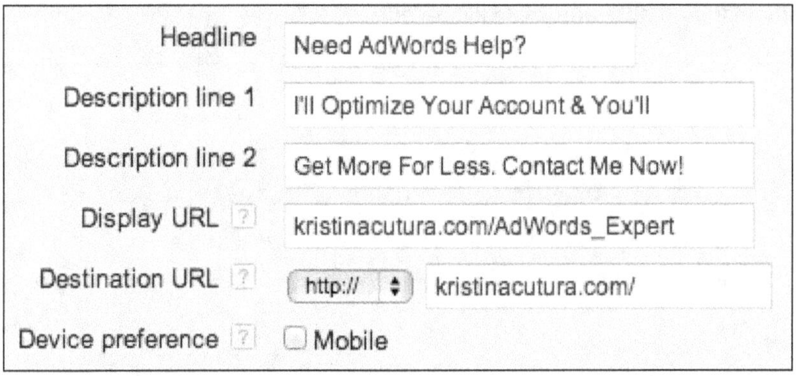

The following table entails the components of the previous screenshot:

Ad component	What it is?	Character limit
Headline	The first line of your ad. Usually the first thing customers look at when searching.	25 characters
Description line 1	The second line of your ad text. Describes your product or service.	35 characters
Description line 2	The third line of your ad text. Continues to describe your product or service along with any special offers or calls-to-action.	35 characters
Display URL	The address of the website that you are promoting. Appears in green and does not have to match the actual address that your visitors will be taken to when they click on your ads.	35 characters

Ad component	What it is?	Character limit
Destination URL	The address of the website the users are redirected to when clicking on your ad. Not visible in your ad but it has to match the display URL's domain.	N/A
Device preference	You can check the device preference mobile box to give an ad preference on mobile devices.	N/A

There's more...

You can write multiple ads within a single ad group and let them run at the same time to test different messaging. I recommend running at least two ads within each ad group to give users some options and test response. Avoid testing more than 3 ads at once within an ad group.

See also

- The *Researching competitors' ads* recipe
- The *Split testing ad copy* recipe

Choosing landing pages

Your landing page or the destination URL is the website's URL you choose to take visitors to after they click on your ad. It should match the user's query and be as general or as specific as the keyword it is matched up with. Most visitors only spend seconds on a website before they decide if they should stay or leave. Taking your visitors to the right landing page helps you ensure that they find what they are looking for and do not bounce after clicking on your ads.

Getting ready

Familiarize yourself with your website's URL structure. Next, match the list of your AdWords keywords to the most relevant sections of your website. You can divide up your keywords into groups or themes and pick a URL on your website that best matches each group or keyword.

How to do it...

Following are the guidelines to keep in mind when choosing landing pages.

Pick a URL that best matches your keywords

Your landing page should be as general or as specific as your keywords. Here is an example of landing pages you might want to pick for different sets of keywords if you sell mobile phones:

Keyword	Correct Landing Page	Incorrect Landing Page
Mobile phones	Home page with all available brands.	Specific brand or specific phone model.
Samsung phones	Samsung brand page with list of all available Samsung phone models.	Home page or specific Samsung phone model, such as Galaxy S4.
Samsung Galaxy S4	Page highlighting the Samsung Galaxy S4 phone, price, and link to buy.	Home page or a list of all Samsung phones.

To check if you picked the right landing page, ask yourself the question, "Does this page match the user's intent?" and monitor your bounce rates through Google Analytics.

Make sure your landing page is conversion friendly

Your landing page should be easy to navigate and conversion friendly. Visitors that arrive to each landing page should easily be able to spot the next step, be it to purchase from you online, download a whitepaper, sign up, or contact you.

The conversion activity should be prominently displayed on your landing page, ideally above the fold. However, I would advise against taking visitors directly to the product signup page or the checkout page as your AdWords destination URL, as most visitors will want to learn more about your products or services first.

How it works...

Your landing page is a part of your Quality Score. You can look up Quality Scores at the keyword level and see if there are issues with your landing page by going to the **Keywords** tab and hovering over the status box.

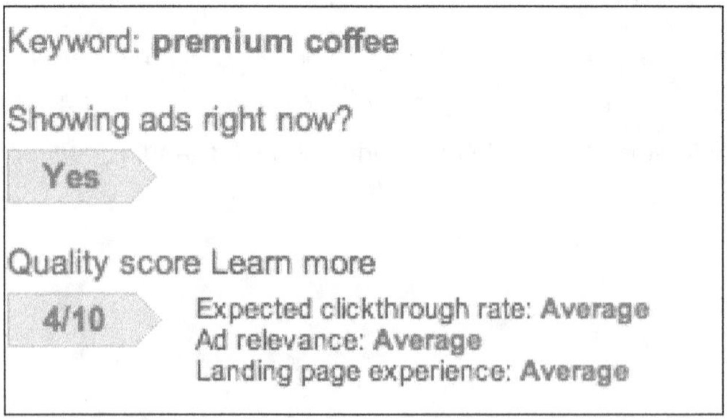

When a landing page doesn't match a user's query, it leads to a poor user experience and low quality ads that don't appeal to users and don't work for advertisers.

To determine your landing page experience, AdWords looks at the content of your page as well as your design. The following are the three most important factors to focus on:

- Relevant and original content that's useful to visitors.
- Transparency about what you do with information you may collect from your visitors. Easy to find contact and business information.
- Ease of navigation without too many links or ads that might be distracting and confusing.

There's more...

You can choose to set landing pages or destination URLs either at the ad group level or at the keyword level. If you properly structure your campaigns into themed ad groups, I recommend you use ad group level destination URLs, rather than keyword level URLs. However, every time you change an ad's destination URL, its history resets, while this is not the case for keyword URLs.

If you are tracking conversions, you can test different landing pages and analyze conversion rates by A/B testing to find the landing pages that work best.

See also

- The *Creating themed ad groups* recipe in *Chapter 4, Structuring Your Account*
- The *Split testing ad copy* recipe
- The *Setting campaign ad rotation* recipe

Implementing dynamic keyword insertion in ads

Dynamic keyword insertion is a tool that allows AdWords advertisers to automate their ads with a single piece of code in the ad copy. Keywords that users are searching on are automatically populated into the ad text, making the ad more relevant, and saving you hours of work. There are many benefits to using keyword insertion, but you should also be careful to avoid ads that don't make sense or aren't converting for you.

Getting ready

If you decide to use dynamic keyword insertion, scrub your keyword lists of the following:

- Misspelled keywords
- Grammatically awkward phrases
- Competitor terms
- Keywords that do not make sense when inserted into your ad text

Keyword insertion should not replace proper account structure or be used with thousands of unrelated keywords all lumped into one ad group. Structure your keywords into relevant themes, and then use keyword insertion to make the ads even more relevant to every individual keyword within a well themed ad group.

How to do it...

To set up dynamic keyword insertion in your ad text, perform the following steps:

1. Enter the following piece of code into your ad: `{KeyWord:Default Text}`.

2. Choose default text that will be inserted into the ad if any of your keywords are not eligible. In the previous example, the default text is `Red Shoes`.
3. Keyword insertion is used most commonly in headlines. However, the code could also be placed in the rest of your ad text, as well as in your display and destination URLs. Keyword insertion in your destination URLs would be mainly used for reporting and tracking purposes.
4. Create separate ad groups with static ads that do not feature dynamic keyword insertion for any keywords that do not make sense when inserted into the ad text or are misspelled.
5. Make sure your landing pages are still relevant to the numerous variations you'll create.

How it works...

Dynamic keyword insertion automatically inserts your keywords into a text ad with the following snippet of code in your ad: `{KeyWord:Default Text}`. The tool can help you generate hundreds or thousands of highly targeted ads instantly. Following is an example of how your ads could appear:

Keyword	Your ad
Red shoes	Buy **Red Shoes** Huge Selection of Stylish Shoes. Shop Today and Get 10% Off! `www.example.com`
Cheap red shoes	Buy **Cheap Red Shoes** Huge Selection of Stylish Shoes. Shop Today and Get 10% Off! `www.example.com`
Red designer shoes	Buy **Red Designer Shoes** Huge Selection of Stylish Shoes. Shop Today and Get 10% Off! `www.example.com`

If the inserted term is too long for the AdWords character limits, the default word or phrase you choose will be inserted. Also, Google will only insert keywords that are actually in your account. For example, if your broad match keyword `shoes` generates an impression on term `tap shoes` that you do not have in your account as a keyword, phrase `tap shoes` will not appear in your ad.

There's more...

You can change the capitalization of the keyword that's inserted into the ad text by modifying the keyword insertion code. Here are the guidelines:

Keyword insertion snippet	How your ad will appear
`{keyword:}`	red shoes
`{Keyword:}`	Red shoes
`{KeyWord:}`	Red Shoes
`{KeyWORD:}`	Red SHOES
`{KEYWord:}`	RED Shoes
`{KEYWORD:}`	RED SHOES

Standard AdWords editorial policies still apply, and you will most likely not be able to use excessive capitalization, unless your keyword is an abbreviation, acronym, or a trademark.

See also

- The *Creating effective ads* recipe

Avoiding common ad copy mistakes

Many advertisers write ads that do not follow best practices and tend to get low clickthrough-rates. Keeping in mind common ad copy mistakes can help you avoid learning the hard way.

How to do it...

The following mistakes can hinder your ad performance:

- **Not using a call-to-action**: Your ads should motivate visitors to take the next step and set the stage for what you would like them to do once they click on your ad.

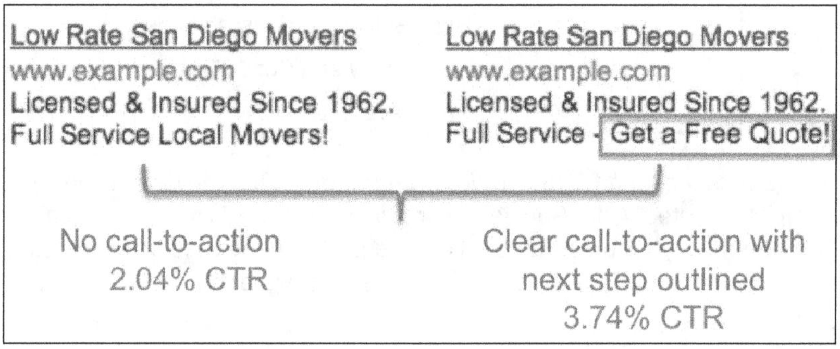

- **Using your company's name in your headline**: Unless you are a prominent brand, your company's name in a headline is wasting space that you could be using to highlight your keywords or special offers. One of the recommended times to use your company's name in a headline is if you are advertising company brand keywords.
- **Not using proper landing pages**: Your ad destination URL should match your keywords and there should not be a disconnect between what your users are searching for and where they'll be taken when they click on your ad. Taking your visitors to a landing page that's too general or too specific will cost you conversions.
- **Not differentiating your company**: Many ads are generic, play it safe, and fail to include why visitors should go with your business rather than a competitor's. If your ads look just like everyone else's, users will have little motivation to click on them and you'll suffer low CTRs.

- **Not prequalifying visitors**: Some advertisers are so focused on squeezing in special offers that they forget to explain what the users will see once they click on an ad. You can save costly clicks and improve your ROI by pre-qualifying your visitors and weeding out those that are unlikely to convert. For example, if you sell high-end furniture, you would benefit from setting the expectation rather than attracting visitors who cannot afford your products.
- **Focusing on product features instead of benefits**: Don't talk about the product feature your customers are already aware of but how they will help their lives. If someone is looking for a lawn mower, they already know that it cuts grass. Think about the benefit to the consumer and play that up in your ads. Take some time to think about what your customers are hoping to find and how to present the solution to them.
- **Not understanding what's working**: After setting up your campaigns, make sure to review performance regularly and take a note of what ad copy is generating clicks and conversions. You can re-use some of the phrases that worked in new ad copy tests and combine them with new discounts or calls-to-action.
- **Not testing**: AdWords can be time consuming and many advertisers are so relieved when they set it up that they simply let the ads they initially created run without much follow-up. However, your savvy competition will be testing and coming back with their strongest offers, and so should you.

How it works...

Ads that get low CTRs not only cost you potential customers but also negatively affect your Quality Scores. Avoiding common pitfalls and writing compelling ads can help:

- Improve CTR
- Improve Quality Score
- Lower average CPC
- Increase conversion rates
- Lower cost per conversion

See also

- The *Creating effective ads* recipe
- The *Split testing ad copy* recipe

Split testing ad copy

Split testing ad copy or A/B testing compares the effectiveness of two different ad variations. Your first ad or the one that you find the most appealing will not necessarily be the one that will attract most of your visitors. Luckily, you get instant feedback on AdWords, where people vote through clicks and conversions to help you choose messaging that works best for you.

Getting ready

Brainstorm ad text elements you'd like to test, such as:

- **Different landing pages**: If you are not sure what landing page would work better for a certain group of keywords, you can run two identical ads that are taking visitors to a different destination URL. Metrics such as conversion data can help you determine which landing page generates a better ROI.
- **Calls-to-action**: Test different phrases that entice users to take your desired action after the click. For example, you can test `Register Now` against `Sign-Up For Free`.
- **Headlines**: You can try static headlines against dynamic keyword insertion. Or, headlines that are phrased as a question.
- **Ad text descriptions**: Test audience specific phrases, such as `Family Friendly` or different ways to describe the product or its benefits. You can also compare different special offers, or using a percentage discount versus a specific price discount.

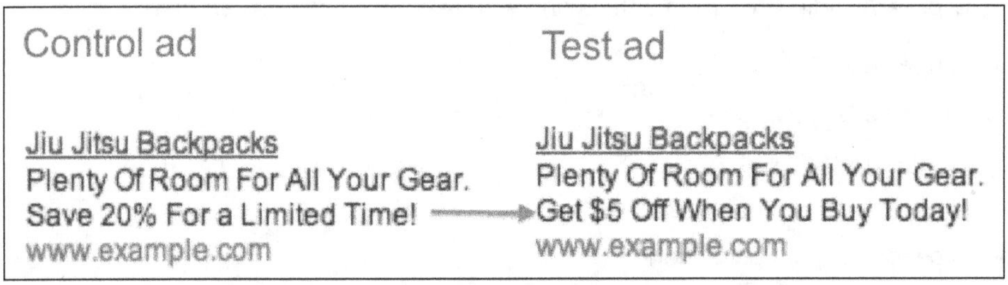

- **Display URL**: Add extra words to your display URL to squeeze in extra language into a limited ad space. For example, you can test `www.example.com` against `www.example.com/Free_Trial` in your display URL. If you do not have enough characters, you can leave out `www.` from your display URL.

Determine your goals or what metric you will be evaluating. If you are looking for more clicks, CTR will be your metric to watch. If your goal is to increase conversions, you should evaluate conversions, conversion rate, cost-per-conversion, and ROI.

How to do it...

To run an A/B split test, perform the following:

1. Choose the campaign and ad group where you would like to run the test. The high-traffic ad groups are a good place to test. You can also create a new campaign and ad group for the test.
2. Set your test campaign's ad rotation settings to **Rotate evenly** so the test ads get even exposure.
3. Choose your control, and determine what ad you would like to use as a baseline. One of your current top performers would be a good choice.
4. Create a test ad within the ad group where you are performing the test. This ad group should only have two ads, your control and your test.
5. Keep the ads you are testing identical, except for the element that you are trying to compare. So, if you are trying to evaluate if one call-to-action will perform better than another, keep the headlines, ad descriptions, and the ad's destination URL the same, except for the call-to-action you are A/B testing.
6. Let the ads compete. Accumulate enough data so the differences are significant. How long you'll need to run the test will depend on how much traffic you'll get. If you'd like to ensure that the data differences between your control and test ads are statistically significant, you can enable **Experiment settings** in AdWords, which you can locate in your campaign **Settings** page.

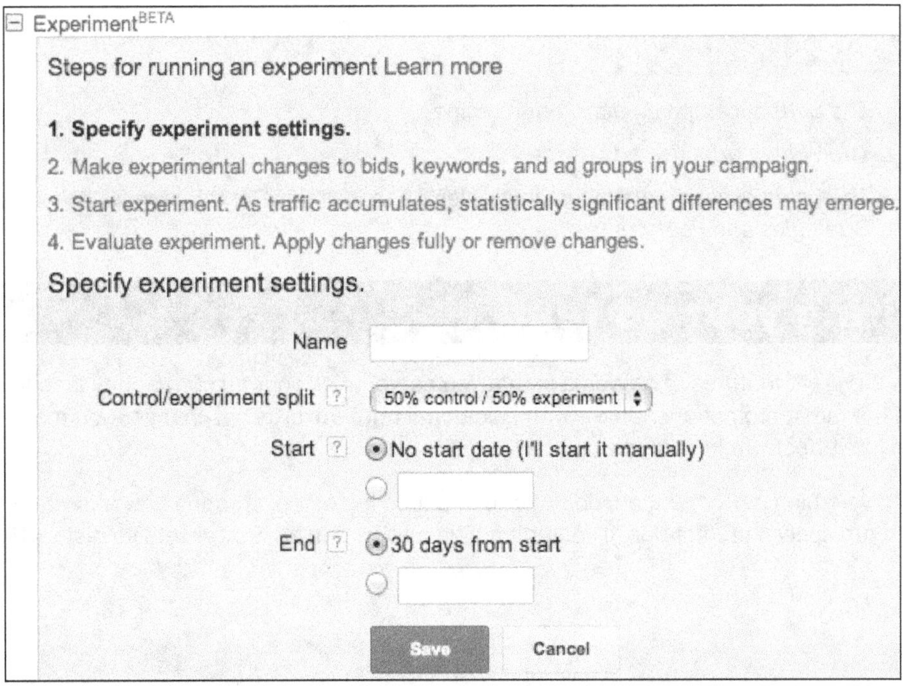

7. Measure test performance; if you are looking for more clicks, compare CTRs. The ad that generates a better CTR will be your winner. If your primary goal is conversions, evaluate conversion metrics.
8. Pause the loser and keep the winner. Decide for yourself what defines a winner. If you have a 0.1 percent increase in CTR, it might not be good enough. Re-iterate and aim for doubling your CTR.
9. Continue testing and refining to stay ahead of your competition.

How it works...

An A/B test involves testing two versions of an ad to compare which ad generates more clicks or more sales. You will see that 50 percent of your visitors are exposed to one version of your ad, while the other 50 percent see another ad version. In the AdWords interface, you can evaluate real time results of each ad to determine which one generates a better ROI. Some tests will show great results, and others won't. However, testing is always better than guessing.

There's more...

Once you test different ad elements, you may wish to implement the winning ad phrases across other ad groups in your account. For example, if you find through ad copy testing that `Save 20%` works better than using `Get $5 Off`, you can apply that learning in your other ads, as appropriate.

See also

- The *Setting campaign ad rotation* recipe
- The *Writing effective ads* recipe
- The *Using experiments to test campaign changes* recipe in *Chapter 12, Advanced Strategies and Features*

Editing your ad text

One of the great features of AdWords is that you can change your ad copy at any time to match the latest promotions. Unlike with traditional print advertising, changes you make can go into effect within minutes.

If you have a high performing ad, do not edit it; pause it instead, creating new ads when you want to run special promotions. If you edit a high-performing ad, that resets its history back to zero.

How to do it...

To edit a single ad, perform the following steps:

1. Navigate to the **Campaigns** tab and click on the **Ads** tab.
2. Hover over the ad you'd like to edit until you see a pencil icon, then click on it. This will bring up the **Edit** window box, where you'll be able to edit any part of your text ad.

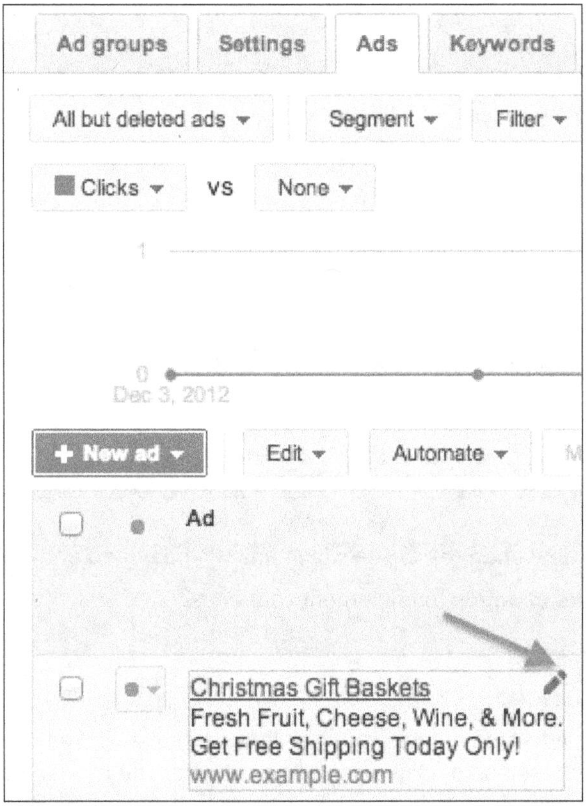

3. Make the necessary edits and click on **Save** to save your ad.

To edit ads in bulk, perform the following steps:

1. Sign in to your AdWords account.
2. Navigate to the **Campaigns** tab and click on the **Ads** tab.
3. In the search box, type in the phrase you'd like to edit. For example search for `Free Shipping`.
4. Select the ads you'd like to edit by clicking the box in the menu bar.
5. Go to **Edit** and choose **Change text ads...**.

6. Choose the type of change you'd like to make. You can **Set text**, **Find and replace**, **Append text**, or **Change case**.

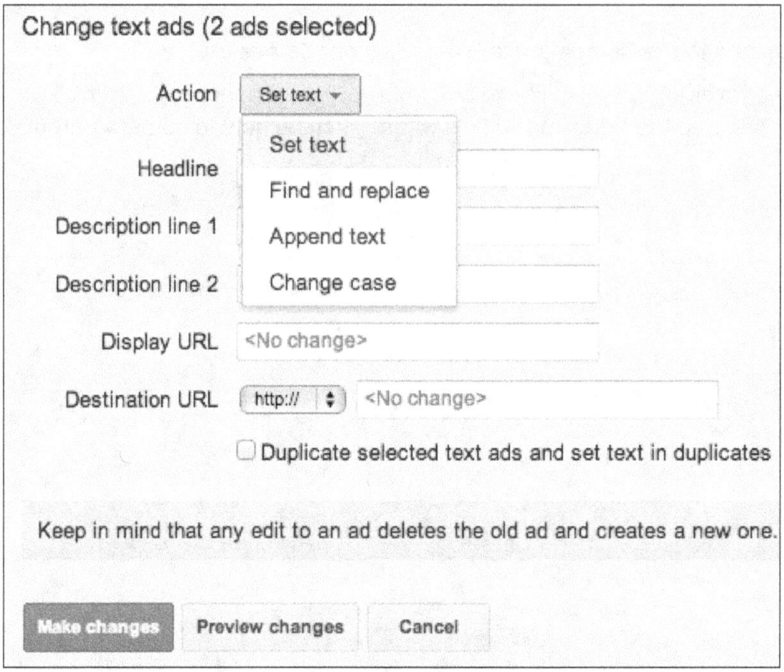

7. You can **Preview changes** to see which ads will be edited and what they will look like.
8. Click on **Make changes** to implement your edits.

How it works...

When you edit an ad, AdWords deletes your previous version and creates a new ad. All of your statistics, such as impressions or clicks, start back at zero. The new ad may still need to go through editorial approval.

See also

- The *Pausing or deleting ads* recipe

Pausing or deleting ads

You can pause or delete ads in AdWords at any time. For example, you may need to pause or delete ads that mention discounts or specials, which may be expiring. You should also periodically review ad performance data and pause low performers, such as ads with low CTR.

Getting ready

Decide if you'd like to pause or delete your ad. If you plan to run this ad again in the future, it makes more sense to pause it, rather than to delete it.

How to do it...

To pause or delete ads, perform the following steps:

1. Sign in to your AdWords account.
2. Navigate to the **Campaigns** tab and click on the **Ads** tab.
3. Select the ads you'd like to pause or delete by clicking the box in the menu bar.
4. Go to **Edit** and choose **Pause** or **Delete**.

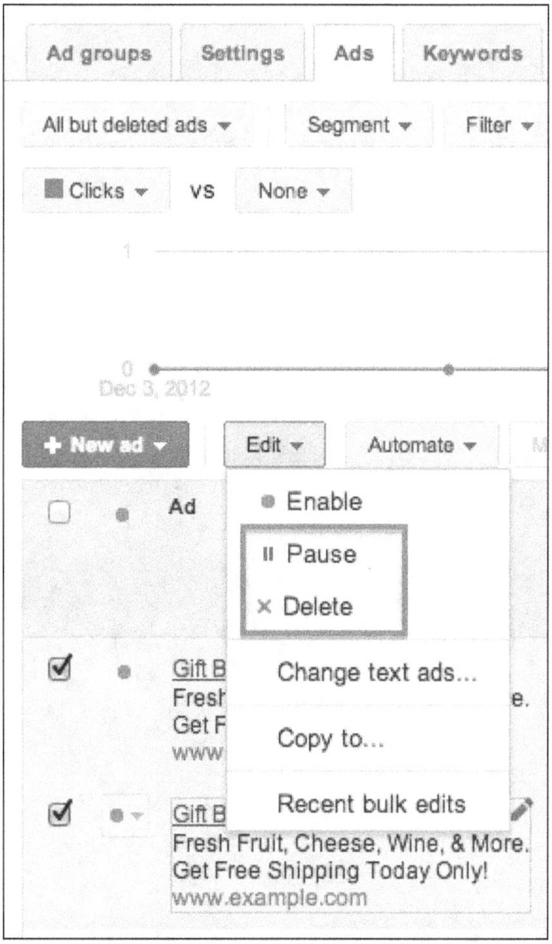

How it works...

When you pause or delete an ad, it stops that ad from showing. If you pause an ad, you can un-pause it at any time. However, if you delete an ad, you will not be able to un-delete it. You can still access a paused or deleted ad's history and performance data within the **Ads** tab.

See also

- The *Editing your ad text* recipe

7

Budgets and Bidding

In this chapter, we will cover the following:

- Setting and adjusting campaign budgets
- Evaluating your current budget and potential impact of budget changes
- Setting and adjusting ad group level bids
- Setting and adjusting keyword level bids
- Enabling enhanced bidding
- Enabling conversion optimizer
- Adjusting CPA bids
- Setting separate bids for calls
- Predicting impact of bid changes using the Bid Simulator
- Modifying mobile bids
- Adjusting location bids
- Adjusting bids based on the day of the week and time of day

Introduction

One of the great selling points of AdWords is that budgets are flexible and you can start advertising and testing the system with only a few dollars. You also choose how much you are willing to pay for individual clicks. Advertisers can lower or increase AdWords budgets and bids at any time, based on changing business needs. This makes for an extremely cost effective advertising solution that's flexible and easy to modify without long-term contracts or budget commitments.

Setting and adjusting campaign budgets

All advertisers have budgets for their various marketing efforts, including AdWords. If you are new to AdWords, your budget should be an amount you are comfortable testing with, while you refine your campaigns and figure out what works for you.

Your AdWords budget controls how often your ads are shown. The greater your budget, the more impressions your ads will receive. However, your budget should still be an amount you are comfortable spending on AdWords.

> Start small while you test keywords and ads that generate the best response. Once you figure out which campaigns convert, you can easily increase your daily budgets.

Getting ready

Decide how much you would like to spend on each product category or service. Are some of your products of greater priority to you? If so, make sure that you have the structure in place to support separate budgets with unique campaigns for each category that should have its own budget.

How to do it...

To set a budget for a new campaign, perform the following steps:

1. Click on **+ New campaign** in the **Campaigns** tab.
2. Scroll to the **Bidding and budget** section of the campaign **Settings** page.

3. Enter the daily budget you would like to set for your campaign in the **Budget** box.

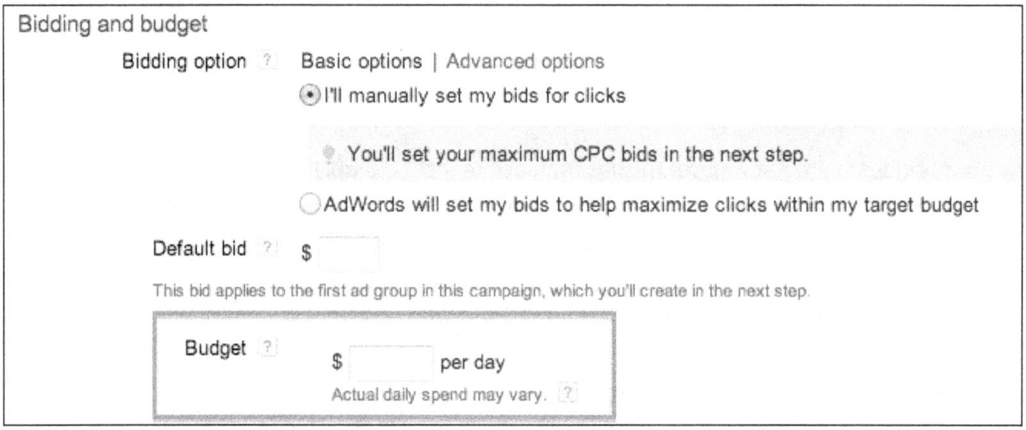

4. Click on **Save and continue**.

To adjust a campaign's budget, perform the following steps:

1. Sign in to your AdWords account, and click on the **Campaigns** tab.
2. In the campaign overview page, hover next to the campaign you'd like to edit and click on the budget amount you'd like to adjust. In this example, we see a $10 daily budget that we can change to a new amount.

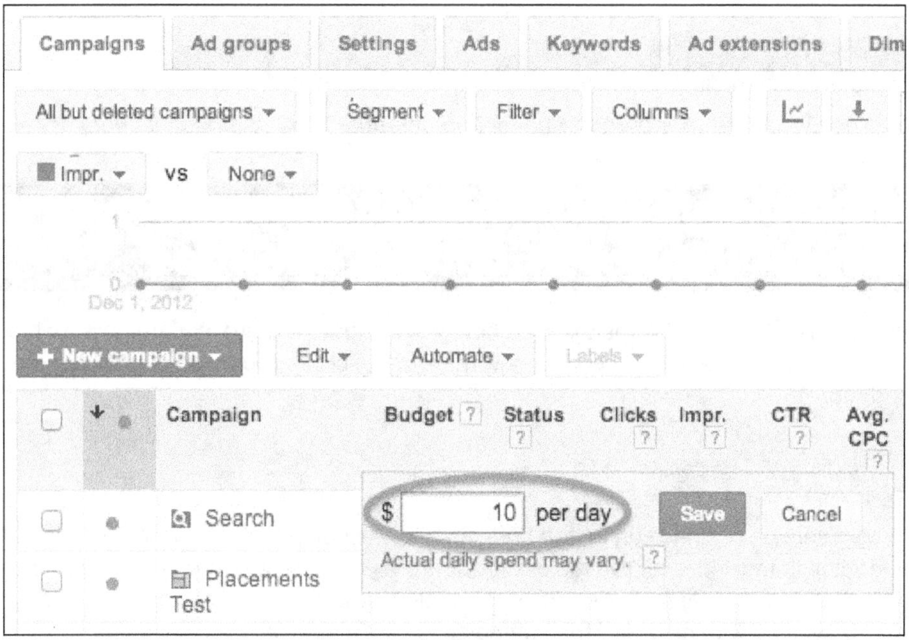

3. You can also adjust a campaign's budget by navigating to that campaign's **Settings** page.
4. Enter the new amount and click on **Save**.

How it works...

AdWords budgets are set per day, rather than per month. Multiply the daily budget amount you choose by days in a month to figure out how much you'll spend in a given month.

Daily budgets are set per campaign and will apply to all ad groups and keywords within that campaign. If you have multiple campaigns, add up each campaign's budget to figure out your total AdWords budget. For example, if you have 5 campaigns with a $10 daily budget each, your total daily budget would be $50 and you should be prepared to spend up to $1500 per month.

Because daily traffic patterns vary, AdWords may deliver more clicks and go over your actual budgets on the busier days when there is more traffic available. This is to make up for the slower days, when the system does not deliver enough traffic to maximize your daily budget.

There's more...

Your budget controls ad delivery or how often your ads will be shown. If your budget is more conservative and less than the recommended amount, AdWords slows ad delivery and shows your ads only intermittently, to avoid going over your set budget. This means that your ads might not be displayed every time a user searches your keywords. Limited budget is one of the most common reasons advertisers are not seeing their ads when searching on `Google.com`.

See also

- The *Evaluating your current budget and potential impact of budget changes* recipe

Evaluating your current budget and potential impact of budget changes

Budget ideas is a tool in AdWords that can help you evaluate if there is more potential for traffic within your campaigns, as well as how many more clicks you could get if you increased your budget.

Getting ready

Most advertisers do not have unlimited budgets and will not be able to afford increasing their spending to maximize all available clicks. Before you increase your budget, make sure a campaign is profitable first. Review your conversions and cost-per-conversion data and consider increasing your budget if the campaign is cost effective.

How to do it...

To evaluate your current budget and potential impact of budget changes, perform the following steps:

1. Click on the **Campaigns** tab, and check if any of your campaigns have the **Limited by budget** message.

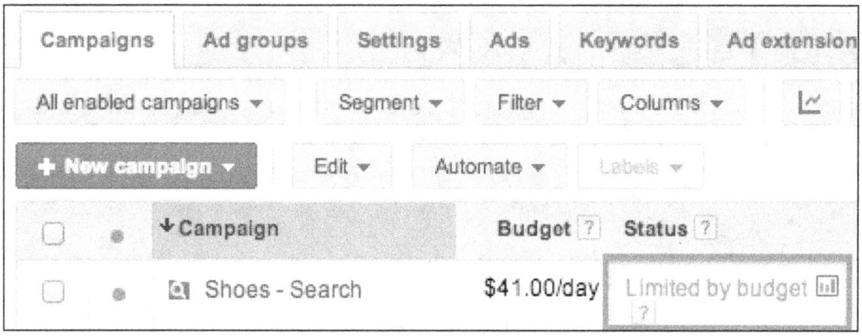

2. Click on the graph icon to the right of the **Limited by budget** message to explore how different budget increases can impact clicks and costs.

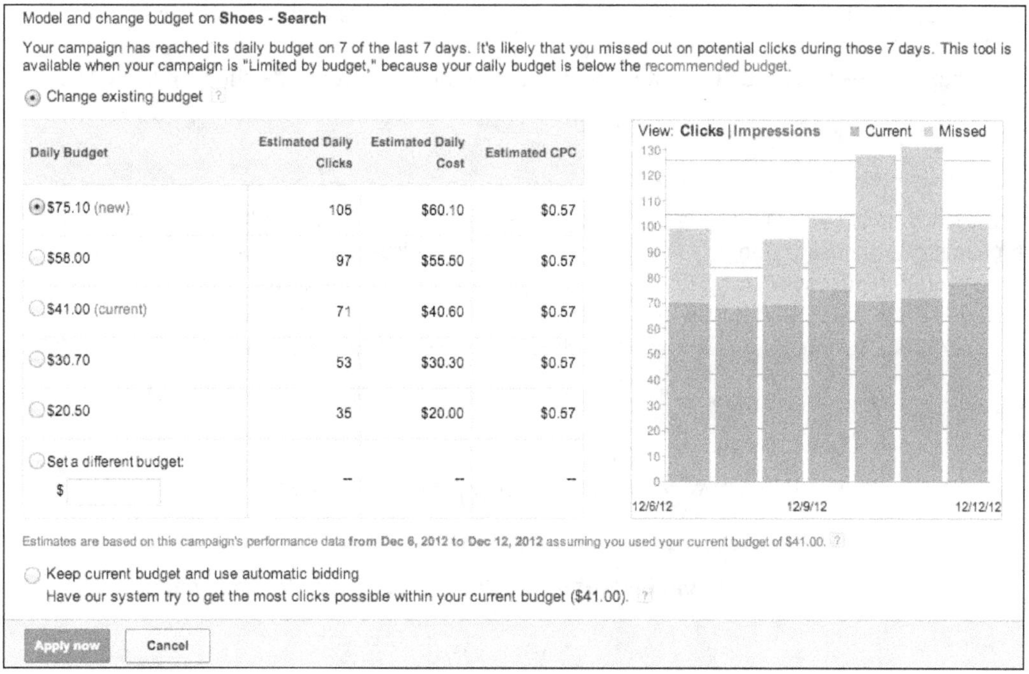

3. Choose your new budget amount and click on **Apply now** to increase your budget.

How it works...

The AdWords **Limited by budget** message means that your ads are not shown as often as they could be if your budget was higher. Your current budget is below the system-recommended amount to maximize impressions and clicks. Your ad delivery slows throughout the day to avoid going over your set budget, and your ads are not showing every time your potential customers are running a search for your keywords.

There's more...

If you are unable to increase your budget to the system-recommended amount, you can also lower your bids to get more clicks out of a limited budget.

See also

- The *Setting and adjusting campaign budgets* recipe
- The *Setting and adjusting ad group level bids* recipe

Setting and adjusting ad group level bids

Bidding competitively in an ad auction is a key ingredient in obtaining your desired ad position and getting traffic to your website. While your budget controls how often your ads are shown, your **Max cost-per-click (CPC)** controls your ad rank, or where your ads show on `Google.com`.

Getting ready

Decide how much you are willing to spend on each set of keywords. Analyze average CPCs for similar terms using Google's keyword tool as well as third-party tools, such as SpyFu, which you can access at `http://www.spyfu.com/`. Keep in mind that SpyFu only provides data for the US and UK. If you need international data, try KeywordSpy at `http://www.keywordspy.com/` or SEMrush at `http://www.semrush.com/`.

How to do it...

To set an ad group bid in a new campaign, perform the following steps:

1. Click on **+ New campaign** in the **Campaigns** tab.
2. Scroll to the **Bidding and budget** section of the campaign **Settings** page.

3. Enter the **Default bid** value, which will apply to the first ad group you create.

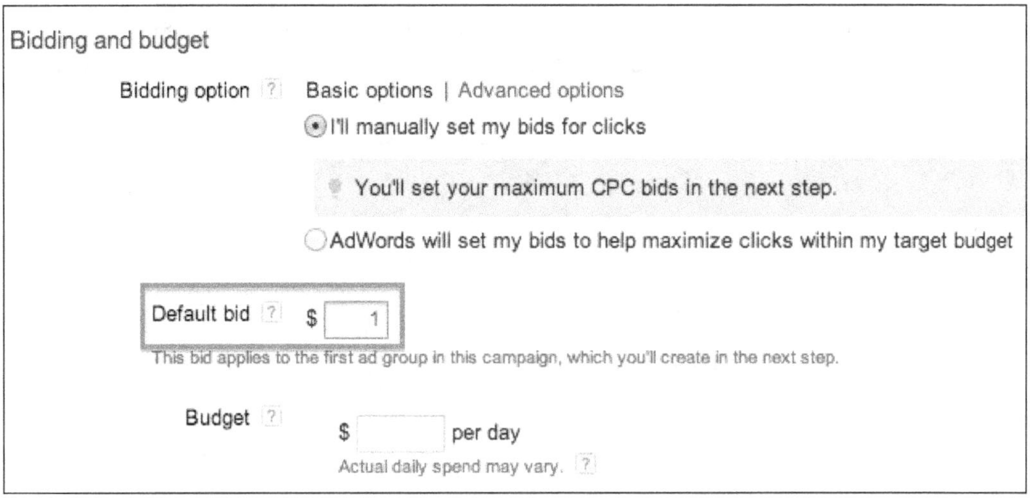

4. Click on **Save and continue**.

To adjust an ad group's bid, perform the following steps:

1. Click on the **Campaigns** tab.
2. And then click on the **Ad Groups** tab.
3. Navigate to the ad group you'd like to edit and click on the **Default Max. CPC** amount you'd like to adjust.
4. Enter the new amount and click on **Save**.

How it works...

Your ad group bid is the most that you are willing to pay per click for all of the ad group's keywords. The ad group's max CPC will apply to all keywords within an ad group, unless you set keyword level bids, which then override ad group bid defaults. The higher your max CPCs, the greater your chances of achieving a better ad rank and a top spot.

There's more...

If you'd like to edit multiple ad groups, you can change bids in bulk. Select all of the ad groups you'd like to adjust bids for and choose **Change bids** from the **Edit** menu. You'll be able to preview changes before they go live.

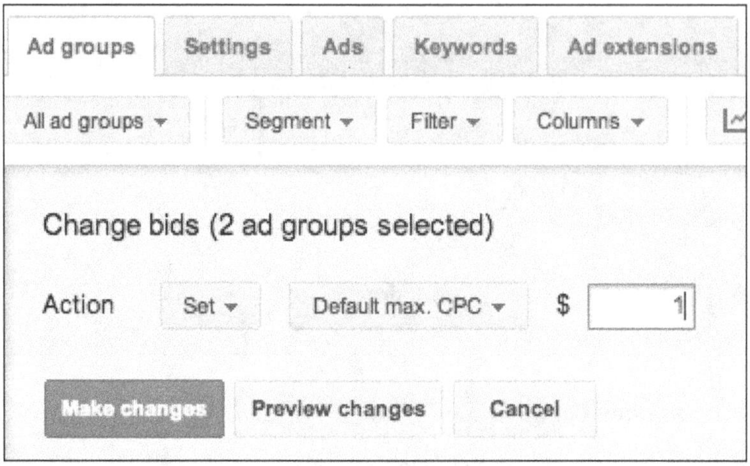

See also

- The *Analyzing budgets and bids to determine market saturation* recipe in *Chapter 1, Researching the Market and Competition and Setting Goals*
- The *Setting and adjusting keyword level bids* recipe

Setting and adjusting keyword level bids

In addition to being able to set ad group level bids, which apply to all keywords within an ad group, you can also set keyword level bids. Individual keywords within an ad group will perform differently, and you'll want to consider increasing bids for low position keywords or decreasing max CPCs for keywords that are not profitable.

Getting ready

Before you adjust bids, research keyword performance. Pay special attention to the following keywords:

- **Costly keywords with no conversions or few conversions**: Decrease bids for keywords that you are spending money on but that are not converting. For example, with a target CPA of $10, decrease bids on keywords that are generating conversions at a $15 CPA.

- **Keywords below first page bid**: Consider increasing bids on keywords that are not shown on the first page of Google's search results.
- **Cost effective keywords**: Increase bids for keywords that are generating profitable conversions to boost ad rank and get more clicks. For example, with a target CPA of $10, increase bids on keywords that are generating conversions at a $7 CPA.

How to do it...

To set or adjust keyword level bids, perform the following steps:

1. Click on the **Campaigns** tab.
2. Click on the **Keywords** tab.
3. Find the keyword you'd like to adjust the bid for and click on the **Max. CPC** field. Enter a new max CPC value and click on **Save**.

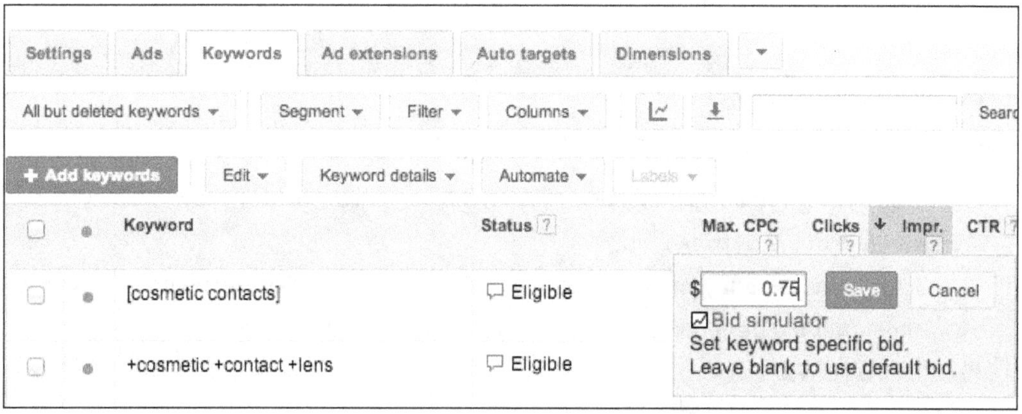

4. You can also adjust keyword bids by selecting one or multiple keywords and choosing **Change bids** from the **Edit** menu.

How it works...

Each ad group has a default bid, which applies to all of the keywords within an ad group, unless you set keyword level bids. If you set a keyword specific max CPC, that bid overrides the ad group level default values.

There's more...

You can change keyword bids in bulk by selecting multiple keywords and choosing the **Change bids** from the **Edit** option on your **Campaign Management** page.

See also

- The *Setting and adjusting ad group level bids* recipe

Enabling enhanced bidding

AdWords offers several tools that help you maximize conversions and get more out of your budget. **Enhanced CPC** (**eCPC**) changes your bids by lowering them on keywords that are less likely to convert, and increasing bids on keywords that do convert.

Getting ready

You will need to have implemented conversion tracking in your AdWords account. There are no minimum conversion requirements to start using eCPC, which means that you can enable this feature as soon as your campaigns start generating conversions.

How to do it...

To enable enhanced bidding, perform the following steps:

1. Click on the **Campaigns** tab, and click on the campaign you'd like to enable eCPC in.
2. Navigate to the **Settings** tab.
3. Scroll to the **Bidding and budget** section of the campaign **Settings** page.
4. Under **Bidding option**, mark the checkbox under **Enhanced CPC**.
5. Click on **Save**.

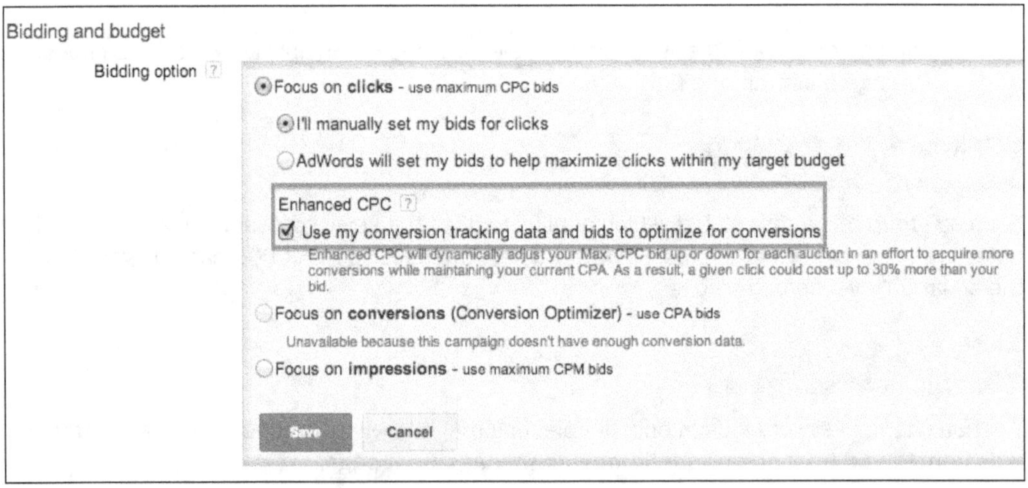

How it works...

Enhanced CPC automatically adjusts your max CPCs up or down for each auction with the goal of increasing conversions while maintaining your CPA. If you enable eCPC, AdWords could increase your bids up to 30 percent more than your original bid.

See also

- The *Creating a conversion goal in AdWords to track leads or sales* recipe in *Chapter 3, Tracking beyond the Click*
- The *Enabling Conversion Optimizer* recipe

Enabling Conversion Optimizer

Savvy advertisers measure conversions and adjust bids based on how much they are willing to pay for each conversion. This can be done manually by regularly reviewing your conversion data, or you can take advantage of **Conversion Optimizer** in AdWords. It uses historical data to predict which clicks are more valuable to you and adjusts bids in real time to maximize conversions without additional work on your part.

Getting ready

In order to use Conversion Optimizer, you will need to implement conversion tracking in your AdWords account and your campaign will need to have received at least 15 conversions in the last 30 days. If your campaign did not generate 15 conversions in the last 30 days, you will not have the option to enable Conversion Optimizer and you will need to wait until you receive the required number of conversions.

How to do it...

To enable Conversion Optimizer, perform the following steps:

1. Click on the **Campaigns** tab.
2. Click on the campaign that you'd like to enable Conversion Optimizer for.
3. Go to the **Settings** tab.
4. Scroll to the **Bidding and budget** section and click to edit **Bidding option**.
5. Select **Focus on conversions (Conversion Optimizer)**. If the campaign is not eligible to use Conversion Optimizer, you will not be able to select this option.

6. Choose from:
   - **Start with recommended bid**: AdWords will show you what target CPA it recommends based on the last 30 days of conversion data. If you are new to CPA bidding, I recommend you go with this option.
   - **Start with custom bid $**: You can enter your own custom target CPA bid you'd like AdWords to optimize for. Maybe you are OK with a slightly higher CPA than the system-recommended bid. If you choose a higher bid than the system-recommendation one, your CPA will increase and you'll also get more clicks. On the other hand, if the most recent CPA average is too high, you can enter a lower target CPA bid. Keep in mind that entering a bid lower than the recommended amount may help lower your CPA but it will also limit your traffic, since Conversion Optimizer will need to bid less to stay within your lower target CPA.
   - **Starts with previous target CPA bids**: If you previously used Conversion Optimizer and disabled it, you can go back to your previous target CPA bids.

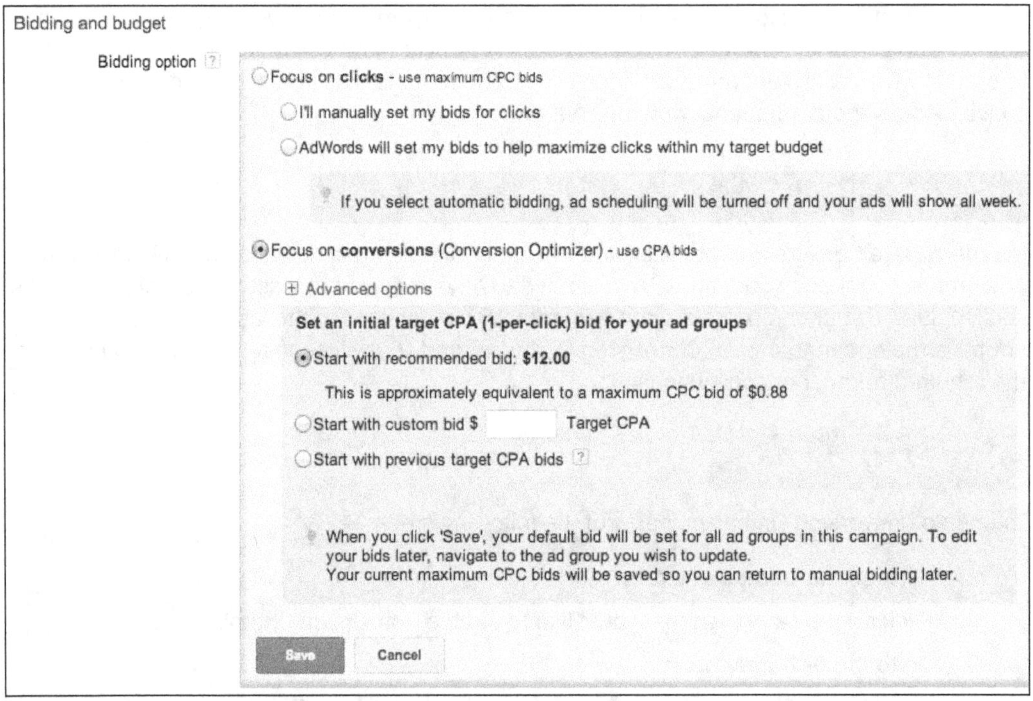

7. Click on **Save** after making your selection.
8. The target CPA bid you choose will be applied to all ad groups within your campaign.

How it works...

Conversion Optimizer adjusts your bids automatically with the goal of getting the most possible conversions out of your budget. It lowers bids on less profitable keywords and increases them on keywords that are more likely to convert.

Conversion Optimizer takes into account historical conversion information, such as the customer's location and times of the day conversions are likely to take place. The more historical conversion data you have, the better the tool is able to predict which clicks are valuable. Advertisers with limited conversion data may not see the best results, so do not rush into using the tool.

If you are not happy with the results that you get while using Conversion Optimizer, you can disable it at any time. Your bids will revert back to the max CPCs you were using prior to implementing Conversion Optimizer.

> It will take a couple of weeks or longer, depending on how much traffic your campaign receives, before you'll be able to gauge the effects of using Conversion Optimizer. Analyze your CPA and conversion rate before and after enabling Conversion Optimizer to assess its effectiveness and if you should implement it across other campaigns.

There's more...

Your conversion rate and average CPA depend partly on other factors, besides the bidding option you are using, such as seasonality, what your competition is doing, changes in your pricing, website, or changes to your keywords and ads. Once you enable CPA bidding, do not make too many changes to your campaign while you evaluate the effects of Conversion Optimizer.

See also

- The *Adjusting CPA bids* recipe

Adjusting CPA bids

If you are using the AdWords Conversion Optimizer, you should continue to adjust CPA bids to get the traffic and results you desire.

Getting ready

Review the ad group's performance within the campaign that's using Conversion Optimizer. You can sort the performance data by various metrics to isolate ad groups that need CPA adjustments.

Ad group performance trend	Recommended CPA change
Converting at a higher CPA than desired	Decrease CPA bid
Generating a lot of clicks and high costs without any conversions	Decrease CPA bid
Converting below CPA target	Increase CPA bid
Not getting enough traffic	Increase CPA bid
Appearing in a low average position within or below CPA target	Increase CPA bid

How to do it...

To edit ad group CPA bids, perform the following steps:

1. Click on the **Campaigns** tab and click on the campaign that's using Conversion Optimizer.
2. Click on the **Ad groups** tab.
3. Identify the ad groups you'd like to adjust, for example, ad groups that are converting at a higher than comfortable CPA.
4. Click on the **Max. CPA** or **Target CPA** field. Enter a new CPA bid and click on **Save**.

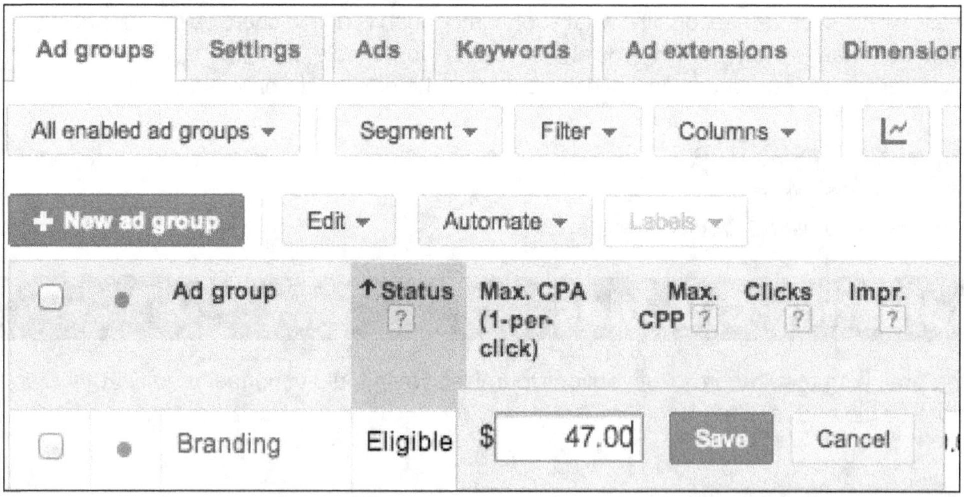

5. You can also change CPA bids by selecting one or multiple ad groups and choosing **Change bids** from the **Edit** menu.

How it works...

Increasing CPA bids will signal to AdWords that you are comfortable with a higher CPA, and AdWords will get you more clicks by increasing your max CPCs. You'll see an increase in conversions at a higher CPA.

Decreasing CPA bids will result in AdWords lowering your max CPCs. You'll get less traffic and fewer clicks but at a lower CPA.

There's more...

The following advanced options are available in your bidding campaign settings for Conversion Optimizer:

- **Max. CPA**: The most you are willing to pay for any particular conversion
- **Target CPA**: This is the average amount you would like to pay for each conversion

You can switch from **Target CPA** to **Max. CPA** at any time in your campaign **Settings** page, depending on which metric you are more comfortable with.

See also

- The *Creating effective ads* recipe in *Chapter 6, Writing Compelling Ads*

Setting separate bids for calls

For many businesses, calls are more important than clicks or even web-based leads. Getting to talk to someone who's considering your product or service directly can make the difference between converting that person to a lifelong customer or losing a sale to a competitor. Because Google understands just how valuable phone calls are, AdWords offers **Max. CPP** (cost-per-phone call), which is the option to set unique bids for calls.

Getting ready

You'll need to enable call extensions in AdWords and choose to use Google's call forwarding. The feature is only available in select countries.

Before you are able to bid separately on calls, you'll also need to meet a number of calls that came via your call extension. If you do not yet meet that threshold, you will see **Ineligible Bid** in the **CPP Bid** column.

How to do it...

To set max CPP bids, perform the following steps:

1. Click on the **Campaigns** tab, and then click on the campaign where you'd like to set unique bids for calls.
2. Click on the **Ad groups** tab.
3. Click directly in the ad group table on the **Max. CPP** row and enter a new max CPP amount for a specific ad group. Click on **Save**.
4. You can also select the ad groups you'd like to edit bids for and choose **Change bids** from the **Edit** tab.
5. Click on **Preview changes** to see which ad groups will be edited, and choose **Make changes** to implement bid edits.

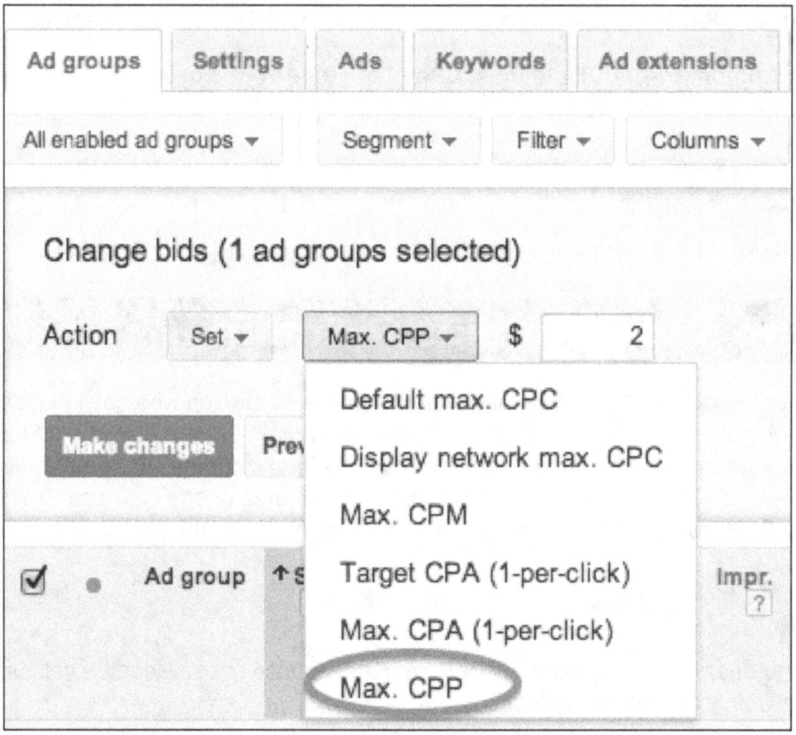

How it works...

Max CPP (cost-per-phone call) is the maximum amount you are willing to pay per phone call through call forwarding. The minimum CPP you can use is $1. Your max CPC, or the most you are willing to pay per click, can be less than your max CPP.

In order to be able to set max CPPs, you'll need to use call extensions with **Google's call forwarding**. With call forwarding, Google shows a toll free phone number in your ads, which forwards to your business phone number.

There's more...

If you decide to use max CPP, you'll only pay if someone decides to call the call-forwarding number from your ad. If a customer clicks through to your website and calls the customer support number on your home page, you will not pay Google for that call.

See also

- The *Setting up call extensions* recipe in *Chapter 12, Advanced Strategies and Features*

Predicting impact of bid changes using the Bid Simulator

Ever wonder how changing your bids might impact traffic? While there is no way to know for sure, Google's Bid Simulator can help you make informed predictions based on your most recent performance.

Getting ready

Choose an ad group or multiple ad groups you'd like to edit bids for. Here are the ad groups you may wish to increase bids for:

- Ad groups appearing in a low position
- Ad groups generating profitable conversions

Ad Groups you may want to decrease bids for include the following:

- Ad groups generating no conversions despite high costs
- Ad groups generating conversions at a high CPA

How to do it...

To use the Bid Simulator, perform the following steps:

1. Click on the **Campaigns** tab.
2. Click on the **Ad groups** tab.

3. Click on the graph icon below an ad group's bid and explore how different bids could have affected your traffic.

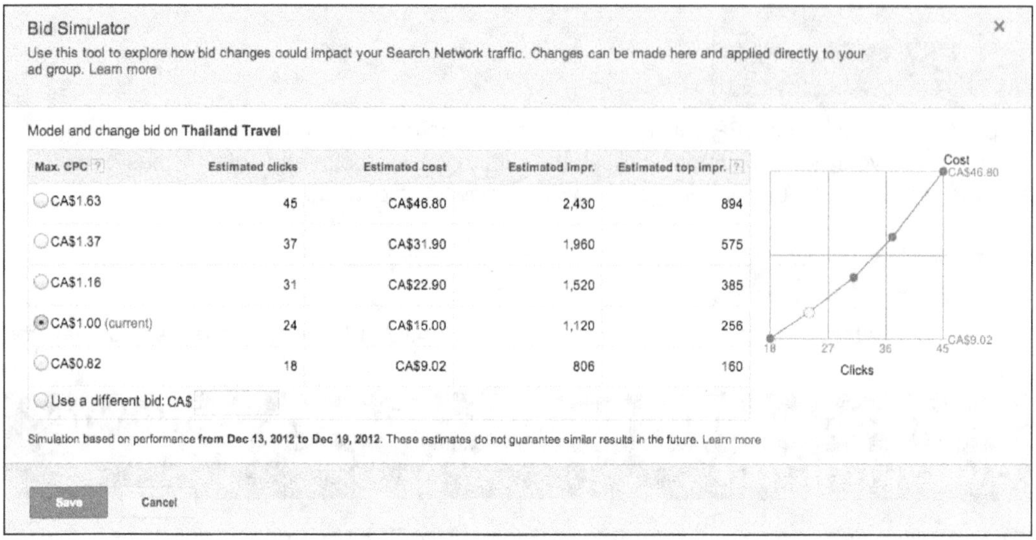

4. Choose a new max CPC and click on **Save** to apply it directly to your ad group.

How it works...

The Bid Simulator allows you to estimate how specific bid changes could impact your traffic. The tool evaluates performance over the last seven days and computes what your performance would have been like over the past week had you used a different bid. You can also see how many top of the page impressions a different bid would have received.

There's more...

The estimates are restricted to the Search network and do not include the Display network.

The Bid Simulator does not work with campaigns that are using automatic bidding or the Conversion Optimizer. It also is not available in limited budget campaigns that have consistently reached the daily budget over the past seven days.

See also

- The *Setting and adjusting ad group level bids* recipe

Modifying mobile bids

The default option for all new advertisers when creating accounts is to have all campaigns opted into all devices, including computers, tablets, and mobile phones. However, you can and should adjust bids for mobile, depending on what types of results you are getting.

Getting ready

Analyze past mobile performances to determine how much traffic you received from mobile and how this traffic has historically converted for you. If conversion rates are on par with computers and tablets, leave mobile bids the same as the default. If mobile conversion rates are much lower, decrease the bids. On the other hand, if you get better performance from mobile, you can also increase bids to capture even more mobile traffic.

Device	Conversion rate	Bid adjustment
Computers	3 percent	Default
Tablets	3.5 percent	Cannot be adjusted
Mobile	1.5 percent	Decrease
Mobile	4 percent	Increase

Visit your website on a mobile device to see if it's mobile friendly. If the user experience is not ideal and it's difficult to navigate your website on a smartphone, decrease bids. Also, consider investing in a mobile-optimized website, which will become increasingly vital as the mobile user's base continues to grow. Explore `http://www.howtogomo.com/` to see how your current website looks in mobile and to find additional resources.

How to do it...

To modify mobile bids, perform the following steps:

1. Go to the **Campaigns** tab.
2. Click on the specific campaign you'd like to edit.
3. Go to the **Settings** tab and select **Devices**.
4. The screen will show you your campaign's past performance for all three devices. Adjust the date range to **All time** near the top of your **Campaigns** tab to include past performance data.

5. Next to **Mobile devices with full browsers**, click in the **Bid adj.** column.

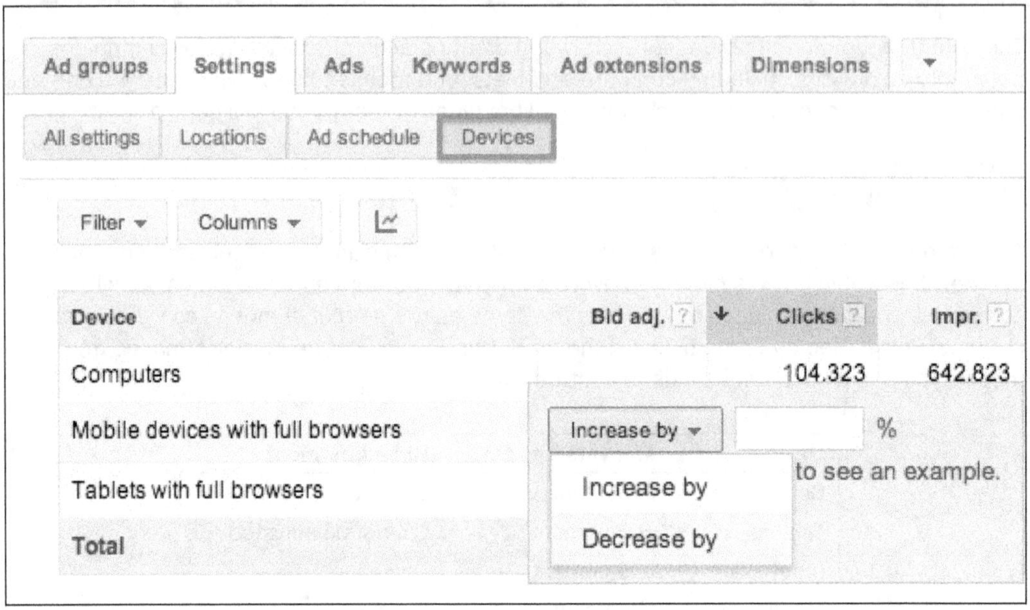

6. Choose from **Increase by** or **Decrease by** and enter your % change.
7. To opt your campaign out of mobile completely, choose **Decrease by** and enter **100%**.
8. Click on **Save**.

How it works...

Mobile bid adjustments help you increase or decrease bids for mobile devices. Bid adjustments are set as a percentage of your default bid.

Mobile bid adjustments are not compatible with Conversion Optimizer, so if your campaigns are taking advantage of CPA bidding, modifying bids will not have any effect. However, you can still opt for a Conversion-Optimizer-enabled campaign for mobile devices by using a 100-percent mobile bid decrease. Mobile bid adjustments are not compatible with Conversion Optimizer since this feature already takes into consideration devices users are searching from when adjusting bids.

There's more...

Currently, AdWords does not provide an option to modify tablet bids. They are the same as the default computer bids.

See also

- The *Optimizing bids for ROI* recipe in *Chapter 11, Optimizing Performance*

Adjusting location bids

With some recent improvements to AdWords, advertisers can now modify bids for different locations all through a single campaign. Location-specific bids can help you achieve higher ad rank in places where you get the best response and spend less in regions and cities that don't work as well. For example, a retailer selling snow tires can set higher bids for customers searching from snowy Colorado than for people who are located in sunny California.

Getting ready

First, you'll need to analyze the results you are getting from you current target locations. To see location specific data, follow these steps:

1. Click on the **Campaigns** tab.
2. Choose a campaign to focus on and click on the **Settings** tab.
3. Click on **Locations**.
4. From the **Location details** drop-down menu choose **What triggered your ad** or **Where your users were**. The option **Where your users were** reports on the physical location of users that saw your ads. The option **What triggered your ad** also includes locations users were searching for or viewing pages about.

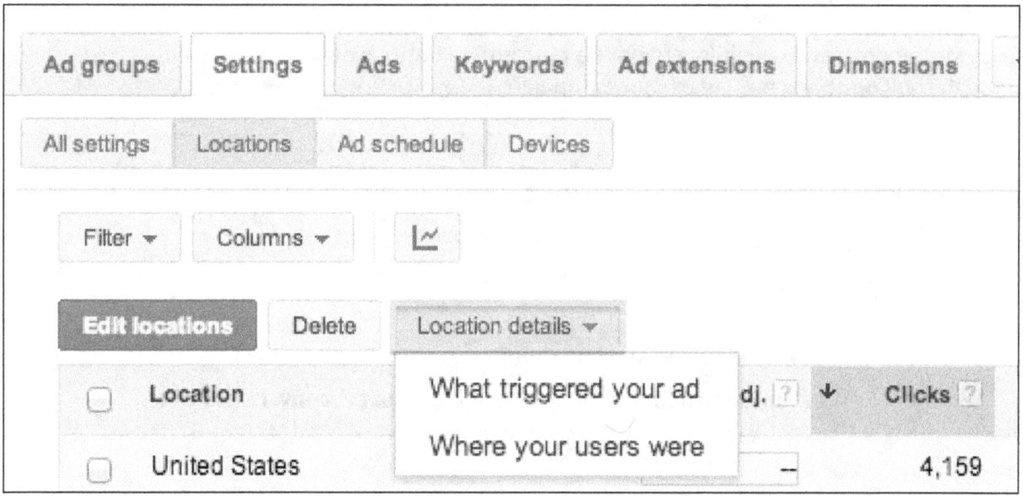

5. Choose the geographic level of detail. Your options are:
    - **Country/Territory**
    - **Region**
    - **City**
    - **Most specific location**

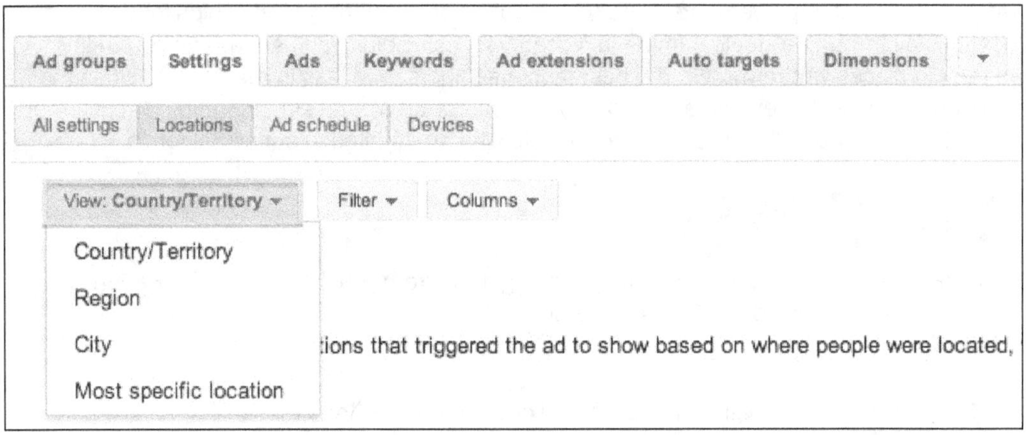

6. Review performance data by geographic level of interest (such as by city), including conversions. Are some regions performing better than others? If you do not have historical data, think about where your products or services are the most successful.

How to do it...

Once you understand which locations are performing better, you'll be able to adjust bids through the **Locations** setting of your campaign.

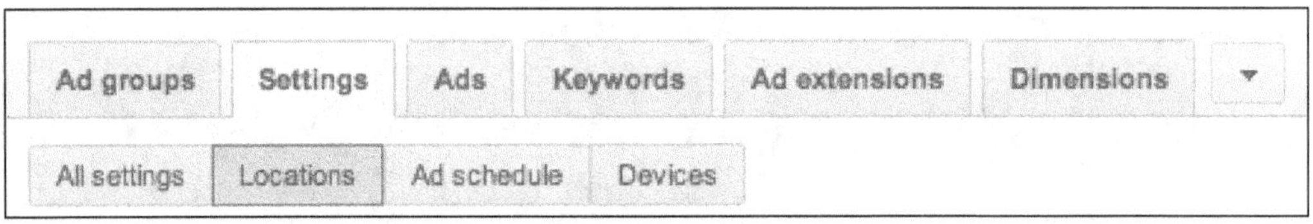

1. Click on **Locations** to see location details.
2. Sort by performance metric of interest, such as **Cost / conv. (1-per-click)**.

3. Select low performing locations and go to **Add targets and set bid adjustments**. For low performers, choose **Decrease by** and enter a % amount. Click on **Add**.
4. Next, select your high performing regions, go to **Add targets and set bid adjustments**, and choose **Increase by** with a specific % amount. Click on **Add**.

Location bids are adjusted at the campaign level and this process will need to be repeated for additional campaigns for which you wish to modify bids.

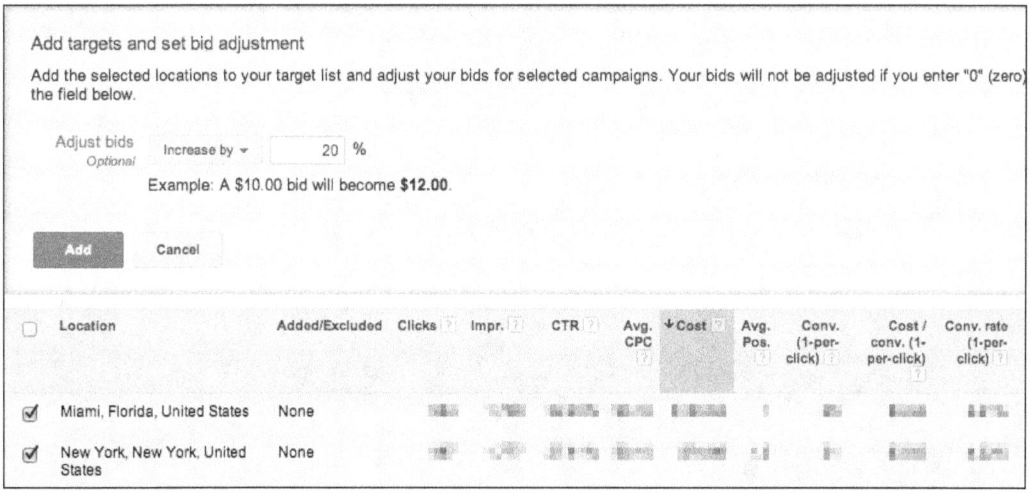

How it works...

Location bid adjustments allow you to increase or decrease bids for specific locations within a single campaign. Bid adjustments are set as a percentage of your default bid.

There's more...

In addition to increasing or decreasing bids, you can also exclude locations to prevent your ads from serving in low performing geographic areas. The following screenshot highlights the **Exclude** option in your **Locations** tab, where you can block specific locations:

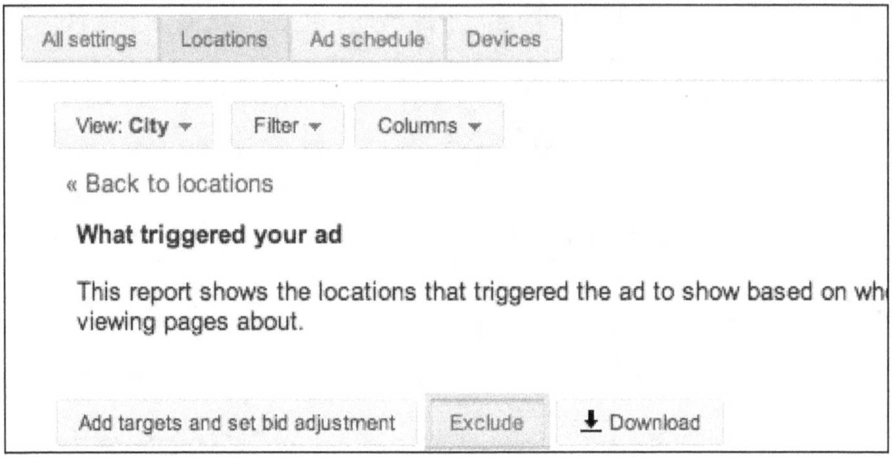

See also

- The *Modifying mobile bids* recipe

Adjusting bids based on the day of the week and time of day

If you find that certain days or times of the day bring more valuable web traffic, you can have AdWords automatically adjust your bids to maximize on these patterns. For example, a coffee shop may want to bid more aggressively during its peak morning hours.

Getting ready

Figure out when you get the most valuable traffic. You can use the **Dimensions** tab in AdWords to analyze performance by day of the week or by hour.

You can also see performance data in your **Ad schedule** campaign settings page. Click on **Schedule details** and choose **Day of the week** or **Hour and day of the week**.

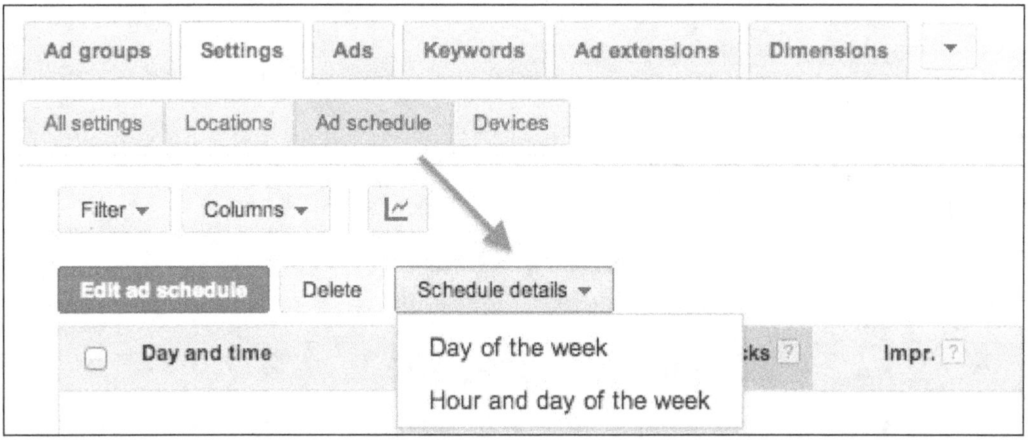

How to do it...

To adjust bids based on the day of the week or time of the day, perform the following steps:

1. Go to the **Campaigns** tab and click on the specific campaign you'd like to edit.
2. Go to the **Settings** tab.
3. Select **Ad schedule**.
4. Click on **Edit ad schedule**.
5. Click on **+ Create custom schedule**.
6. Choose the days when you'd like your ads to run. To make different bid adjustments for different hours of the day, you'll need to create multiple ad schedules and then adjust bids for them. In our coffee shop example, we'll create three different time slots.

Time slot	Bid adjustment
6:00 - 10:00	10 percent bid increase
10:00 - 15:00	No bid adjustment
15:00 - 18:00	10 percent bid decrease

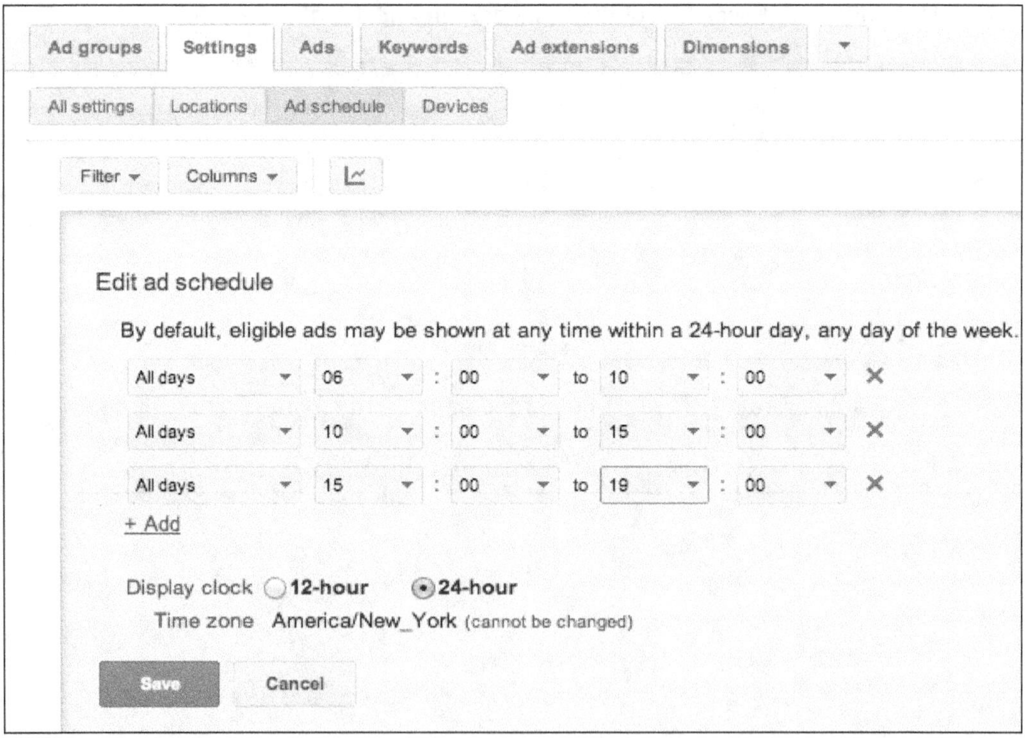

7. Click on **Save** after you have selected your desired days and hours.
8. Next, you'll see a list of the days and times your ads will be running. Clicking on the **Bid adj.** column next to each time slot will allow you to increase or decrease bids.

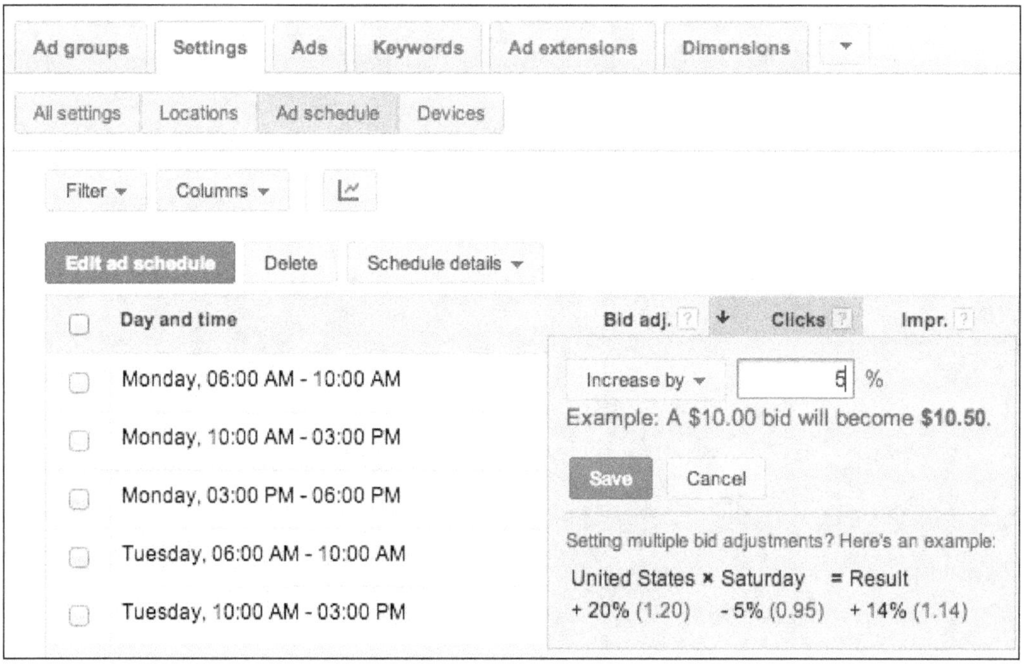

9. Click on **Save** after modifying each time slot's bid. Bids you do not modify will remain at 100 percent of the default.

How it works...

Ad scheduling bid adjustments help you increase or decrease bids for certain days of the week or hours of the day to maximize ad exposure during important time periods. Bid adjustments are set as a percentage of your default bid.

There's more...

If you are using Conversion Optimizer as your bidding strategy, you will not be able to set up ad-scheduling bid modifications. Conversion Optimizer is a robust AdWords tool that already takes into account when your conversions are happening and optimizes bids to maximize ROI.

See also

- The *Enabling Conversion Optimizer* recipe

8
Running Display Ads

In this chapter, we will cover the following:

- Creating an automatic placements campaign
- Creating a managed placements display campaign
- Researching and adding display placements
- Targeting display sites based on topics
- Excluding irrelevant and poorly performing placements
- Avoid displaying your ads on certain pages
- Excluding categories of sites and potentially sensitive topics
- Adding image ads to display campaigns
- Creating rich image ads with Display Ad Builder
- Analyzing relative CTR to benchmark display performance

Introduction

The **Google's Display network** (**GDN**) helps advertisers reach a greater audience through ads that show on websites outside of `Google.com`, such as news, blogs, and a variety of popular or niche websites. The Display network can be a great supplement to search campaigns. It helps advertisers reach customers who may not be searching for products and services, but can still be enticed by relevant ads as they browse the Internet. A well-executed display campaign can lift your search performance and helps build trust as people move through the purchase funnel.

Before creating display campaigns, define who you would like to reach. As a best practice, always keep search and display campaigns separate, so that you can use separate budgets and analyze and maximize each network's potential.

If you are mainly interested in branding, you have the option to pay for impressions on GDN through maximum CPM (cost-per-thousand impressions) bidding. With CPM bids, you pay for impressions rather than clicks. However, for advertisers who are interested in sales or leads (most advertisers), max CPC bidding is the recommended bidding option for display.

Creating an automatic placements campaign

If you are new to Google Display, I recommend you start with automatic placements. This is where AdWords shows your ads on relevant websites based on your keywords and other factors. You have the option to simply opt a search campaign into the Google Display network, however, that is not the recommended setup. I recommend creating a new AdWords campaign targeting Google Display only, so you can allocate a separate budget and customize other settings for display.

Getting ready

Decide how much of your budget you'd like to allocate for testing display. Start with a smaller budget until you evaluate if display will work for you while you optimize your campaign.

How to do it...

To create an automatic placements display campaign, perform the following steps:

1. Click on the **Campaigns** tab.
2. Click on **+ New campaign** to create a new campaign.
3. Choose **Display Network only**:

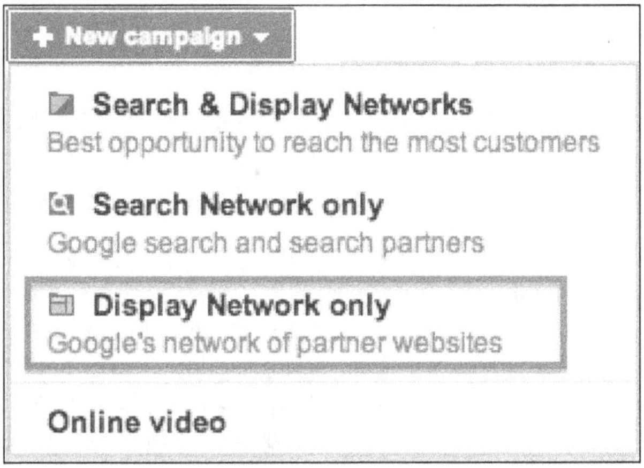

4. Name your campaign. I recommend including `Display` in your naming convention for easier reporting and analysis.
5. Choose your target locations and languages.
6. Choose your bidding option. I recommend you start with **I'll manually set my bids for clicks** for greater control over how much you bid on each ad group.
7. Set a daily **Budget**. Start small while you optimize and evaluate the effectiveness of display.
8. Click on **Save and continue**.
9. Next, you'll create your first display ad group. Choose an ad group name that reflects the theme of the keywords you'll add.
10. Choose your **Default bid** value. This is the most you are willing to pay for clicks in an ad group.

11. Under **Choose how to target your ads**, select **Display Keywords**:

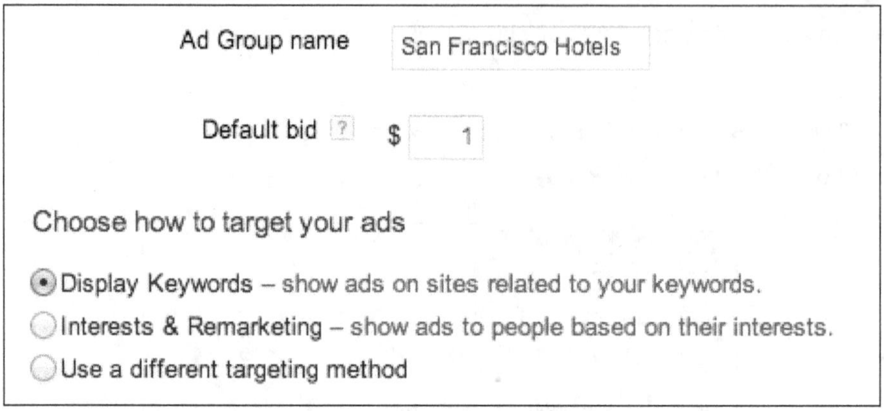

12. Enter your keywords into the keyword box and click on **Find related keywords** for additional ideas. Select a small, targeted keyword list of 3 to 5 keywords and no more than 20 keywords. Smaller keyword lists tend to work better on the Display network. Keywords are used to identify websites with similar themes and therefore function very differently from keywords in your search campaigns. You do not need to use misspellings or be too specific with your keyword lists, as this might filter out too many relevant websites.

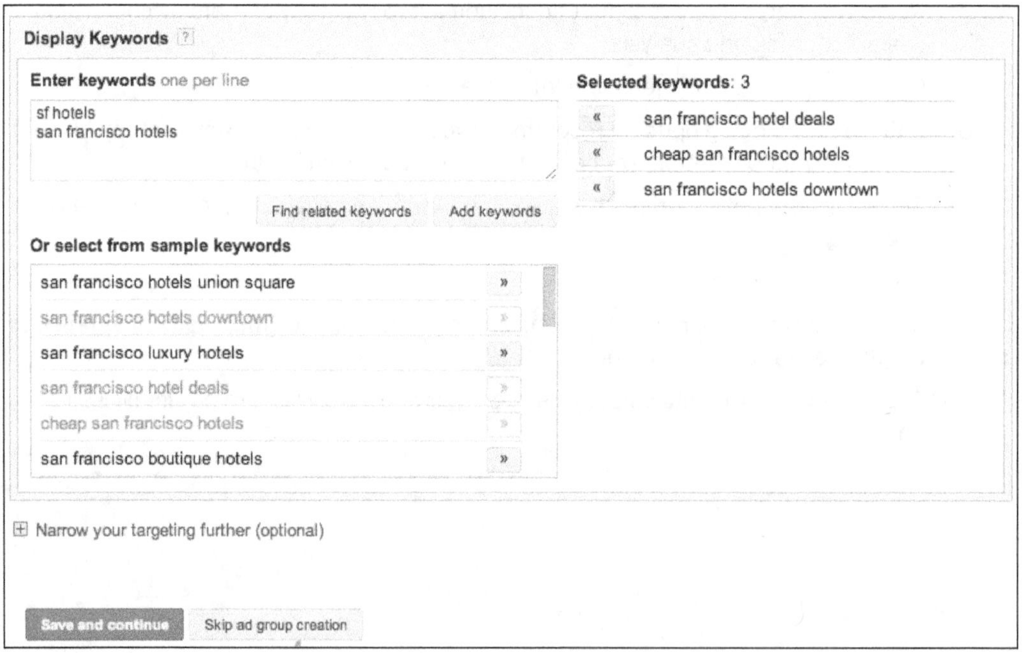

13. Click on **Save and continue**.
14. Next, create an ad. You can run image, display rich media, text, and video ads in your display campaigns. If you have image or video ads, you can add them to your campaign.
15. If you do not have an image ad, you can use the **Display ad builder** feature to create one. Keep your ad targeted to your keyword list and follow other ad copy best practices, such as including calls-to-action and special offers. You do not need to add all ad formats at once and can come back to add in additional ad formats at a later time.
16. Click on **Save ads** when you are done.
17. Create additional ad groups following the same guidelines of small keyword lists and targeted ads. I recommend you start with several display ad groups, rather than just one, as they will likely perform differently based on the keywords and ads you choose.

How it works...

With automatic placements, AdWords uses your keywords and other factors to match your ads to relevant placements that are part of Google's Display network. Rather than choosing specific placements to show ads on, AdWords places your ads based on your ad group's theme, matching it up to relevant websites on the Display network through contextual targeting. For example, if you have an ad group with keywords related to dog toys, your ads could show next to an article that discusses dog training techniques.

There's more...

The easiest way to get started with AdWords display is to create a campaign that's a mirror version of your search campaign, customized for the Display network. You can quickly create a duplicate version of your search campaign with AdWords Editor. Copy and paste an existing campaign and make sure to select the appropriate networks for your new display campaign under the **Campaigns** tab. You might need to make some edits to your keywords, removing keyword misspellings and keywords that are too specific, keeping your keyword lists small and targeted. Keyword match types are not relevant for display campaigns, so you should just use the broad match modifier.

See also

- The *Creating a managed placements display campaign* recipe
- The *Adding image ads to display campaigns* recipe
- The *Copying campaigns or ad groups with AdWords Editor* recipe in *Chapter 13, Managing Campaigns*

Creating a managed placements campaign

In addition to letting AdWords contextually target ads based on your keywords (automatic placements), you can choose specific websites you'd like to show ads on (managed placements). This is a good strategy for advertisers who only want to show ads on specific websites and want more control over where their ads are shown.

Getting ready

Brainstorm websites or types of websites where you'd like your ads to be shown. These properties may or may not be part of Google's Display network, but you'll be able to research them and find similar websites as you create your campaign.

How to do it...

To create a managed placements display campaign, perform the following steps:

1. Go to your **Campaigns** tab.
2. Click on **+ New campaign** to create a new campaign.
3. Choose **Display Network only**.
4. After choosing all of the relevant campaign settings and your budget, click on **Save and continue**.
5. Name your new ad group and choose the **Default Bid** value. This bid will apply to all placements you choose within this ad group, unless you set placement-specific bids, which will override the default ad group bid.
6. Under **Choose how to target your ads**, select **Use a different targeting method** and select **Placements**:

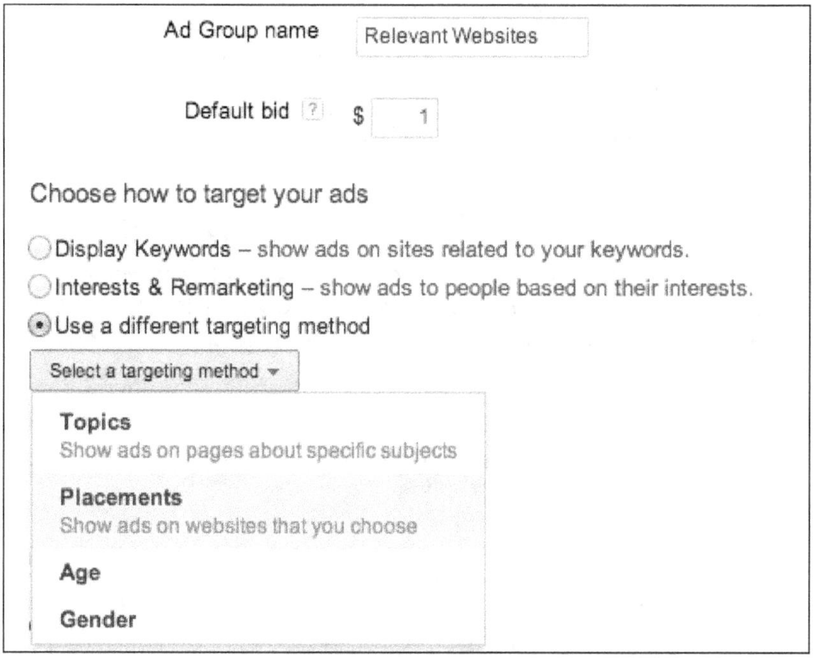

7. In the next step, you'll be able to search for placement ideas by entering a word, phrase, or website. The tool provides data on how many impressions each placement receives as well as what ad types (text ad, image ad, audio ad, or In-Stream ad) each placement accepts. The In-Stream ads are video ads that appear as an ad break before or during YouTube partner videos.

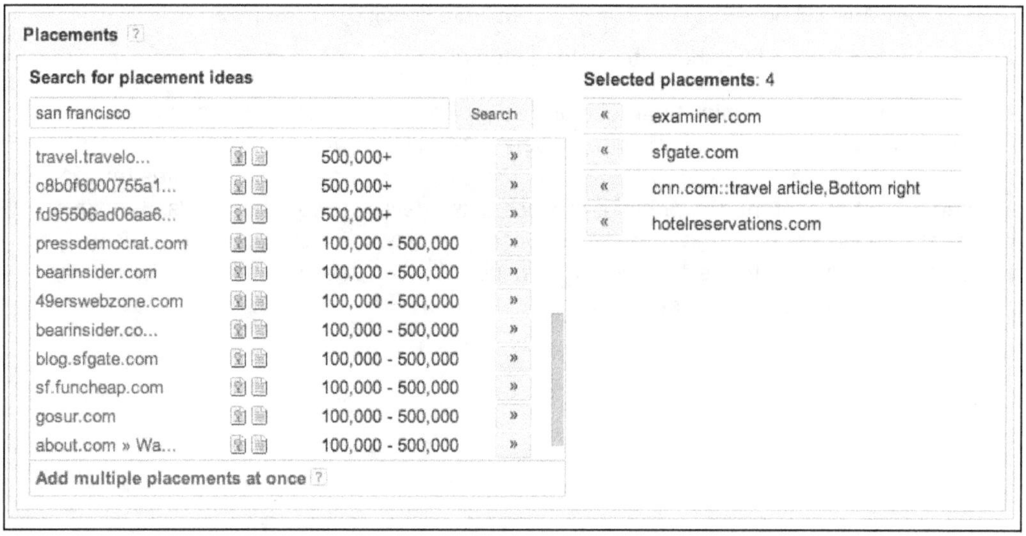

8. Select the placements you'd like to add and click on **Save and continue**.
9. Add text, image, display, or video ads to your ad group. Add a combination of different ad formats for greatest reach.
10. You can create additional ad groups with different placements or types of websites.

How it works...

Placements are websites, specific pages on a website, app, or ad units within a webpage where AdWords shows ads. A website needs to be part of Google's Display network to be eligible as a placement. You'll also need to win a bid in each ad auction in order for your ads to be shown.

> To maximize reach, set competitive bids, especially if you are targeting popular websites.

There's more...

In addition to selecting specific placements to show ads on, you can narrow your targeting further by the following criteria:

- **Display keywords**: Ads will be shown on websites relevant to keywords you add
- **Audiences**: Ads will be shown to people based on their interests, types of websites they visit, and if they previously visited your website (remarketing)
- **Topics**: Ads will be shown on pages about specific topics or sub-topics
- **Age**: Ads will be shown to people that fall into specific age ranges
- **Gender**: Ads will be shown to males or females

If you combine multiple display targets in one ad group, you restrict your ads to be shown only to those users who meet all of your chosen targets. For example, if you use keywords and placements in one ad group, your ads will only be shown on specific websites that you selected when the content of a publisher's website is relevant to your keywords. Keep in mind that if you layer on too many targets at once, you may be restricting your ad visibility to a very narrow audience. In the following screenshot, you can see an example of how using placements and keywords together in one ad group can restrict your reach:

See also

- The *Creating an automatic placements campaign* recipe
- The *Adding image ads to display campaigns* recipe

Researching and adding display placements

If you are not yet ready to create a display campaign, but would like to research available placements or check if specific websites are part of Google's Display network, you can use Google's **Placement Tool**. You can also use this tool if you have already created a display campaign that you'd like to build on and expand with additional placements.

Getting ready

Put together a list of websites you'd like to show ads on. Also, prepare keywords and product categories to search for additional available placements.

How to do it...

To find placements, perform the following steps:

1. Sign in to your AdWords account.
2. Go to **Tools and Analysis** and choose the **Placement Tool** option.
3. You can search for placement based on one of the following criteria:
    - **Word or phrase**
    - **Website**
    - **Category**
4. Once you enter your search criteria, you can filter further by locations, languages, and devices under **Advanced Options and Filters**.
5. Click on **Search** to see if the specific placement you are interested in is available, or to find placements relevant to searched phrases and categories.

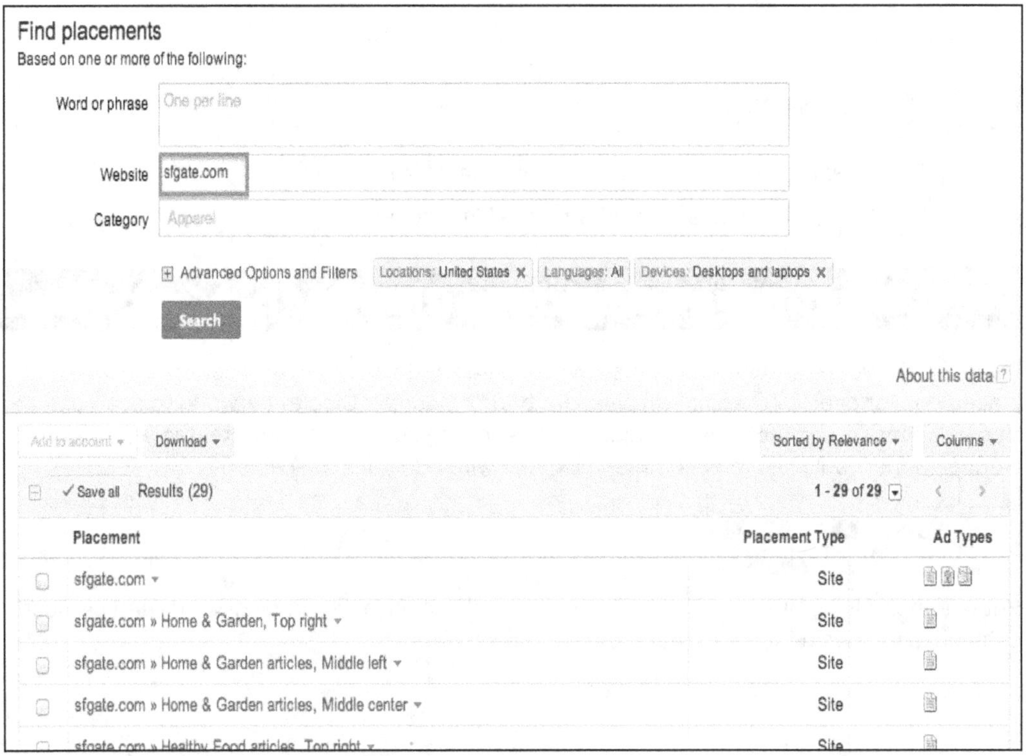

6. You can further filter placements by type. Uncheck any that you are not interested in showing your ads on. The following placement types are available:
    - **Site**
    - **Video**
    - **Feed**
    - **Game**
    - **Mobile App**
    - **Audio**

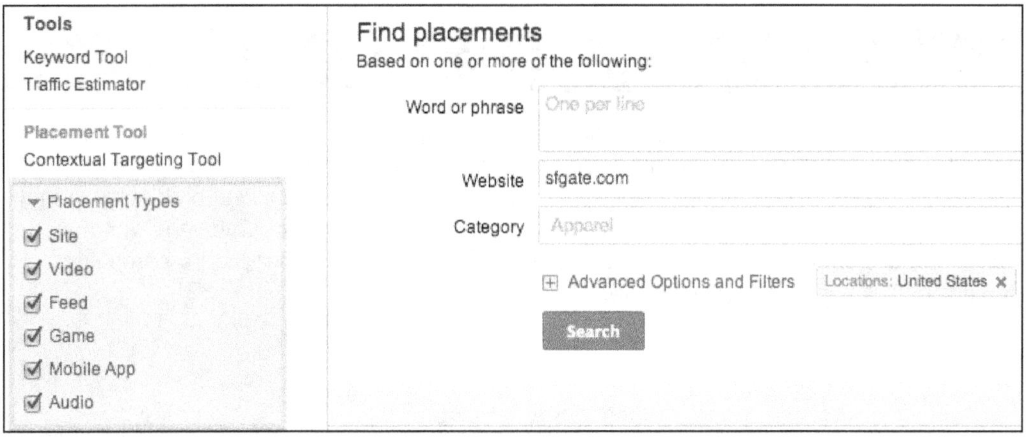

7. If you'd like to find out more about a specific placement, click on it from within the placement tool. You'll see additional information about it, such as what ad formats it accepts, or an example page where your ads could show.
8. Select **Impressions Per Day** under the **Columns** drop-down button to see how many daily impressions each placement receives:

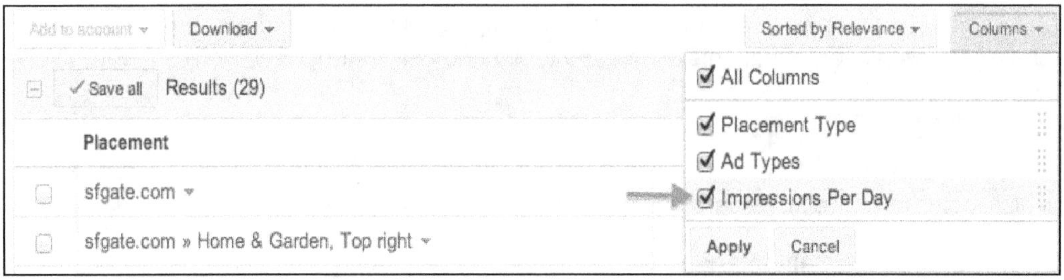

9. Check the box next to the placements you would like to save to **My placement ideas**, add them directly to your account, or download into a spreadsheet.

How it works...

The **Placement Tool** option helps you find websites on Google's Display network to show your ads on. It provides example pages where your ads could appear, as well as the types of ad formats each placement accepts. Once you find placements you like, you can add them to your campaigns directly from the **Placement Tool** option.

See also

- The *Creating a managed placements campaign* recipe

Targeting display sites based on topics

If you would like to cast a wider net on display and show your ads to a collection of websites related to certain topics, such as travel or news, you can do so through AdWords display. This is a good option for those who are not sure what specific websites to target on display or may not have the time to research and add individual placements to their campaigns. You may also want to try this approach if you are not getting enough traffic from your display campaigns, and if your CPA goals are more flexible.

Getting ready

Think about topics that would be relevant to your business. Do not limit yourself to just the most specific topics, but try other, more loosely related topics as well as ones that your target customers are likely to browse. For example, if you sell diet products, you may want to target:

- **Weight Loss**
- **Fashion & Style**
- **Food & Drink**

While you can add topics to an existing display campaign, I recommend creating a separate campaign for topic targeting. This allows you to bid and use your budget more effectively.

How to do it...

To add topics to your display campaign, perform the following steps:

1. Click on the **Campaigns** tab.
2. Click on **+ New campaign** to create a new campaign.
3. Choose **Display Network only**.

4. After choosing the relevant campaign setting, including target locations, languages, bidding options, and your budget, click on **Save and continue**.
5. Name your new ad group and choose the **Default Bid** value. This bid will apply to all topics you choose within this ad group, unless you set topic–specific bids, which override the default bid.
6. Under **Choose how to target your ads**, select **Use a different targeting method** and select **Topics**.
7. On the next screen, you'll be able to search for topics with your key phrases, or you can browse available topics. There are also numerous sub-topics that you can pick and choose from:

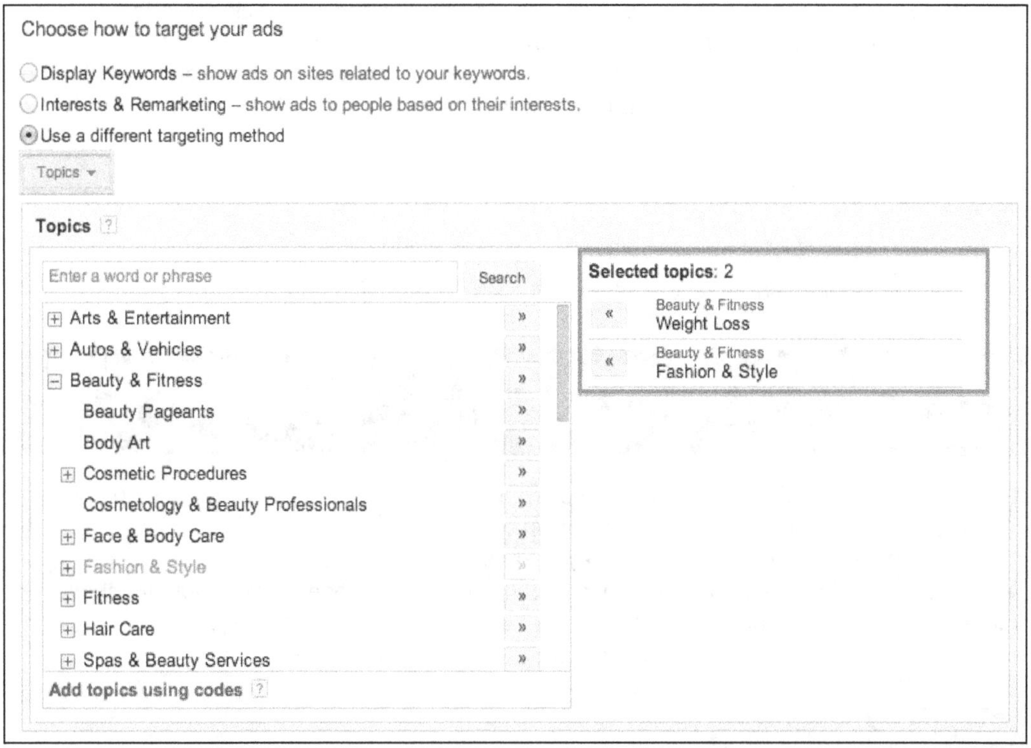

8. Select the topics you want to add and click on **Save and continue**.
9. Add ads to your ad group.

How it works...

Topic targeting on the Google's Display network lets you show ads on websites related to specific topics, such as finance or biotech. Google analyzes the keywords on a page to determine the topic of the page, categorizing it into topics and sub-topics. If you choose to target via topics, your ads will be shown on websites related to topics you choose to add to your campaign.

There's more...

You can further pre-qualify topic targeting by layering on keywords or specific placements in addition to topics. If you choose to use keywords in combination with topic targeting, your ads will only show on pages that meet both criteria you selected. For example, if you choose the **Finance** topic and add keywords about agriculture, your ads could show on the finance section of a local news website featuring an article about agricultural stock prices.

See also

- The *Creating an automatic placements campaign* recipe
- The *Creating a managed placements display campaign* recipe

Excluding irrelevant and poorly performing placements

If you are running display campaigns, you should periodically review performance on specific placements to ensure that your ads are shown on quality pages that meet your goals. This is especially important if you are running keyword-based, interest- or topic-targeted campaigns, where AdWords places your ads on pages you may not have chosen. If your ads are shown on low-quality placements, or placements that generate clicks without any conversions, you can exclude them in AdWords and block such websites from displaying your ads.

Getting ready

Before you start excluding specific placements, review their performance. Specifically, pay attention to the following:

- High-cost placements that generated zero conversions.
- High CPA placements.
- Low-quality or irrelevant placements.
- Placements with high bounce rates and low time on site. You will need to access your Google Analytics to find this data.

How to do it...

To review and exclude placements, perform the following steps:

1. Go to your **Campaigns** tab.
2. Click on a display campaign you'd like to analyze.
3. Click the **Display Network** tab and select the **Placements** sub-tab.
4. Below, you will see a list of managed and automatic placements along with relevant data, such as clicks, costs, and conversions.
5. Sort the results by clicks or cost, to first review the placements that generate the most traffic. If a placement generated a large number of clicks without any conversions, consider excluding it.

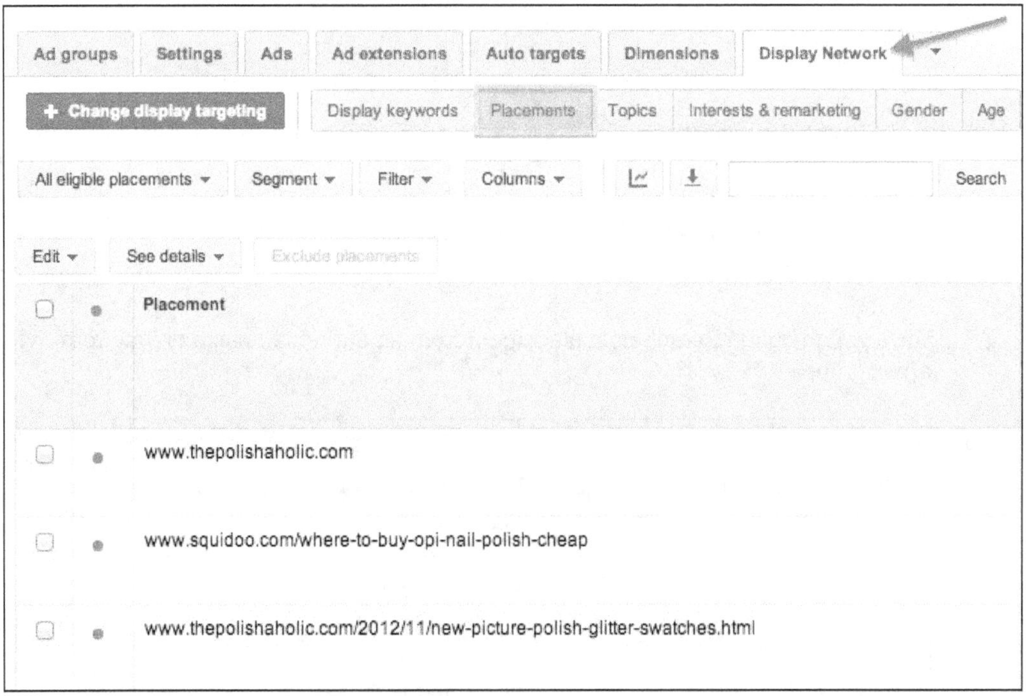

6. To exclude a placement, mark a checkbox on the left of a placement and choose **Exclude placements**:

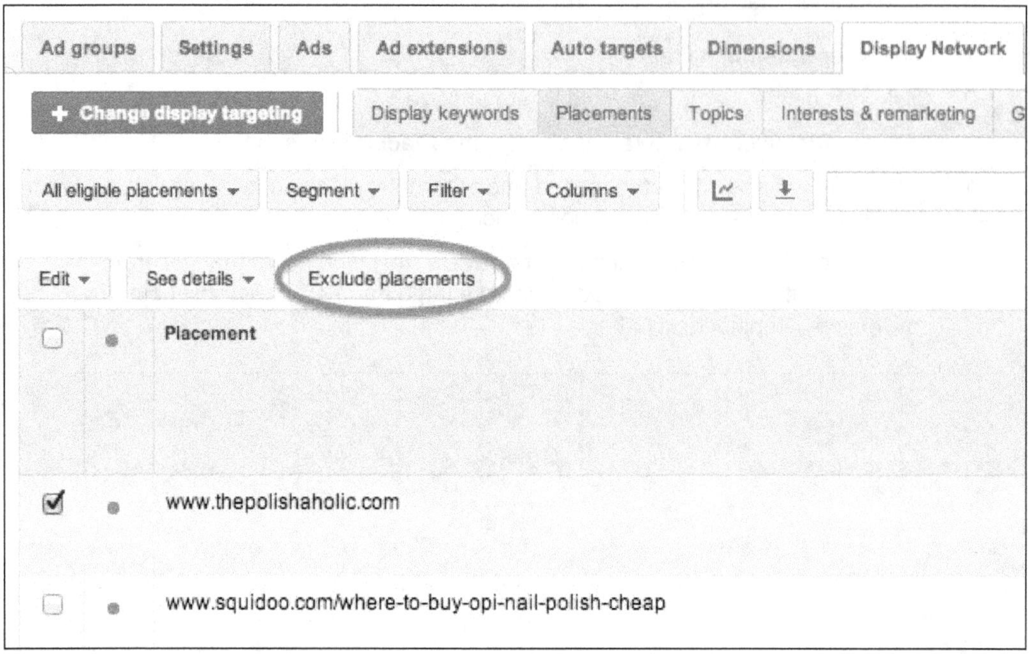

7. You'll get an option to exclude a placement from an entire campaign or just from an ad group:

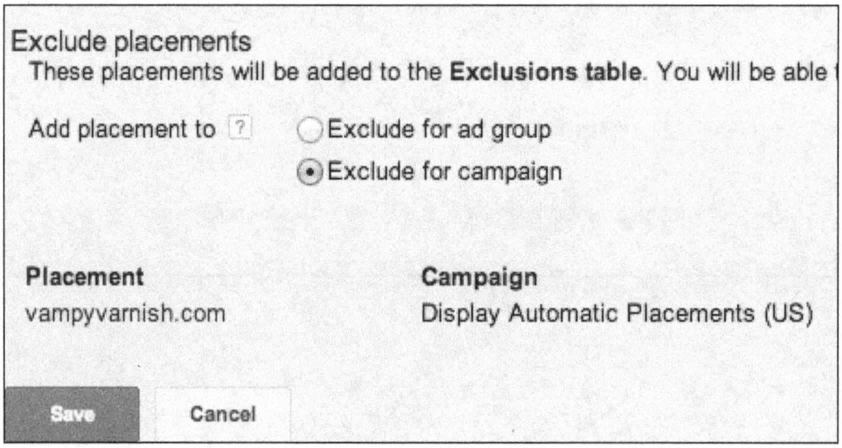

8. Click on **Save**.

How it works...

By excluding a placement, you can ensure that your ads are not shown on specific websites. You can exclude placements from an ad group or from a campaign, which will affect all ad groups within a campaign.

> The display data for individual placements from the last 48 hours may not be available. Select a wider date range (such as last 7 days or last 30 days) in your analysis.

There's more...

To see specific pages on various websites that your ads appeared on, click on **See details**. Choose **Selected** to see pages related to a specific domain you selected or choose **All** to see all pages:

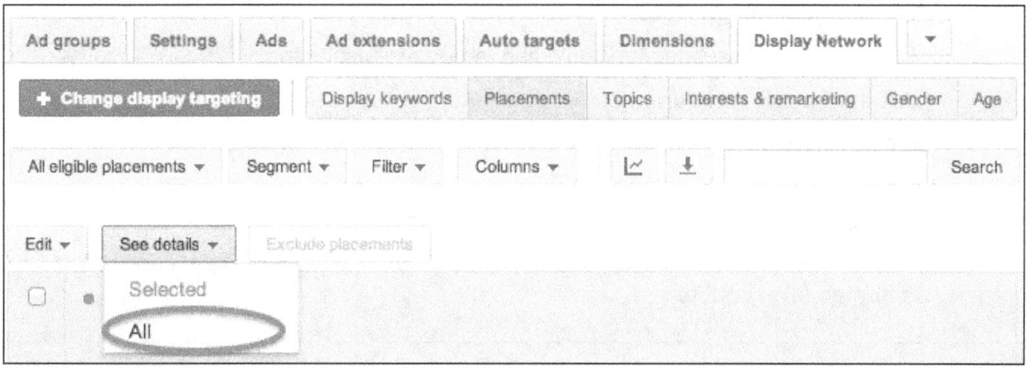

See also

- The *Creating an automatic placements campaign* recipe
- The *Targeting display sites based on topics* recipe

Avoid displaying your ads on certain pages

You can exclude an entire set of topics from showing your ads on Google's Display network. This strategy can help you get more out of display by blocking all irrelevant websites related to certain subjects at once.

Getting ready

Review the campaign's performance and individual display placements where your ads have appeared. If you notice that certain types of websites, such as gaming websites, show your ads but are not relevant to your audience, consider excluding gaming topics.

How to do it...

To exclude topics, perform the following steps:

1. Go to your **Campaigns** tab.
2. Click on the display campaign you'd like to add exclusions to.
3. Click the **Display Network** tab.
4. Scroll down to the bottom of the screen and click on **Exclusions**.
5. Select the **Topics** tab.
6. You can add exclusions at the ad group level or at the campaign level. If a certain group of websites is not applicable to any ad group in your campaign, choose the **Campaign level** option:

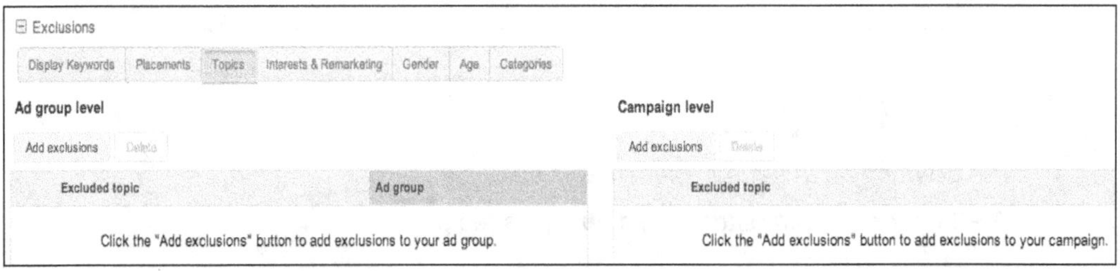

7. Click on **Add exclusions**.

8. Choose topics or sub-topics you'd like to exclude and click on **Save**:

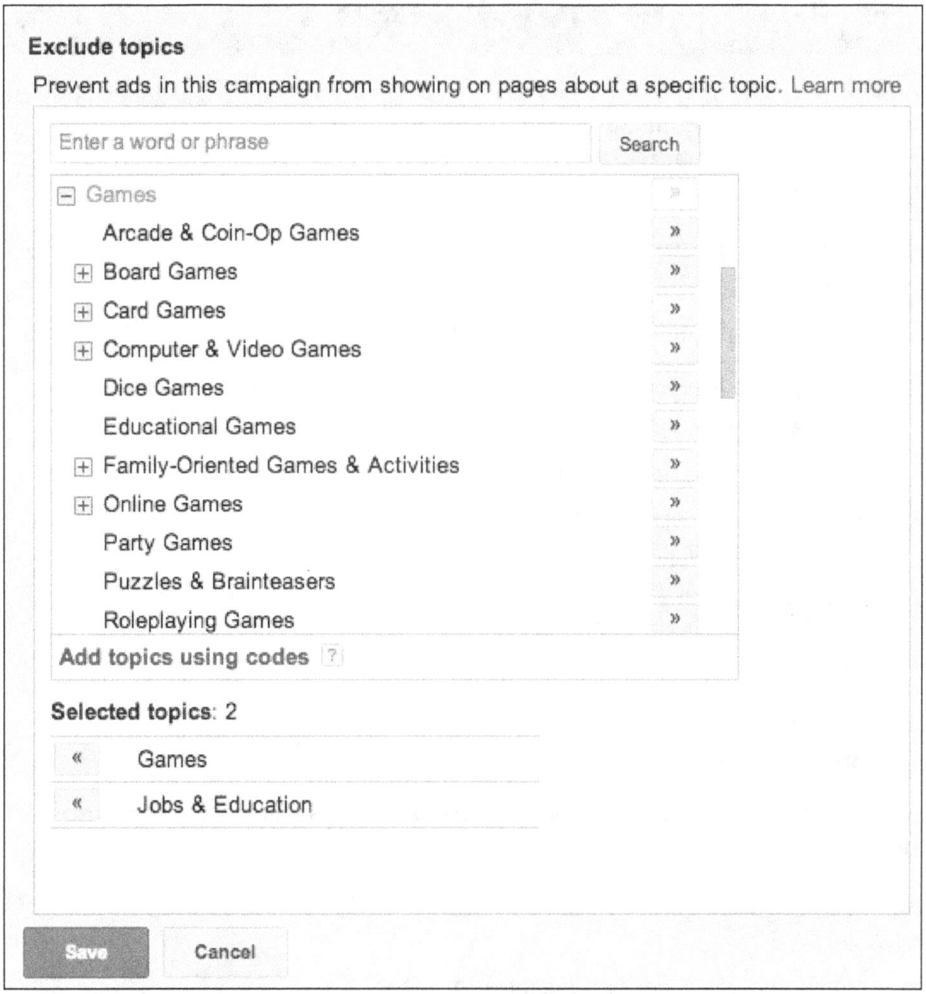

How it works...

By adding topic exclusions, you block all websites related to your excluded topics from showing your ads. For example, as a lawyer who is advertising legal services to clients, you may want to block all websites related to "jobs" to prevent irrelevant clicks from other lawyers looking for employment.

See also

- The *Excluding categories of sites and potentially sensitive topics* recipe

Excluding categories of sites and potentially sensitive topics

If you are showing ads on the Display network, you can exclude entire categories of websites and pages, which discuss potentially sensitive topics from showing your ads. Your display traffic will be more efficiently targeted and you'll prevent your ads from appearing on questionable pages.

Getting ready

The category exclusions that are most pressing to exclude are:

- **Crime, police & emergency**
- **Death & tragedy**
- **Military & International Conflict**
- **Juvenile, gross & bizarre content**
- **Profanity & rough language**
- **Sexually suggestive content**

You may also want to consider excluding the following:

- **Error pages**
- **Parked domains**

Review ad performance on **Error pages** and **Parked domains** before you decide to exclude them.

How to do it...

To add negative categories, perform the following steps:

1. Click on the **Campaigns** tab.
2. Go into a campaign targeting display.
3. Navigate to the **Display Network** tab.
4. Scroll down to the bottom of the page and open up **Exclusions**.
5. Select the far right box that says **Categories**. Under **Campaign level**, click on the box that says **Add Exclusions**:

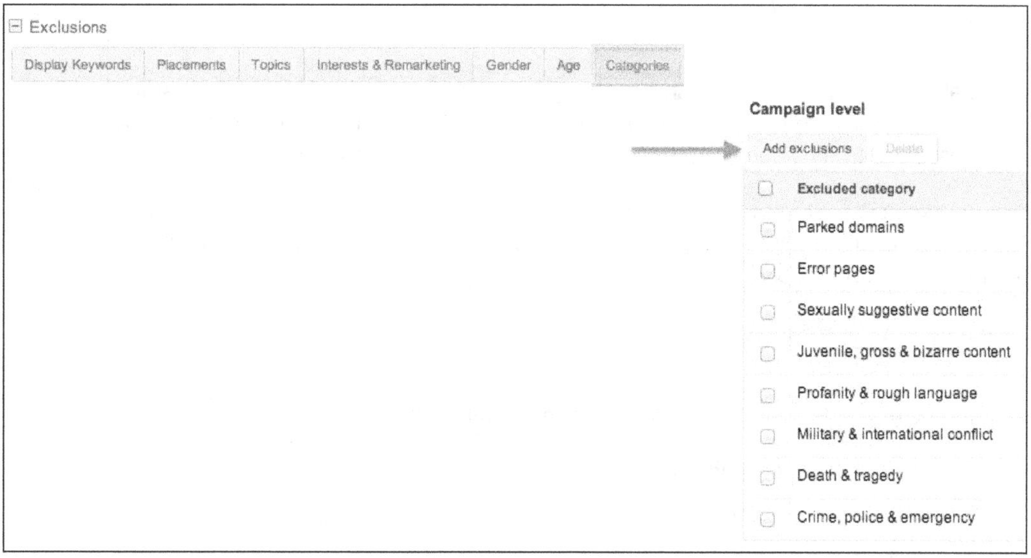

6. Check the categories you would like to exclude and click on **Save**.
7. Repeat for each display campaign.

How it works...

Excluding categories prevents your ads from showing on certain potentially sensitive categories of web pages, such as pages about crime, death, and sexual content. You can also block your ads from showing on certain types of websites, such as parked domains, error pages, games, social networks, and more.

> AdWords cannot guarantee that your ads will never show on pages related to the topics or categories you excluded. Review placement data regularly and exclude individual pages you do not want your ads to show on.

See also

- The *Avoid displaying your ads on certain pages* recipe

Adding image ads to display campaigns

One of the great benefits of Google's Display network is that you can run engaging and visually powerful banners on websites that are part of Display network. Image ads can help you grab the user's attention better than standard text ads, and they can help you boost your brand's presence on many different websites across the Internet.

Getting ready

If you already have image or flash ads that you'd like to add to AdWords, make sure they follow the technical requirements outlined in the *How it works...* section of this recipe. Save them to your computer from which you'll be able to upload them into your AdWords campaigns.

The images must be relevant and clear, and text must be legible. Blurry or poor quality images are against policy, as are any ads that try to trick a user into clicking them, such as system warnings or error messages.

How to do it...

To add image ads to your campaign, perform the following steps:

1. Click on the **Campaigns** tab.
2. Go into a campaign targeting display.
3. Click on the ad group to which you'd like to add image ads to.
4. Navigate to the **Ads** tab.
5. Click on **+ New ad** and select **Image ad** from the drop-down menu.
6. Click on **Upload an ad** and locate the ad saved on your computer.
7. Write an **Ad name** value and enter your **Display URL** and **Destination URL** values:

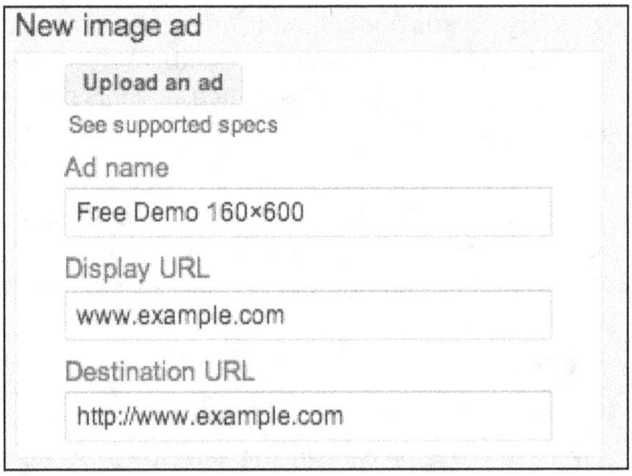

8. Click on **Save**.
9. To maximize reach, add image ads in various sizes.

How it works...

Image ads use a picture or interactive graphic to present your products and services visually. They generally follow the same policies as text ads and also have the technical requirements outlined at `http://support.google.com/adwordspolicy/bin/answer.py?hl=en-AU&answer=176108`. The following table outlines some of those requirements:

	File type	File size	Image size	Animation length and speed

Non-animated image ads	`.jpeg`
	`.jpg`
	`.png`
	`.gif`
		150 KB or smaller	Mobile leaderboard: 320 x 50
			Banner: 468 x 60
			Leaderboard: 728 x 90
			Square: 250 x 250
			Small square: 200 x 200
			Large rectangle: 336 x 280
			Inline rectangle: 300 x 250
			Skyscraper: 120 x 600
			Wide skyscraper: 160 x 600
			Half-page: 300 x 600	

Animated image ads	`.gif`	150 KB or smaller	Banner: 468 x 60 Leaderboard: 728 x 90 Square: 250 x 250 Small square: 200 x 200 Large rectangle: 336 x 280 Inline rectangle: 300 x 250 Skyscraper: 120 x 600 Wide skyscraper: 160 x 600 Half-page: 300 x 600	Animation length must be 30 seconds or shorter. Animations can be looped, but the animations must stop after 30 seconds. Animated GIF ads must be 5 fps or slower. Animated GIFs cannot be used in mobile or tablet ads.
Flash ads	`.swf`	150 KB or smaller, except for half-page ads, which can be as large as 200 KB	Banner: 468 x 60 Leaderboard: 728 x 90 Square: 250 x 250 Small square: 200 x 200 Large rectangle: 336 x 280 Inline rectangle: 300 x 250 Skyscraper: 120 x 600 Wide skyscraper: 160 x 600 Half-page: 300 x 600	Animation length must be 30 seconds or shorter. Animations can be looped, but the animations must stop after 30 seconds. Flash ads must be 20 fps or slower.

There's more...

All image ads must be approved as family safe in order to show on GDN. Any ads containing sexual content or nudity will be deemed as non-family or adult, and will not be eligible to be shown. You do not need to take any action besides submitting your ad to get your ads approved. If an ad is disapproved, you'll be notified via e-mail.

See also

- The *Creating rich image ads with Display Ad Builder* recipe

Creating rich image ads with Display Ad Builder

Google's Display Ad Builder is a tool that helps you easily create image ads without any prior graphic design experience. The tool is available for free to all advertisers using Google AdWords.

Getting ready

Prepare product images or company logos you'd like to use. Make sure that you own or have the necessary permissions to use the images you plan to leverage.

Review your search ad text performance to find descriptions, special offers, and call-to-action phrases that perform best for you. You'll want to add these phrases to your image ads as you build them with the Display Ad Builder tool.

How to do it...

To create image ads using Google's Display Ad Builder, perform the following steps:

1. Navigate to the **Ads** tab.
2. Click on **+ New ad** and select **Display ad builder** from the drop-down menu. Here, you'll be able to choose a template from one of the many different themes and formats.

3. Choose one of the ad templates provided by AdWords. Search by **Industries**, **Seasons and events**, or select **General Purpose** for more generic templates. The **Advanced** section contains ad formats, which allow you to showcase multiple images with different URLs or expandable ads that show additional information at the click of a button:

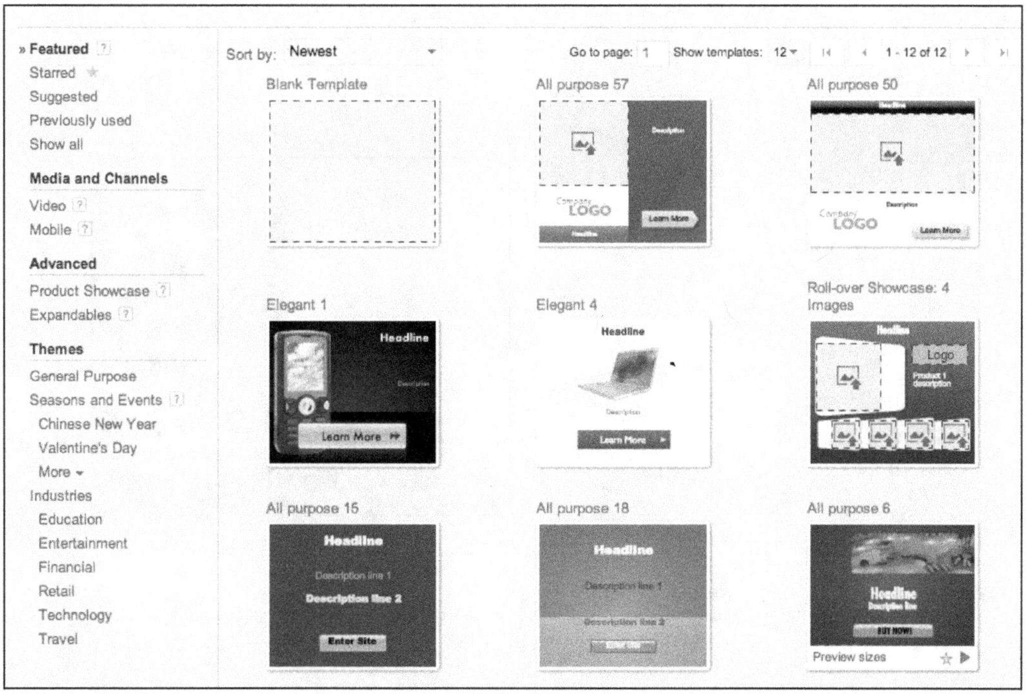

4. Once you have selected a template you'd like to use, follow the screen prompts to create your ad. The elements you'll need to fill in will vary, depending on the template you choose.

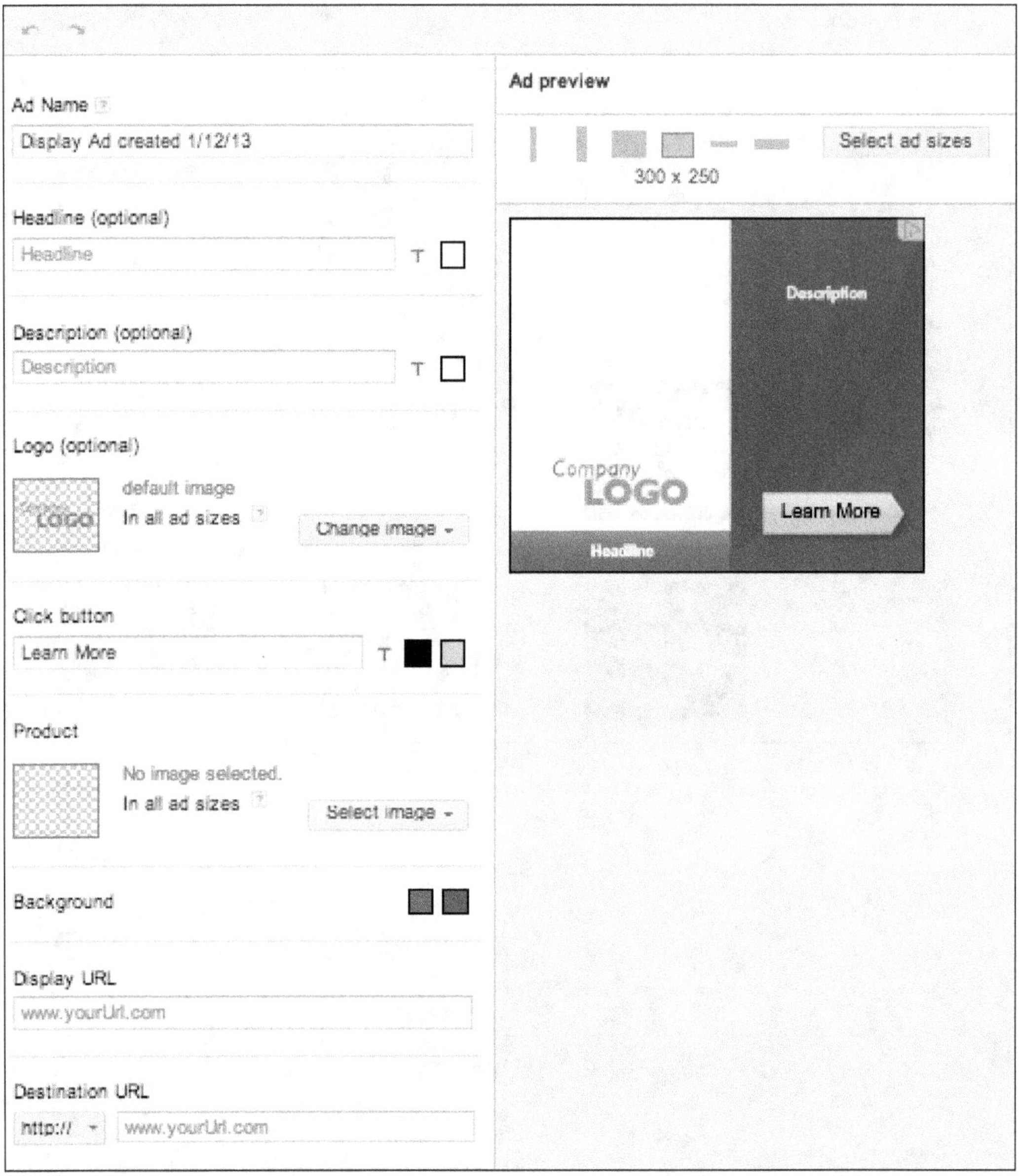

5. Generally, you'll need to first name your ad. Choose a name that's descriptive of the products or offers you are promoting.

6. Write a headline and description in the **Headline** and **Description** fields. Follow the same best practices as for text ads. Be informative and descriptive and include special offers and calls-to-action. You can customize text colors and fonts, if necessary.
7. Add a company logo.
8. Customize your **Click button** field with language that best fits your offer. You can also change the button font and color.
9. Add a product image or multiple images, depending on your template.
10. Customize background colors, if you'd like to adjust the color scheme provided in the template.
11. Write in your **Display URL** and **Destination URL** values.
12. Always use the **Ad preview** feature to see what your ads would look like in all available ad sizes. Your images or logos might be difficult to see or even illegible in some ad sizes, or the text might not fit properly together. Some of the templates allow you to adjust the various text and image elements by ad size. Make sure to go through each ad size in the **Ad preview** screen and make any necessary adjustments.
13. Click on **Preview and Save**. If you do not like how your ad appears in a specific ad size, you can unselect that ad in the **Ad preview** screen.
14. Once you click on **Save**, AdWords will populate your ad group with all of the display ad sizes you have chosen.

You can edit the ads you created with the Display Ad Builder tool at any time, if you need to update your images or text. Continue to experiment with additional templates to test alternate formats, colors, and messaging.

How it works...

Google's Display Ad Builder is a free tool that helps advertisers create professional looking display ads. Advertisers can choose from hundreds of available templates, different fonts, colors, and images, or upload their own logos, images, and video. Each template also allows for text to be customized and easily updated directly in your AdWords account.

There's more...

The **Suggested ads** feature in the Display Ad Builder will scan your website and automatically generate relevant ads by pulling in text and images into multiple ad variations you can choose from. You can further refine and customize the ads by clicking on one of the suggested options.

See also

- The *Adding image ads to display campaigns* recipe

Analyzing relative CTR to benchmark display performance

CTR on display is typically much lower than CTRs you're used to seeing from your search campaigns. Instead of comparing your display CTR to your search CTR, a more useful metric would be to understand how your display ads fare against other display campaigns. To help you analyze and benchmark how your display CTR compares to other ads, AdWords provides the Relative CTR metric in your account.

How to do it...

To view relative CTR, perform the following steps:

1. Click on the **Campaigns** tab. You can also view **Relative CTR** at the ad group level.
2. Click on **Columns** and choose **Customize columns**.
3. Under **Competitive metrics**, scroll until you see **Relative CTR**:

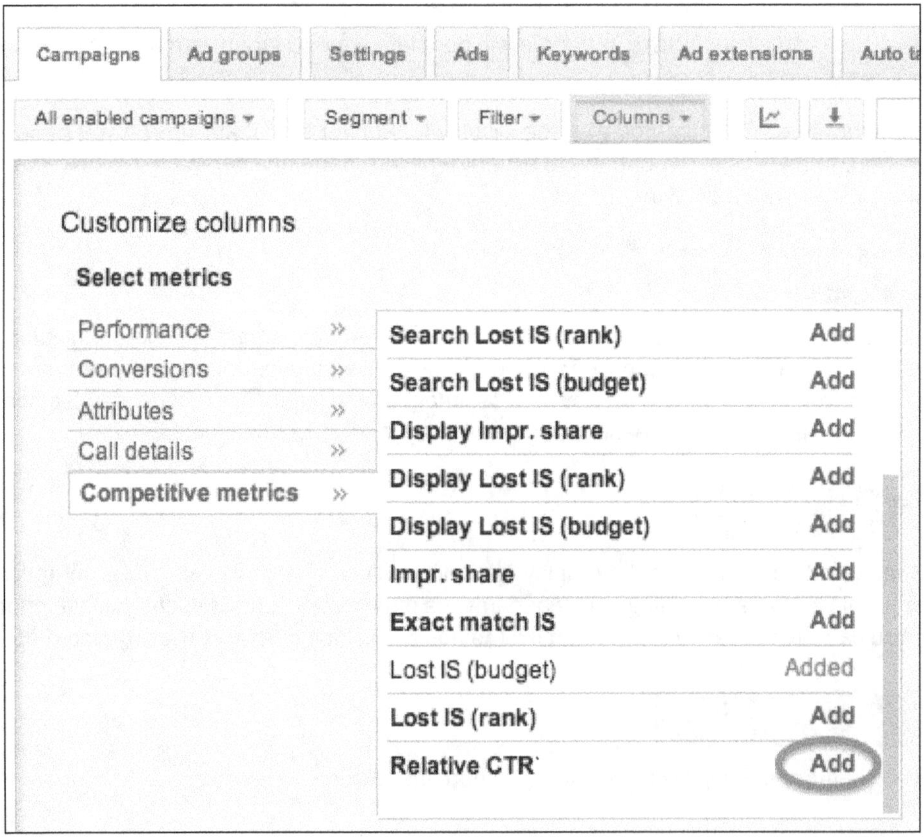

4. Click on **Add** to add the metric to your dashboard and click on **Apply** to save your settings.
5. You should now see **Relative CTR** as a metric in your campaign dashboard. The average Relative CTR is 1x, and you should aim above that (such as 1.5x). If your Relative CTR is under 1x (such as 0.5x), consider optimizing your display campaign.

How it works...

Relative CTR is a measure of how your ads perform on Google's Display network when compared to other ads appearing on the same pages. It's calculated by dividing your CTR by the average CTR of all advertisers appearing on your placements.

The average Relative CTR is 1x, which means that your CTR equals the average CTR of all advertisers on the same pages. If your Relative CTR is higher than 1x (such as 2x), your ads are getting better clickthrough-rates than other ads on the same placements.

Relative CTR is available at the campaign and ad group levels, however, it doesn't work with campaigns that use CPM bidding as a bidding strategy.

There's more...

Search and Display Quality Scores are completely separate. On Google's Display network, AdWords also considers your performance on a site, in addition to your ad's relevance and your landing page. Like on Google Search, a more relevant and high CTR ad on the Google Display network will help you be more competitive in an ad auction. If your CTR is lower than average, you may want to take the following actions:

- Exclude low performing and irrelevant placements. These include any placements that have lower CTRs than other placements, but make sure to not exclude placements that are generating profitable conversions.
- Add new ads, pausing the lower performing ad copy.
- Add image and rich media ads, in addition to text ads.
- Create more themed ad groups to allow AdWords to better target your ads to relevant placements.
- Pause low performing keywords, if you are running a display campaign that uses keywords to target.

See also

- The *Customizing columns to personalize data views* recipe
- The *Excluding irrelevant and poorly performing placements* recipe

9

Remarketing to Past Visitors

In this chapter, we will cover:

- Generating the remarketing code
- Creating remarketing audiences in AdWords
- Creating custom remarketing combinations via rules
- Setting up a remarketing campaign
- Setting remarketing bids
- Setting frequency caps to limit how often ads show
- Increasing traffic to your remarketing campaign
- Remarketing to YouTube viewers

Introduction

Have you noticed ads that seem to just know what you want to buy, following you around the Web? I recently searched for "tennis shoes," visiting various websites but did not buy from any of them. Over the next few days, wherever I went on the Internet, be it my favorite news website or a blog I regularly read, I kept seeing ads for tennis shoes that I recently researched. This is called **remarketing** and is also referred to as **retargeting** in the world of online marketing.

Remarketing allows you to reconnect with users who previously visited your website as they go on to browse the Display network, setting you up for a second chance to convert. Remarketing can be an extremely powerful method of reminding your potential customers of your brand or reconnecting with them as they click on your ads but navigate away from your website without performing the desired action. This can help you look like a big brand, even if you are on a small budget.

If you are advertising with Google, you can set up remarketing through your Google AdWords campaigns. To get started, you'll need to place some code on your website, define your audiences or who you'd like to target, and create a separate campaign for remarketing.

Generating the remarketing code

The first step of setting up remarketing is adding the remarketing code to your website. You'll need to access this code in your AdWords account, where it might be pre-populated already for you. If not, you can easily set it up.

You can also create remarketing lists through Google Analytics by editing your Analytics tracking code. For additional details about setting up remarketing lists through Google Analytics, see the article at `https://support.google.com/analytics/answer/2611270?hl=en&ref_topic=2611283`.

Getting ready

You'll need to have an AdWords account to use Google's remarketing. You'll also need to add the code to your website, so make sure you have access to the website's code or get in touch with your webmaster, if someone else edits your website for you.

How to do it...

To generate the remarketing code in your AdWords account, follow these steps:

1. Sign in to your AdWords account.
2. Click on the **Shared library** link at the bottom-left corner of your campaign management page.
3. Click to **View** the shared settings for **Audiences**.

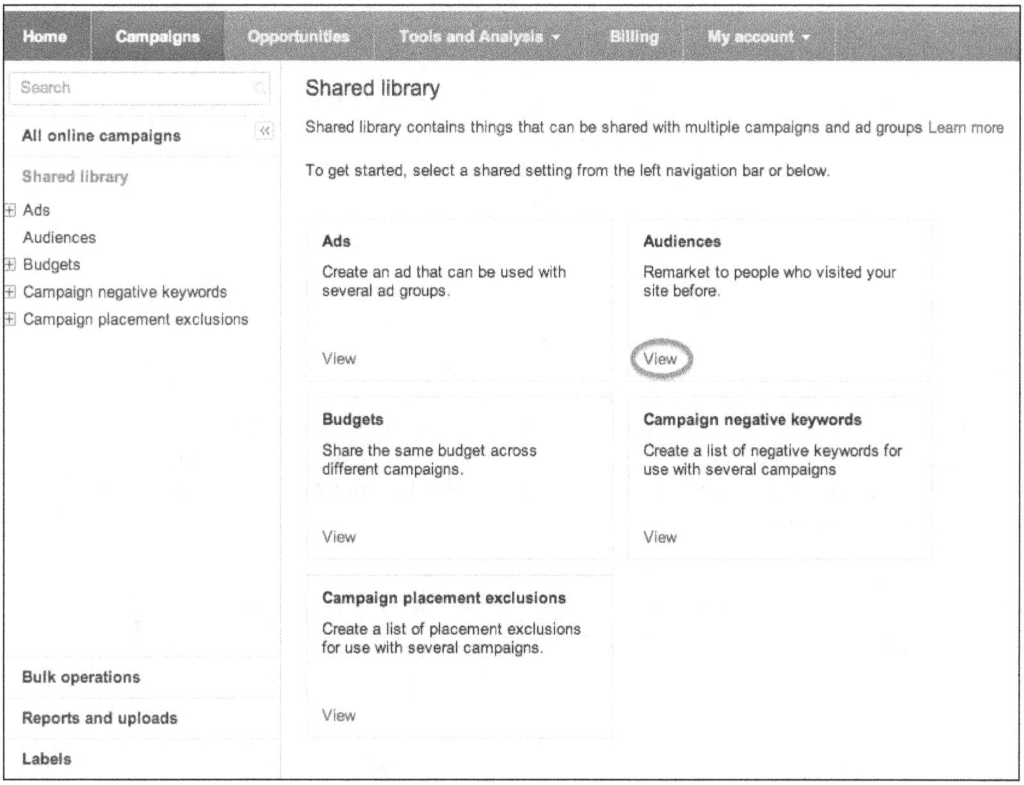

4. Click on the **Set up remarketing** prompt to set up remarketing.

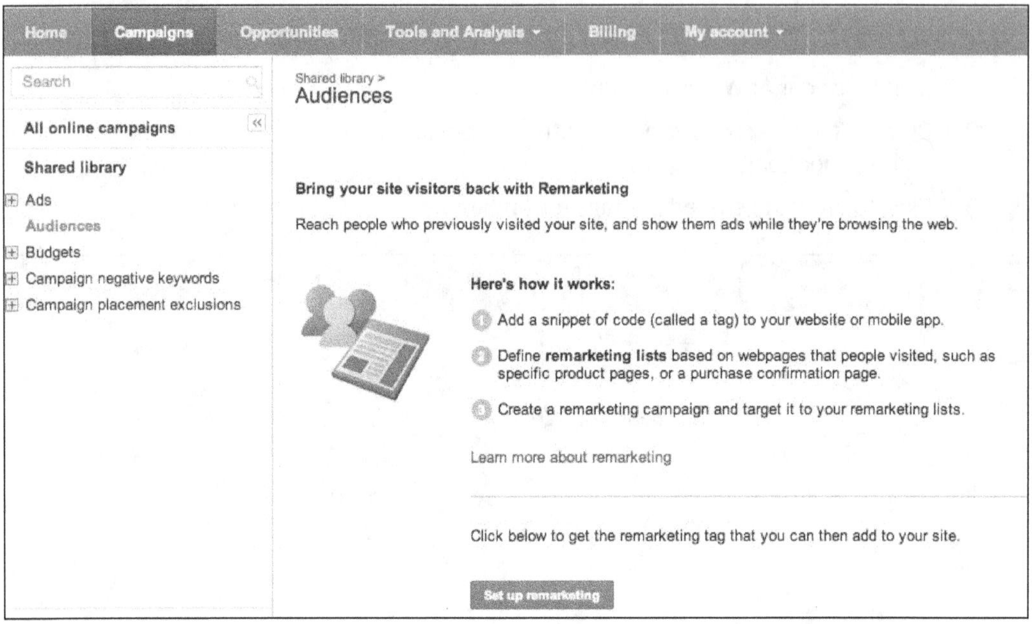

5. Next, AdWords will show you the code that you'll need to add to every page of your website, right before the `</body>` tag. You can copy and save this code for later, or send it to your webmaster. This is your **Main list** that AdWords automatically generates for you.

> Do not use the code from the example below. Your remarketing code is unique to your AdWords account.

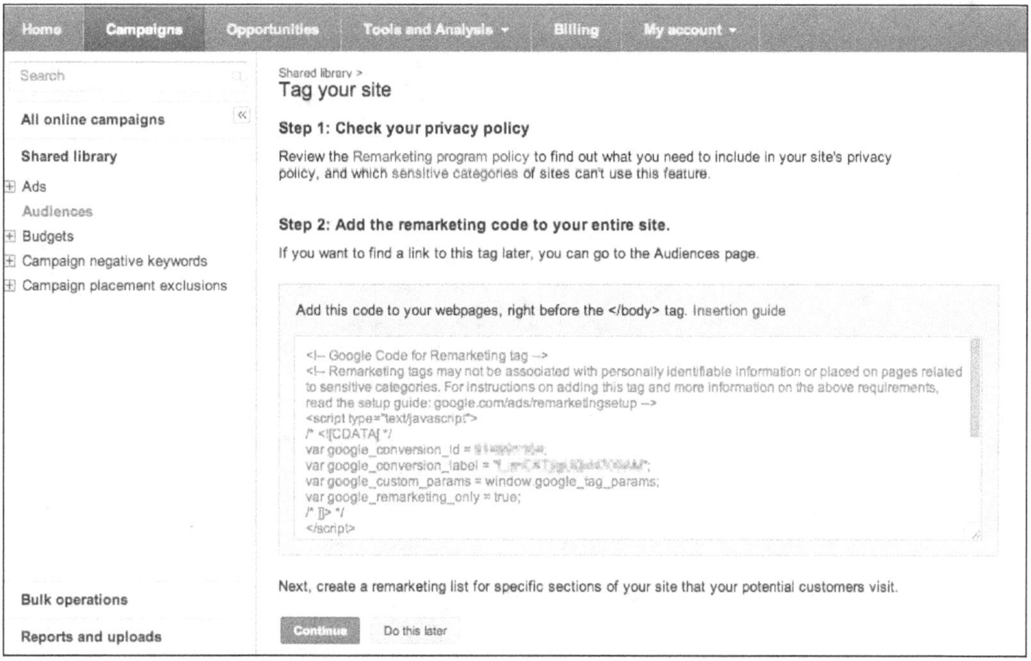

6. Click on **Continue** to create specific audiences you'd like to reach with your ads.

How it works...

AdWords automatically pre-populates a Main remarketing list that you can access in your shared library. Once you add this single tag to your entire website, you'll be able to create as many lists as you want based on sections of your site that people visit.

There's more...

If you don't see a Main list, you can create one by following these steps:

1. Click on the **Shared library** link at the bottom left of your campaign management page.
2. Click to **View** the shared settings for **Audiences**.
3. Choose **+ New audience** and select **Remarketing list**.
4. Choose the second option, **Define a list of site visitors by placing a new tag on your site**.

5. Click the **+New tag** button.

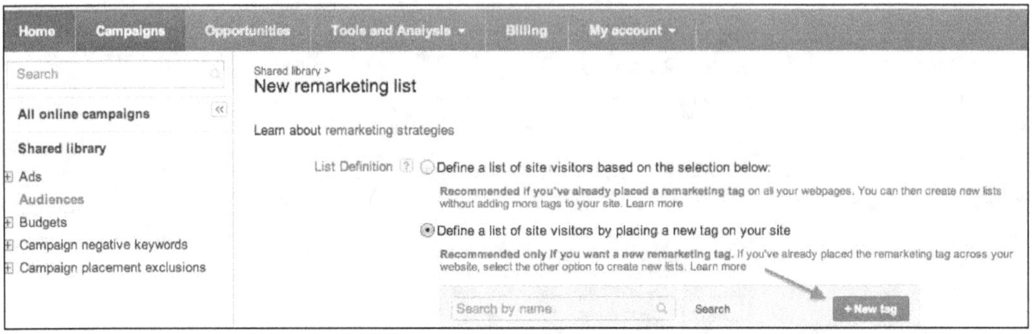

6. Name your new list `Main list` and choose your membership duration. Membership duration refers to the number of days a cookie stays on your remarketing list with the maximum being 540 days. You can leave the default 30 days and also enter an optional list description, such as `All visitors`.

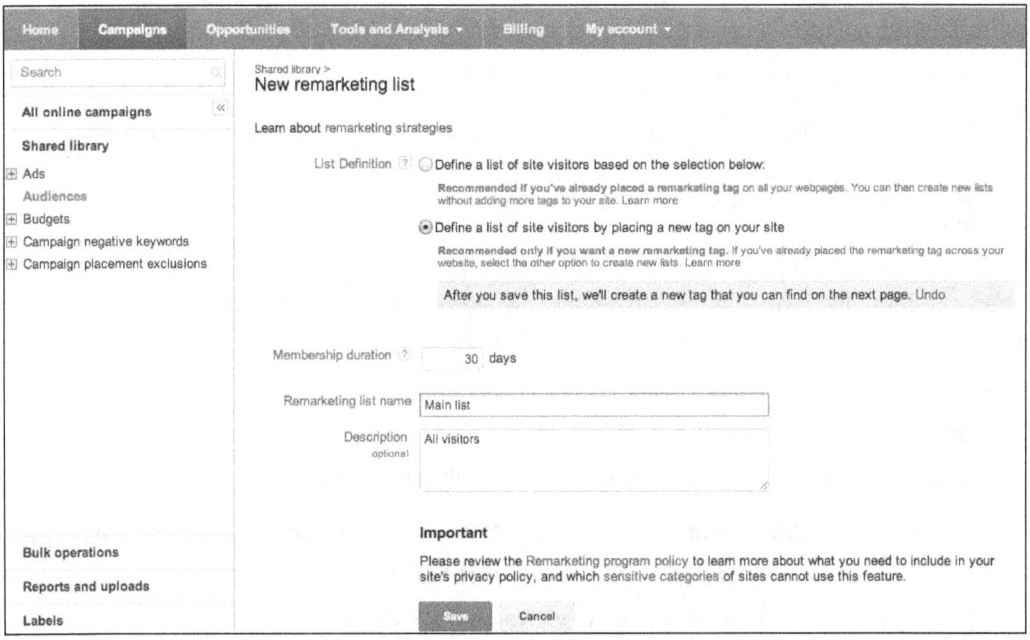

7. Click on **Save** and you'll be taken to the screen where you can see your audiences and access their tags. Click on the Main list **[Tag]** to copy and paste the remarketing code snippet at the bottom of each webpage, just before the closing `</body>` tag in your source code.

See also

- The *Creating an AdWords account* recipe in *Chapter 2, Setting up Your Account*
- The *Creating remarketing audiences in AdWords* recipe

Creating remarketing audiences in AdWords

With AdWords, you have the option to target broad as well as highly specific audiences via your remarketing campaigns. For example, you can target all visitors or only those who browsed certain product pages but did not convert. Segmenting who you remarket to allows you to tailor your ads to visitors you already know are interested in your website. You can further customize messaging with personalized ads based on what content someone browsed on your website.

Getting ready

If you have not done so already, go through the prompts to enable remarketing in your account and generate the **Main list** remarketing code. Add this code to all pages of your website.

Next, define your audiences or what segments of visitors you'd like your ads to reach. Here are some recommended audiences:

- **All visitors**: Anyone who came to your website. This is the most basic and simple way to set up remarketing but also the least targeted.
- **By products or services**: You could target users who visited specific pages on your site with custom ads and messages. You could take this further and only target visitors to specific pages who did not convert.
- **Converters**: You could target those who already purchased a product or became a lead and continue to nurture your relationship with past customers.
- **Non-converters**: All visitors minus those that purchased a product or became a lead. Targeting such audiences can remind your non-converting visitors of your brand and entice them to come back to your site and convert.
- **By membership duration**: You can segment visitors by the number of days a cookie stays on your remarketing list. For example, you could create a shorter 7-day audience list to show one message, and a longer 30-day list audience for a different message or offer.

How to do it...

In this section, I'll go through examples of how to create an audience of users who visited specific product pages and an audience of all visitors who converted.

To create a remarketing audience for users who visited specific product pages, follow these steps:

1. Go to your **Campaigns** tab.
2. Click on **Shared library** at the bottom-left corner of your screen.
3. Click on **View** to view your **Audiences**.
4. Choose **+ New audience** and select **Remarketing list**.
5. Select the first option, **Define a list of site visitors based on the selection below**.
6. Next, define what URLs should be included in this audience. You'll be able to choose if your URL contains or does not contain the specified parameters. If your URLs are descriptive and contain words such as "roses" or "tulips" you can use these words to include all URLs with these terms in them. If your URLs are not descriptive, you can still create audiences around common parameters within your URL structure. You can also be more specific by including a specific URL for your audience by choosing the **equals** option. Here are all of the available options to define your list:

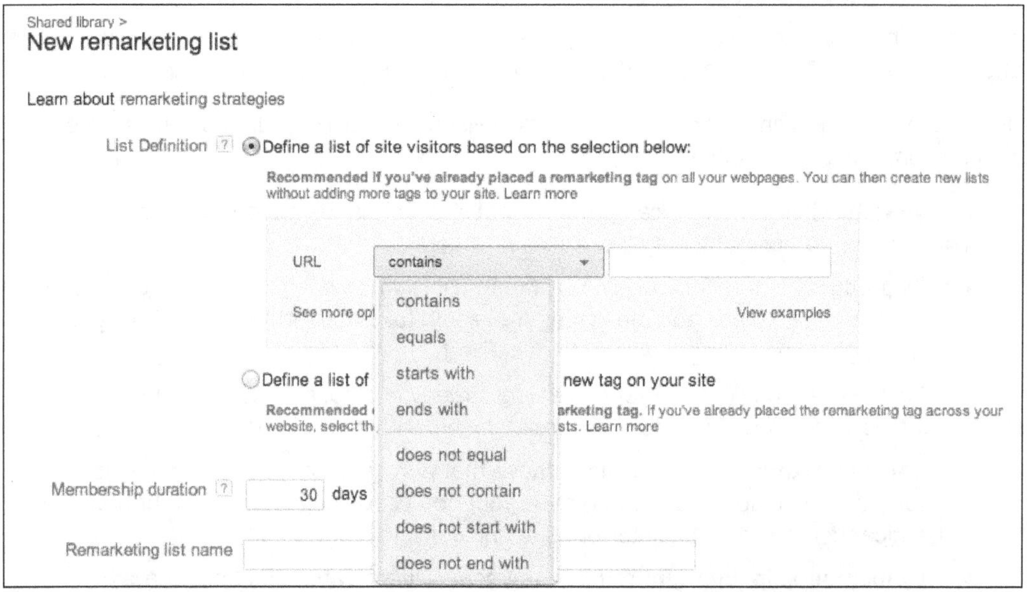

7. After defining your URL parameters, choose your membership duration. The default is 30 days, but you can choose up to 540 days. Your membership duration should follow your sales cycle. For example, if you have a short sales cycle of a few days, your ads should not follow your customers long after they have decided not to buy. However, if you have a typically longer sales cycle of a few months, such as expensive machinery, longer remarketing membership duration is more appropriate.

8. Name your list under **Remarketing list name** and write an optional description.
9. Under **Initial list size**, choose if you'd like to **Include past visitors who match your list definition** or **Start with an empty list.** If you choose to include past visitors, the list will include visitors from up to the past 30 days that still fit your list definition.

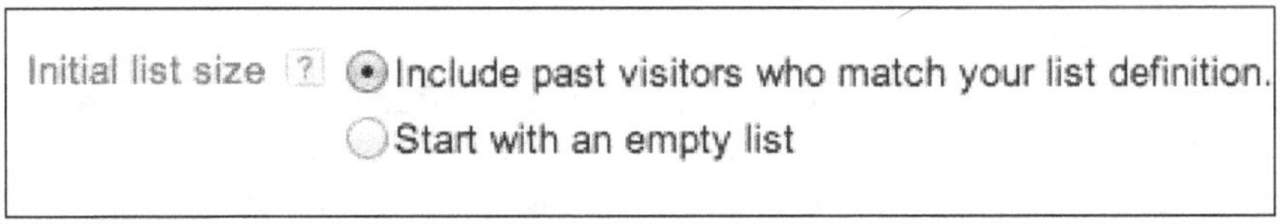

Click on **Save**.

If you track conversions in AdWords, you can easily create a remarketing audience for users who converted:

1. In your shared library's **Audiences** section choose **+ New audience** and select **Remarketing list**.
2. Select the second option, **Define a list of site visitors by placing a new tag on your site**.
3. In the box below, you'll see all of your current tags, including your conversion action. Click on **Add** next to the tag that defines converted users. You might want to double-check the name of your active conversions by going to **Tools and Analysis** and choosing **Conversions**.

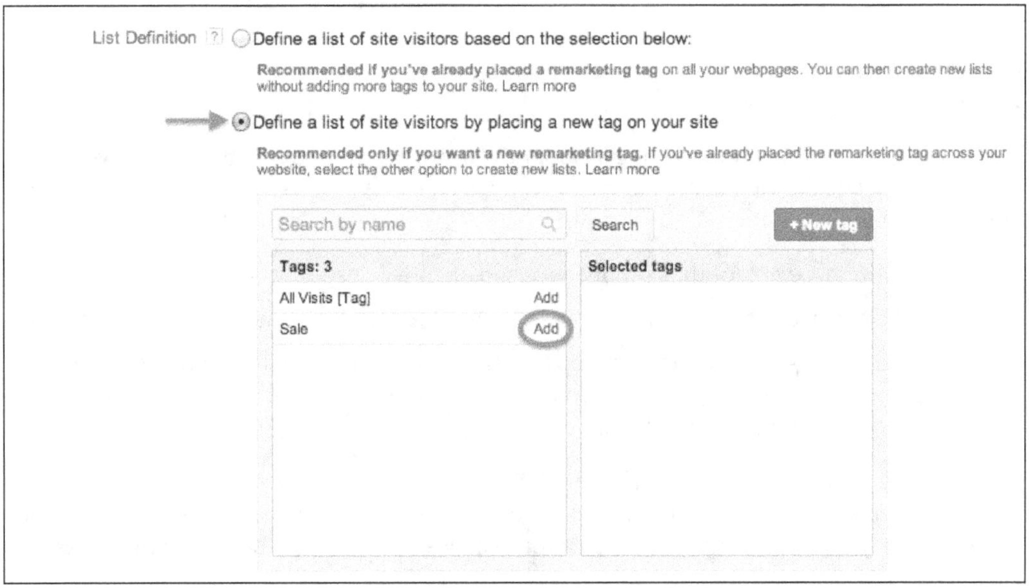

4. Choose your membership duration, name the list (such as "Converters" or "Sale"), and write an optional description.
5. Click on **Save**.

How it works...

Defining remarketing audiences allows you to show customized ads to visitors who browsed specific pages on your website. You can choose specific parameters, such as URLs visited as well as how long a cookie should stay on your remarketing list. Once you define remarketing lists, you can create separate ad groups and show different ads to each audience.

See also

- The *Generating the remarketing code* recipe
- The *Setting up a remarketing campaign* recipe

Creating custom remarketing combinations via rules

Custom combinations enable advertisers to further define and segment visitors based on multiple criteria. For example, they allow you to remove customers that already converted from your remarketing list and avoid spamming existing customers who already purchased your product.

Getting ready

You'll need to first enable remarketing in your AdWords account and add the code to your website. Then, decide what custom audiences you'd like to target. I suggest you start with one of the following:

- All visitors except for those that converted already.
- Visitors to specific pages or categories of pages except for those that converted already.
- Visitors who abandoned the shopping cart. This is one of the most effective ways to target via remarketing, as you can reach someone that was already considering a purchase but did not yet complete it.

If you'd like to create custom combinations for the above audiences who did not convert, you'll first need to create remarketing lists for all visitors, visitors to specific pages, and shopping cart visitors. Then, you'll exclude anyone that's already converted from your custom combination.

How to do it...

To create a custom combination, follow these steps:

1. Go to your **Campaigns** tab.
2. Click on **Shared library** at the bottom-left corner of your screen.
3. Click on **View** to view your **Audiences**.
4. Choose **+ New audience** and select **Custom combination**.
5. Name your new combination and write an optional description. For example, `Shopping cart abandoners`.
6. Under **Users included or interested in...** choose **each of these audiences (AND)** from the drop-down menu.

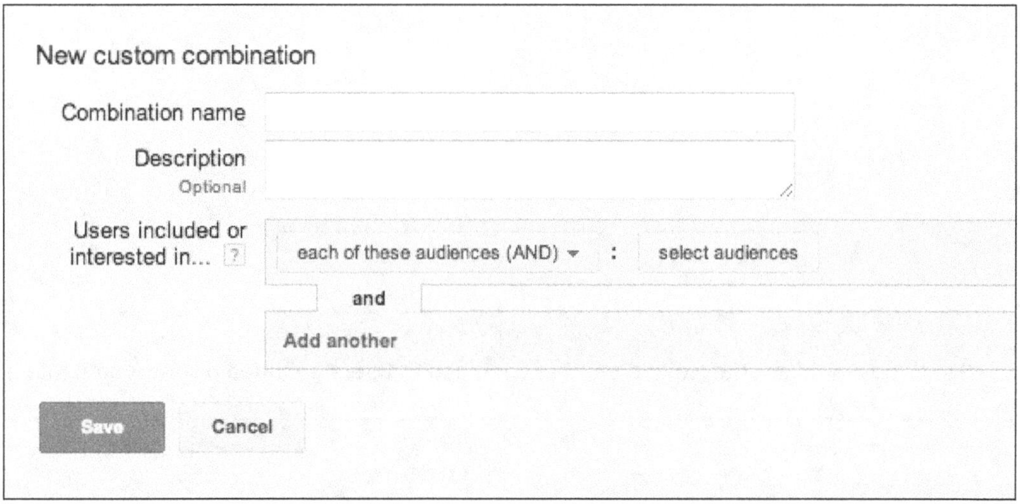

7. Click on **select audiences** and from the drop-down menu choose **Remarketing lists**.

8. Click on the arrow to select the **Shopping cart** list or another list you'd like to create a combination around. Click on **OK**.

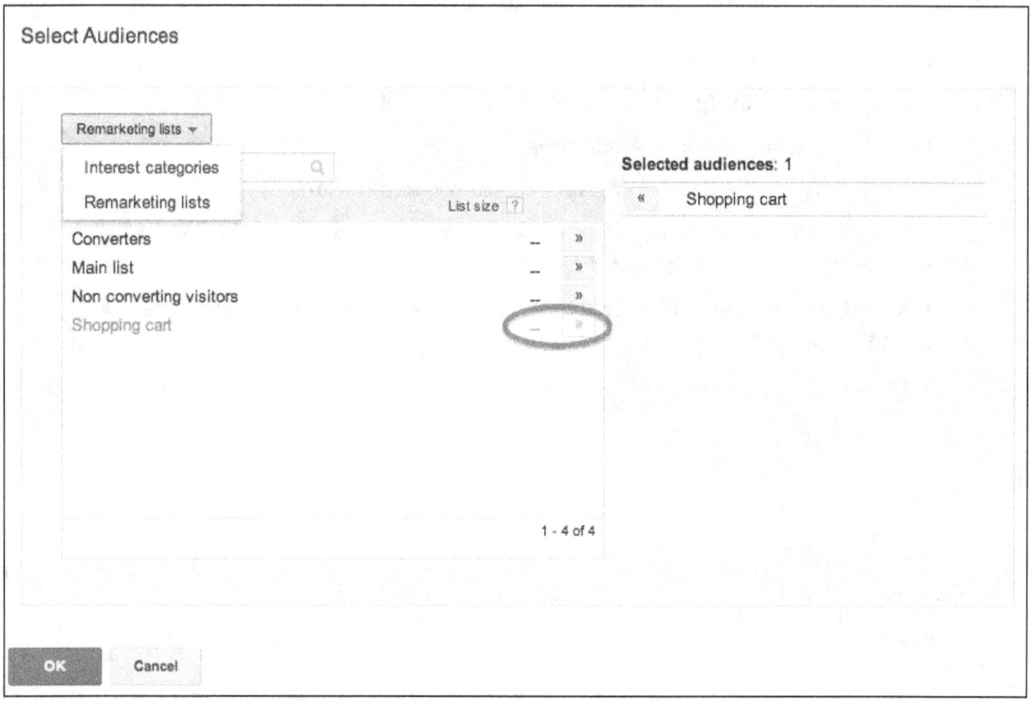

9. Choose **Add another** to add another condition to **Users included or interested in...**.

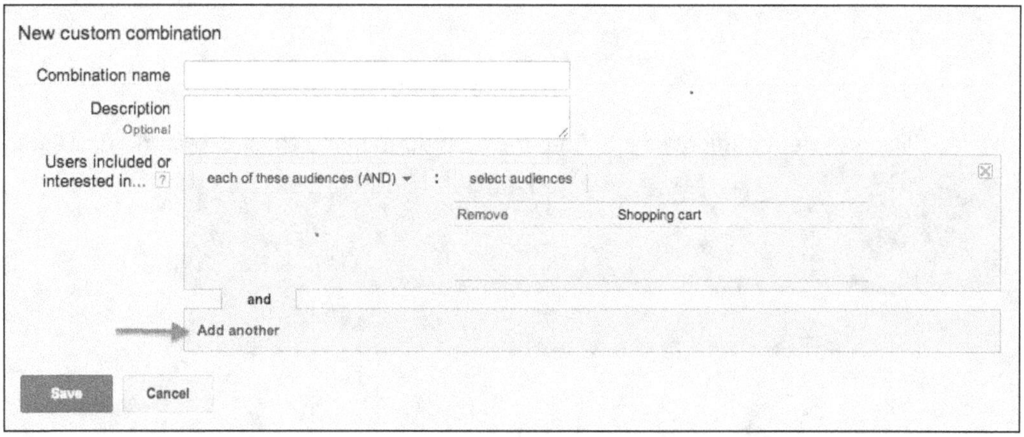

10. Select **none of these audiences**, proceed to **select audiences**, and switch to **Remarketing lists**. Then, select **Converters** or however you named your list of users who completed a purchase. Click on **OK**.
11. Now you have your custom combination with anyone that's visited your shopping cart but did not convert.

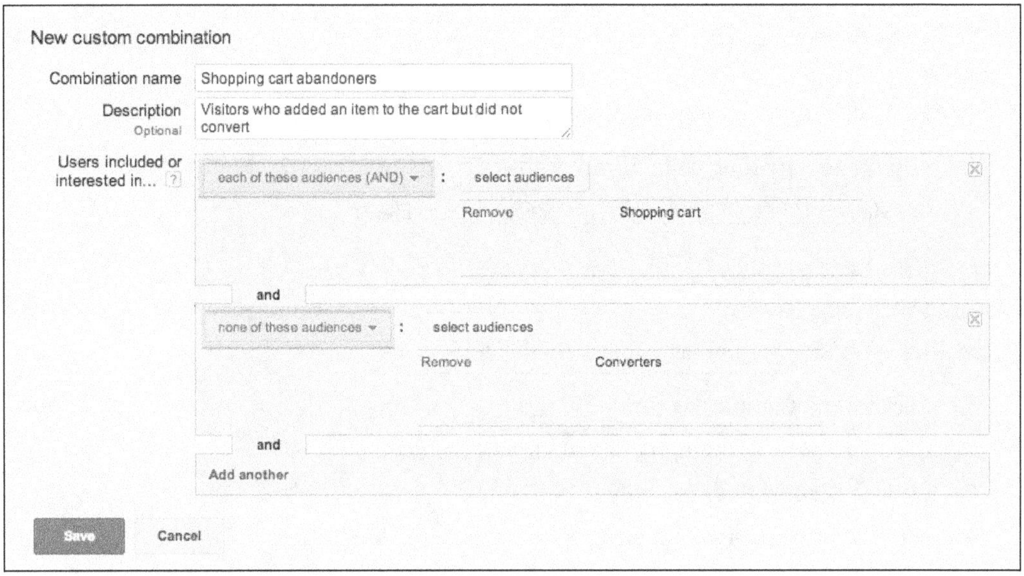

12. Click on **Save**.

How it works...

Custom combinations allow you to create rules to include, exclude, or combine different audiences. You can use the following combinations:

- Any of the audiences (OR)
- Each of these audiences (AND)
- None of these audiences

Using the above parameters, you can choose to create a custom combination to show ads to users who visited the shopping cart but did not convert, for example.

See also

- The *Generating the remarketing code* recipe
- The *Creating remarketing audiences in AdWords* recipe

Setting up a remarketing campaign

In order to show remarketing ads, you'll need to set up a separate campaign in AdWords. This campaign should target the Google Display network (rather than Google Search) and will not require keywords, but should be built around audiences you'll add to individual ad groups.

Getting ready

Before setting up a remarketing campaign, you'll need to:

- Add the remarketing code to your website
- Create remarketing audiences for visitors you'd like to target

How to do it...

To create a remarketing campaign, follow these steps:

1. Click on the **Campaigns** tab.
2. Click on **+ New campaign** to create a new campaign.
3. Choose **Display Network only**.
4. Name your campaign and pick your locations and languages.
5. Under **Bidding and budget** in your campaign settings page, **choose I'll manually set my bids for clicks** and enter your budget.
6. Click on **Save and continue**.
7. Next, create your first ad group. Your remarketing campaign should have separate ad groups for your different remarketing audiences. For example, your campaign could have the following remarketing ad groups:
    - **Ad group #1**: All visitors
    - **Ad group #2**: All visitors except for those who converted
    - **Ad group #3**: All shopping cart abandoners
    - **Ad group #4**: Specific product or category shopping cart abandoners (for example, Levi's 501 jeans shopping cart abandoners)
8. Name each ad group after the remarketing audience you'll target. This will allow you to prioritize bids and evaluate performance based on each remarketing segment.
9. Set a **Default bid**, keeping in mind that the higher your bid, the greater the likelihood that your ads will show.
10. Under **Choose how to target ads**, select **Interests & Remarketing**.

11. From the **Remarketing lists** section, choose the audience you wish to target. Do not add multiple lists into one ad group.

12. Click **Save and continue.**
13. Write a text ad on the next step. You can also add image or video ads, or build an ad using Google's Display ad builder.

> Use a combination of text and image ads for greatest reach. Your message should be customized to the audience you are trying to reach. For example, if you are targeting visitors who did not convert, your ads should remind them why your brand is awesome or you can offer customers special discounts for coming back.

14. Create additional ad groups for other remarketing lists you wish to target.

How it works...

Remarketing allows you to show ads to users who previously visited your website after they leave and go on to browse other websites on the web. After adding a piece of remarketing code to your website, you can create custom lists to target specific segments of visitors and deliver them customized messages.

The costs are the same as for other AdWords campaigns. You only pay when someone clicks on your remarketing ads or sees them (depending on if you're using CPC or CPM bidding methods) and you set your own bids and budgets.

There's more...

After you set up remarketing, continue to test and experiment with audiences and campaign settings while keeping a close eye on results. As you tailor the campaign to your many unique audience segments, you can make powerful connections with your customers and improve your ROI.

See also

- The *Generating the remarketing code* recipe
- The *Creating remarketing audiences in AdWords* recipe

Setting remarketing bids

You'll need to bid competitively on your remarketing ad groups in order for your ads to show on Google's Display network. You'll be competing against all of the other advertisers who are running remarketing campaigns as well as against other ads targeting the Display network. Keep in mind the purchase cycle and your different remarketing audiences as you decide how much to bid on each segment.

Getting ready

You'll need to create a remarketing campaign and multiple ad groups for your different audiences. Creating separate ad groups for each remarketing audience will allow you to better segment and bid separately based on priority.

How to do it...

1. First decide if you'd like to use Max **Cost-Per-Click** (**CPC**) or **Cost Per 1000 Impressions** (**CPM**) bids. I recommend going with CPC bids if you are direct response focused. You can choose and adjust your bidding strategy at the campaign level in your remarketing campaign setting page.

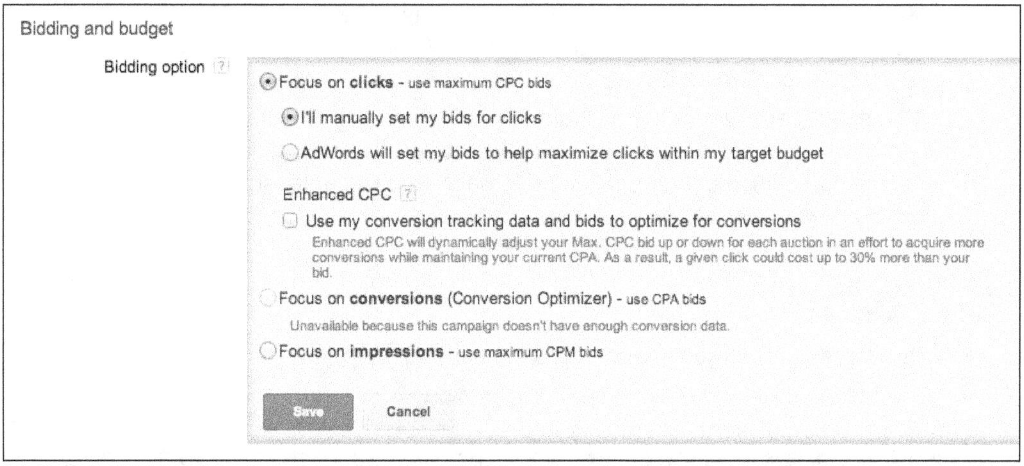

2. Once you have chosen your bidding strategy at the campaign level, you'll set actual bids at the ad group level. Start with a higher initial bid to be competitive in the ad auction.
3. Set different bids for individual ad groups with your different remarketing audiences. Your bids should be lower for lower funnel audiences (such as `All Visitors`) and higher for audiences further along the conversion cycle (such as `Shopping cart abandoners`). Here is an example of how you might want to set your initial bids based on the different remarketing segments:

Remarketing Ad Group	Max CPC
All visitors	$2
All visitors except for those who converted	$2.1
All shopping cart abandoners	$2.2
iPhone 5 shopping cart abandoners	$2.3

4. Monitor impressions, clicks, and conversions, and adjust based on results. If you are not getting enough impressions and clicks, try increasing your Max CPCs. If your ad groups are getting a large number of clicks without any conversions, lower Max CPCs.

How it works...

The following bidding strategies are available for remarketing campaigns:

- **Max CPC**: The maximum amount you are willing to pay for each click. Your Max CPC affects your ad rank on Google's Display network. Increasing Max CPC increases your ad rank and improves your chances of ads appearing.
- **Max CPM**: The maximum amount you are willing to pay for 1,000 impressions. You pay for impressions, rather than clicks. CPA bidding is most appropriate for advertisers focused on branding.
- **CPA**: specify a Target or a Maximum CPA bid and Google's Conversion Optimizer will help you maximize conversions within your targets based on historical information. Your remarketing campaign will need to have received at least 15 conversions in the last 30 days to be eligible.

See also

- The *Creating remarketing audiences in AdWords* recipe
- The *Setting up a remarketing campaign* recipe

Setting frequency caps to limit how often ads show

Many advertisers considering remarketing campaigns are concerned about inundating their visitors. In fact, you could alienate your customers by spamming them with ads that constantly follow them around. To protect your brand, you can set frequency caps in AdWords, which by default Google does not enable in your campaigns. However, it's easy to set this up and it can make the difference between a highly effective remarketing ad and a customer never purchasing from you again.

Getting ready

Decide how often you'd like your ads to show to past visitors. Advertisers differ on how often they like to show their ads to past visitors, and I recommend testing different frequency caps to find what produces the best results. There is no right or wrong impression cap limit, and you'll want to test to figure out what's most effective for you. I recommend starting with 3 to 5 impressions per day and adjusting from there.

You can limit impressions by the following criteria:

- Campaign
- Ad group
- Ad

I like to set my impressions caps per campaign to ensure all ads within a remarketing campaign show only a predefined number of impressions. However, your strategy will differ based on your goals, and I recommend you experiment with different settings.

> Keep in mind that just because an impression was served, that does not mean that someone actually saw your ad. The ad could have appeared below the fold, or the person simply may not have noticed it while browsing the Google Display network.

How to do it...

To set impressions caps in your remarketing campaign, follow these steps:

1. Click on the **Campaigns** tab.
2. Click on your remarketing campaign and go to **Settings**.
3. Scroll down to **Advanced Settings** and click to expand the section **Ad delivery: Ad rotation, frequency capping**.
4. Click on the **Edit** option under **Frequency capping**.
5. Set your desired impression cap and choose if you'd like to limit impressions per day, per week, or per month. Also choose if you'd like to limit impressions for the entire campaign, an ad group, or per ad.

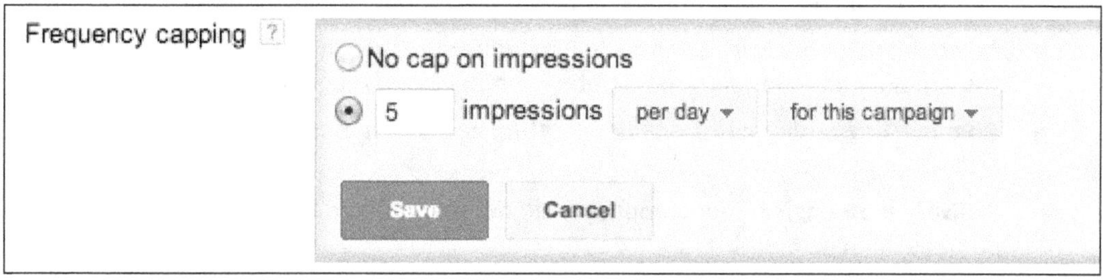

6. Click on **Save**.

How it works...

Frequency capping in AdWords limits the number of times your ads show to each user on the Google Display network over a given time period. By limiting how often ads show to the same person, you can protect your brand and ensure remarketing ads are not spamming your customers.

You can set impression caps per day, per week, or per month. You can also cap impressions by campaign, ad group, or an ad.

See also

- The *Setting up a remarketing campaign* recipe

Increasing traffic to your remarketing campaign

If your remarketing campaign is not getting enough impressions and clicks, you can make some changes to increase reach and ensure your ads are showing as much as possible. Since with remarketing you are reaching users who already showed interest in your website, your settings can be less restrictive while still reaching an extremely targeted set of visitors.

How to do it...

To ensure maximum visibility, try making some of the following changes:

- **Budget**: Is your remarketing campaign consistently reaching or is close to reaching its daily budget? Try increasing it to get more impressions and clicks.
- **Bids**: Increase bids to be more competitive in the ad auction against other advertisers.
- **Location and language targeting**: Relax your location and language targeting settings.
- **Frequency capping**: Try increasing impression caps (if you have frequency capping enabled) to increase impressions or how often ads show to each user.
- **Ad scheduling**: Review ad scheduling to make sure ads show all days and hours and you are not restricting your remarketing campaign too much.
- **Remarketing audiences**: Consider creating new remarketing audiences to capture additional visitors.
- **Delivery method**: Set your campaign's ad delivery method to Accelerated, so ads show as soon as possible.

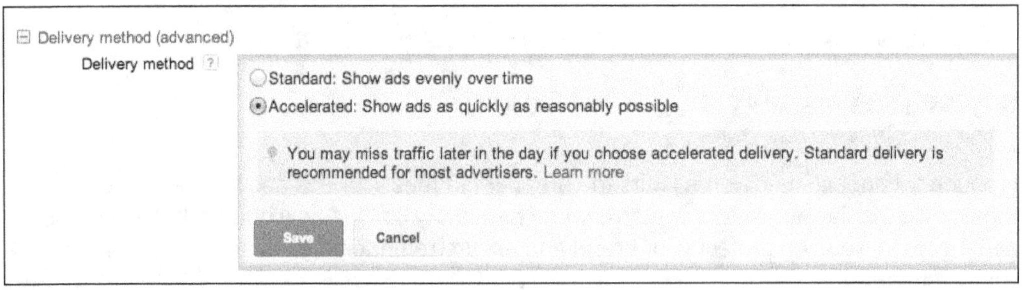

How it works...

By relaxing your remarketing campaign settings and increasing budgets and bids, you can help increase overall impressions and clicks. Make sure to monitor conversions to ensure any additional traffic results in positive ROI.

See also

- The *Setting frequency caps to limit how often ads show* recipe

Remarketing to YouTube viewers

AdWords remarketing now allows you to reach viewers who interacted with your YouTube videos, helping you strengthen your brand and relationship with your YouTube audience. By showing tailored ads to viewers who chose to interact with your videos or your YouTube channel, you can increase ROI with custom ads unique to YouTube interactions.

Getting ready

To get started, you'll need to link your AdWords and YouTube accounts first, if you have not already. To link your YouTube account to AdWords, choose to create a new online video campaign in your AdWords account.

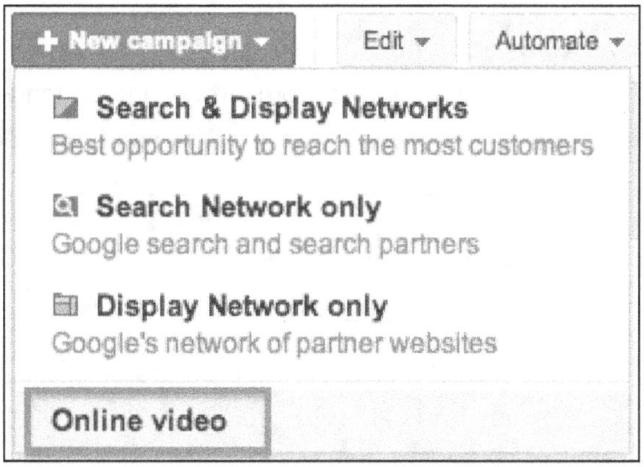

After you choose this new campaign type, you'll see an option to link your YouTube account to AdWords. You'll need to enter your YouTube credentials using the e-mail address and password on the account that owns your YouTube channel.

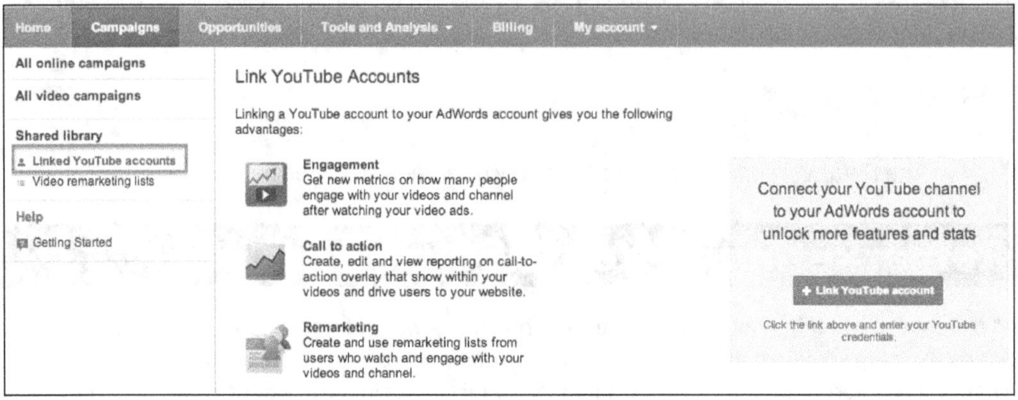

Once you sign in, you'll be automatically redirected to AdWords, and you should see your channel linked to your AdWords account.

How to do it...

Once your YouTube and AdWords accounts are linked, you'll need to access your video remarketing lists.

1. Sign in to your AdWords account.
2. Click on **All video campaigns** at the bottom left of your campaign management page.
3. Access the **Video remarketing lists** under the **Shared library** section.

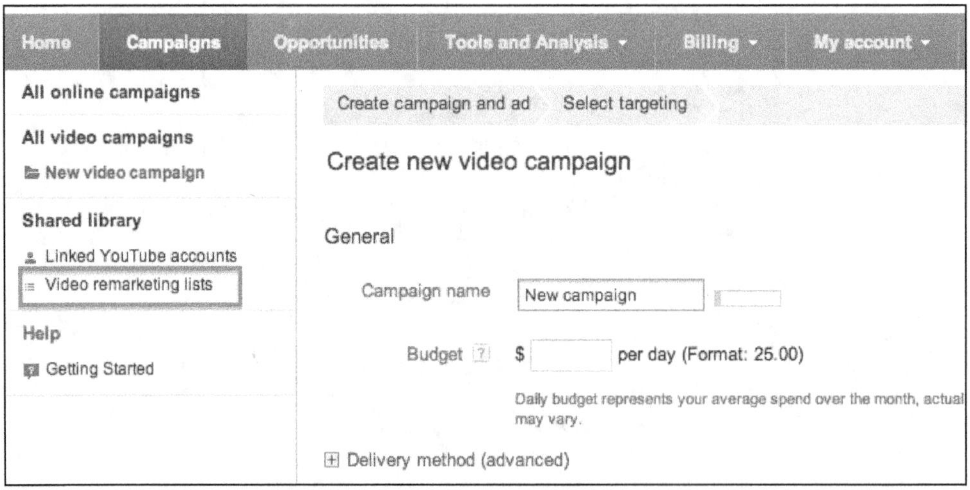

4. Click to create a new remarketing list and choose from one of the already defined audiences, which AdWords automatically populates for you.

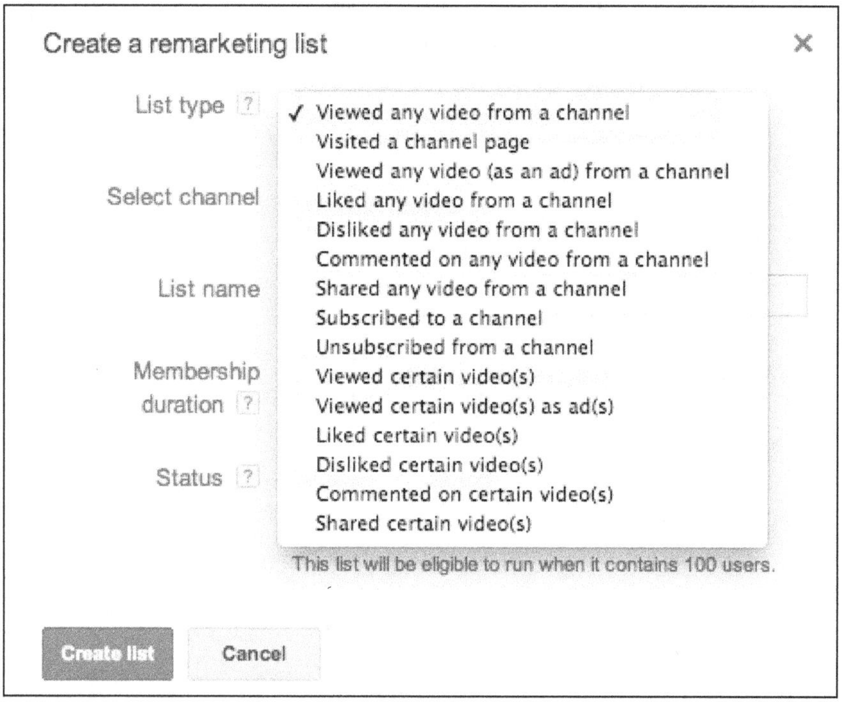

5. After choosing your list type, click on **Create list** and fill in the list name, membership duration, and any other necessary parameters.
6. Once you've decided who you'd like to remarket to and have created your audiences, set up a new remarketing campaign, adding the YouTube audiences you just created as your targets. Make sure to customize ad messaging for the audience you are reaching and include relevant offers and calls-to-action.

How it works...

YouTube remarketing helps you reach viewers based on their past interactions with your videos and your YouTube channel. With YouTube remarketing you can automatically create remarketing user lists without adding any additional pixels to your website. You can choose to remarket to users who watched or liked specific videos, and subscribed or unsubscribed from your channel. You can even create custom audiences and combinations to further subdivide who sees what message. For example, you can remarket to anyone that's viewed a video but did not yet convert through your site.

See also

- The *Setting up a remarketing campaign* recipe
- The *Creating remarketing audiences in AdWords* recipe

10

Reporting and Analysis

In this chapter, we will cover:

- Running and scheduling reports
- Customizing columns to personalize data views
- Analyzing the days and times when ads perform best
- Analyzing geographic performance
- Reviewing call details
- Finding out where on display your ads are appearing
- Segmenting performance reports
- Creating filters to customize reporting
- Viewing data in graph format
- Evaluating sitelink extensions
- Using impression share metrics to increase conversions

Introduction

AdWords offers rich and detailed reporting to help you analyze ad performance and get the most out of your investment. For example, you can find out where your most valuable clicks are coming from and use that data to set up regionally targeted campaigns. You can also analyze how your website visitors using different devices (such as tablets versus mobile) convert and make adjustments to your campaigns based on trends you observe. Successful advertisers review their reports regularly and react to the traffic and conversion patterns. This chapter highlights some of the key reports to pay attention to as well as ways to react to the data to maximize your ROI.

Running and scheduling reports

Running reports in AdWords is easy and can be done in the campaign management section of your account. In addition to seeing the data in the interface, you can choose to download reports to one of the many available formats (such as `.pdf` or Excel `.csv`) as well as schedule reports to be e-mailed on a regular basis to account users.

Getting ready

If you would like to schedule reports to be automatically e-mailed to specific e-mail addresses, make sure they are listed as users on your AdWords account. If they are not, you will need to invite them.

Here are the basic reports I recommend you run on a regular basis:

- Campaigns
- Ad groups
- Keywords
- Ads

How to do it...

To view, schedule, and download AdWords reports, follow these steps:

1. Navigate to the **Campaigns** tab.
2. One of the most basic reports you'll want to analyze on a regular basis is an account summary of all of your campaigns. However, you can also run reports on your ad groups, keywords, ads, and many other segments using the same steps outlined in the following example.
3. Adjust the date range at the top-right corner of your campaign management page to reflect the period you are interested in analyzing. You can choose to review all time data, or most recent performance, such as this week or the last 30 days. You can also enter custom date ranges and turn on the **Compare dates** feature to compare recent performance to the same period last year, for example.

4. Customize columns to include performance metrics you care about in your report, such as conversions.

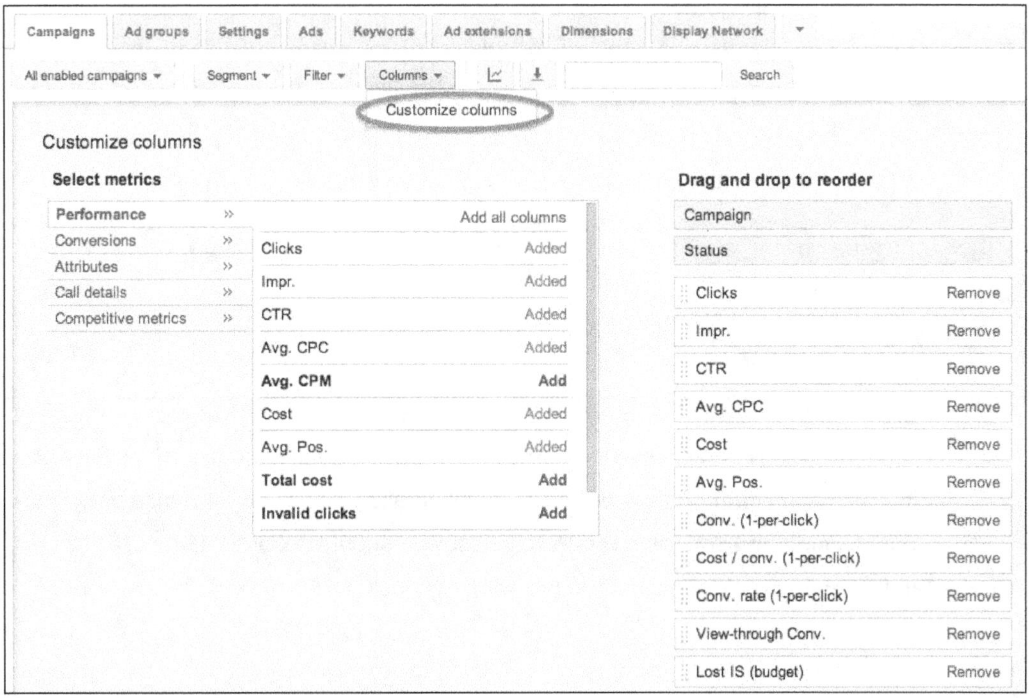

5. Click on the **Download Report** button to bring up the option to export, e-mail, and schedule your report.

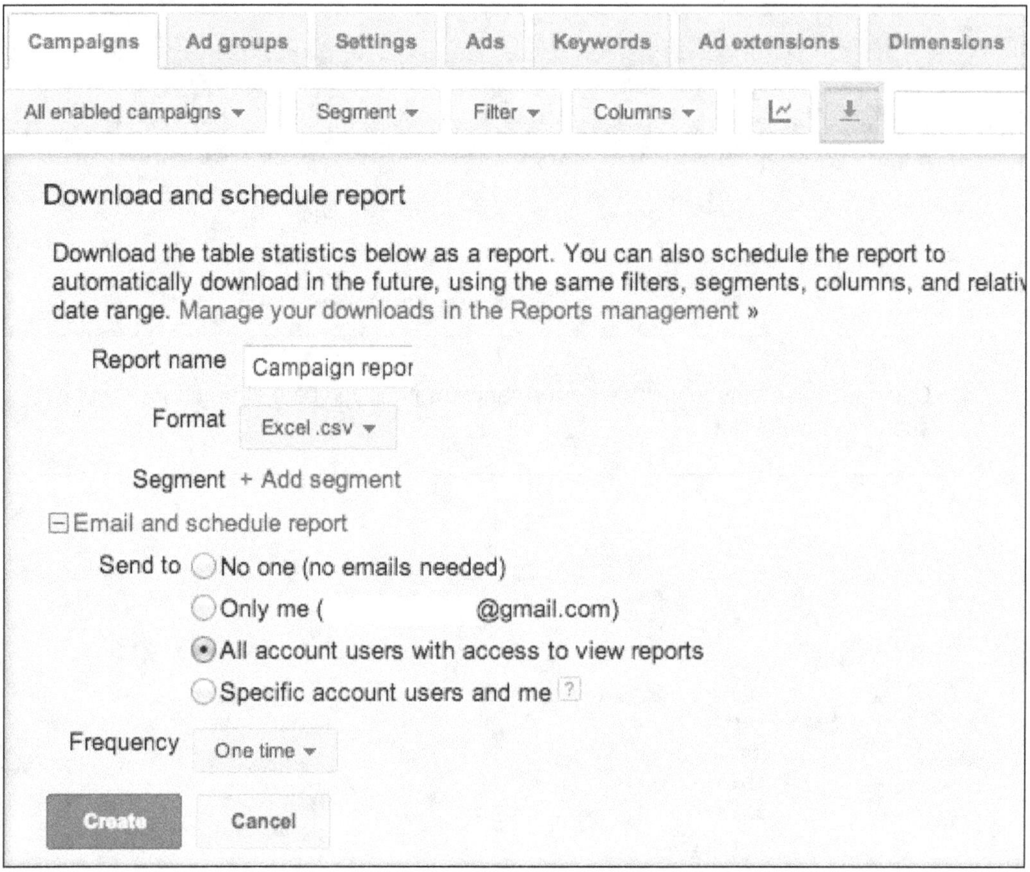

6. Name your report and choose the format you'd like to download it to, such as **Excel.csv**.
7. Click on **+ Add segment** to layer on additional details, such as performance by network.
8. Choose **Email and schedule report** to select who should receive this report.
9. Select **Frequency** from one of the following options:
    - One time
    - Daily
    - Every Monday
    - First day of the month
10. Click on **Create**. If your report is a one-time report, it will download right away.

How it works...

Reporting is not real time. Clicks and impressions can be delayed by up to three hours, while the following metrics are updated only once per day:

- Search terms
- Automatic placements
- Geographic
- Demographic
- Destination URL

Additionally, if you are importing Google Analytics goals as conversions into your AdWords account, they may not be reflected in AdWords for 24 to 72 hours.

There's more...

You can adjust settings of previously scheduled reports at any time by clicking on **Reports** at the bottom-left corner of your campaign management page. You can change the report download format, adjust the date range, change who receives it, run the report again, create a similar report, or delete a report.

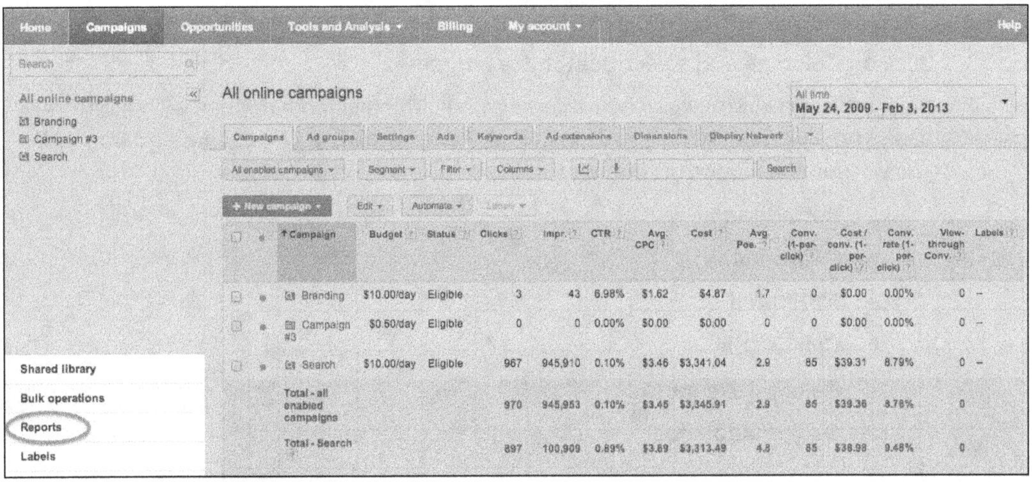

See also

- The *Inviting other users to access your account* recipe in *Chapter 2, Setting up Your Account*
- The *Customizing columns to personalize data views* recipe

Customizing columns to personalize data views

Once your campaigns have been set up, there are many different pieces of data that you can analyze in AdWords. AdWords allows rich customization of your campaign management page, so that you are looking at data that is most pertinent to your analysis. The default view will most likely not include all of the information that you'll need as you review performance and optimize, and you'll need to customize the views to include the metrics of interest.

Getting ready

Think about what data is useful for a particular analysis. For example, you may wish to review performance data at the campaign level so that you can decide which campaigns are generating the most clicks and conversions.

How to do it...

To personalize your data views, follow these steps:

1. Click on the **Campaigns** tab.
2. Choose the sub tab you are interested in, such as **Campaigns** or **Keywords**.
3. Click on **Columns** and select **Customize columns**.
4. Select the metric you wish to further segment. The available metrics will be different based on what sub tab you are looking at. For example, in your **Campaign** sub tab, you will see the following options:
    - **Performance**
    - **Conversions**
    - **Attributes**
    - **Call details**
    - **Competitive metrics**
    - **Google Analytics**

5. Once you select the metric of interest, you'll be able to further select columns within each metric. Click on **Add** to see the data you are interested in.

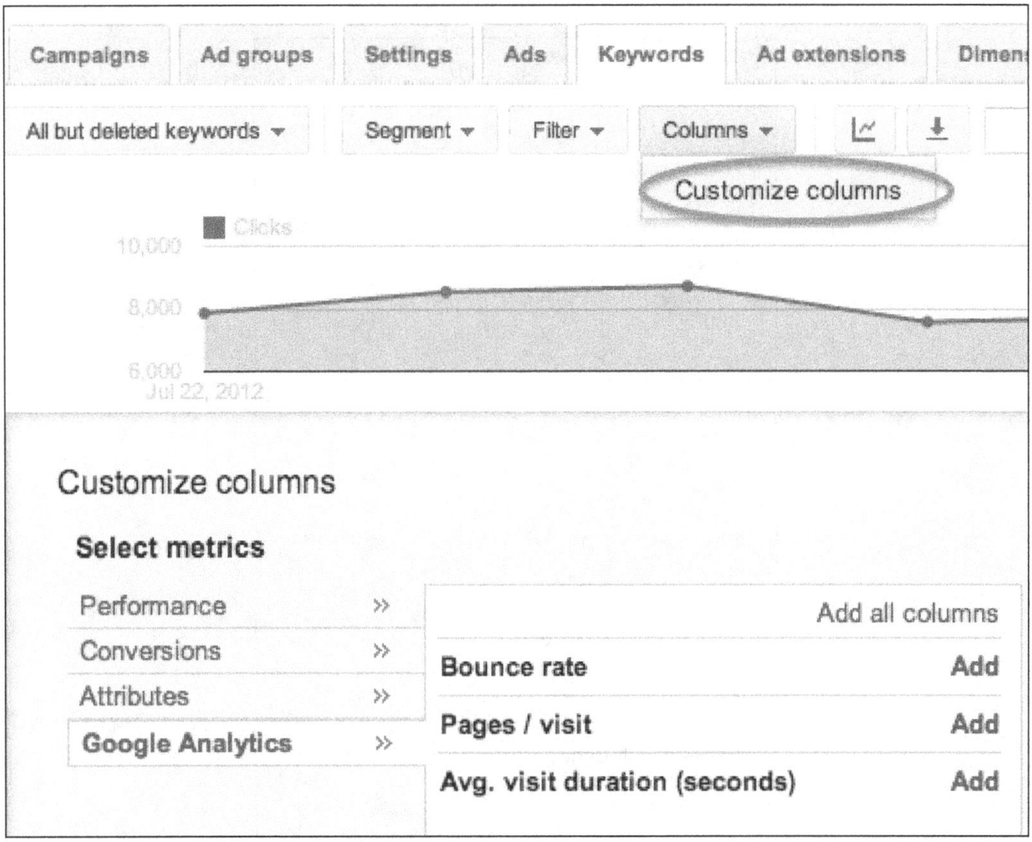

It can be overwhelming and distracting to look at all possible columns at once, so limit your views to the information that's most pertinent to the analysis at hand.

How it works...

Users with access to your account have their own custom campaign management views based on their unique settings. You cannot customize data views for other users. However, once you select your settings, you will see the same columns the next time you log in.

There's more...

You can save your preferred view or create multiple views for different types of goals and toggle back and forth between those settings. This can be useful for different types of analyses, such as analyzing Google Analytics data or analyzing competitive metrics.

You can also remove certain data from being shown or re-order the metrics at any time so the views reflect the data in the order that makes the most sense to you. Simply drag-and-drop the individual columns.

See also

- The *Viewing or hiding paused or deleted items* recipe in *Chapter 12, Managing AdWords*

Analyzing the days and times when ads perform best

Curious if your customers are searching for you more during the week or on weekends? How people interact with your website likely depends on the day of the week and even the time of the day. For example, if you sell pizzas, people are more likely to search for you in the evenings than early in the morning. To help you figure out your traffic patterns, AdWords provides a report where you can analyze impressions, clicks, and conversions by day and hour.

Getting ready

In order to run this report, your campaigns will need to have accumulated some data. If you are already restricting your campaigns to show only during certain days and hours via ad scheduling, keep that in mind, as it will skew your totals.

How to do it...

To view performance by day or hour of the day, follow these steps:

1. Click on the **Campaigns** tab.
2. Go to the **Dimensions** tab.
3. From the **View** drop-down menu, choose **Time** and select from one of the available options:
    - **Day of the week**
    - **Day**
    - **Week**
    - **Month**
    - **Quarter**
    - **Year**
    - **Hour of day**

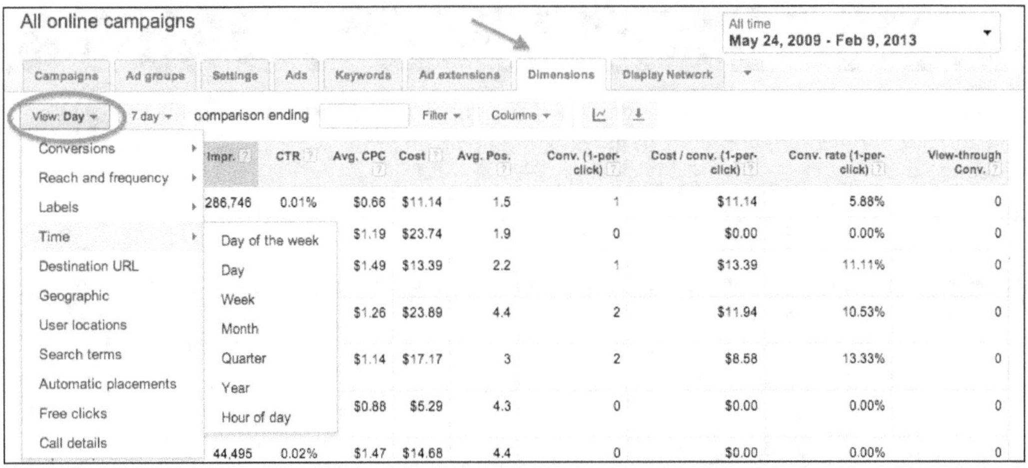

4. Make sure to adjust the date range for the account at the top-right corner of the campaign management page to reflect dates you are interested in analyzing.

5. You can apply these segments to the entire account or select individual campaigns and ad groups. You can view data for a specific campaign's ad groups by selecting them from the left navigation menu in your campaign management page.
6. You can sort your data by your chosen time segment or by performance metrics, such as impressions, clicks, or conversions. Customize your columns, adding additional metrics of interest to see the data that's most important to you.
7. If you find that certain days of the week or hours of the day bring you more traffic or convert better and your budget is limited, you can implement ad scheduling to take advantage of these patterns and maximize clicks during high traffic periods. Schedule ads to run during key days and times through your campaign settings page.

How it works...

The **Dimensions** tab allows you to analyze data across different periods of time, such as by day of the week or by hour of the day for your entire account or by campaign or ad group.

See also

- The *Analyzing geographic performance* recipe
- The *Customizing columns to personalize data views* recipe
- The *Scheduling ads to run during key days and times* recipe in *Chapter 11, Optimizing Performance*

Analyzing geographic performance

Wonder where your clicks are coming from? The geographic report can help you find out so you can fine-tune your campaigns to maximize visibility in areas where ads perform better.

Getting ready

Your AdWords campaigns will need to have been running for some time and will need to have accumulated some data first.

How to do it...

To view geographic performance, follow these steps:

1. Click on the **Campaigns** tab.
2. Go to the **Dimensions** tab.
3. Adjust the date range to reflect the period you are interested in analyzing.
4. From the **View** drop-down menu, choose **Geographic**.

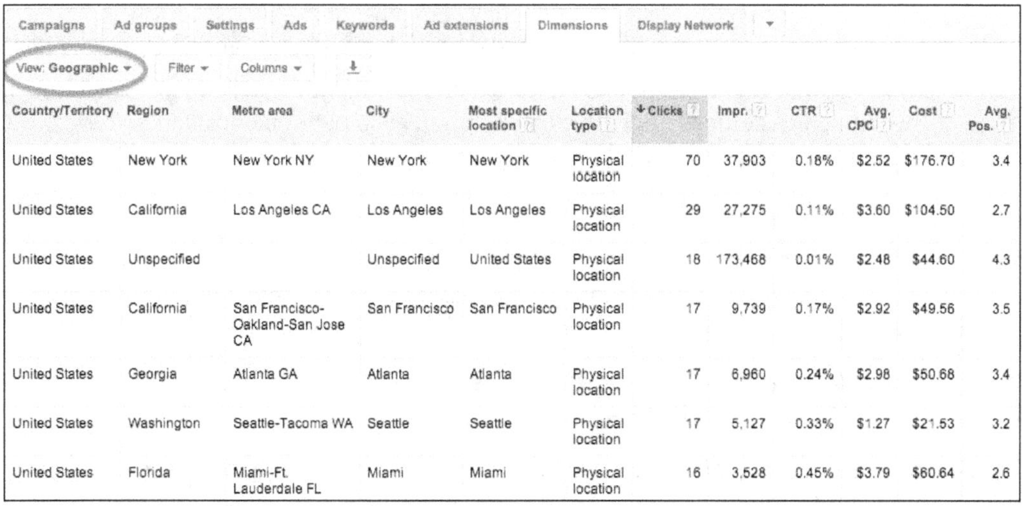

Country/Territory	Region	Metro area	City	Most specific location	Location type	Clicks	Impr.	CTR	Avg. CPC	Cost	Avg. Pos.
United States	New York	New York NY	New York	New York	Physical location	70	37,903	0.18%	$2.52	$176.70	3.4
United States	California	Los Angeles CA	Los Angeles	Los Angeles	Physical location	29	27,275	0.11%	$3.60	$104.50	2.7
United States	Unspecified		Unspecified	United States	Physical location	18	173,468	0.01%	$2.48	$44.60	4.3
United States	California	San Francisco-Oakland-San Jose CA	San Francisco	San Francisco	Physical location	17	9,739	0.17%	$2.92	$49.56	3.5
United States	Georgia	Atlanta GA	Atlanta	Atlanta	Physical location	17	6,960	0.24%	$2.98	$50.68	3.4
United States	Washington	Seattle-Tacoma WA	Seattle	Seattle	Physical location	17	5,127	0.33%	$1.27	$21.53	3.2
United States	Florida	Miami-Ft. Lauderdale FL	Miami	Miami	Physical location	16	3,528	0.45%	$3.79	$60.64	2.6

5. Next, customize **Columns** to include the level of detail you care about, such as region, metro area, and city. Add all columns you would like to see in your report and click on **Apply**.

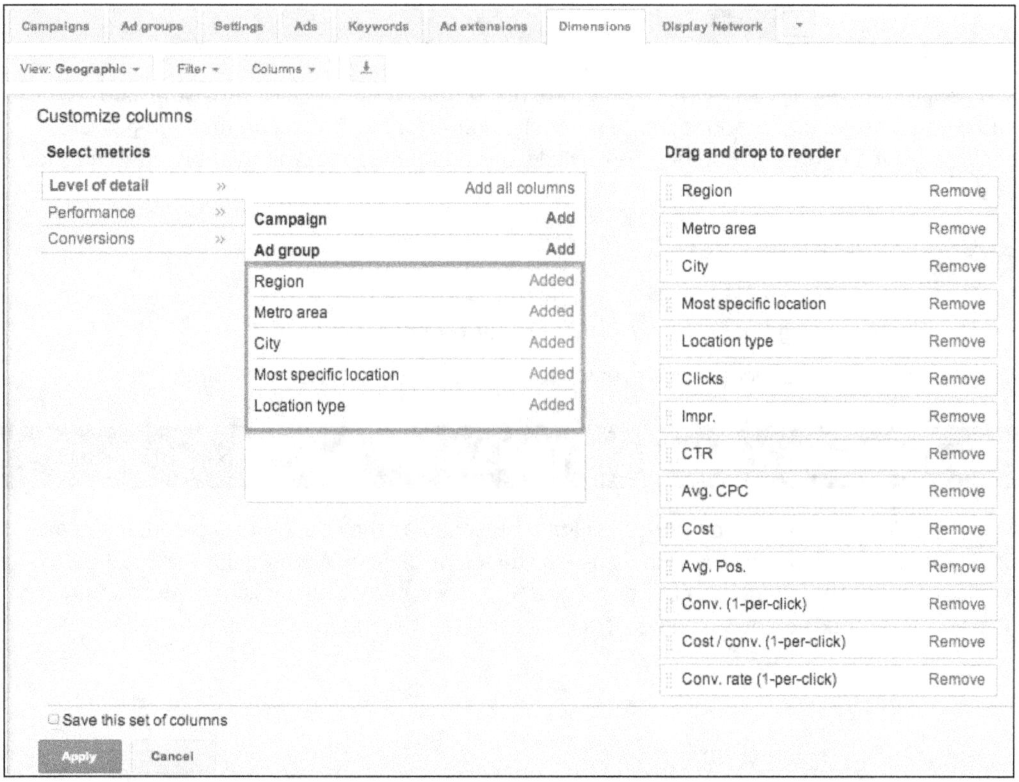

6. Sort by impressions or clicks to figure out where most of the search activity is concentrated. Sort by conversions to find out which geographic areas convert the best.
7. If you find that certain locations perform better for you, you can increase bids through your campaign settings page. This can help you get a better ad position and even more clicks from your most important locations.

How it works...

The geographic report allows you to analyze performance across different countries, regions, metro areas, or cities.

The **Most specific location** column shows the most detailed information available, such as the postal code (the most specific location data varies by country).

The **Location type** column indicates whether an impression was matched by physical location (where a user was physically located) or location of interest (location a user was searching for or viewing content about).

Geographic performance data is available for the entire account or you can choose to analyze individual campaigns and ad groups.

There's more...

The geographic report can help you fine tune performance by concentrating your budget and bids on areas that produce the best results, For example, if you find that you get a lot of clicks from a certain region but these clicks are not converting, you might want to exclude this region.

See also

- The *Analyzing the days and times ads perform best* recipe
- The *Adjusting location bids* recipe in *Chapter 7, Budgets and Bidding*

Reviewing call details

Many people searching online prefer calling a business as they do their research. If you are using AdWords call extensions with Google's call forwarding, AdWords will record call data associated with the phone number that appeared in your AdWords ads. This information can help you measure the effectiveness of your campaigns beyond just the click-based metrics.

Getting ready

You'll need to be using call extensions with Google's call forwarding number to get detailed call reports. Google's call forwarding extensions are currently only available to advertisers in the US, UK, and Germany.

How to do it...

To review call details for calls that came through Google's call forwarding number:

1. Click on the **Campaigns** tab.
2. Go to the **Dimensions** tab.
3. Adjust the date range to reflect the period you are interested in analyzing.
4. From the **View** drop-down menu, select **Call details**.

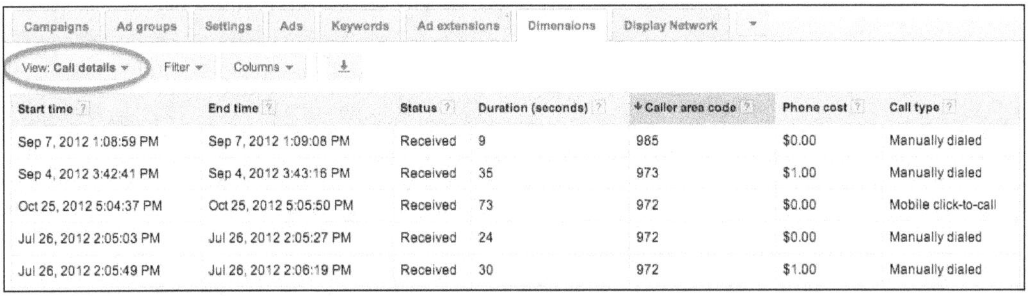

Start time	End time	Status	Duration (seconds)	Caller area code	Phone cost	Call type
Sep 7, 2012 1:08:59 PM	Sep 7, 2012 1:09:08 PM	Received	9	985	$0.00	Manually dialed
Sep 4, 2012 3:42:41 PM	Sep 4, 2012 3:43:16 PM	Received	35	973	$1.00	Manually dialed
Oct 25, 2012 5:04:37 PM	Oct 25, 2012 5:05:50 PM	Received	73	972	$0.00	Mobile click-to-call
Jul 26, 2012 2:05:03 PM	Jul 26, 2012 2:05:27 PM	Received	24	972	$0.00	Manually dialed
Jul 26, 2012 2:05:49 PM	Jul 26, 2012 2:06:19 PM	Received	30	972	$1.00	Manually dialed

5. The report will show you information, such as if and when the call was received, how long it lasted, and the caller's area code.
6. You can analyze call details for all of your campaigns or select specific campaigns and ad groups.
7. Call details are also available in your campaign and ad group tabs. You'll need to customize columns to see call data in your dashboard summary page. The following columns are available:
   - **Phone impressions**: The number of times your ad was shown with a Google call forwarding number
   - **Phone calls**: The number of valid calls received through your Google call forwarding number
   - **PTR**: Phone-through-rate or the number of calls received divided by the number of times your phone number was shown
   - **Phone cost:** Total costs accrued for calls received through Google's forwarding number

- **Avg. CPP:** Average cost-per-phone-call is the average amount you pay for each call received through Google's call forwarding number

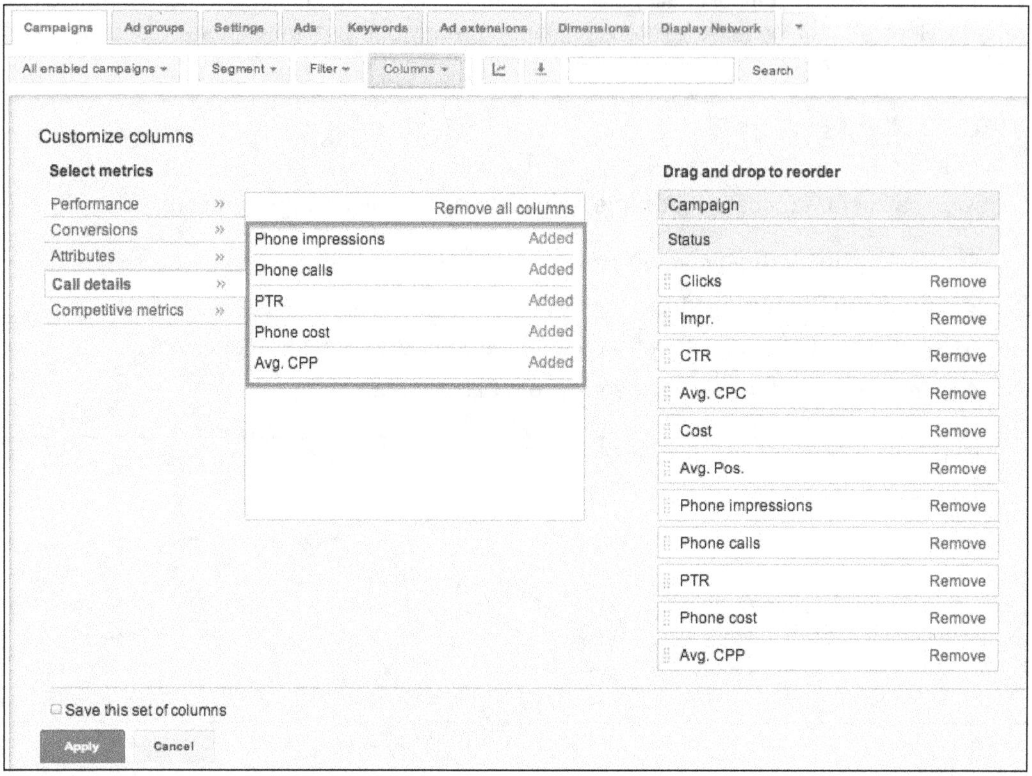

[Set **Max CPP bids** to **Bid separately on calls**, especially if calls are more valuable to you than clicks.]

How it works...

The call details report provides data on calls received through a Google call forwarding number via desktops, tablets or high-end mobile devices. You can access call details data in your campaign or ad group reporting dashboards or through the dimensions tab.

See also

- The *Setting up call extensions* recipe in *Chapter 12, Advanced Strategies and Features*
- The *Setting separate bids for calls* recipe in *Chapter 7, Budgets and Bidding*

Finding out where on display your ads are appearing

If you are running display campaigns, you'll want to periodically analyze where your ads are appearing. You may want to pause or exclude some of the websites your ads appear on, such as irrelevant placements or pages you are getting a lot of clicks on without any conversions.

Getting ready

You'll need to be running display campaigns to run this report.

How to do it...

To review domains and pages your ads have appeared on, follow these steps:

1. Go to the **Campaigns** tab.
2. Select your display campaign and go to the **Display Network** tab.
3. Click on sub tab **Placements**.

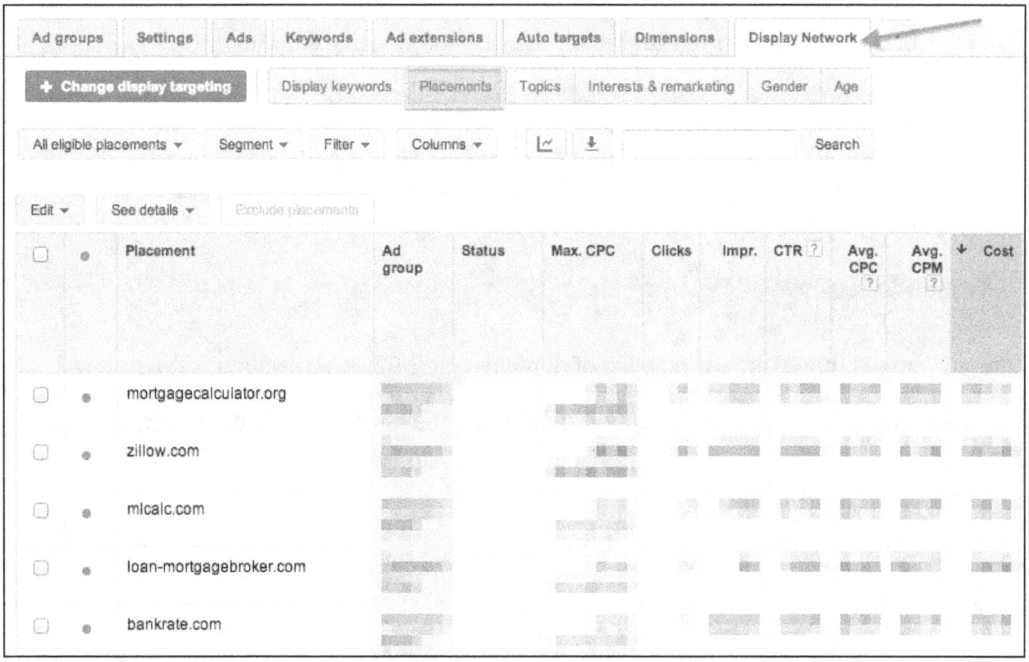

4. To find out even more information, such as the actual pages (rather than just domains) your ads have shown on, click on the **See details** button and choose **All**.

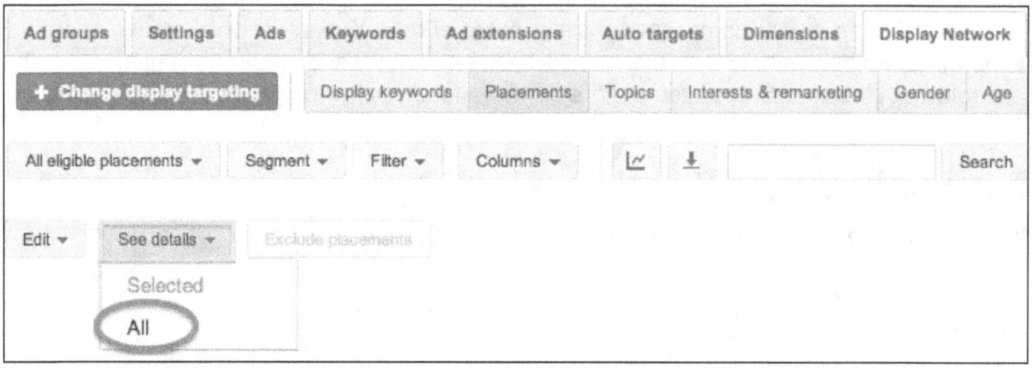

5. You can also see URLs for specific placements rather than all by selecting the checkbox next to a domain in your placements report and choosing **Selected** from the **See details** drop-down menu.
6. Customize your columns to see additional data, such as conversions and cost/conversion.
7. Consider excluding irrelevant and poorly performing placements.
8. Consider adding relevant placements and those that convert to your managed placements.
9. You can choose to download your data into an excel file or schedule it to be emailed to you on a recurring basis, so you can always stay on top of your display performance.

How it works...

The placements report shows you a list of domains and URLs where your ads have shown.

Reporting is not real time and placement data may not available until the next day.

There's more...

Reviewing a large number of websites and pages your ads appeared on can be a little daunting as you look for opportunities to optimize. However, you can sort your data by metrics that are important to you to identify opportunities. Here are a few ways you can analyze placements:

- Sort placements data by impressions to see where your ads are appearing the most
- Sort placement data by cost to see which placements you are spending the most money on
- Sort by conversions to analyze which placements are generating sales or leads

See also

- The *Excluding irrelevant and poorly performing placements* recipe in *Chapter 7, Running Display Ads*

Segmenting performance reports

Segments in AdWords allow you to further split up your performance data and take your reporting to the next level. For example, you can segment how your campaigns perform on Google Search versus Search Partners or compare performance by device. Segments arm you with the tools necessary to pinpoint trouble areas or what's working for you.

How to do it...

To segment your AdWords data, follow these steps:

1. Go to the **Campaigns** tab.
2. Click on the tab you are interested in examining further. Most tabs have segments but the available segments will vary depending on if you are analyzing your campaigns, ad groups, ads, keywords, or display.

3. Click on **Segment** and choose one of the available options, such as **Network**.

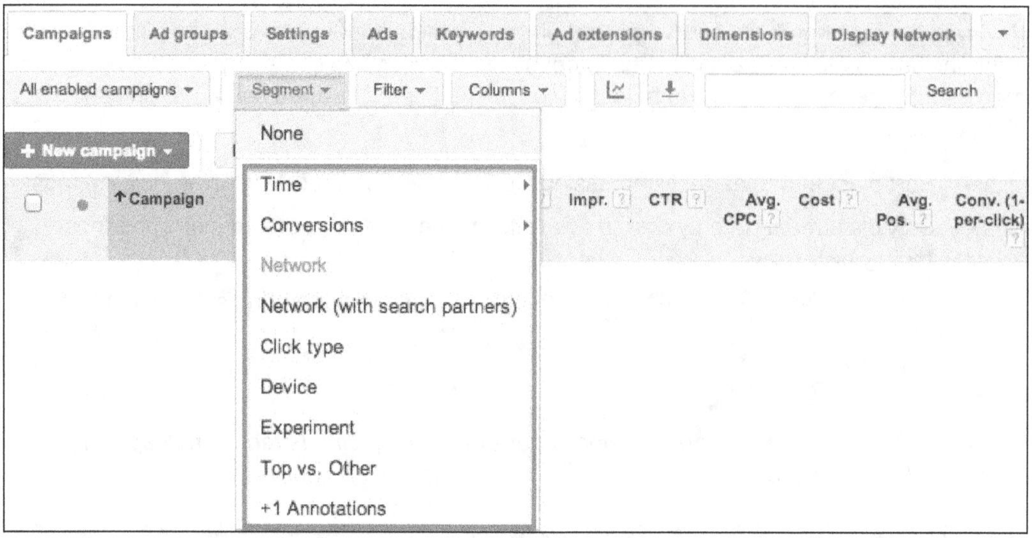

4. Adjust the reporting date range to see data for the periods of time you are interested in analyzing.
5. Select **None** from the **Segment** drop-down menu to remove the segment or apply a different one.
6. Make changes based on what you learn from your segments. For example, if you find out that clicks from mobile devices do not perform as well as clicks from computers, decrease mobile device bids.

How it works...

Segments allow you to split up reports into multiple rows to further analyze various aspects of your AdWords performance. The segment options you'll see will vary depending on which tab in your campaign management page you are analyzing.

The following segments are available:

- **Time**: Analyze data by day, week, month, quarter, year, day of the week, or hour of the day.
- **Conversions**: Choose from action name or conversion tracking purpose.
- **Network**: Find out if the impressions came from Google Search, Search partners, or the Google Display network.
- **Keyword/Placement**: Segment available for ads showing which keyword or placement triggered impressions and clicks.

- **Search terms match type**: See if the ad was triggered by broad, phrase, or exact match.
- **Click type**: If you received clicks to your headline, sitelink, if it was a mobile click-to-call, or a click on "Get direction" from your Google Places extension.
- **Device**: Performance data for computers, tablets, and mobile devices.
- **Experiment**: If you previously set up experiments, you can see how experimental ads did against control ads, for example.
- **Top vs. Other**: Where you ads appeared on Google.com and search partner pages. Ads that appear above organic search results are classified as "Top" while all other ad positions are listed under "Other".
- **+1 Annotations**: How your ads performed when shown with different types of social annotations.

Some of the segments are only available to be downloaded as a report rather than viewed in the interface. When you make your selection, you'll get a notification and a message to use the download report button, indicating a particular segment can be downloaded as a report only.

See also

- The *Running and scheduling reports* recipe
- The *Modifying mobile bids* recipe in *Chapter 7, Budgets and Bidding*

Creating filters to customize reporting

Filters can help you further slice your reports to identify areas of improvement or to analyze how certain sets of campaigns or strategies are performing. For example, you may wish to filter out in your reports poorly performing keywords, evaluate how branded versus not branded campaigns perform, or analyze ads featuring special promotions.

Getting ready

You'll need to name your campaigns by using common terms that will help you filter. For example, name all campaigns that do not include non-branded keywords with NB. Alternatively, you can create labels to group certain campaigns together and apply a label to each campaign that should be included.

Evaluate your goals, such as desired CPA and maximum CPA you are willing to tolerate. Keep these goals in mind when you set up various performance centered filters.

How to do it...

To create a filter to isolate groups of campaigns, follow these steps:

1. Click on the **Campaigns** tab.
2. Adjust the date range at the top right of your campaign management page.
3. From the **Filter** drop-down menu choose **Create filter**.
4. In this example, we'll create a filter to analyze all non-branded campaigns. In the previous step we renamed all campaigns that do not include branded keywords by appending a common identifier such as NB to the campaign name. Next, after clicking to create a filter, choose **Campaign name**, select **contains**, and write in NB or any other words you wish to filter campaigns by. If you are using labels, you can also filter just by your NB label.
5. Check **Save filter** to access it again at a later date and click on **Apply**.

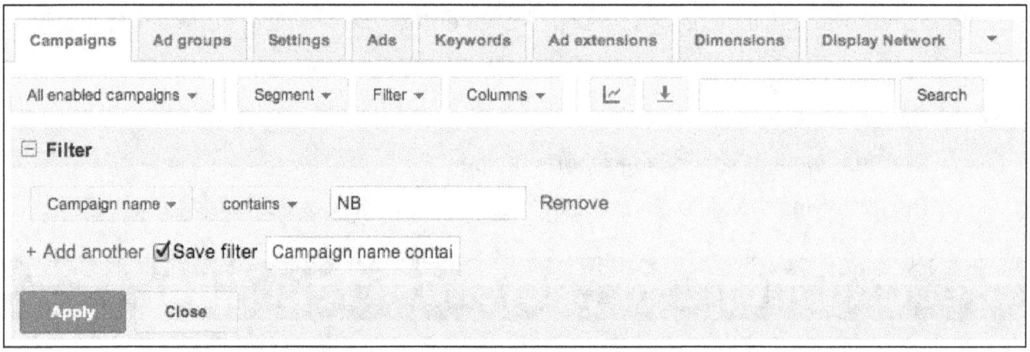

In the next example, we'll create a filter to isolate costly keywords that are not converting.

1. Go to your **Keywords** tab and click on **Create filter**.
2. From the **Conversions** drop-down choose **Conversions (1-per-click)**, select **<=**, and enter in 0.

3. Click on **+ Add another** and from the **Performance** drop down choose **Cost** and write in a specific amount. For example, if you target CPA is $10, you may wish to analyze all keywords that have accumulated over $10 but have not converted.

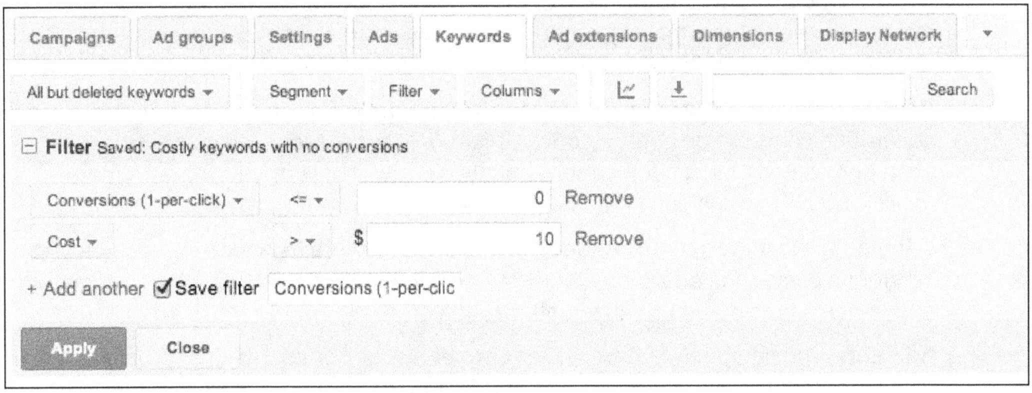

Save the filter if you plan to use it again, and click on **Apply**.

> Save your most commonly used filters to easily access them at any time and use them with different date ranges. Filters you create are user-specific and will not be available to another user who has access to your account.

How it works...

Filters help you isolate campaigns, ad groups, keywords, or other account segments by predefined criteria to help you better analyze performance. AdWords may provide certain predefined filters in your account or you can create custom filters to focus on metrics specific to your goals.

You can add multiple layers to each filter and save these filters for future use and analysis.

There's more...

Here are a few common filters you may wish to set up and review regularly:

- **Keywords below first page bid**. This is a predefined filter that you can access in your keywords tab. It shows you all of the keywords with ad rank below the first page. Consider raising your bid and work on improving your Quality Score. For example, refine your ad or add negative keywords to increase CTR.

- **Cost-effective keywords**. Create a filter to review keywords that are converting within your desired CPA. Consider raising your Max CPC to get more traffic out of keywords that are working for you.
- **Costly keywords without any conversions**. Keywords that accumulate a certain amount in spending without generating any conversions. Consider lowering bids, creating new ads, adding negative keywords, or pausing these keywords.
- **Keywords converting above your target CPA goal**. Review keywords that are generating conversions but are converting above your target cost/conversion. Consider lowering bids, adding more negative keywords, restructuring with more specific ad copy, or pausing these keywords.
- **Campaign or ad group performance filters**. Create filters to isolate campaigns and ad groups converting above or within your target CPA. Use this data when budgeting and to help you bid and prioritize optimization efforts.
- **Ad filters**. You can analyze how certain sets of ads performed against others. For example, you may wish to review how ads featuring "Free Download" fared against ads that used the call-to-action "Download Now."

See also

- The *Running and scheduling reports* recipe
- The *Creating filters to customize reporting* recipe

Viewing data in graph format

Your AdWords campaign management page offers the option to view various performance metrics in graph format. This visual analysis of performance trends can help you identify issues as well as spot when your campaigns perform better.

How to do it...

To view performance graphs, follow these steps:

1. Click on the **Campaigns** tab.
2. Adjust the date range at the top-right of your campaign management page.
3. Click on the graph icon (see highlighted image in the following screenshot) above your data summary table.
4. Choose the metrics you'd like the graph to display. You can choose one or two metrics to see how they relate to one another. For example, you can compare click trends versus conversions to zero in on days when your clicks are converting better or worse.

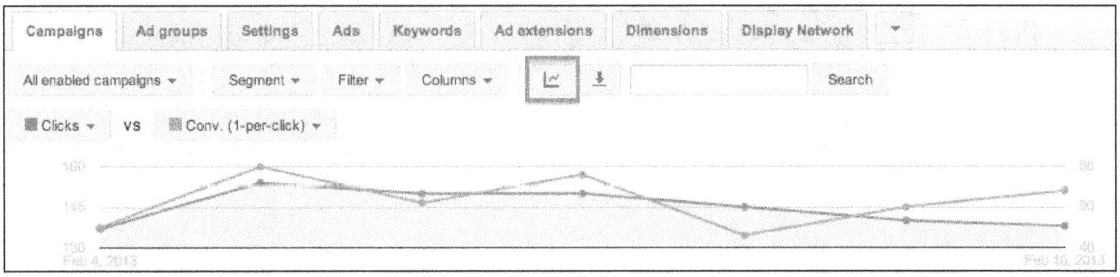

5. You can see graphs for your entire account or graph specific campaigns and ad groups.
6. If you notice important trends, such as an increase in conversions on Mondays, for example, make changes to your settings to maximize on this information.

How it works...

AdWords campaign management offers graphical data of your performance for your chosen date ranges. You can select up to two metrics to compare trends in several campaign management tabs. Available graph metrics include:

- Performance
- Conversions
- Competitive metrics

Graphs are available for the entire account, or specific campaigns and ad groups. You can also use custom filters to only see graphs for sets of campaigns, such as all non-branded campaigns.

There's more...

The following data trends are useful to note:

- A decrease in CTR can signal the need to test new ad copy and add negative keywords.
- If you notice a decrease in Avg. Pos., consider raising your bids.
- An increase in Cost/Cov. may warrant re-examining your account structure.
- A boost in conversions is a great sign that you are doing something right. Consider testing similar strategies across your other campaigns.
- Consistent decrease in impressions over the weekend, for example, can mean that people are searching for you more during the week. Adjust your bids and ad scheduling to maximize this trend.

See also

- The *Creating filters to customize reporting* recipe

Evaluating sitelink extensions

Sitelink ad extensions can help boost your CTR and make your ads stand out with additional relevant page links. However, some sitelinks perform better than others and there are some sitelinks that may need to be re-worded or eliminated completely based on performance.

Getting ready

First, you'll need to set up sitelink extensions in at least one of your campaigns and your extensions will need to have been approved to run. Your sitelinks may not show all the time, depending on performance and ad position. Also, each sitelink needs to direct customers to a unique landing page. If a sitelink stops showing, check if it was disapproved and make the necessary edits.

How to do it...

1. Click on the **Campaigns** tab.
2. Go to the **Ad Extensions** tab.
3. Select **Sitelinks Extensions** from the **View** drop-down menu.
4. Each of your sitelinks will have impression, click, cost, and other data you choose to view. Make sure to customize columns to include conversion data and other metrics on interest.

Sitelink	Status	Clicks	Impr.	CTR	Avg. CPC	Cost	Avg. Pos.	Conv. (1-per-click)	Cost / conv. (1-per-click)	Conv. rate (1-per-click)
Site Link 1	Approved	20	1,409	1.42%	$1.60	$32.05	1.1	2	$16.02	10.00%
Site Link 2	Approved	20	1,353	1.48%	$1.60	$32.05	1.1	2	$16.02	10.00%
Site Link 3	Approved	19	1,344	1.41%	$1.68	$31.95	1.1	2	$15.98	10.53%
Site Link 4	Approved	10	1,117	0.90%	$1.80	$17.96	1.2	0	$0.00	0.00%
Total - all sitelinks		32	3,612	0.89%	$1.85	$59.24	1.1	3	$19.75	9.38%

5. Next, go to **Segment** and choose **Click type** to see sitelink specific data. Segmenting by click type shows you how many people are choosing to click on a particular sitelink versus your headline.
6. From the **Segment** drop-down menu, choose **This Extension vs. Other** to see how an individual sitelink performs against another sitelink extension you are using.

> If you notice that some of your sitelinks have low CTRs, consider rephrasing the sitelink text with more appealing descriptions or calls-to-action. If a sitelink is getting plenty of clicks but no conversions, consider deleting it, as it could be distracting users from the desired conversion path.

How it works...

AdWords sitelink ad extensions expand your text ads with additional page links, providing your visitors with other navigation options. AdWords reports on the performance of each extension you create so you can analyze the effectiveness of each sitelink.

See also

- The *Creating sitelinks* recipe in *Chapter 12, Advanced Strategies and Features*

Using impression share metrics to increase conversions

If your AdWords campaigns are profitable, make sure you are not losing impression share and missing out on sales. Review your competitive metrics on a regular basis to identify if you are losing traffic due to budgets and bids and to prioritize your optimization efforts.

Getting ready

You'll need to customize columns to see competitive metrics, currently available in campaign and ad group tabs.

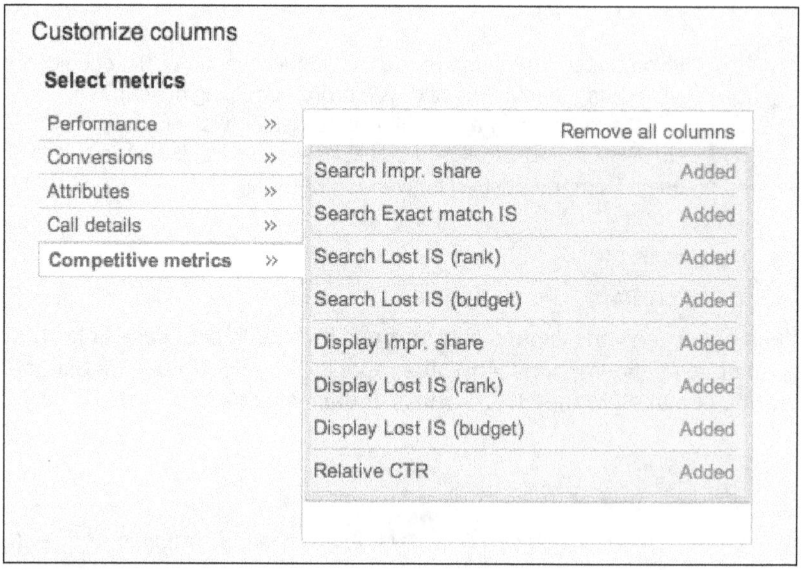

Once you customize your data columns to include competitive metrics, your campaign and ad group tabs will include extra impression share (IS) columns for the metrics you have chosen.

How to do it...

Search Lost IS (budget) and Display Lost IS (budget):

The **Search Lost IS (budget)** and **Display Lost IS (budget)** columns help you identify if you need to increase your campaign budgets. If the number is greater than 0 percent, this means that your ads did not show on the Search or on the Display network because your budget was low. For example, if your Search Lost IS (budget) is 50 percent, your ads were eligible but did not show to 50 percent of the user searches because of your budget.

- Sort your campaigns by **Search Lost IS (budget)** or **Display Lost IS (budget)** columns to see which campaigns are losing the greatest share of impressions.

Campaigns | Ad groups | Settings | Ads | Keywords | Ad extensions | Dimensions | Display Network

All enabled campaigns | Segment | Filter | Columns | Search

+ New campaign | Edit | Automate | Labels

Campaign	Budget	Status	Enhanced	Clicks	Impr.	CTR	Avg. CPC	Avg. Pos.	Cost / conv. (1-per-click)	Cost	Search Lost IS (budget)
Campaign 1	$122.00/day	Limited by budget	Legacy	256	19,796	1.29%	$8.96	4.8	$52.12	$2,293.28	15.77%
Campaign 2	$35.00/day	Limited by budget	Legacy	50	1,675	2.99%	$9.20	4.1	$34.49	$459.96	12.08%

- Next, review your **Cost/Conv.** data for all campaigns that have high percentages of lost impressions due to budget. If a campaign is within your target **Cost/Conv.** but is losing impression share, consider increasing budget.
- Segment data by hour of the day to analyze how your coverage varies throughout the day or by device to analyze coverage for computers, tablets, and mobile devices.

Campaign	Budget	Status	Enhanced	Clicks	Impr.	CTR	Avg. CPC	Cost / conv. (1-per-click)	Cost	Avg. Pos.	Search Lost IS (budget)
7				1	297	0.34%	$16.36	$0.00	$16.36	4.5	6.81%
8				4	510	0.78%	$7.84	$0.00	$31.37	4.9	7.56%
9				14	974	1.44%	$9.36	$26.21	$131.03	4.9	6.91%
10				17	1,485	1.14%	$7.37	$125.21	$125.21	4.9	5.84%
11				45	2,223	2.02%	$8.78	$131.74	$395.23	4.8	2.62%
12				42	2,801	1.50%	$8.76	$40.86	$367.71	5	2.60%
13				23	2,566	0.90%	$9.70	$37.18	$223.07	5.1	4.74%
14				33	2,621	1.26%	$9.86	$65.10	$325.52	4.7	5.75%
15				18	1,701	1.06%	$10.84	$97.58	$195.17	4.9	15.39%
16				13	1,437	0.90%	$9.27	$60.26	$120.52	4.5	19.21%
17				11	739	1.49%	$10.00	$55.01	$110.02	4.5	30.14%
18				9	637	1.41%	$7.03	$21.09	$63.27	4.7	33.51%
19				9	396	2.27%	$7.94	$35.71	$71.42	4.5	44.07%
20				3	282	1.06%	$7.57	$11.35	$22.70	4.5	50.19%
21				5	381	1.31%	$4.62	$23.12	$23.12	4.7	46.72%
22				5	146	3.42%	$7.58	$0.00	$37.90	5.1	64.22%

Search Lost IS (rank) and Display Lost IS (rank):

- The **Search Lost IS (rank)** and **Display Lost IS (rank)** columns help you identify impressions you're missing out on due to low ad rank. For example, if your **Display Lost IS (rank)** number is high, such as 62%, this means that your ad was eligible but did not show on Google's Display network 62% of the time due to low ad rank.
- The actions you can take to improve lost impression share due to ad rank include raising your bids and improving your Quality Score. However, if your **Cost/Conv.** is outside your target CPA, raising your bids is not recommended. In that case, focus on improving Quality Score by refining structure, keywords, and ads.

Search Exact match IS:

Search Exact match IS helps you understand your impression share for just the keywords you have chosen. If you are using broad match keywords, your ads could be showing on variations of the keywords you have entered.

Sort campaigns or ad groups by **Search Exact match IS** and focus efforts where the number is low. A high number means you're getting high quality clicks on keywords you obviously found relevant enough to add to your campaigns.

If the number is low, run a search query report to analyze what queries are triggering clicks. Add the relevant queries as keywords and add negative terms to weed out irrelevant clicks.

How it works...

Impression Share (**IS**) is the number of impressions you received divided by impressions you were eligible to receive in your AdWords campaigns and ad groups. IS helps you analyze your share of voice with your current settings (such as your location targeting) and Quality Score.

Available IS metrics include:

Search Impression share: The percentage of time your ads were shown out of the times that your ads were eligible to show on the Search network.

Search Exact Match IS: The percentage of time your ads were shown for queries that exactly matched your keywords divided by exact match impressions you were eligible for.

Search Lost IS (rank): Search impressions you are missing out on due to low ad rank.

Search Lost IS (budget): How often your campaign's ads did not show on Google's Search network because of a limited budget.

- **Display Impression share**: The percentage of time your ads were shown out of the times that your ads were eligible to show on the Display network.
- **Display Lost IS (rank)**: Display impressions you are missing out on due to low ad rank.
- **Display Lost IS (budget)**: How often your campaign's ads did not show on Google's Display network because of a limited budget.

See also

- The *Customizing columns to personalize data views* recipe
- The *Analyzing relative CTR to benchmark display performance* recipe in *Chapter 10, Running Display Ads*

11
Optimizing Performance

In this chapter, we will cover the following topics:

- Improving relevance and Quality Score
- Improving ad rank
- Changing keyword match types
- Scheduling ads to run during key days and times
- Expanding your keyword list
- Analyzing ad copy performance and picking top performers
- Adjusting budgets to maximize traffic and conversions
- Tips to increase traffic
- Running search term reports to optimize keywords
- Optimizing bids for ROI
- Optimizing keywords to improve ROI
- Excluding IP addresses from seeing your ads
- Optimizing your landing pages

Introduction

The most successful advertisers continuously refine and optimize their campaigns to keep them profitable. Your initial keywords and ads will need to be regularly updated, paused, and refined to stay on top of the latest trends in your market. Also, you'll need to adjust bids and other settings to keep on target with your goals such as a specific ad position or CPA.

Improving relevance and Quality Score

AdWords rewards advertisers who choose relevant keywords and write compelling ads with good Quality Scores. The better your Quality Scores, the less you'll need to pay for each click, resulting in more profits for you. This ecosystem evolved to benefit users, Google, and advertisers. If the ads on Google were irrelevant and of poor quality, users would get frustrated and not click on them, and Google would lose revenue. From an advertiser's perspective, when users click on irrelevant ads, they tend to leave your website, costing you money and not contributing to your bottom line. AdWords was designed to encourage high-quality ads, and as an advertiser you'll reap many benefits from optimizing them to improve relevance.

Getting ready

First, check your Quality Scores to identify low quality keywords to focus on.

1. Go to the **Campaigns** tab.
2. Click on the **Keywords** tab.
3. Go to **Columns** and choose **Customize columns**.
4. From the **Attributes** section, choose **Qual. score**.

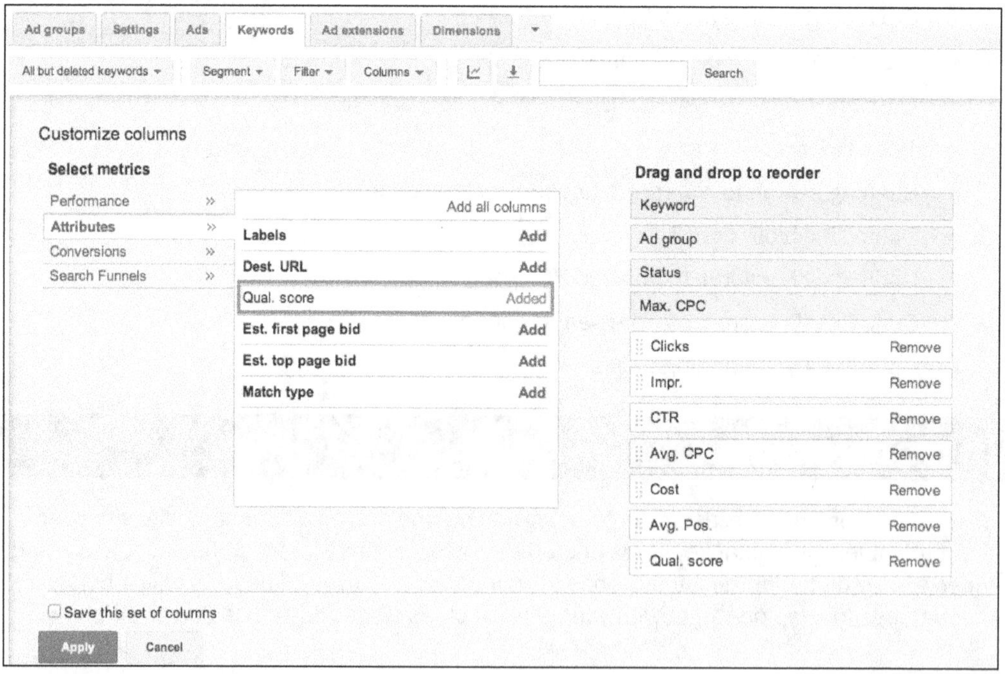

5. Click on **Apply** and you will see an extra column with your Quality Scores.
6. In your **Keywords** tab, sort the **Qual. score** column to review low Quality Score keywords. Generally, Quality Score 1 to 3 is considered low, 4 to 6 is average with room for improvement, 7 to 9 is good, and 10 is considered great.
7. Another way you can identify low-quality keywords is with filters. Create a keyword filter to see all keywords that are below a certain Quality Score. Download this report to have an easy to refer to summary of all keywords you'll need to focus on.

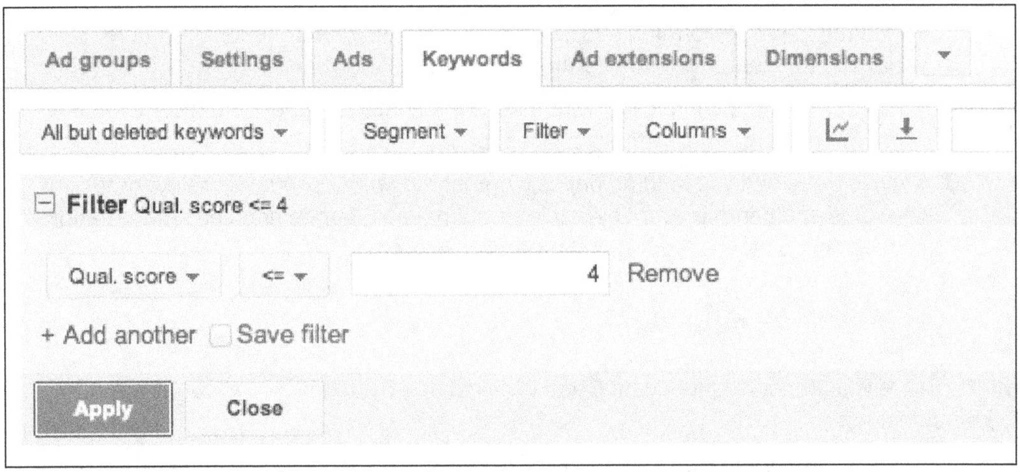

How to do it...

To improve your Quality Scores, follow these 10 tips:

1. Start with low Quality Score keywords that get the most impressions. This is where you'll have the biggest impact.
2. Re-organize your keywords into more tightly themed ad groups. If a keyword has a low Quality Score, try moving it to its own ad group with more specific ad text and its own negative keywords.
3. Your broad match keywords may be getting expanded to irrelevant variations. Try changing them to a more specific match type.
4. Add negative keywords to eliminate irrelevant impressions and increase your CTR. For example, add `free` as a negative keyword to eliminate someone looking for free products and services online. Run a search terms report to see what queries are triggering clicks and get new negative keyword ideas.

5. Some of your low quality keywords may not be relevant to your website. If a keyword has a very low Quality Score and rarely shows, it could be negatively impacting the rest of your account. Consider deleting it.
6. Write new ads for your low Quality Score keywords, placing each keyword in your ad text, ideally in your headline.
7. Test multiple ad versions to see which one resonates better with your customers. Experiment with different calls-to-action, promotions, and ways to describe the unique benefits of your products and services.
8. Pause the lower performing ads in each ad group, if you are testing multiple variations to ensure that ads getting a better CTR show more often.
9. Try implementing dynamic keyword insertion to have AdWords automatically insert your keywords into the ad titles or description lines.
10. Choose more specific landing pages. Your landing page should be relevant to your keywords and contain your keywords on the page. If it does not, consider creating new landing pages for your most important keywords.

How it works...

Quality Score is a measure of relevance and is calculated by taking into account the following factors:

- **Your keyword's CTR**: Your CTR is like an online voting system; people in the search auction vote on how relevant your ads are with their clicks.
- **Your display URL's CTR**: Your display URL's past CTR affects your Quality Scores.
- **How relevant your keywords are**: Some keywords you choose will be more relevant to your business than others. If you sell snowboards, but would like to run on a keyword like "snow," a generic term that's not as relevant to your business, you will receive a much lower Quality Score. Pick specific keywords that clearly describe your products and stay away from general keywords that could apply to many different businesses.
- **The relevance of your ads to your keywords**: Your ads need to include your keywords in the ad text. If you have too many keywords for them all to be reflected in your ad copy, create additional, smaller ad groups. When a searched **keywords** is included in an ad text, that term is highlighted by Google in your ad, helping it stand out even more on the Google search results page.
- **Landing page quality**: The keywords you choose should be included in your ad text and further mirrored on your landing page. In addition to your landing page being relevant to your keywords, it also needs to be transparent and easy to navigate.

- **Historical account performance**: Advertisers who continue to choose poor quality keywords will receive low Quality Scores when adding new keywords. This system helps Google discourage advertisers who continue to choose irrelevant keywords and encourage advertisers who create relevant, quality keywords and ads.
- **Performance in the regions you are targeting**: The regions you target via your campaign settings page will affect your Quality Scores.
- **Performance on the devices you are targeting**: You may get different Quality Scores on mobile and tablet devices, if your keywords perform differently depending on device.

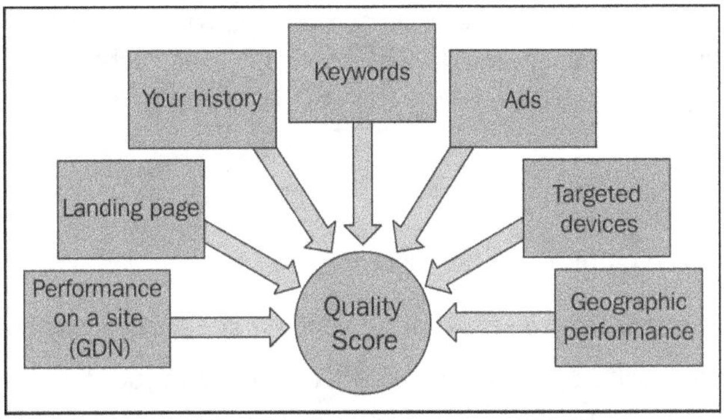

Quality Score is dynamic and is calculated every time a search triggers your ad. In order to achieve better Quality Scores, you'll need to focus on tying together all of the various elements that comprise Quality Score. Increasing relevance helps you achieve a better ad rank and pay less for each click. The Quality Score algorithm is designed to reward relevancy and encourage advertisers to create high-quality accounts, which will in turn help you achieve better ROI with AdWords.

There's more...

The more general your keywords are, the more difficult it will be to obtain a high Quality Score for them, even after following all of the recommended AdWords best practices. In such cases, you'll need to weigh if the lower Quality Score is worth the traffic and conversions you get from these keywords. Keep in mind that if you continue to choose low-quality keywords, this will hurt your overall account performance.

See also

- The *Generating negative keywords* recipe in *Chapter 5, Creating Relevant Keywords*
- The *Running search term reports to optimize keywords* recipe

Improving ad rank

Your ad position is going to heavily impact visibility and traffic, with the top-ranked ads receiving the most clicks. Obviously, the more competitive your keywords are, the more costly it will be to have your ads show in the #1 spot. However, there are specific short- and long-term strategies that will help you obtain the best possible ad rank.

Getting ready

First, isolate the keywords that are not ranked optimally:

- Identify keywords that are not showing on the first page of Google's search results
- If you have a specific ad position in mind, use filters in your **Keywords** tab to see which keywords are not meeting this criteria

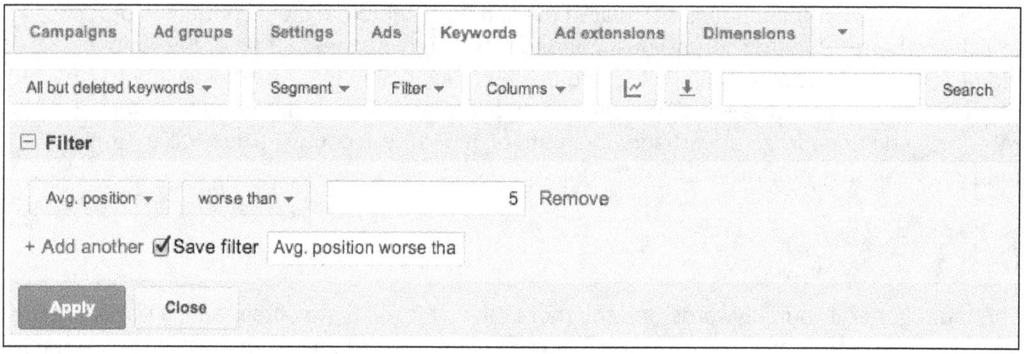

Quickly diagnose your keywords to figure out if they are showing or are restricted by Quality Scores and bids. On your **Keywords** tab, click on **Keyword details** and select **Diagnose keywords**.

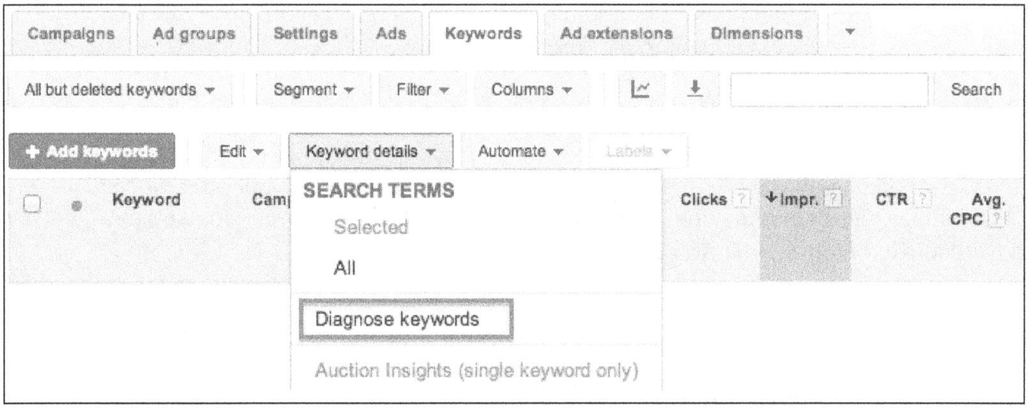

How to do it...

To improve your ad rank, you can:

1. Increase your bid
2. Improve your Quality Score

Increasing your bids is the easy fix short-term solution. However, continuing to increase how much you spend on each click when your ad rank slips is not going to be profitable in the long run.

The long-term strategy to improving ad position is to raise your Quality Scores. To improve Quality Score, start with the following:

1. Refine your campaign structure, breaking out related keywords into their own ad groups, which will help you write more relevant ads.
2. Refine ads with more compelling ad copy, using keywords in ad text.
3. Pause lower CTR ads if you are running multiple ad variations.
4. Add negative keywords to weed out impressions that are not relevant and are weighing down your CTR.

How it works...

Your ad rank determines your ad position, or where your ads show in relation to other advertisers. The ad rank formula consists of your Quality Score and your bid:

Ad Rank = Quality Score x Max CPC

Ad rank is calculated each time your ad enters the ad auction. This means that for each new query your ads could appear in a different position.

There's more...

The higher your Quality Score, the less you'll need to bid to maintain your ad rank. This strategy helps AdWords ensure high quality ads on Google.com and encourages advertisers to optimize their accounts.

See also

- The *Improving relevance and Quality Score* recipe

Changing keyword match types

Keyword match types control who sees your ads and how the keywords you have chosen are expanded to match other relevant queries. Using too many of your keywords in the most restrictive match types can limit your traffic, while using too many broad keywords can generate some or a lot of irrelevant clicks.

Getting ready

Determine which keywords you might want to change match types for. Here are a couple of common edits advertisers make:

- Broad match keywords with low Quality Scores and no conversions. Change to phrase or exact match to restrict variations.
- Exact match keywords with no impressions. Change to more general match type to broaden reach.

How to do it...

To change a single keyword's match type:

1. Go to the **Campaigns** tab.
2. Click on the **Keywords** tab or click on a specific campaign and ad group first.

3. In your keyword table, click on the keyword you'd like to edit. Before you can proceed, you might need to agree to the system warning by clicking on **Yes, I understand**. The system warns you that if you edit a keyword, it will be deleted and treated as a new keyword in AdWords. You can check the **Don't show this message again** checkbox so you don't have to see this warning each time you edit a keyword.

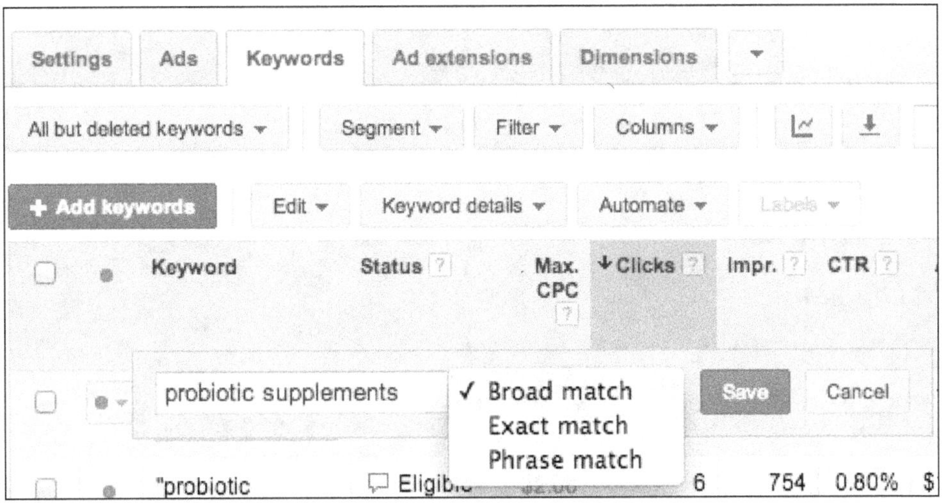

4. Next, you'll be able to choose a different match type from the drop-down menu. In this screenshot, we are choosing to change a broad keyword to a more specific match type.
5. Click on **Save**.

To change match types for multiple keywords:

1. From your **Keywords** tab, check all of the keywords you'd like to edit.
2. From the **Edit** drop-down menu, choose **Change match type**.
3. Choose what you'd like to change your match type from and to.
4. Since changing a match type deletes the old keyword and creates a new one, you have the option to create duplicate versions of the keywords you have selected and add them in the new match types. To use that option, check **Duplicate keywords and change match type in duplicates**.
5. You can preview your changes before they go live by clicking on **Preview changes**.

6. Click on **Make changes**.

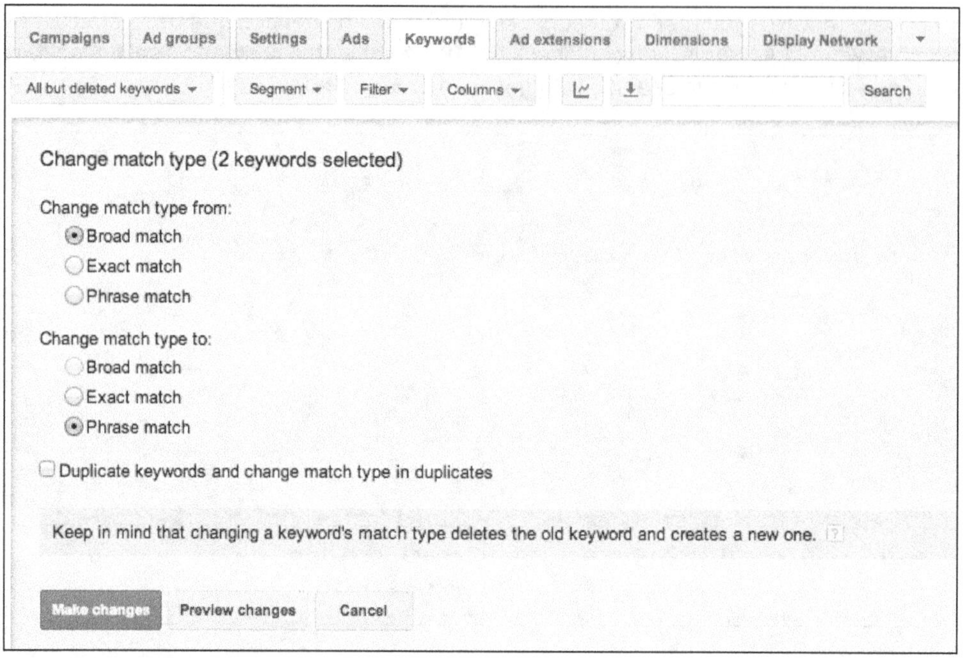

How it works...

Changing a keyword's match type deletes the old keyword and creates a brand new keyword in your account. It also resets a keyword's history to `0`, but performance data will still be available for all deleted keywords.

See also

- The *Improving relevance and Quality Score* recipe
- The *Optimizing keywords to improve ROI* recipe

Scheduling ads to run during key days and times

Many advertisers choose to run AdWords campaigns only during hours when they have customer support available. If you have a limited budget, you might want to focus your ad budgets on days and times your customers are most likely to be looking for you.

Getting ready

Determine if ad scheduling is necessary and appropriate for your business. Advertisers that may benefit from this include businesses that operate primarily during specific hours. For example, a website with customer support available to take calls during business hours only, or a pizza delivery service that only delivers evenings.

Review performance by day and hour of day, keeping in mind that you will see fewer clicks and impressions during less busy times, so you have focus on conversion rates and CPA instead. Some advertisers get great conversion rates during off peak hours, late at night and in the early mornings, when fewer advertisers are competing in the ad auction.

Keep in mind how your customers interact with you. If you rely on calls and only have customer support during specific hours, make sure your ads are focused on when you have the proper support available.

How to do it...

To enable ad scheduling:

1. Go to the **Campaigns** tab.
2. Click on the specific campaign you'd like to edit.
3. Go to the **Settings** tab.
4. Select **Ad schedule**.

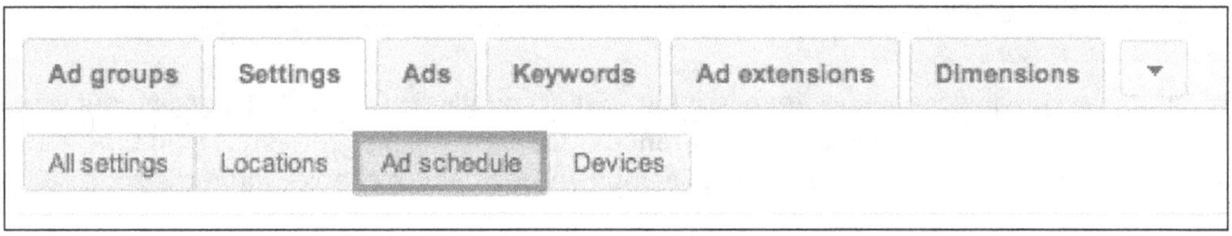

5. Click on **Edit ad schedule**.
6. Click on **+ Create custom schedule**.
7. From the drop-down menu, choose to create a schedule for all days, Monday through Friday, or specific days of the week, and then set your hours.
8. Click on **+Add** to add additional parameters.

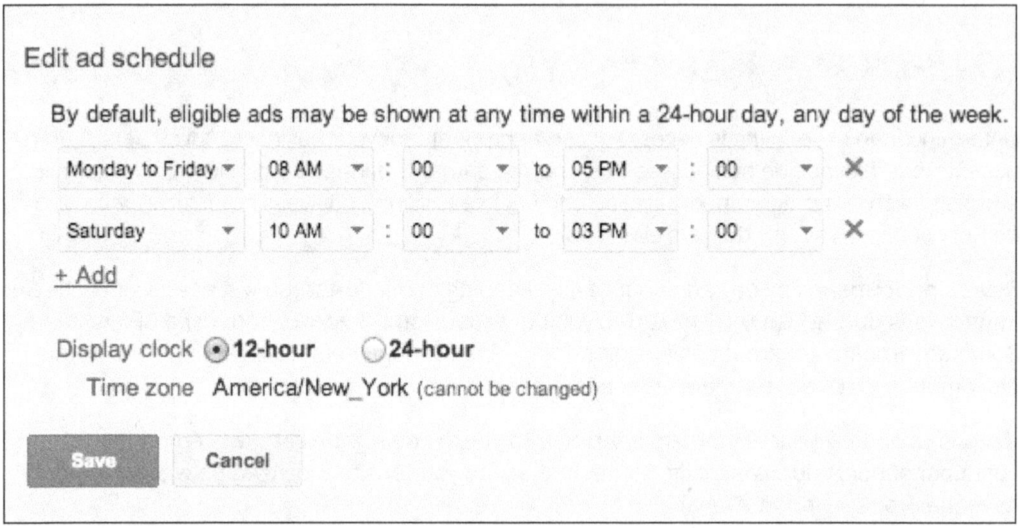

9. Click on **Save**.

How it works...

Ad scheduling helps you control when your ads appear to potential customers. Ad scheduling is set at the campaign level, which means that it applies to all keywords and ads within a single campaign. By default, AdWords campaigns are set to run all days of the week and all hours of the day.

There's more...

When you set up ad scheduling, keep in mind your account's time zone. You can find out your time zone by going to **My Account** | **Preferences**. AdWords will also reference your time zone as you create a custom schedule for each campaign. You cannot change your time zone.

See also

- The *Analyzing days and times ads perform best* recipe in *Chapter 10, Reporting and Analysis*

Expanding your keyword list

Expanding your keywords will be one of your main strategies to increase clicks as well as conversions. Just as markets evolve and search patterns change, your keywords also need to be updated in order not to become stagnant. Here we will discuss several tools you can use to build up and refresh your keyword list.

Getting ready

Review your website and compare your list of products and services to your AdWords account. Are your current keywords covering all of the categories you specialize in? Are there other ways to describe some of your key offerings? Who are your main competitors and are they doing PPC?

How to do it...

To expand your keyword list, try one of the following strategies.

Automated keyword suggestions

To see automated keyword ideas relevant to your website, follow these steps:

1. Click on the **Campaigns** tab.
2. Go into a specific campaign and ad group.
3. Clock on **+ Add keywords** above your ad group's current keyword summary.
4. AdWords will suggest new sample keywords based on a scan of your website grouped into related categories.

5. Click to expand each category and review the suggested keywords. If you like a keyword, click on **Add** to move it to the **Add keywords** box. Do not simply add all of the automated suggestions, as not all of them will be specific enough. You as a business owner know your audience best and should pick and choose only the keywords that are the most relevant. Make sure that you are not adding keywords that may be already present in your other campaigns or ad groups.

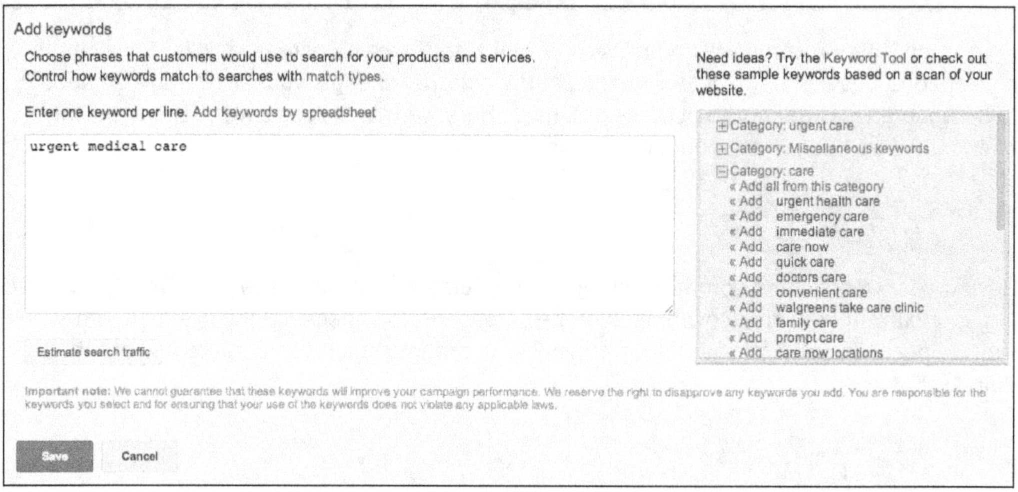

6. Click on **Save** after adding all of the relevant keywords.

Search terms report

Review your search terms report regularly and add any relevant keywords that resulted in clicks and conversions. Click on **Add as keyword** recipe after viewing your search terms to add them to your account.

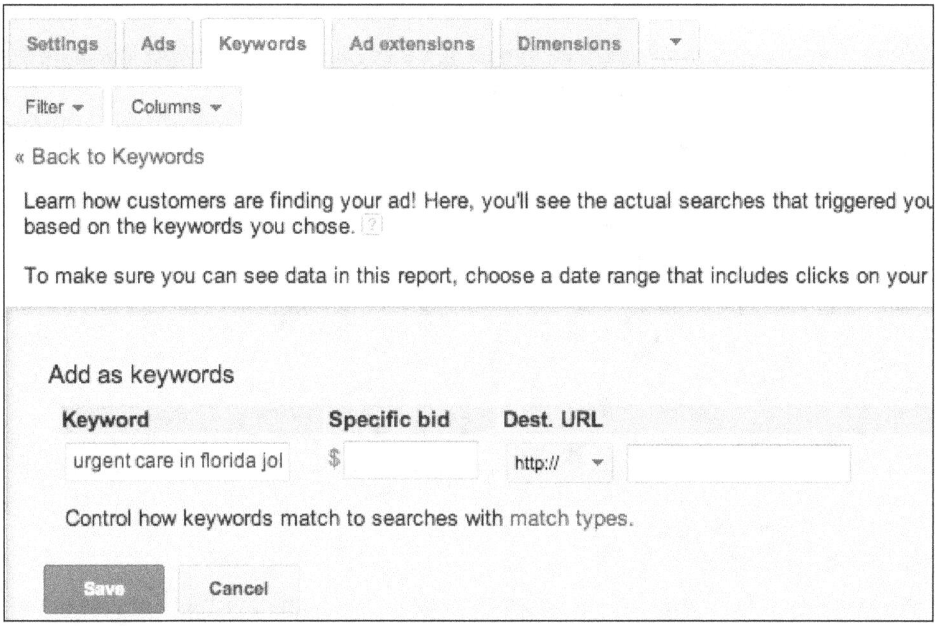

Competitor keywords

Use websites such as spyfu.com to see what keywords your competitors' ads are appearing on and to download their keyword lists. Enter a competitor's URL into the search box to uncover profitable keywords you missed.

You can download a competitor's full keyword list, sort, and filter it, or export it to an AdWords-friendly format. The tool can even organize a domain's keywords into targeted ad groups so you have less manual work to do.

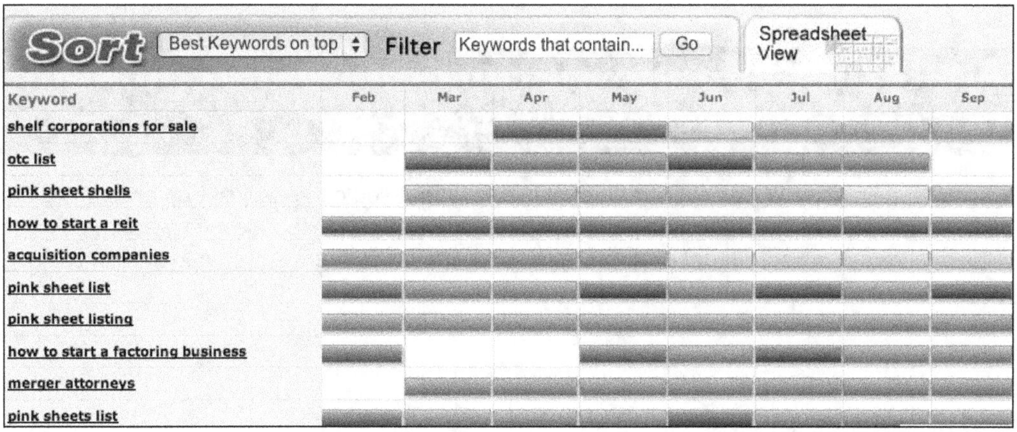

Google's keyword tool

In addition to entering your own domain into Google's keyword tool, try typing in a competitor's website and see what keywords are being recommended.

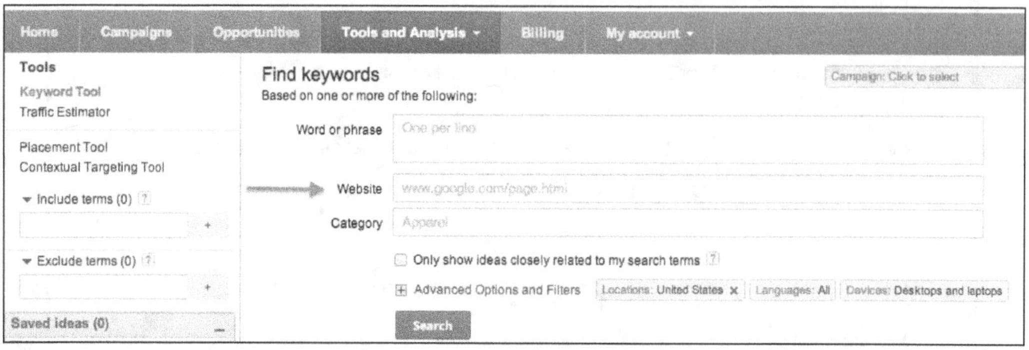

How it works...

Adding new relevant keywords to your AdWords account will help drive more impressions and clicks. With new and unique keywords, you can capitalize on previously untapped opportunities to drive new leads and sales.

See also

- The *Running search term reports to optimize keywords* recipe
- The *Finding relevant keywords* recipe in *Chapter 5, Creating Relevant Keywords*
- The *Analyzing competitor keywords from spyfu.com and similar tools* recipe in *Chapter 5, Creating Relevant Keywords*

Analyzing ad copy performance and picking top performers

A big advantage of AdWords over traditional media is that you can easily set up and run multiple ad versions in just minutes. Even better, you'll get fast responses via real-time votes or clicks from your actual customers on what speaks to them so you can fine tune your message to reach even more qualified visitors.

Getting ready

In order to compare ads against one another, you'll need to set up multiple ads within an ad group. Create no more than 2 to 3 ads per ad group while you are testing. Let your ads accumulate some impressions and clicks before you make decisions about the effectiveness of each ad.

How long you'll need to wait before analyzing your tests will vary greatly based on how many impressions and clicks you receive, which will partly depend on your budgets. The general rule of thumb is to have at least 1000 impressions per ad copy before analyzing performance.

Set your campaign's ad rotation to rotate evenly to get an even split in impressions to each ad.

How to do it...

To analyze multiple ads within an ad group:

1. Go to the **Campaigns** tab.
2. Click on the campaign you're looking to analyze and choose an ad group.
3. Click on the **Ads** tab.
4. If the ads you are analyzing are low in impressions and clicks, allow for more time, until you have ~1000 impressions per ad version.
5. Review multiple metrics, rather than basing your decision on just one metric, such as only CTR or just conversion rates. The following table shows an example of two ads being tested within an ad group:

Ad	Clicks	Impress-ions	CTR	Avg CPC	Cost	Avg pos	Conver-sions	Cost/ Cov	Cov. rate
1	6,804	38,889	17.50%	$0.39	$2,638	1	567	$4.65	8.33%
2	5,588	34,095	16.39%	$0.54	$3,030	1	466	$6.50	8.34%

6. In the preceding example, Ad 1 is the winner. It has a higher CTR, lower average CPC, and even though it's converting at about the same rate as Ad 1 it costs less to convert a visitor through Ad 1.
7. In some instances, you'll see clear winners, such as ads that are clearly getting a better CTR and are converting at better rates. However, the ad with the best CTR will not always have a better conversion rate, and you'll need to review other metrics to determine your next steps.

8. If an ad is getting a high CTR but no conversions, it might not pre-qualify visitors enough and it might in fact be too appealing. Pausing it might lower your CTR, but if another ad is converting better and your goal is to have more conversions, pausing the high CTR ad without conversions might be a cost effective decision.
9. Once you determine a winner and a loser, pause the lower performing ad.
10. Some tests will have a major positive impact and others will fall flat. Continue to add new ad text variations to keep your message fresh and learn about what your customers will find compelling.

How it works...

Pausing low-performing ads helps you get more impressions and clicks on ads that work better. Even if you turn on **Optimize for clicks** or **Optimize for conversions** ad rotation settings, your low performers will continue to show occasionally. Figuring out which ads are meeting your goals and pausing the ones that don't ensures that the ads that work are shown to more users.

See also

- The *Creating effective ads* recipe in *Chapter 6, Writing Compelling Ads*
- The *Split testing ad copy* recipe in *Chapter 6, Writing Compelling Ads*

Adjusting budgets to maximize traffic and conversions

Most advertisers, except for large companies with unlimited funds, have specific budgets for AdWords that will need to be managed and redistributed among the different campaigns. This section discusses the key considerations and data to review as you decide where to focus your funds.

Getting ready

Keep in mind your overall ad budgets. Also, review your current performance and outline your goals. Are your conversion rates and cost per conversion acceptable and you'd like to get more such traffic? Or, are your current CPAs a bit outside your comfort zone and you need to improve on that?

How to do it...

1. First, determine which campaigns are limited by budgets.
2. In your main **Campaigns** tabs, some campaigns may show a **Limited by budget** message, indicating that they could earn more impressions and clicks if you raised your daily budget. Sort your campaigns by the **Status** column to see which campaigns are limited by budget.
3. You can also review competitive metrics **Search Lost IS (budget)** and **Display Lost IS (budget)** to find out which campaigns are losing impression share due to low budgets. Customize your column views to see those metrics and sort the data to highlight campaigns where ads are not capturing all possible impressions. The higher the percent, the more impression share you are losing due to insufficient funds.
4. Next, analyze conversion rates and cost/conversion for each campaign that's limited by budget.
5. If a campaign is within your target CPA and is losing impression share, move some funds over from a less profitable campaign.
6. If a campaign is outside your target CPA and it's limited by budget, it might not make sense to raise its budget, since this would further increase your overall CPA.

Here is an example of how you might want to redistribute a budget of $100/day based on performance with a CPA goal of $10:

	Current budget	**Limited by budget**	**CPA**	**Recommended budget action**
Campaign #1	$30	Yes	$10	Increase budget
Campaign #2	$30	No	$9	Leave budget as is
Campaign #3	$30	Yes	$15	Decrease budget, move funds to Campaign #1

How it works...

With AdWords, you have the flexibility to adjust budgets across your different campaigns at any time and as often as you would like. Performance varies and shifts all the time, which is why budgets should be monitored and adjusted regularly to maximize returns.

There's more...

You can change your budgets in bulk if you have a large number of campaigns that will need to be adjusted. After selecting your campaigns, click on the **Edit** button and choose **Change budget**.

Then, choose to set your budgets to a specific amount, or increase or decrease budgets across selected campaigns by a specific percent. You can set an upper or lower budget limit to make sure your budget changes are not going above or below what you are comfortable with.

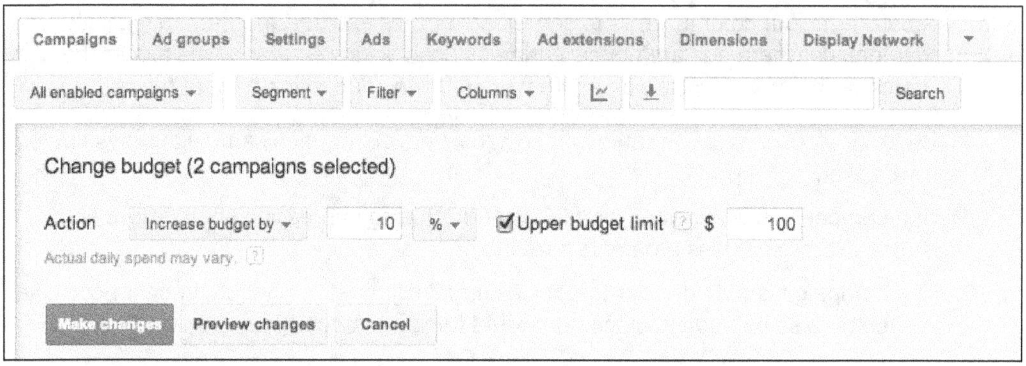

See also

- The *Optimizing bids for ROI* recipe
- The *Using impression share metrics to increase conversions* recipe in *Chapter 10, Reporting and Analysis*

Tips to increase traffic

If you're getting great results from AdWords, chances are you would like more traffic. Be cautious as you expand and implement the proposed strategies, focusing on a select few at a time to keep your ROI steady.

Getting ready

Review your current campaigns and figure out which ones are meeting your ROI goals. You'll want to start your optimization efforts there.

Catalog your current strategies and campaigns:

- Are your campaigns targeting all of the relevant locations?
- Are you advertising all of your current products and services?
- Have you tried running ads on Google's Display network?

How to do it...

To increase traffic, try the following strategies:

1. Increase your budgets on campaigns that are restricted by budgets and not showing ads as often as possible. Check lost impression share and move more funds to campaigns that have high Lost IS (budget) percentages. Lost IS (budget) metrics show you how often your campaign's ad did not show due to a limited budget.

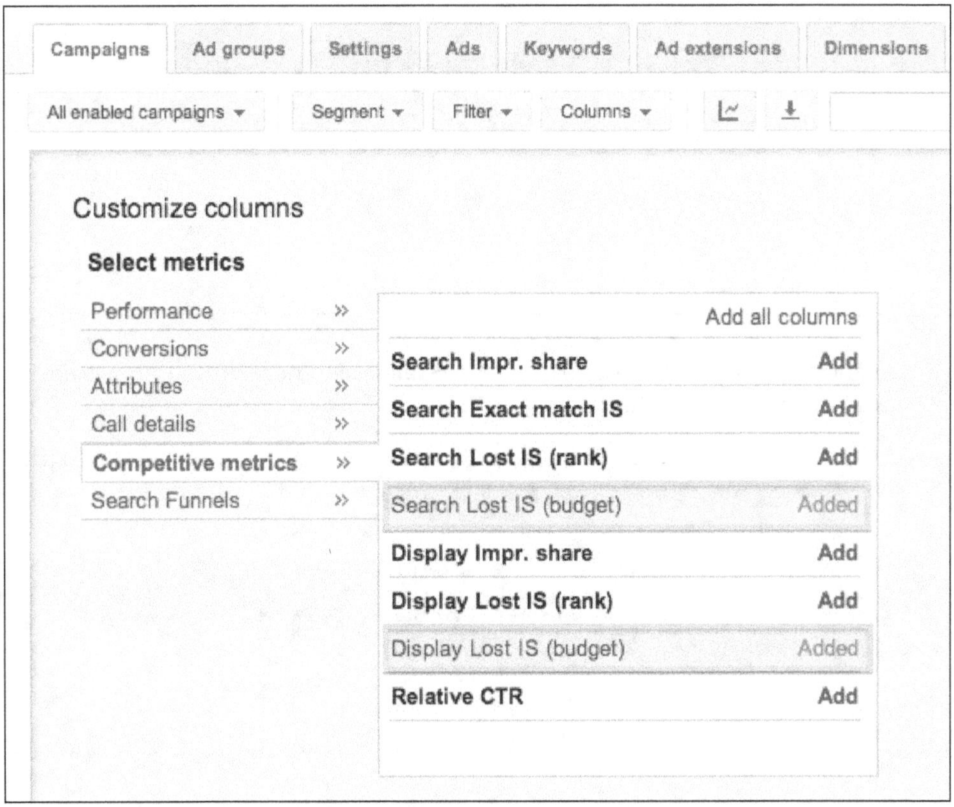

2. Raise bids on ad groups that are losing impressions share (Lost IS (rank) metrics) due to low ad rank. Focus on ad groups that are generating conversions within your CPA goal.

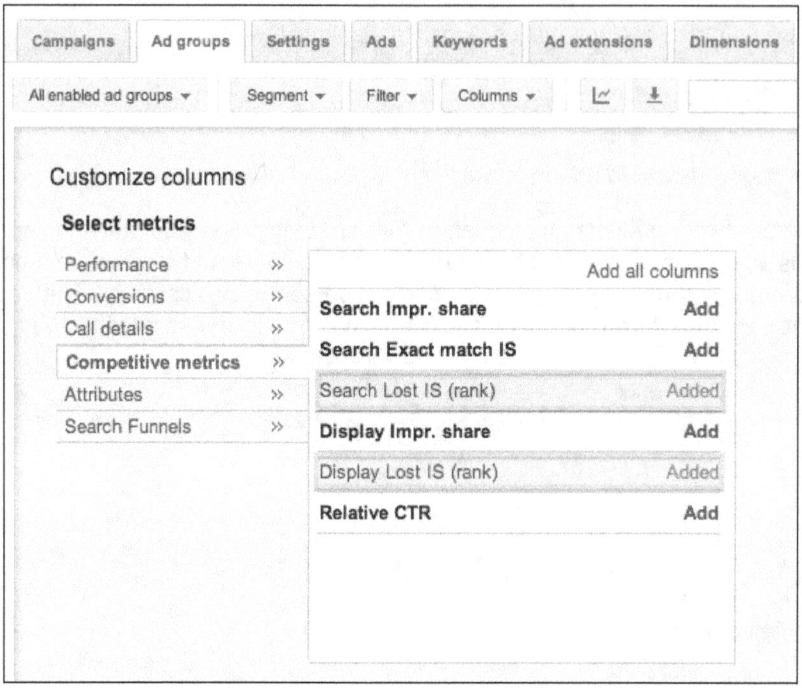

3. Change your campaign's ad delivery from **Standard** to **Accelerated,** so ads are displayed as soon as possible.

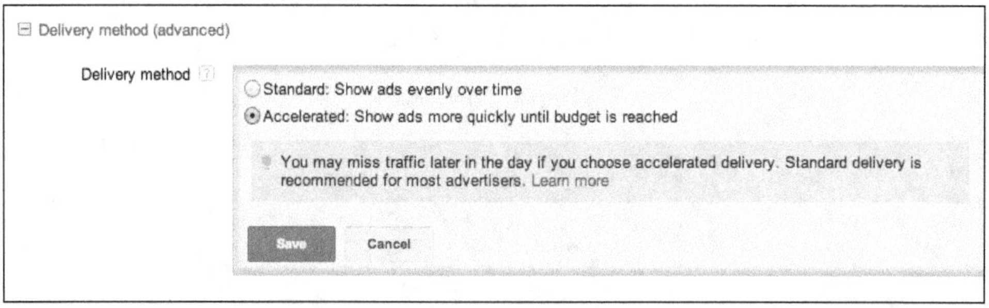

4. Expand your keywords with additional relevant terms. Create new ad groups for the new keywords to stay organized and keep your campaigns themed and your Quality Scores high.

5. Add new campaigns and ad groups for products and services you are not currently advertising. For example, if you sell car parts and are only advertising your Honda car parts through AdWords, add campaigns for additional brands you feature, such as Toyota or Mercedes.
6. Test the various targeting options available through Google's Display network. If you are already running display campaigns, consider adding some of the less frequently used campaign types. For example, you can target display ads through interest categories to reach users visiting pages about specific topics.

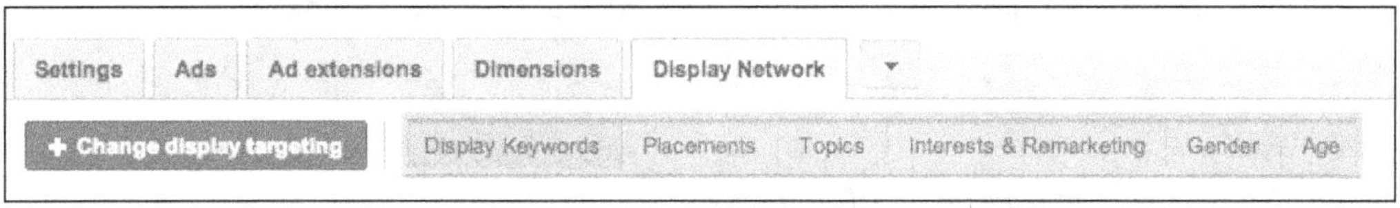

7. Consider expanding your locations to additional relevant geographic locations where your customers are located as well as targeting additional appropriate languages.

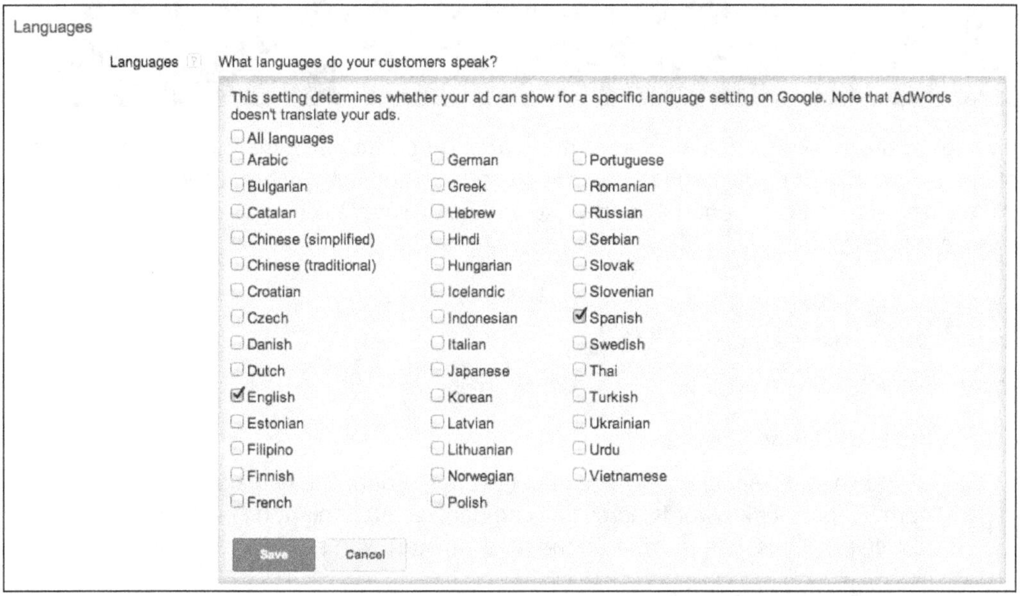

How it works...

Raising your bids and budgets helps you achieve a better ad rank and increases your ad delivery with your ads showing more throughout the day.

Adding new campaigns and keywords helps to increase your impressions and clicks through new terms that you were not previously bidding on.

Loosening some of your campaign settings, such as location and language targets, can help you reach additional customers not captured through your previous settings.

See also

- The *Expanding your keyword list* recipe
- The *Using impression share metrics to increase conversions* recipe in *Chapter 10, Reporting and Analysis*

Running search term reports to optimize keywords

If you are using keywords in match types other than exact, your ads are showing on a number of other variations that you should be aware of. You can find out what these variations are through the search terms report and use it to add new relevant keywords or exclude the irrelevant queries.

How to do it...

To run a search terms report:

1. Go to the **Campaigns** tab.
2. Go down into a specific search campaign or ad group. You can also run a search terms report for keywords across all campaigns, but it might be overwhelming and difficult to focus. It is recommended that you start with specific campaigns instead.
3. Go to the **Keywords** tab.
4. This recently changed in AdWords. This sentence should read "Click on the **Details** button and select **All** under **SEARCH TERMS**.

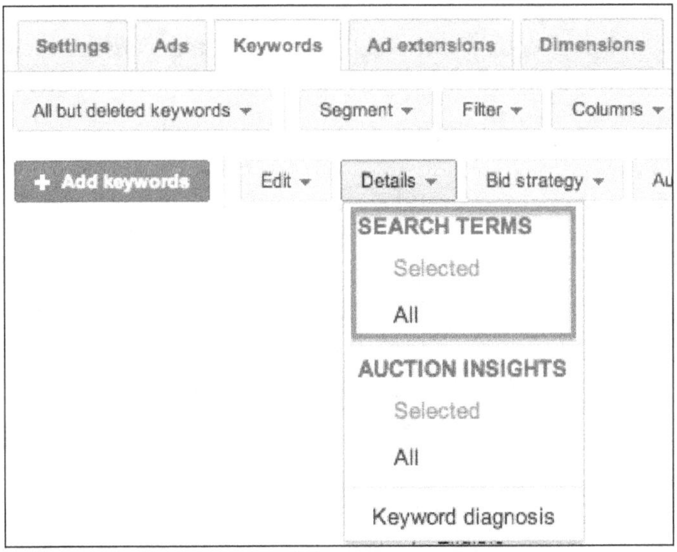

5. Next, you'll see a list of search terms that triggered your ads as well as CTRs and other performance data.
6. Column **Added/Excluded** tells you if a keyword is already a part of your keyword list (**Added**), if you previously excluded it (**Excluded**), or if it triggered your ads but you have yet to add or exclude it (**None**).

Once you know what search terms are triggering your ads, you have three options:

1. If a keyword has solid performance, such as a high CTR or has generated conversions, add it to your account. You can do so easily from within the AdWords interface by selecting the high performing keyword and clicking on the **Add as keyword** button above the report.
2. If a keyword is irrelevant to your business, has low CTR, or has not generated any conversions despite high costs, exclude it from your keyword list. Be careful not to use negatives that could prevent your relevant keywords from showing. Select the low performing keyword and click on the **Add as negative keyword** button. You will need to select whether the exclusion should apply to just the individual ad group or to an entire campaign.

3. You can choose to download your search terms into an Excel file or other convenient format as well as schedule it as an ongoing report that can be e-mailed to you.

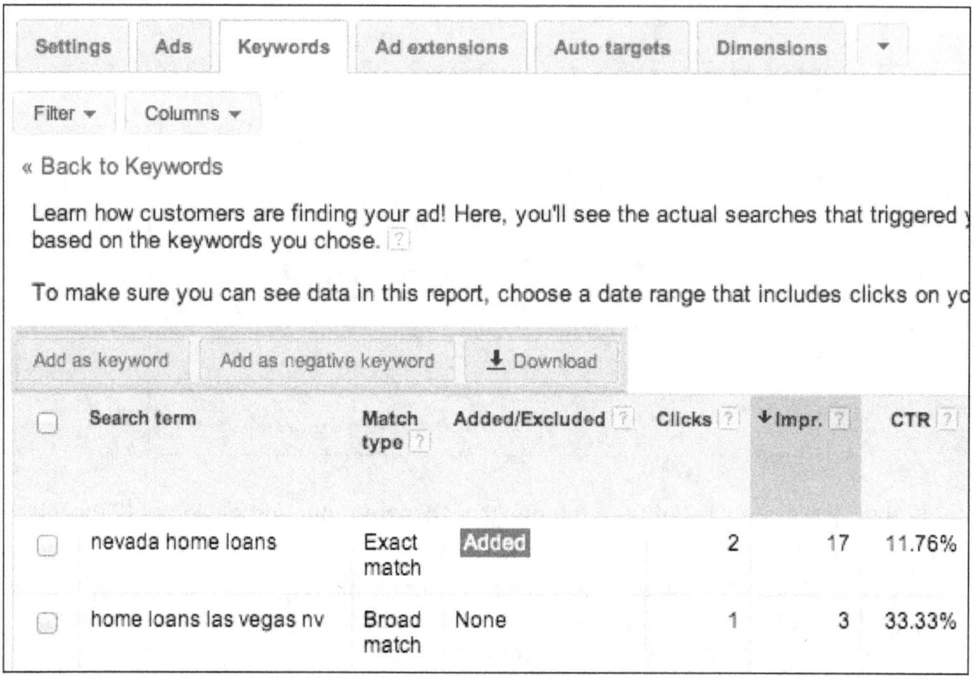

How it works...

The search terms report shows you the exact queries that triggered your ads and led to the clicks. It is available for searches performed on Google.com and Google's Search Partners.

Search terms reports are not real time; they have a one-day delay before you see the data. You will only see impression data if a search term generated at least one click in the last 30 days.

There's more...

If you'd like to eliminate clutter in your search terms report and only focus on keywords that you have not added or excluded already, you can create a filter after viewing your keyword details. Saving this filter will allow you to access it again the next time you log in.

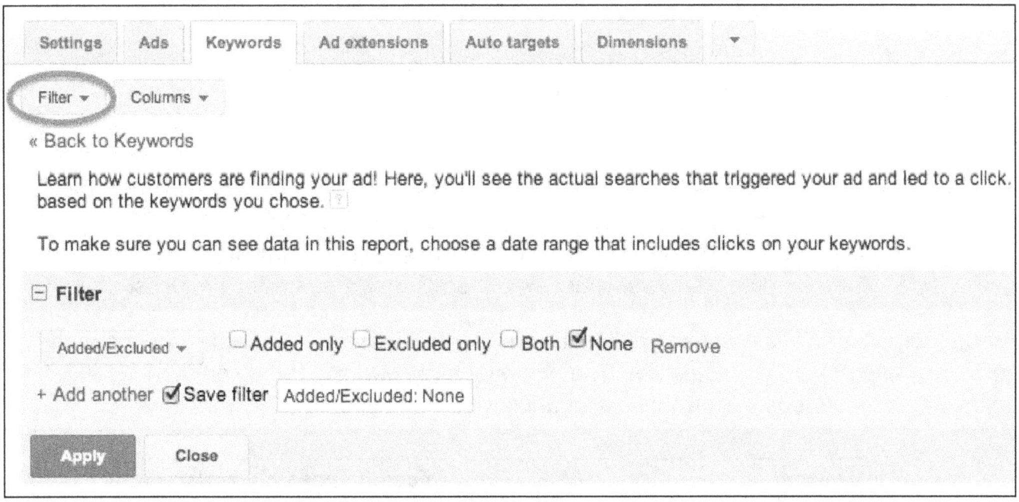

See also

- The *Using keyword matching options effectively* recipe in *Chapter 5, Creating Relevant Keywords*
- The *Generating negative keywords* recipe in *Chapter 5, Creating Relevant Keywords*

Optimizing bids for ROI

ROI focused bid optimization is the key to keeping your conversion rates high and CPA as low as possible. Many advertisers get distracted by ad position and keep increasing their bids to stay above their competitors. That's not always the optimal strategy, when it comes to ROI. This recipe focuses on identifying which keywords to adjust bids for and how to adjust them based on conversions.

Getting ready

In order to optimize for ROI, you will need to implement conversion tracking and your keywords will need to have accumulated some data that you can work with.

Also, keep in mind your overall CPA goal. That goal will help you identify ad groups and keywords outside and within a profitable range.

How to do it...

You can optimize bids at the ad group level as well as at the keyword level. The rule of thumb is as follows:

- Increase bids on ad groups and keywords that are converting within your target CPA, so you can get a better ad rank and more clicks.
- Decrease bids on ad groups and keywords that are converting outside of your target CPA. This can help you lower your CPA on terms that are currently not cost effective.

For the purposes of this exercise, we'll focus on keyword bid strategy, but the same general guidelines apply to ad groups as well. The following table outlines the recommended bid adjustments for various performance scenarios with a CPA goal of $10.

Keyword	CPA	Recommended bid action
New car	$15.34	Decrease bid
Honda dealership	$12.67	Decrease bid
Honda civic	$9.35	Leave the bid as is
Honda civic best price	$5.36	Increase bid

Here are four ways you can interact with your AdWords data and use the various AdWords tools to prioritize bid optimization efforts:

- Sort keywords by **Cost/conv. (1-per-click)** to see the most costly and highest CPA terms first. Decrease bids on the worst offenders. You can start with a 20 percent decrease, but if the CPA is way outside of your target, you might want to decrease bids even more.
- Create a filter that isolates all cost effective keywords. Increase bids if the CPA is well within your target.

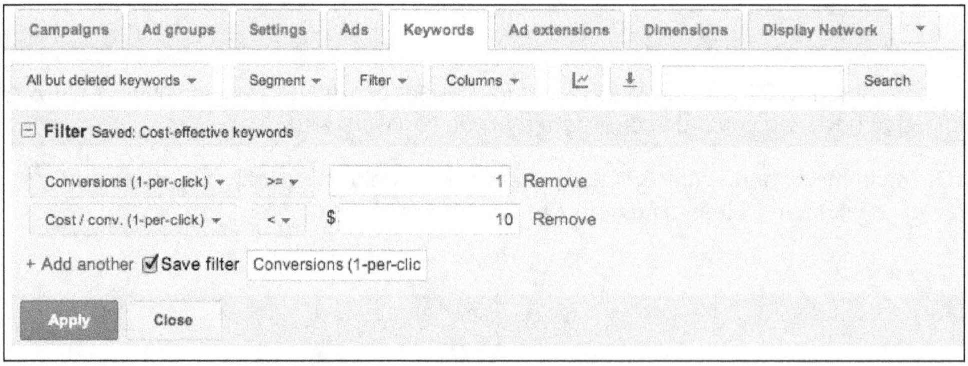

- Create a filter to isolate all costly keywords with no conversions to see where you are spending money without any results. Decrease bids on these terms or pause them.

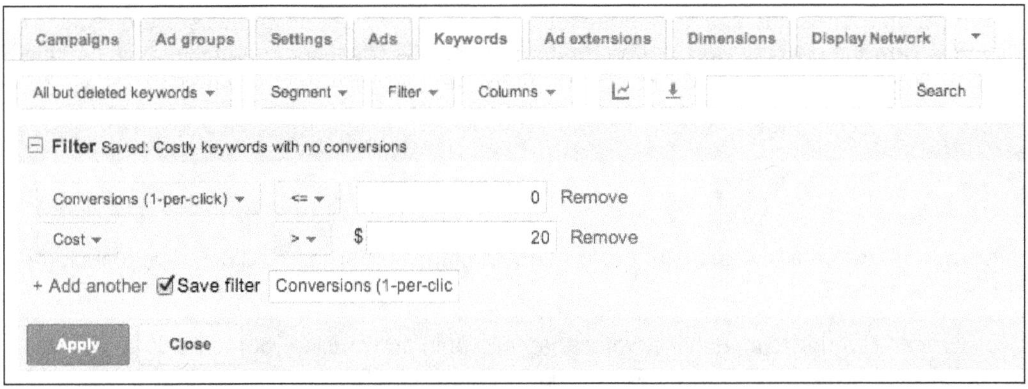

- Monitor and adjust bids on a regular basis to ensure CPAs stay within your targets. You can even set up automated rules to increase and decrease bids regularly (such as each week or every day) based on performance.

How it works...

Increasing and decreasing your bids based on prior conversion data will help you bid more on keywords that are working for you, and less on keywords that do not convert.

There's more...

To automate the process of adjusting bids, you can test CPA bidding in AdWords to let the system adjust bids for you based on a specific CPA goal. Make sure to watch results closely after you implement conversion optimizer, as it does not work for all advertisers. If CPA bidding does not produce the desired results, you can also try enhanced bidding.

See also

- The *Creating filters to customize reporting* recipe in *Chapter 10, Reporting and Analysis*
- The *Enabling Conversion Optimizer* recipe in *Chapter 7, Budgets and Bidding*
- The *Automating actions based on rules and goals* recipe in *Chapter 12, Advanced Strategies and Features*

Optimizing keywords to improve ROI

You've set up your campaigns and added lots of keywords, and people have started clicking on your ads. Now the ongoing work of fine tuning begins. A key aspect of optimization is making sure that the keywords that work for you get the most possible exposure while the keywords that do not are properly identified.

Getting ready

First, understand your low and high performers. Customize your keyword columns to include conversion metrics.

Use filters and sorting to identify keywords that fall within and outside your CPA goals. Download keyword data into an Excel file, or another easier to work with format.

How to do it...

First, focus on your top performers:

1. Create separate campaigns for your best keywords to set a unique budget for top performers. This will help you ensure that your other, less profitable, keywords are not taking impressions away from your highest ROI terms.
2. Increase bids on keywords that are profitable but are not appearing in the top position. This will help you get a better ad rank and more clicks from keywords that you know do well.

Next, make changes to keywords that are underperforming:

1. Lower bids for keywords that are converting at high costs or on keywords that have accumulated lots of clicks without any conversions.
2. Add negative keywords to improve CTR and quality of your low performing keywords.
3. Restructure by moving poor performers into their own ad groups with custom ads.

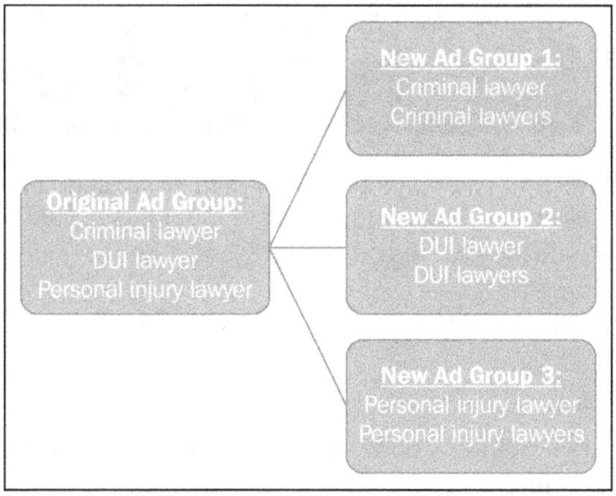

4. Try using different, more specific landing pages that better match your keywords.
5. Change the keyword match type to a more specific keyword matching option. This can help you reduce impressions and improve CTR.
6. If a keyword continues to under-perform, pause it. Click on the green status button to the left of the keyword you wish to pause and change the status from **Enabled** to **Paused**.

How it works...

Optimizing keywords based on your historical conversion data helps you improve performance and maximize ROI, since you can assume similar patterns from future searches. Optimizing keywords for ROI involves maximizing ad visibility and ad rank on keywords that work and refining keywords that have not performed well in the past.

See also

- The *Optimizing bids for ROI* recipe
- The *Editing, pausing, or deleting keywords* recipe in *Chapter 5, Creating Relevant Keywords*

Excluding IP addresses from seeing your ads

Are you worried that competitors are clicking on your ads? The good news is that AdWords offers a comprehensive click-fraud system that will in most cases filter out those clicks from your bill. However, you can also exclude competitors and other suspicious IPs from seeing your ads to further protect yourself.

Getting ready

AdWords does not provide IP address data for impressions and clicks you receive. However, you can get this information from your web logs.

How to do it...

To exclude specific IP addresses:

1. Go to the **Campaigns** tab.
2. Go to the **Settings** tab of a specific campaign you'd like to add IP exclusions to.
3. Scroll down to the **Advanced Settings** until you see **+ IP exclusions** and click to expand this section.
4. Click on the **Edit** link.

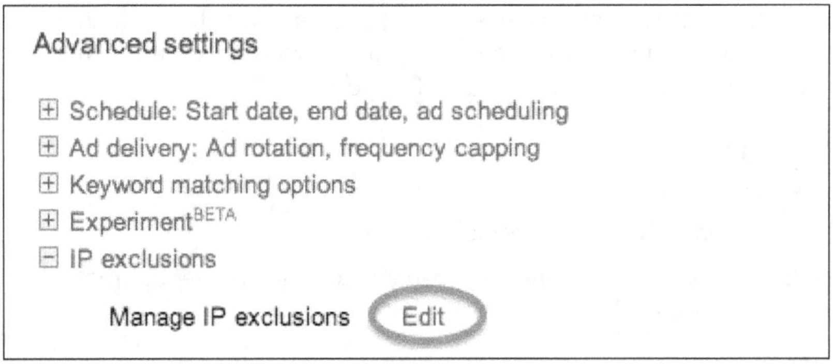

5. Enter one IP address you'd like excluded per line.

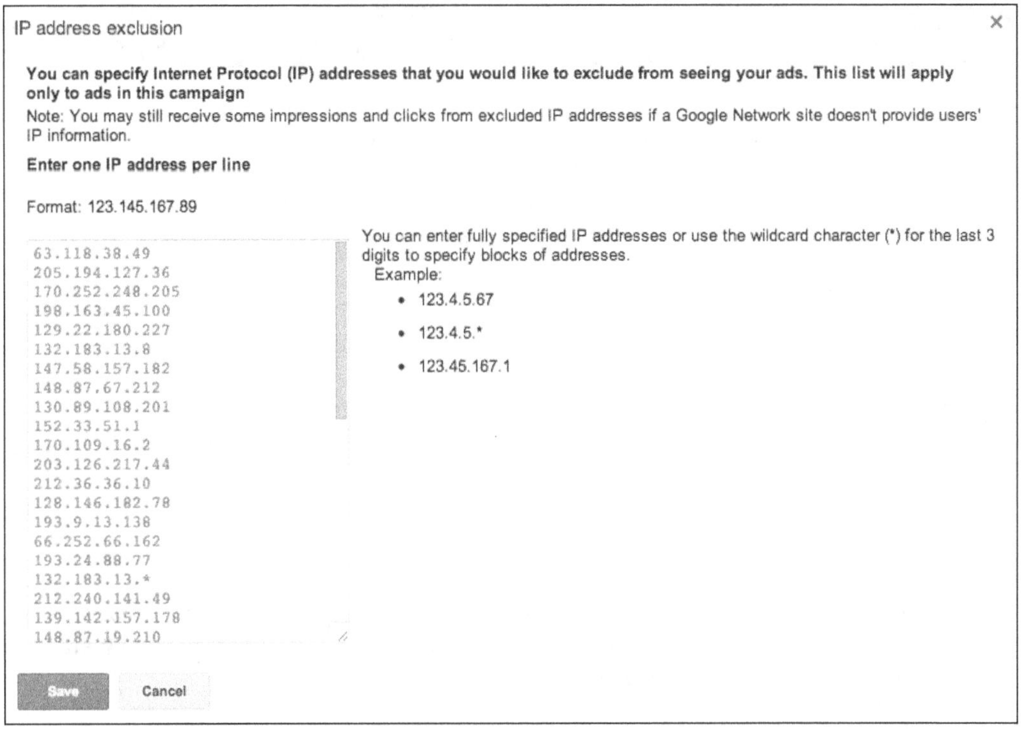

6. Click on **Save**.

How it works...

IP address exclusion in AdWords blocks your ads from showing on related computers and networks. You can exclude up to 500 addresses.

> Be careful about excluding certain generic IPs that internet service providers (such as AOL) assign to a large number of their users.

See also

- The *Excluding locations from seeing your ads* recipe in *Chapter 4, Structuring Your Account*

Optimizing your landing pages

Your landing pages are a key part of the sales process and need to convince the visitors who clicked on your ads not only to stay, but to continue browsing your website and buy what you are selling. A typical visitor stays on a website only a few seconds before deciding to bounce, and it is the job of your landing page to keep potential customers from leaving. Even if you have chosen the best keywords and ads, your online campaigns will not be a success without an effective landing page.

Getting ready

Analyze your bounce rates and time on site through Google Analytics. Figure out if specific campaigns and ad groups have higher bounce rates than others and zero in on the landing pages you are using.

How to do it...

First, make sure that you are taking visitors to the most appropriate pages on your website. Perhaps you are taking your visitors to a page that's too general or too specific, and there is a section that is a better match for your keywords.

Next, consider some of the landing page optimization best practices to help improve engagement and conversions:

- Customize your landing page's headline to your keywords. This will help reassure the users that they have arrived at the right place and will help boost your AdWords Quality Scores.
- Keep important information above the fold, including your heading and any other important elements.
- Make your conversion activity prominent and easy to spot. If you are capturing leads, your lead form should not be below the fold where many visitors might not even look. If you sell products, the product "Buy" button should be big and enticing.
- Keep your forms short and only require users to fill out the most essential information. Each additional form field you add reduces the chances that the form will actually be completed.
- Include customer testimonials on your landing page to build trust and showcase what others love about your business.
- Include affiliations, guarantees, awards, privacy, security statements, and other reassurances that help build trust and reassure your customers of your credibility.

- Focus on a single call-to-action. Your landing page should have a single purpose. Do not distract visitors with too many options, such as a newsletter sign-up, whitepaper download, and a demo request all at once.
- Experiment with "Submit" button text, trying more enticing and non-intimidating language. For example, avoid the commitment-heavy "Subscribe Now" and try the less committal "Unlimited Access" instead.
- Show your products and services being used in context.
- Reduce unnecessary language and navigation, keeping the steps to complete a conversion short. Write succinct and to the point copy using easy-to-read bullets.

Keep testing and reiterating until you find what works best for you. There is no one size fits all approach when it comes to landing pages.

How it works...

Landing pages are a part of Google's Quality Score formula, affecting your overall ad performance. Your landing pages need to reflect your keywords but also be transparent and easy to navigate.

There's more...

To test different versions of your website and the impact of changing various landing page elements, set up Google Analytics Content Experiments. Content Experiments help you figure out which landing page elements work better for your predefined goals, such as signups or purchases. You can read more and find out how to get started at `http://support.google.com/analytics/answer/1745147?topic=1745207`.

See also

- The *Analyzing time on site data and bounce rates* recipe in *Chapter 3, Tracking beyond the Click*
- The *Choosing landing pages* recipe in *Chapter 6, Writing Compelling Ads*

12
Advanced Strategies and Features

In this chapter, we will cover:

- Creating sitelinks
- Setting up call extensions
- Implementing social extensions
- Setting up location extensions
- Promoting application downloads
- Setting up dynamic search ads
- Creating product ads
- Using experiments to test campaign changes
- Using advanced negative match keywords
- Automating actions based on rules and goals
- Common AdWords mistakes

Introduction

AdWords offers a variety of advanced features many advertisers overlook, such as ad extensions that show your business phone number or links to other relevant pages on your website. You can also explore other ad formats such as product listings ads and video ads to get more traffic and engage with your customers through different channels. Not all of the advanced features and strategies will be applicable to your business, but hopefully a few can help your ads stand out in a saturated marketplace and give your campaigns the edge over your competition.

Creating sitelinks

An AdWords ad can only have one destination URL where visitors are taken after clicking on your ad. But, in many cases, there are actually multiple pages on your website that could potentially be applicable and relevant to a list of keywords. AdWords sitelinks help solve for that by allowing you to show alternate URL options in addition to your ad's main destination URL. However, they can also distract visitors from your target conversion activity, so be careful when adding sitelinks and monitor results after implementing them.

Getting ready

Brainstorm the additional page URLs you'd like to highlight in your ads. Here are some ideas for pages on your website you can promote via sitelinks:

- About us
- Contact us
- Store locator
- Testimonials
- FAQ
- Signup page
- Related or similar products
- Link to coupons or special promotions

How to do it...

To set up sitelinks, follow these steps:

1. Click on the **Campaigns** tab.
2. Go into a campaign you wish to edit. Set up sitelinks at the campaign level or go into a specific ad group if you wish to create sitelinks unique to an ad group.
3. Go to the **Ad extensions** tab.

4. From the **View** drop-down menu, select **Sitelinks Extensions**:

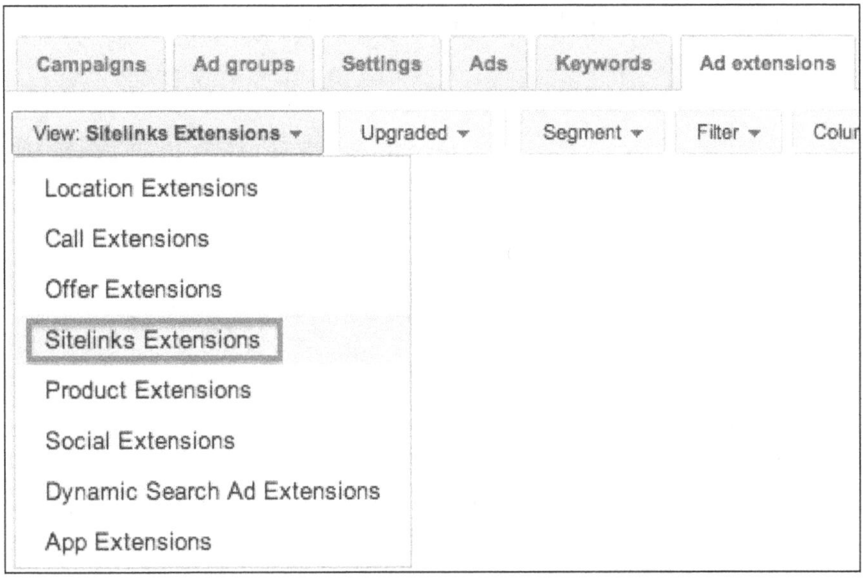

5. Click on **Edit** to edit the **Sitelink extension** setting:

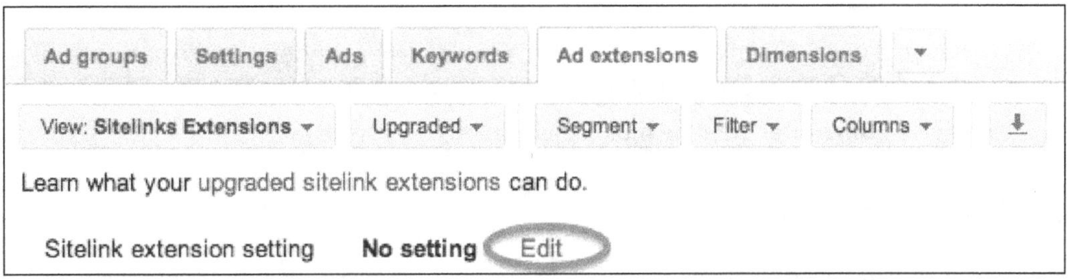

6. Click on **+ New sitelink**.

7. Write in the link text (25 character limit) and enter a link URL. Make your sitelinks compelling and interesting. For example, if you plan to use your testimonials page as a sitelink, say something like **See Why Customers Love Us**.

8. Click on **Save**.
9. Create additional sitelinks for other URLs you wish to promote. Add as many sitelinks as possible to increase your chances of sitelinks appearing.
10. Click on **Save** after creating multiple sitelinks.

How it works...

Sitelinks allow you to show links to other pages on your website in addition to your main ad destination URL. They only appear if your ad is ranked at the top or at the bottom of Google's search results.

Sitelink text needs to be 25 characters or less. You can create sitelinks at the campaign level, but can also set unique sitelinks for each ad group. You can add up to 10 sitelinks but not all of them will show.

There's more...

You can customize your sitelinks for mobile devices if you prefer to show certain sitelinks only on mobile devices.

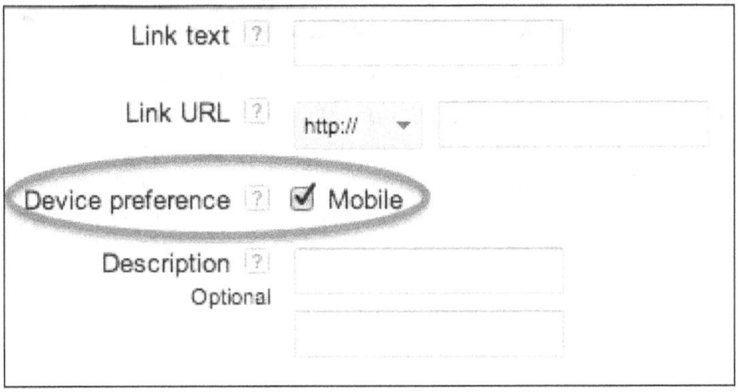

You can also enable ad scheduling to show sitelinks during certain days and times only. For example, you can choose specific dates on which an ad extension can show up with your ad (for example, only for special holiday promotions).

See also

- The *Evaluating sitelink extensions* recipe in *Chapter 10, Reporting and Analysis*

Setting up call extensions

If you are in a business that values calls more than website visits, you should be taking advantage of call extensions in AdWords. When you set up call extensions, your ad text is extended with an extra line of text for your phone number on computers and tablets. Additionally, when you set up "click-to-call", people searching for you on their mobile devices have the option to call you instead of clicking through to your website, saving customers the extra step of having to go to your website to look up your phone number.

Getting ready

Decide if you'd like to show your own business phone number or use Google's call forwarding. If you use Google's call forwarding, Google will assign a toll-free number that will dial through to your phone number. The advantage of using Google's free call forwarding is the ability to see data about calls that are dialed through this call extension (such as call area code and duration) and the option to track calls as conversions.

How to do it...

To set up call extensions, follow these steps:

1. Click on the **Campaigns** tab.
2. Go into a specific campaign. You can set-up call extensions at the campaign level and at the ad group level. To set them up at the ad group level, go into a specific ad group.
3. Go to the **Ad extensions** tab.
4. From the **View** drop-down, select **Call Extensions**.
5. Click to **Edit** the **Call extension setting**:

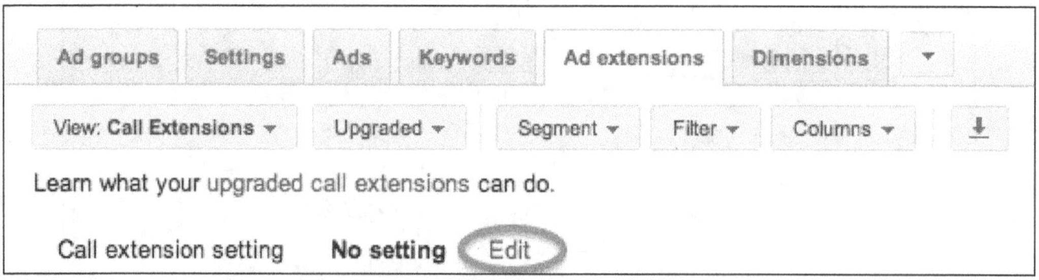

6. Click on **+ New phone number**:

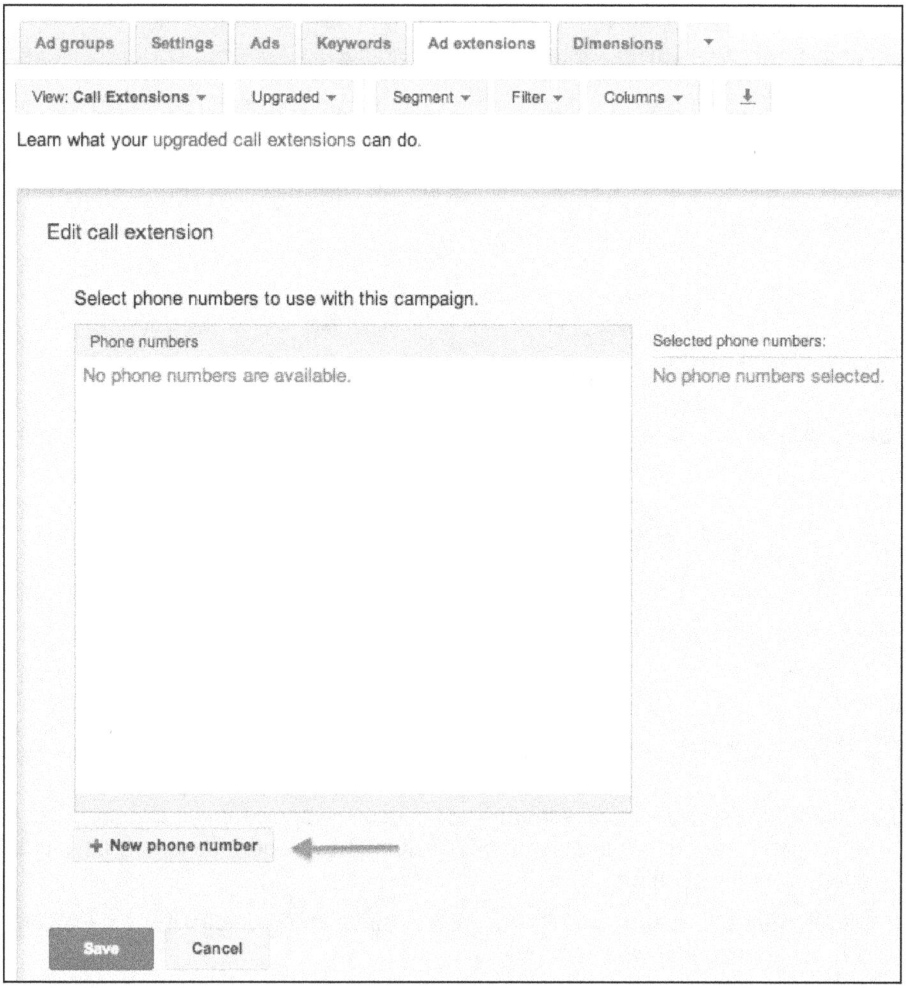

7. Choose your country and enter the phone number.
8. Next, decide if you'd like to use Google's call forwarding or show your own phone number.
9. Under **Show the following links**, pick if you would like to show both a link to your website and your phone number, or just the phone number. The default is to show both options, since that gives your customers more flexibility to choose what they prefer. With the second option, only the phone number will be clickable when your ad is shown on mobile devices capable of making phone calls. This option is most appropriate for businesses that need to talk to their customers first, such as a salon that makes all appointments over the phone.

10. Under **Report phone call conversions**, you can choose to count any calls that last longer than a certain amount of time as conversions. Keep this option checked and adjust your desired call duration (default is 60 seconds). This option is only available for call extensions using Google's call forwarding.

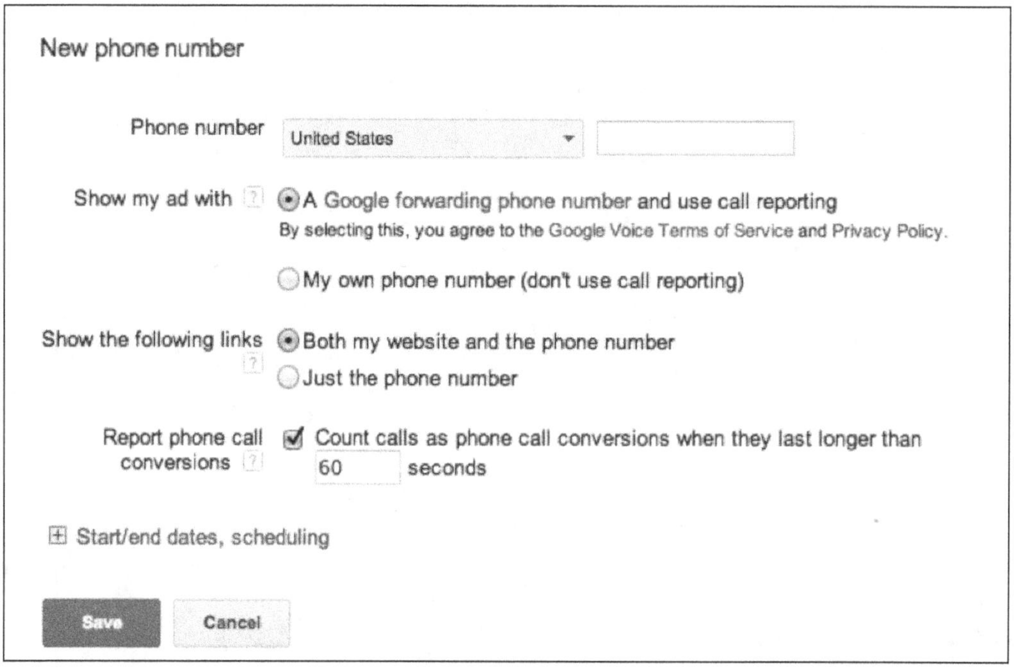

11. Expand **+Start/end dates, scheduling** to choose when your call extensions can run. Set a specific schedule when your phone number will show if you only have customer support during set hours.
12. Click on **Save** to keep your call extension settings and then click on **Save** again to add this call extension to your campaign.

How it works...

Call extensions extend your text ads with an extra line of text that shows a phone number on all devices. You can create call extensions at the campaign and ad group levels.

Advertisers can choose to show their business number in ads or use Google's free call forwarding, which provides additional reporting to help you evaluate calls that are coming through AdWords.

See also

- The *Reviewing call details* recipe in *Chapter 10, Reporting and Analysis*

Implementing social extensions

If you have a Google+ page, you can link it to your AdWords campaigns to show Google+ endorsements in your ads. This feature can help your ads stand out, increase credibility if you have a strong Google+ presence, and can help improve CTR.

Getting ready

You need to have a Google+ page. This page and your website need to be linked in order to prove that the Google+ page belongs to you. You can link your Google+ page and your website by adding your website's URL to your Google+ page. You will also need to add your Google+ URL to your website.

How to do it...

To set up social extensions, follow these steps:

1. Click on the **Campaigns** tab.
2. Go into a specific campaign and go to **Ad extensions**.
3. From the **View** drop-down menu, select **Social Extensions**.
4. Click on **+ New extension**:

5. Enter the URL of your Google+ page. To find your URL, go to your Google+ page and copy the URL from your browser. It should include the domain `https://plus.google.com/`, and your unique Google+ page ID.

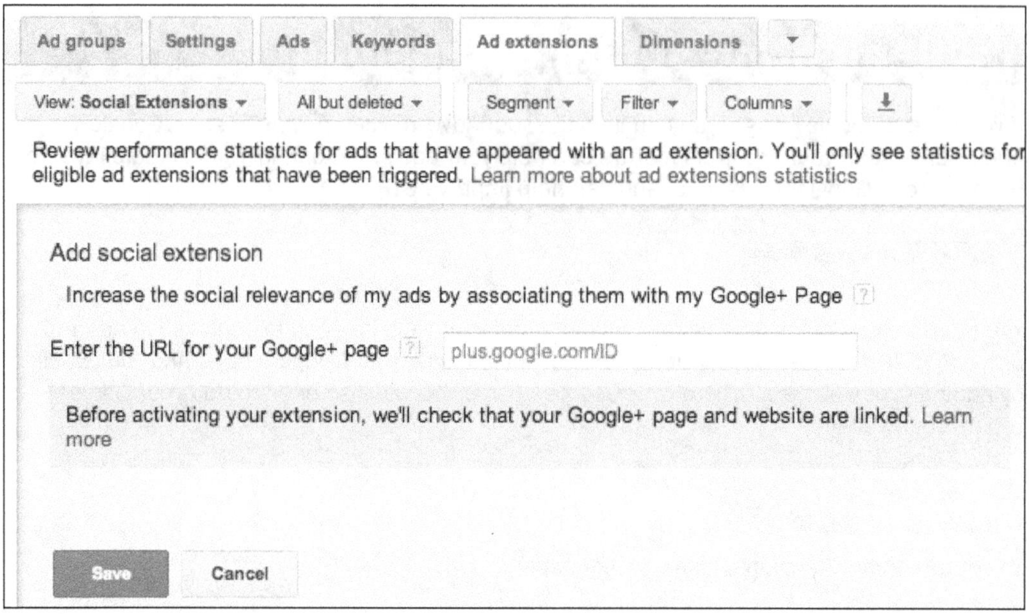

6. Click on **Save**.

How it works...

Social extensions allow you to associate your ads with your Google+ page and show Google+ endorsements in your ads. Social extensions are set up at the campaign level, show on all networks, and are available in all countries.

See also

- The *Setting up call extensions* recipe

Setting up location extensions

Location extensions highlight your business address and help you set yourself apart as a local business. They show a link to Google Maps with your phone number and the option to get directions to your location.

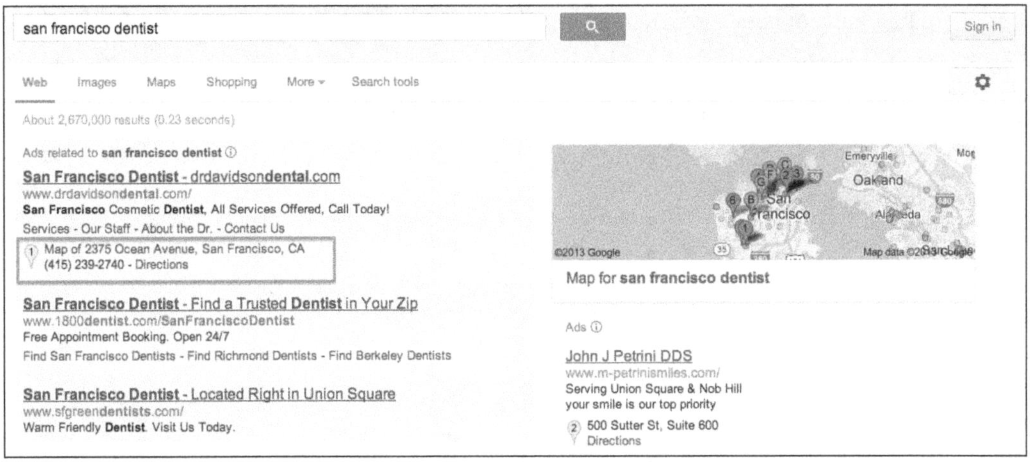

Getting ready

Decide how you'd like to enable location extensions:

- By using addresses from Google Places
- By manually entering addresses

If you have a business listing with Google Places, you'll need your username and password to connect it to your AdWords account. To create your listing for free on Google Places for business, go to `www.google.com/placesforbusiness`.

If you do not have a Google Places account, you can still take advantage of location extensions by entering your business address manually into AdWords.

How to do it...

To set up social extensions, follow these steps:

1. Click on the **Campaigns** tab.
2. Go into a specific campaign and go to the **Ad extensions** tab.
3. From the **View** drop-down menu, select **Location Extensions**.
4. Click on **+ New extension**.

5. To use your Google Places account, choose **+ Addresses from Google Places** and enter your Google Places username and password.
6. Pick a map icon to represent your industry from one of the existing icons or upload your own.
7. If you have multiple businesses in Google Places but would only like to show certain addresses with your ads, use the advanced **Filter** option to exclude business names, categories, or countries and territories.
8. Click on **Save**.

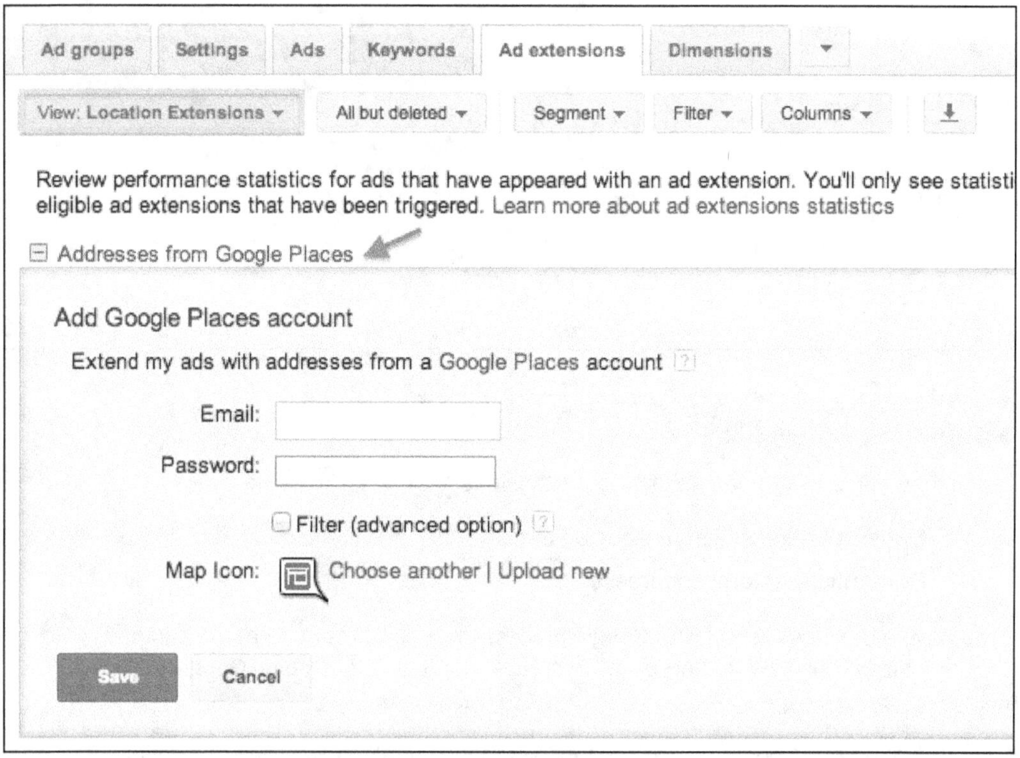

9. If you do not have a Google Places account, click on **+ Manually entered Addresses** and then click on **+ New extension**.

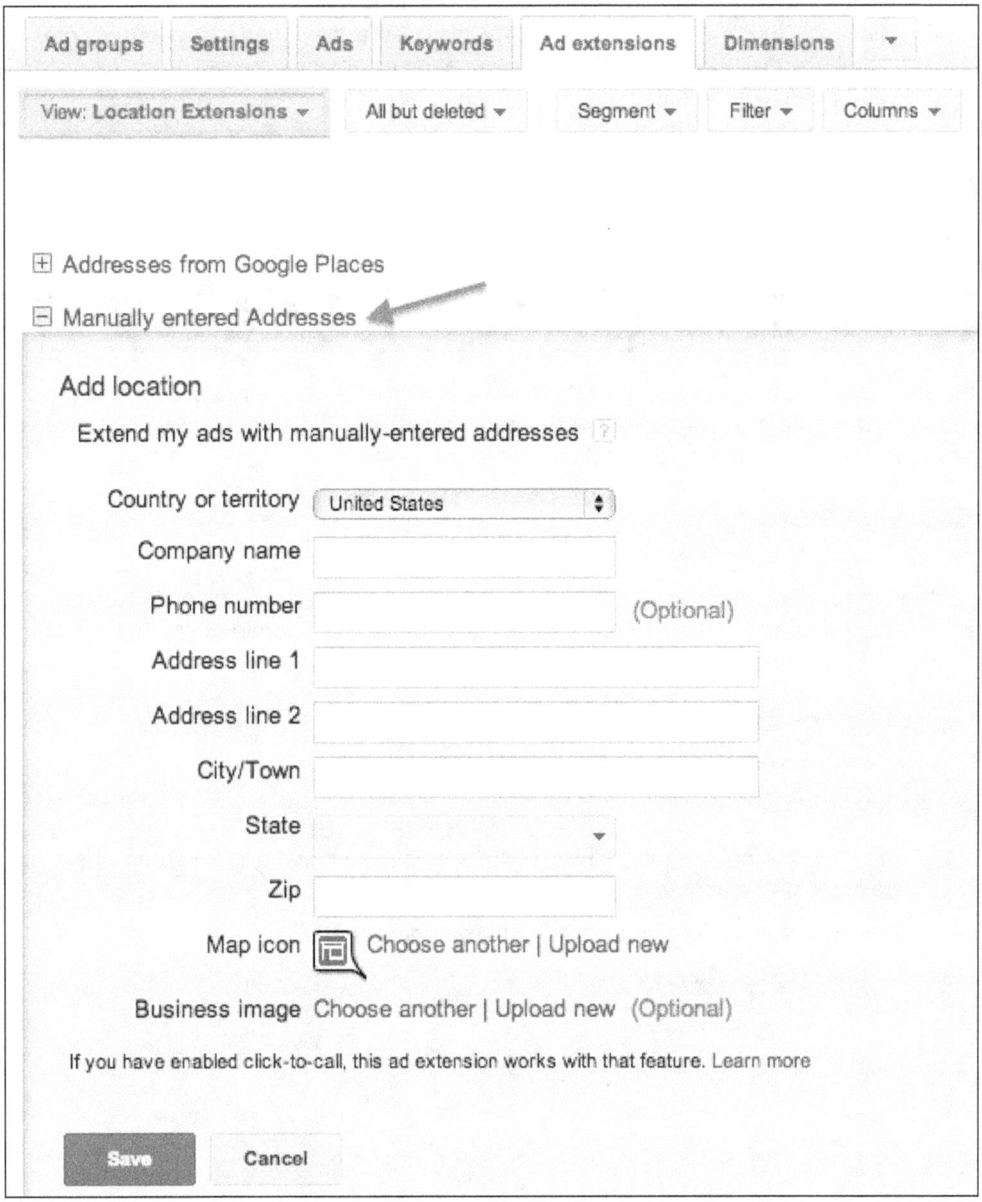

10. Choose your country, enter your business name, phone number, and address.
11. Pick a **Map icon** and upload an optional **Business image**.
12. Click on **Save**.

How it works...

Location extensions help you promote your business address and shows an extra line of ad text with a link to a Google map. If you have multiple business locations, the address most relevant to each user will show up in your ads. Location extensions are set up at the campaign level and you'll need to enable this option for each campaign.

See also

- The *Setting up call extensions* recipe

Promoting application downloads

Application promotion ads extend your AdWords ads with a link to your application to drive downloads. Customers can choose to click on the application link instead of on your ad text headline to learn more about the application and download it.

Getting ready

You'll need to have an iOS or an Android app live on iTunes or on the Google Play store. You may also need your App ID (for iOS apps) or Package name (for Android apps), though you can also look up this information as you're setting up the ad.

How to do it...

To set up app extensions:

1. Go to the **Campaigns** tab and click on a specific campaign and ad group where you'd like to create an app ad.
2. Click on **+ New ad** and choose **App/digital content ad**.
3. Select **App promotion ad**:

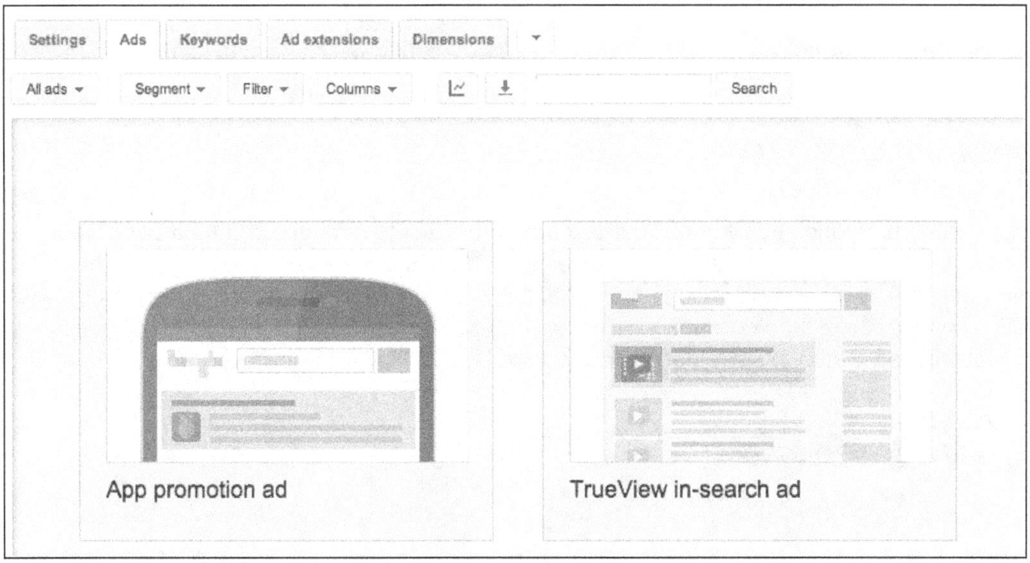

4. Select your **App platform** and enter your **App ID** or **Package name**. You can also look up your app information by name, ID, or by publisher.

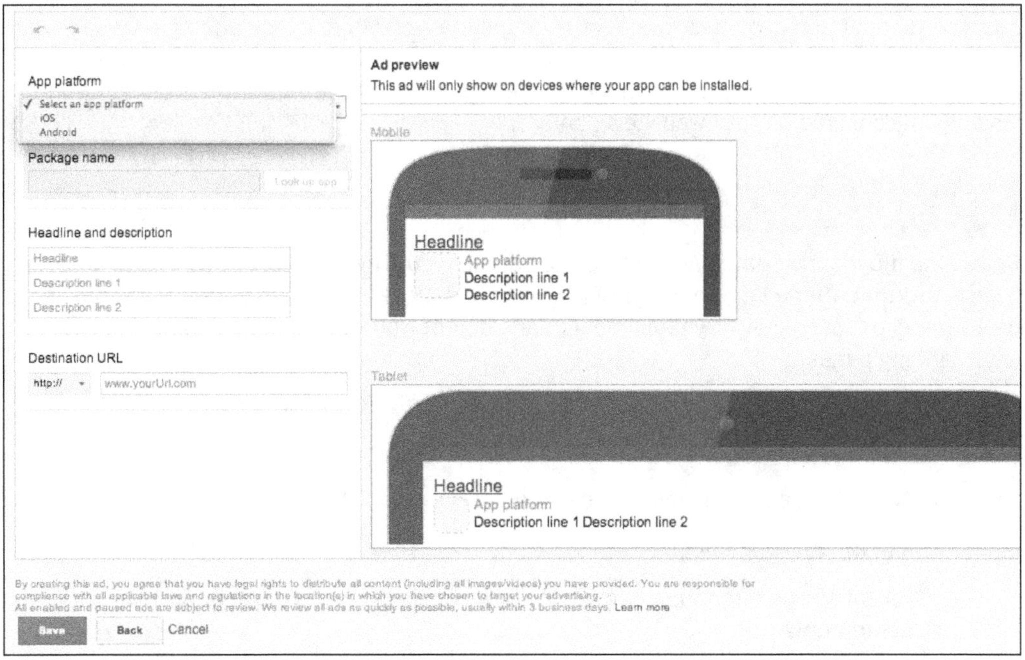

5. Write a headline and description, and choose your destination URL.

6. Click on **Save**.
7. Create additional ads following these steps if your app is available on both app platforms.

How it works...

Application promotion ads extend your text ads with a link to a mobile or a tablet application. The ads you create will only show on devices that the app can be downloaded from. For example, if a user is searching on an iPhone, only the ad you created for the iOS platform with a link to your iTunes app download will show. If a user is searching on an Android device, only the ad with an option to download your app from Google Play will show up.

See also

- The *Creating sitelinks* recipe

Setting up Dynamic Search Ads

If you sell a large number of products and would like to automate the process of creating and managing AdWords ads, you could benefit from a new campaign type called **Dynamic Search Ads**. You do not need to pick keywords or write unique ads with custom landing pages for your various products, and you don't need to pause products that are out of stock. AdWords does this work automatically for you, matching up the appropriate keywords to the most relevant landing pages based on your website's content.

Getting ready

Determine if Dynamic Search Ads are appropriate for you. This campaign type works best for businesses that offer a large number of products or services that change frequently based on inventory or seasonality. Dynamic Search Ads do not work as well for smaller websites with fewer landing pages.

How to do it...

To set up Dynamic Search Ads, follow these steps:

1. Go to the **Campaigns** tab.
2. Click on **+ New campaign** to create a new campaign and choose **Search Network only**.
3. Choose **Dynamic Search Ads** from the list of available campaign types:

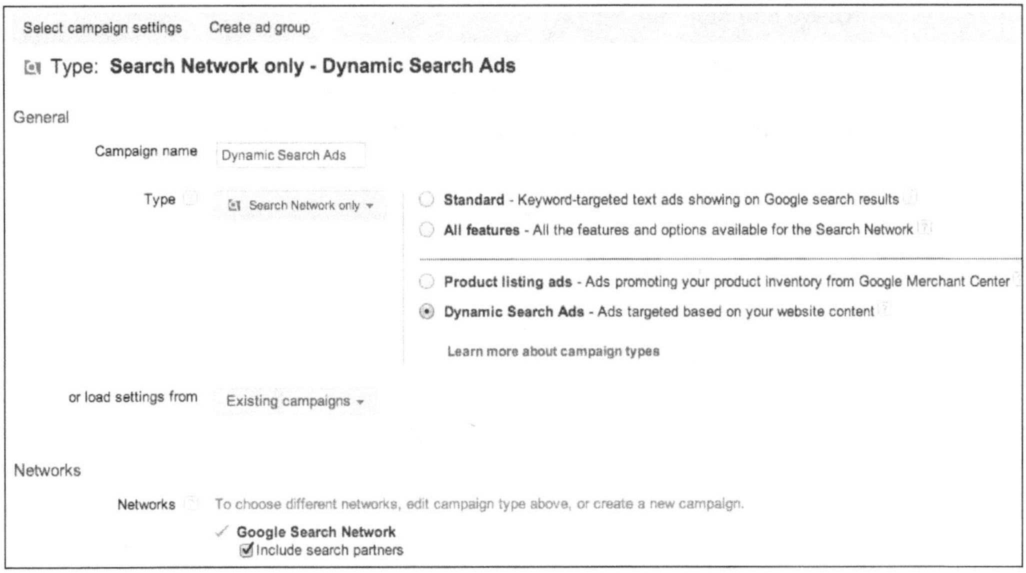

4. Choose your target locations, languages, pick your bidding option (for greater control, choose **I'll manually set my bids for clicks**), enter a default bid and set your daily budget.
5. Under **Ad extensions**, leave **Dynamic search ads** checked to allow AdWords to use your website content to target ads.
6. Enter your **Website domain** and choose your domain's language:

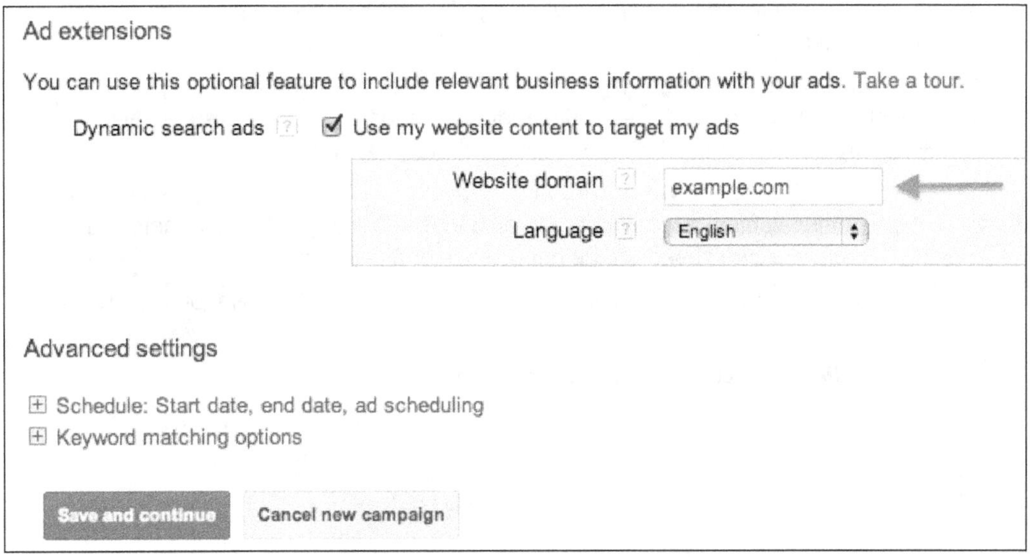

7. Click on **Save and continue**.
8. Now, create an ad group. You'll need to customize your description lines and your display URL. Your headlines will be dynamically generated for you.
9. Under **Auto targets**, keep **All pages** checked to allow AdWords to include all pages from your website domain:

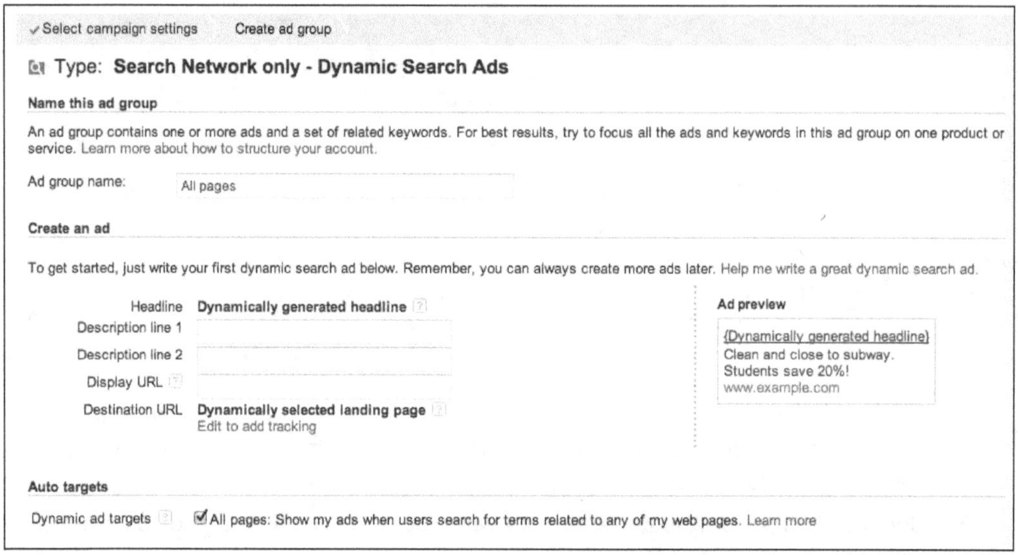

10. Adjust your **Default bid**, if necessary, and click on **Save ad group**.
11. You can add multiple ads to dynamic ad groups to test how different description lines perform.
12. Create additional ad groups if you'd like to target specific groups of pages and further customize bids and ads for specific products. Go to the **Auto targets** tab and click on **+ Add dynamic ad target**. Choose from the following available options:
    - **CATEGORY**: AdWords may automatically pre-populate categories based on your website's content, after you choose this target. This can help you bid up or down based on the importance of a category.
    - **URL**: Enter specific pages or a string of words and underscores to denote a page.
    - **PAGE_TITLE**: Use a specific page title to focus on a key product.

- **PAGE_CONTENT**: Define what pages should be included with words describing page content.

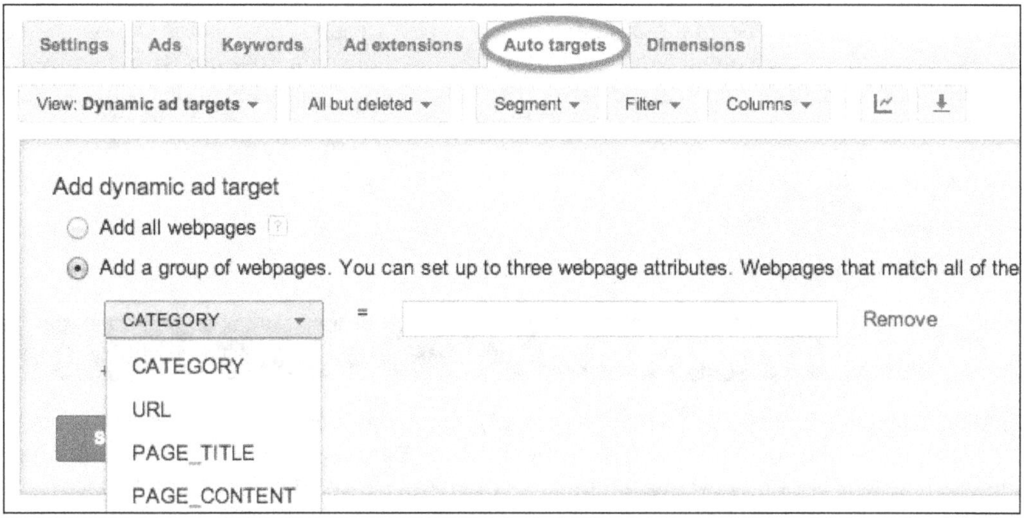

How it works...

Dynamic Search Ads automate AdWords campaign management by serving ads based on your website's content. Unlike standard search ads, where you have to pick keywords and write unique ads, with Dynamic Search Ads, Google determines which keywords are relevant and matches them up to the appropriate landing pages.

Additionally, Google creates a custom headline for each ad using content from the landing page being served. While the headline is generated dynamically, you still need to write ad description lines.

You can choose if you would like AdWords to create ads for all of the products on your website or just specific pages or categories.

There's more...

Continue to monitor search terms that are triggering your ads to ensure that the searches are relevant to your website. Go to the **Dimensions** tab of your Dynamic Search Ads campaign and review search terms data on an ongoing basis. If you find that some irrelevant searches are triggering your ads, or certain searches are generating a lot of traffic without any conversions, you can add them as negative keywords.

See also

- The *Creating product ads* recipe

Creating product ads

Product listing ads are a powerful ad format available through Google which allows retailers to showcase merchandise through images on Google.com. Because users can already see what the products look like and how much they cost, it's an extremely effective and profitable way to advertise with often better conversion rates than your standard text ads.

Getting ready

You'll need to have an account and a data feed submitted with Google's Merchant Center. The Merchant Center allows retailers to submit products, which show on Google Shopping, Product Listing Ads, and on Google Commerce. If you do not have a Merchant Center account, you can get started at `www.google.com/merchants`.

You'll need to create, upload, and regularly update a formatted feed with all of your products. There are feed management companies that specialize in creating and optimizing your feeds, including `http://godatafeed.com/` and `https://www.singlefeed.com`.

How to do it...

First, you'll need to link your Merchant Center account to your Google AdWords account. To do this, follow these steps:

1. Sign in to your Merchant Center account at `www.google.com/merchants`.
2. Click on **+ Settings**.
3. Click on the **AdWords** link.
4. Add your 10-digit AdWords Customer ID and click on **Link account**:

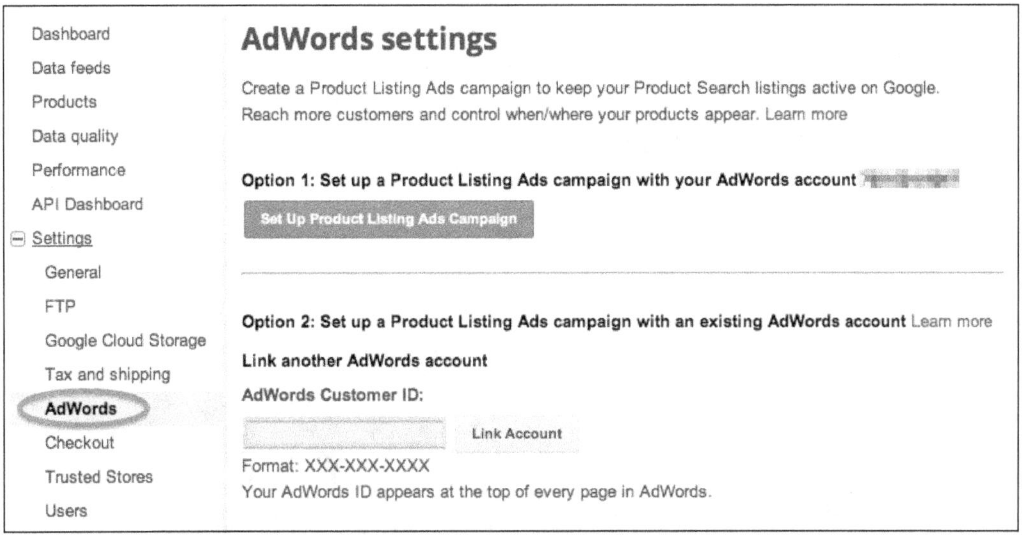

5. Next, you'll need to link the two accounts through AdWords.
6. Sign in to your AdWords account.
7. Go to the **Campaigns** tab and click on a specific campaign.
8. Click on the **Ad extensions** tab and from the **View** drop-down menu select **Product Extensions**.

Click on **+ New extension** after which you should see the option to select your Merchant Center ID:

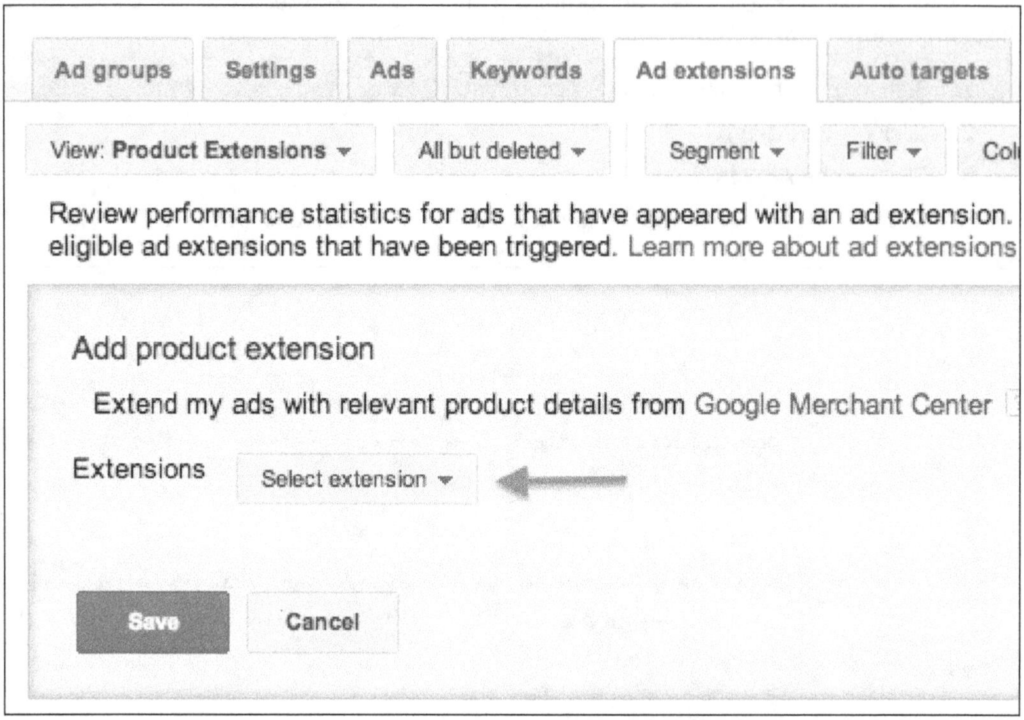

9. Click on **Save**.

Now that your accounts are linked, you can set up Product Listing Ads and enable product extensions in your AdWords account. Download your Merchant Center feed first to mirror AdWords targets to your Merchant Center attributes.

1. To enable product extensions in your existing campaigns, follow the preceding steps to link your Merchant Center ID to campaigns you are already running through Ad extensions.
2. Next, create a separate campaign for Product Listing Ads. In your AdWords account, go to the **Campaigns** tab and click on **+ New campaign**.
3. Choose **Search Network only**.

4. From the list of available campaign types, choose **Product listing ads**:

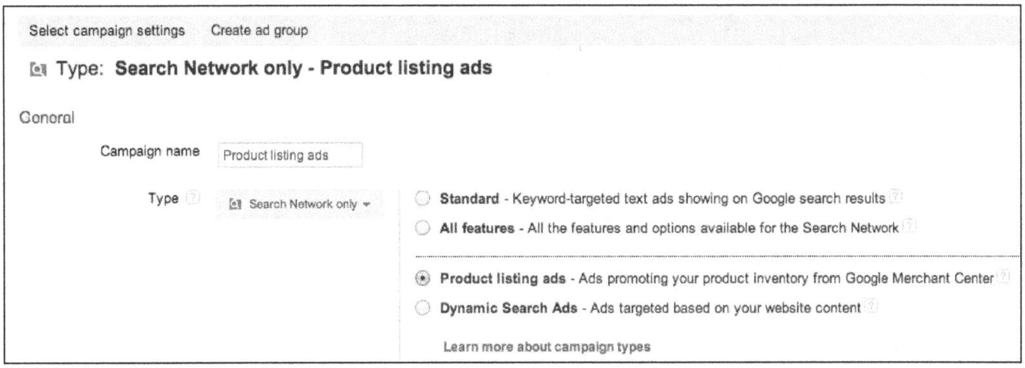

5. Choose your target locations, languages, and select a bidding option (it is recommended to select **I'll manually set my bids for clicks**). Enter a default bid and set your daily budget.
6. Under **Ad extensions**, select your product extension, which should allow you to select your Merchant Center ID.

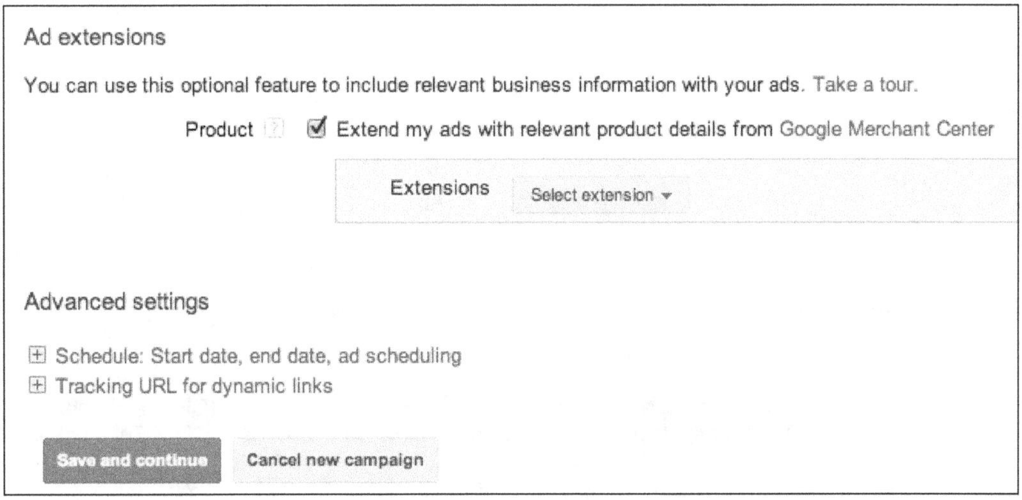

7. Click on **Save and continue**.
8. Next, you'll create your first ad group. This first ad group should capture all of your data feed products. You can name it `All products`. This ad group ensures that all of your products are eligible to show when users are searching for them.
9. Under **Create an ad**, write an optimal ad promotion, if you'd like to highlight any special discounts and coupons.

10. Under section **Auto targets**, keep **All products** checked.
11. Enter a default bid and click on **Save ad group**:

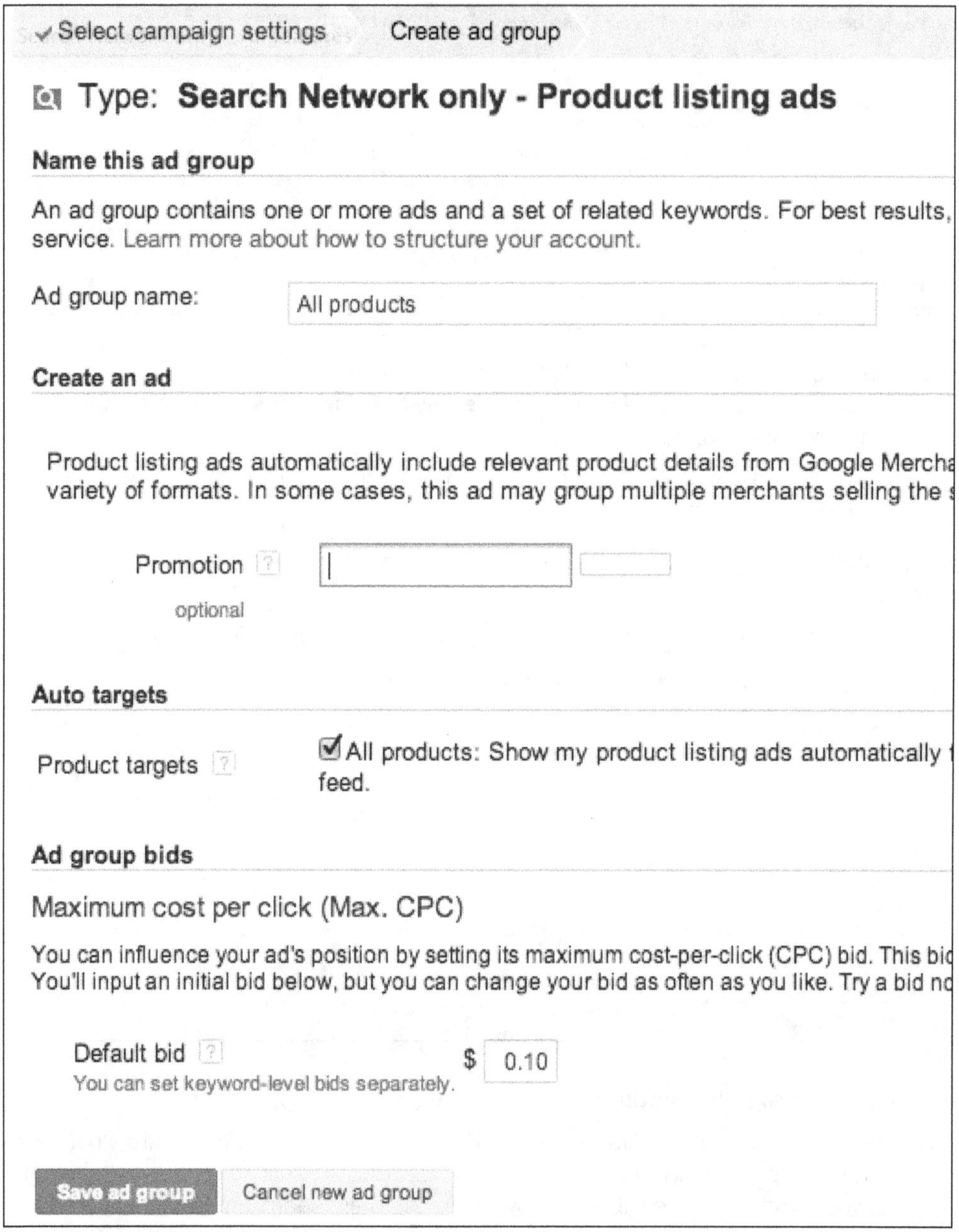

12. You do not need to add any keywords, as AdWords automates this for you based on your data feed. Your ads are shown to users typing in relevant queries that match your products.
13. Now that you have your main ad group for all products, you can create separate ad groups for your different brands and products based on merchant center targets.
14. Use different product targets to tailor bids to a group of products based on priority. Your `All products` ad groups should have lower bids than other targets' bids.
15. Here are the different ways you can target your data feed ad groups through the **Auto targets** tab:
    - All products
    - ID
    - Product type
    - Brand
    - Condition
    - AdWords labels
    - AdWords groupings

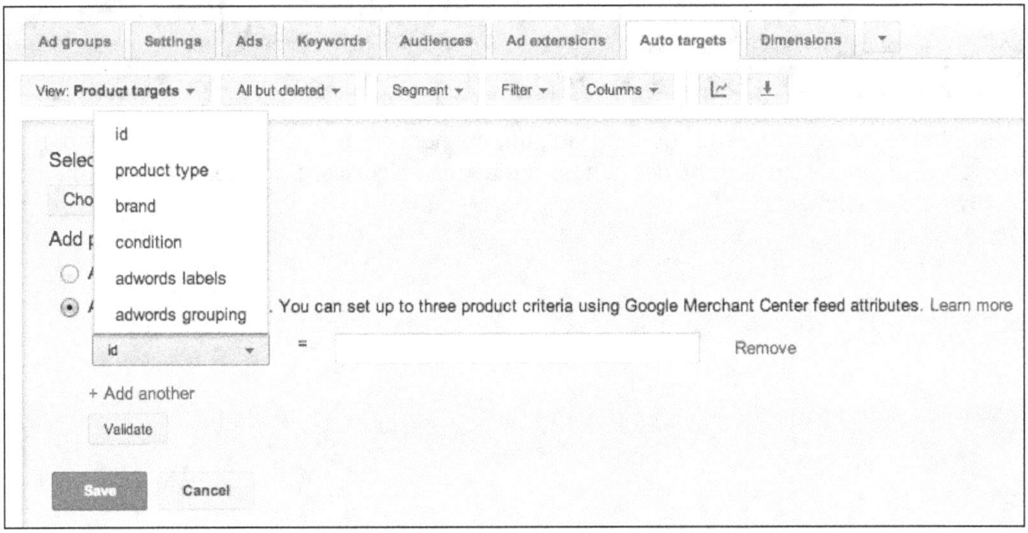

How it works...

Product ads include specific product information such as an image, price, and retailer's domain. The data feed is managed through your Merchant Center account, while the ad campaigns are managed through AdWords.

Ads include a product image, price, domain, and an optional promotional message, which is limited to 45 characters.

There's more...

As of this writing, product ads are not yet available in all countries. For a complete list of countries, please see `http://support.google.com/merchants/bin/answer.py?hl=en&answer=160619`

See also

- The *Setting up Dynamic Search Ads* recipe

Using experiments to test campaign changes

If you plan to make changes to your account, but are not sure how to analyze impact and would like to make sure that the differences are actually significant, you can take advantage of AdWords experiments.

Getting ready

Decide what you'd like to change and measure. Here are a few ideas:

- Create new ad variations to run against current ad text. You can experiment with using special offers, discounts versus price points, different calls-to-action, extra words in your Display URL, and many other ad elements.
- Make changes to ad group or keyword bids. You can start with ad groups that are losing impression share due to ad rank.
- Add new keywords to existing ad groups. Focus on ad groups that are not getting enough traffic.
- Add new ad groups to an existing campaign. Try new categories or match types.

Keep in your mind your goal metrics that are important to your business, such as conversions.

How to do it...

To set up an experiment, follow these steps:

1. Go to the **Campaigns** tab and click on a specific campaign that you plan to make changes to.
2. Click on the **Settings** tab and choose **All Settings**.
3. Scroll down to **Advanced settings** and click to expand the **+ Experiment** section.

4. Click on **+ Specify experiment settings**:

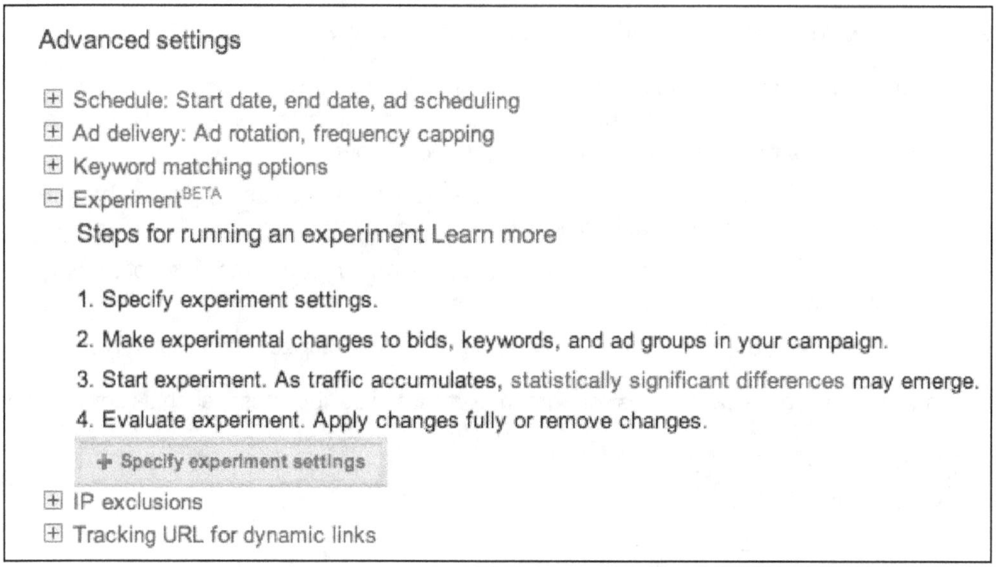

5. Give your experiment a name.
6. Choose your **Control/experiment split** or the percent of users exposed to your control versus your experiment.
7. Choose your start and end dates or if you would like to start the experiment manually.
8. Click on **Start running experiment** if you did not choose a specific start date:

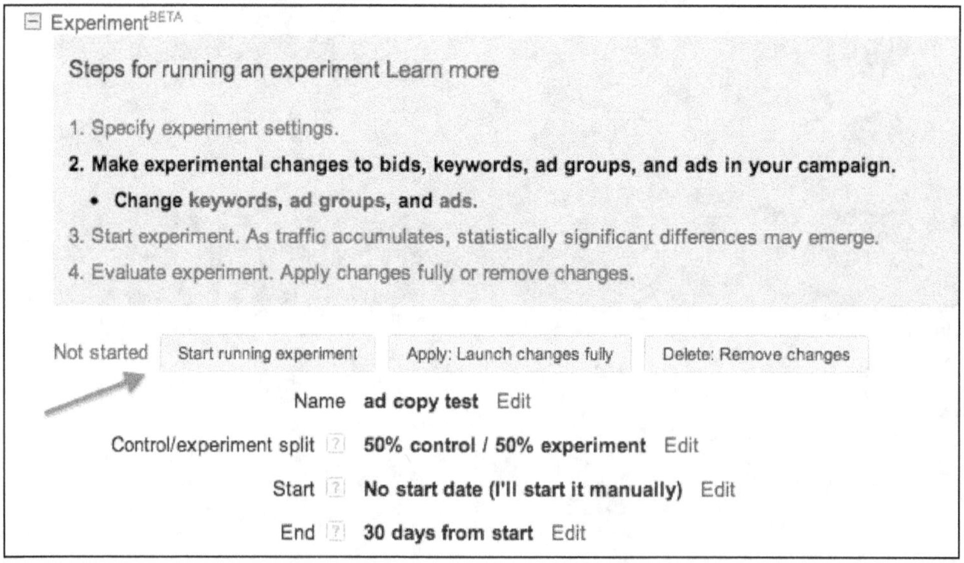

9. Next, go to your campaign and make changes to ad groups, bids, your keywords or ads.

10. For the purposes of this example, we'll create an experiment ad to test against the current ad copy. Go into a specific ad group and click on the **Ads** tab. Click on **+ New ad** and write a new text ad. Before saving your experiment ad, mark **Add as experiment-only ad**:

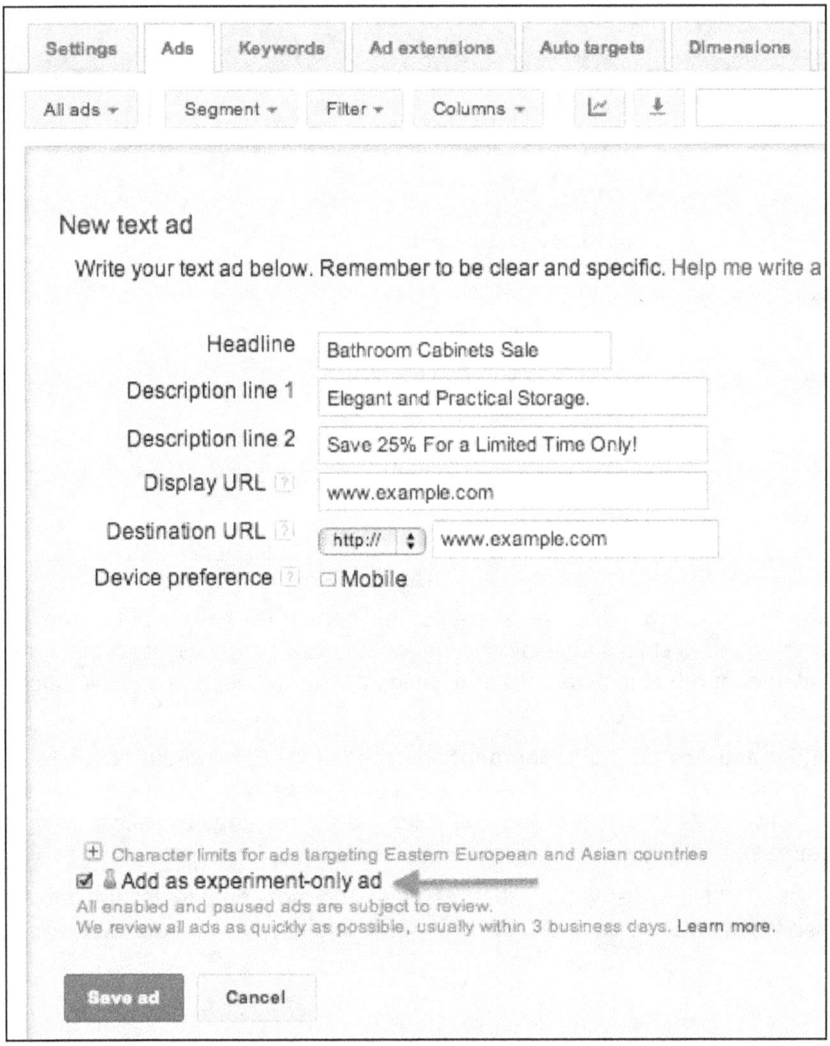

11. Go back to your original ad and hover over it to change it to **Control only**:

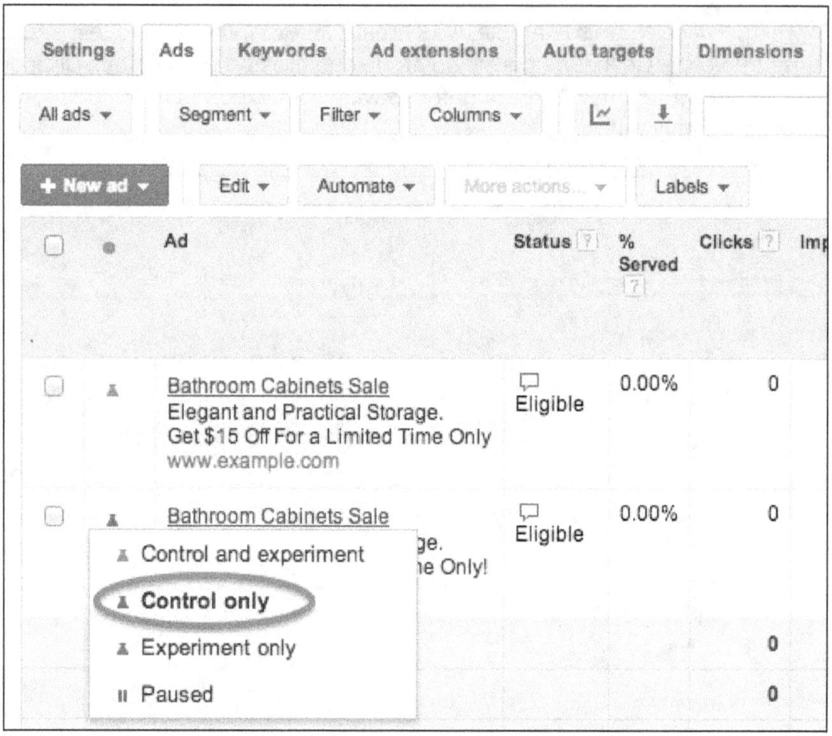

12. Now that you have your experiment set up, monitor the results to see how your experiment ad stacks up against your control. How long you'll need to let the experiment run to get statistically significant data will depend on how much traffic you get. The general rule of thumb is to allow for 2 to 4 weeks.
13. Under your **Ads** tab, go to **Segment** and choose the **Experiment** option to see data for your control and experiment ads, as well as if the results are statistically significant. Make sure that you are looking at a date range specific to when you started the experiment, rather than at all time data, for example.
14. If you would like to stop the experiment or need more time to accumulate statistically significant data, adjust the experiment end date in your campaign settings page.

15. If the experiment was successful and you would like to implement the changes, click on **Apply: Launch changes fully**. If the experiment underperformed and the control did better, choose **Delete: Remove changes**. Choosing to delete the changes will pause the experiment ad. If you apply the experiment changes, your control ad will be paused and your experiment ad will remain active.

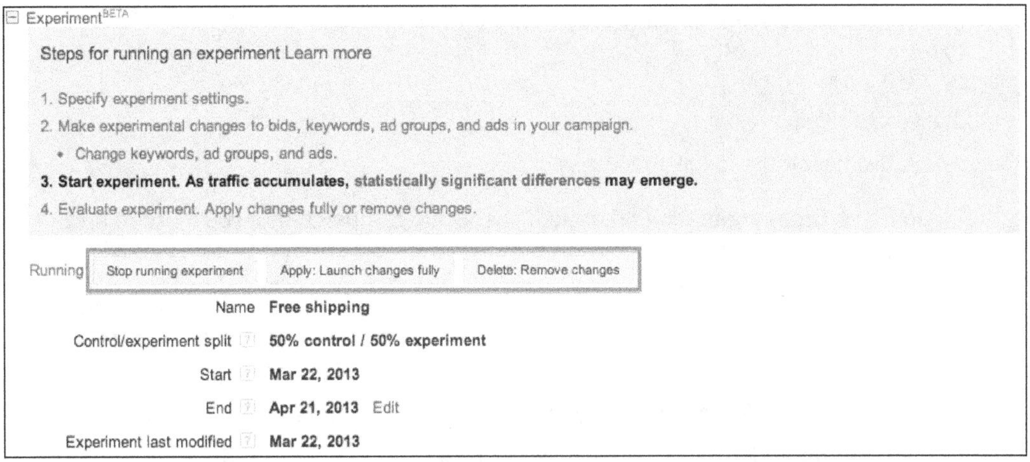

How it works...

Experiments in AdWords allow you to test the impact of changes you are considering making to your AdWords account. With experiments, you can evaluate if the differences you are seeing are statistically significant, or unlikely to have occurred by chance. You can make experimental changes to ad groups, bids, keywords, and ads. You can also choose how many people will be exposed to your experimental changes with the option to start and stop your experiment at any time.

See also

- The *Split testing ad copy* recipe in *Chapter 6, Writing Compelling Ads*
- The *Segmenting performance reports* recipe in *Chapter 10, Reporting and Analysis*

Using advanced negative match keywords

Advanced negative keyword match types allow you to further refine and exclude irrelevant traffic and get only the most relevant clicks. Negative match options include broad, phrase, and exact match.

Getting ready

Review your search terms reports to see what searches are triggering your ads. This is one of the best sources of new negative keywords with data specific to your account.

If you are in the planning stages of your keyword lists, use Google's keyword tool to research keywords and note any words or phrases that are irrelevant.

How to do it...

To add negative keywords, follow these steps:

1. Go to the **Campaigns** tab and click on a specific campaign that you'd like to add negative keywords to.
2. Click on the **Keywords** tab.
3. Scroll all the way down to the bottom of your keyword list and click on **+ Negative keywords**.
4. Choose if you'd like to add ad group or campaign negatives.
5. Click on **Add** and enter your negatives as follows:
6. For Negative Broad, just enter the word or phrase.
7. For Negative Phrase, enter the phrase with quotations around it.
8. For Negative Exact, enter the word or phrase with brackets around it.

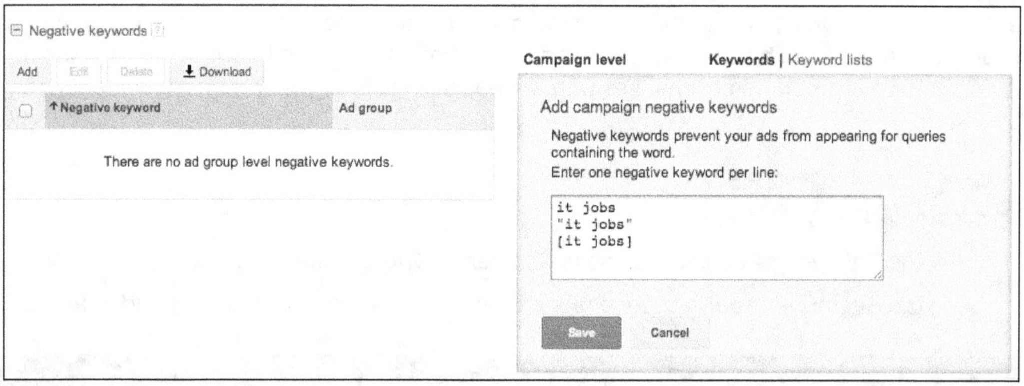

9. Click on **Save**.

How it works...

Negative Broad match is the default negative option that will exclude any query that includes your negative broad terms. Word order does not matter but misspellings and variations are not included. For example, if you have a negative broad keyword "it jobs" your ads would not appear on a query like "jobs it" but traffic for another irrelevant query like "information technology jobs" would not be filtered out. Ideally, you would add "jobs" as a negative broad keyword to exclude any query containing that term.

Negative Phrase match allows you to exclude specific phrases from triggering your ads by including quotations around the phrase. The word order is preserved, meaning if someone searches for a negative keyword you are using in a different word order, your ads could still appear. For example, if you have a negative phrase "it jobs," your ads would not show on query "find it jobs," but could show on a query such as "jobs in it."

Negative Exact match allows you to exclude a specific phrase only by including brackets around a word or phrase. Any additional words, variations or queries in a different order would still potentially trigger your ads. For example, if you have [it jobs] as a negative exact, your ads could still show on searches like "find it jobs" or "it job."

The following table highlights how the different match types would help you filter traffic and what queries would and would not trigger your ads based on your negative match type:

Search Query ✓ Ads show ✗ Ads do not show	**Negative Broad** **-jobs**	**Negative Broad** **-it jobs**	**Negative Phrase** **-"it jobs"**	**Negative Exact** **-[it jobs]**
It jobs	✗	✗	✗	✗
It job	✓	✓	✓	✓
Information technology jobs	✗	✓	✓	✓
Jobs it	✗	✗	✓	✓
Find it jobs	✗	✗	✗	✓
Jobs in it	✗	✗	✓	✓
It career	✓	✓	✓	✓

There's more...

Review your list of negative keywords regularly to ensure you are using negative match types correctly and are not excluding any relevant traffic. Since misspellings, plurals, or other variations are not included with any of the negative match types, expand your negatives by including all related phrases.

See also

- The *Running search terms reports to optimize keywords* recipe in *Chapter 11, Optimizing Performance*
- The *Generating negative keywords* recipe in *Chapter 5, Creating Relevant Keywords*

Automating actions based on rules and goals

Automated rules in AdWords can save you time managing and optimizing your account by performing changes to your campaigns based on the criteria you specify. For example, you can adjust bids based on specific goals and latest performance or pause ads when a certain promotion is set to end.

Getting ready

Plan how to best take advantage of automation. Here are a few ways you can use automated rules:

- Adjust bids based on ad position, conversions, and other factors. For example, you can increase bids on your top converting keywords.
- Pause or activate campaigns, keywords, or ads that feature special promotions. For example, if you have a free shipping promotion running for a few days only, you can activate and schedule ads to be paused automatically on specific start and end dates.
- Adjust campaign budgets based on performance. For example, you can schedule campaign budgets to automatically increase when a campaign is losing impression share due to budget.
- Pause low performing ad groups or keywords. For example, you can pause poor Quality Score keywords that are not generating any conversions.

How to do it...

To set up automated rules, follow these steps:

1. Go to the **Campaigns** tab and click on a campaign where you'd like to set up automated rules.
2. Go to the tab where you'd like to make changes. For example, if you would like to automate budget changes, click on the **Campaigns** tab. To automate keyword bid changes, click on the **Keywords** tab.
3. Here, we'll walk through how to schedule all ads containing a special promotion to be paused on a specific date. To make changes to ads, we'll go to the **Ads** tab.
4. Click on **Automate** and choose **Pause ads when...**:

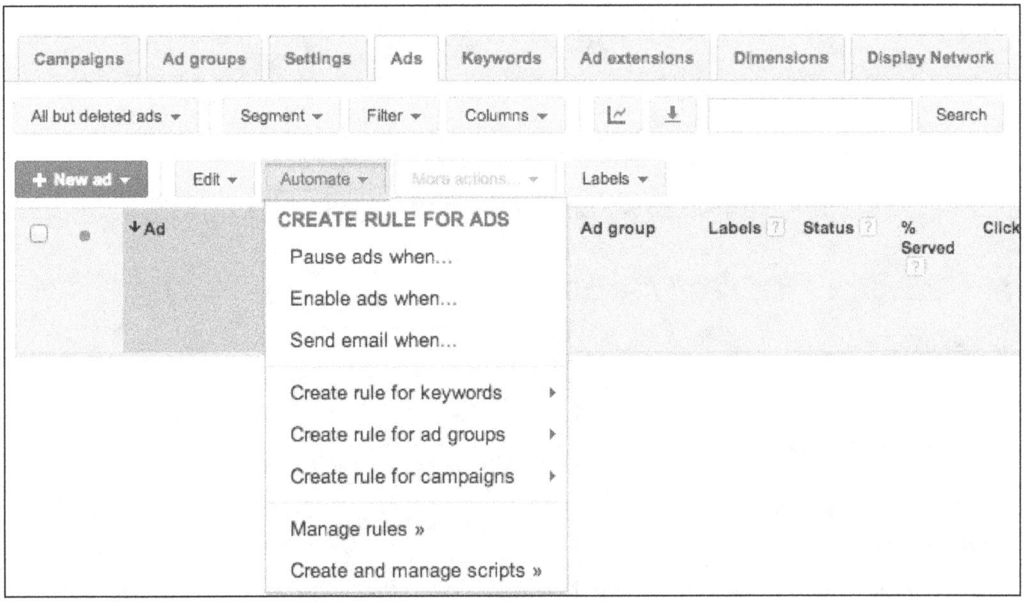

5. Select your requirements. Click on **+ Add another** to layer on additional criteria.
6. Choose your **Frequency** or when your rule will run. Our rule will be a one-time rule, but you can set-up daily, weekly, or monthly rules as well.
7. Choose a **Rule name**, keeping it descriptive to the action that will be performed.
8. Under **Email results**, pick if and how you would like AdWords to notify you when this rule runs.

9. Preview the results to see what would change if your rule ran.

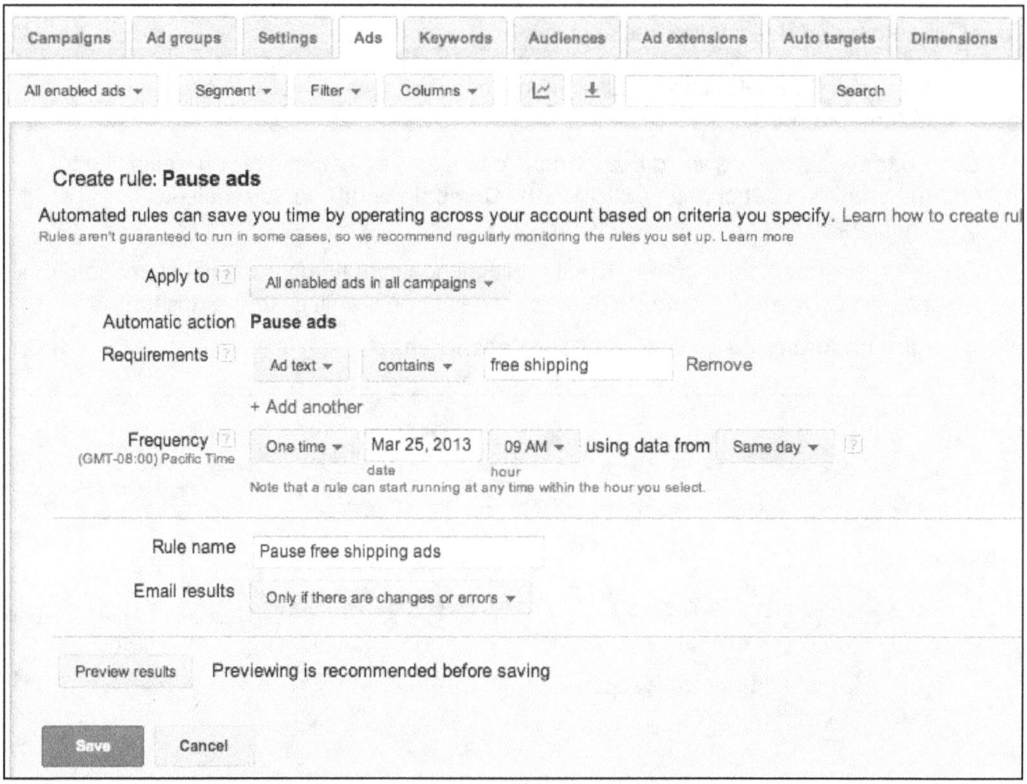

10. Click on **Save**.

How it works...

Automated rules help you perform account changes based on criteria you specify. They can save time and automate tasks based on your goals and changing business needs. You can edit or pause your automated rules at any time. Additionally, you can view details of edits that were made and undo the latest changes. If you are not comfortable with changes being implemented in your account, you can instead choose to receive emails based on your requirements.

There's more...

Monitor your rules on a regular basis and edit them when necessary. In your **Campaigns** tab, click on **Bulk operations** at the bottom left of the screen and choose **Manage rules**. Click on **Edit rule** to revise your settings.

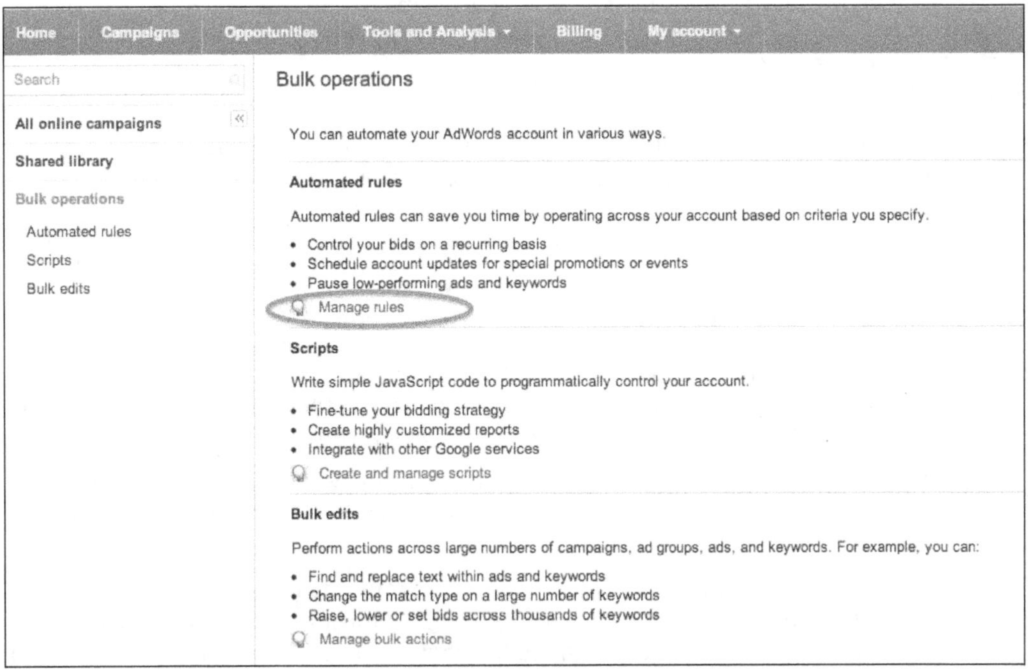

Logs provide data on changes that were made and allow you to undo the latest changes.

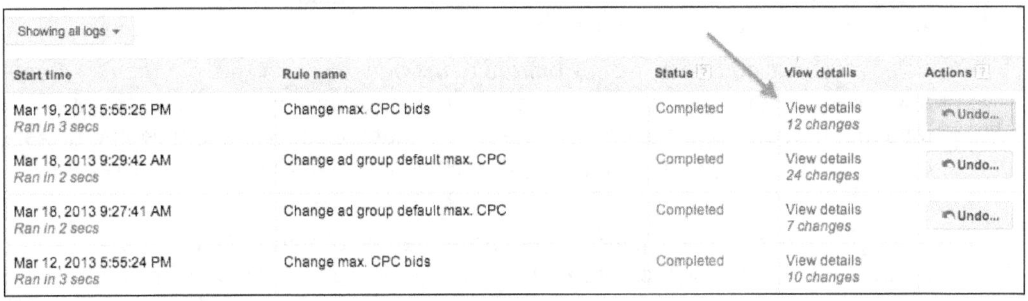

See also

- The *Setting and adjusting ad group level bids* recipe in *Chapter 6, Budgets and Bidding*
- The *Setting and adjusting keyword level bids* recipe in *Chapter 6, Budgets and Bidding*

Common AdWords mistakes

In this section, we'll discuss some of the common mistakes advertisers make with AdWords. Google AdWords offers so many features and options that it's easy to overlook a few key components. Review the following list and compare them to your campaigns to ensure you are following AdWords best practices and not committing some of the common errors.

Getting ready

Review your campaigns and revisit of structure, keywords, budgets and bids. Prepare to take note of any issues and opportunities based on the following list.

How to do it...

Here are 10 common mistakes I see advertisers make with AdWords:

- *Not separating campaigns by network*. Having separate campaigns for search and display allows you to control your budget more precisely and help you ensure that the network that's performing better gets more of your ad dollars.
- *Poor ad group structure*. Most businesses starting out with AdWords create one campaign and one ad group with many only loosely related keywords. This practice results in low Quality Scores and costly clicks.
- *Picking the wrong keywords*. Monitor conversion rates, bounce rates and time on site to ensure keywords you have chosen bring engaged visitors to your website. Keywords that are too general, such as one-word keywords, can use up a lot of your budget and lower your Quality Scores.
- *Forgetting about negative keywords*. Negative keywords are a key tool you can use to achieve better Quality Scores, CTR and conversion rates. Failing to add negative keywords means you are paying for some unqualified clicks and losing money.
- *Using a generic ad that is not customized to the ad group and keyword themes*. Some advertisers split up their keywords into multiple ad groups, but they often forget to take that next step and customize the ads. Ads that are specific to your keywords get better CTRs and help with your Quality Scores, reducing how much you need to pay for each click.
- *Setting default bids not adjusted based on actual performance*. Ad group and keyword bids should be modified regularly based on position, conversions and other key metrics.
- *Forgetting to implement ad extensions, such as sitelinks, social annotations or call extensions*. Adding these extra elements help your ads stand apart by adding extra relevant lines to your ad text.

- *Not monitoring your competition*. Use third-party tools to keep track of any changes to keywords and test any new terms your competition is trying out. Also keep track of changes to competitors' ad copy to make sure your ads are unique and appealing.
- *Making changes to your account without keeping your end goal in mind*. For example, you might get distracted with the need to be in the #1 position for some of your keywords, when those keywords might not be profitable for you. Keep your business goals first and foremost as you make changes.
- *Set and forget it mentality*. Not every campaign and strategy you try in AdWords will actually work for you. After launching any new keywords, ads or other features, monitor performance to ensure you're getting the traffic that you want. Schedule reports to be emailed to you on a regular basis to help you stay on track.

How it works...

Not following best practices and monitoring your campaigns can hurt your AdWords performance. Go through the list of common errors periodically, to make sure you are not committing some of the typical mistakes advertisers make.

See also

- The *Common ways to structure campaigns* recipe in *Chapter 4, Structuring Your Account*
- The *Creating themed ad groups* recipe in *Chapter 4, Structuring Your Account*
- The *Finding relevant keywords* recipe in *Chapter 5, Creating Relevant Keywords*
- The *Generating negative keywords* recipe in *Chapter 5, Creating Relevant Keywords*
- The *Creating effective ads* recipe in *Chapter 6, Writing Compelling Ads*
- The *Running and scheduling reports* recipe in *Chapter 10, Reporting and Analysis*
- The *Setting and adjusting ad group level bids* recipe in *Chapter 7, Budgets and Bidding*
- The *Setting and adjusting keyword level bids* recipe in *Chapter 7, Budgets and Bidding*

13
Managing AdWords

In this chapter, we will cover:

- Troubleshooting why your ads are not showing up
- Finding out your ad's approval status
- Creating custom alerts to monitor performance
- Reviewing past changes and revisions
- Viewing or hiding paused or deleted items
- Getting started with AdWords Editor
- Making changes to campaign settings via AdWords Editor
- Reviewing account statistics through AdWords Editor
- Copying campaigns or ad groups with AdWords Editor
- Adding keywords in bulk using AdWords Editor
- Updating ads in bulk using AdWords Editor

Introduction

The numerous account management tools in AdWords can help you troubleshoot and make changes to your campaigns more efficiently. From figuring out why your ads are not showing, to making large-scale edits to keywords and ads, there are free tools available to you that will make day-to-day account tasks more manageable.

Troubleshooting why your ads are not showing up

There are a variety of reasons why your ads might not be showing on Google, with the most common issue being a limited budget. To help you take the guesswork out of this process, AdWords provides the Ad Preview and Diagnosis tool.

Getting ready

Take note of keywords that you are concerned about, as well as locations and devices you are searching from.

How to do it...

To diagnose why your ads are not showing up on Google, follow these steps:

1. Click on **Tools and Analysis** and choose the **Ad Preview and Diagnosis Tool**.
2. Choose your domain, language, location, and device.
3. Enter your keyword into the search box and click on **Preview**.
4. Once you click on **Preview**, your diagnosis for the searched keyword will load and you'll see if your ads are showing under **Showing ads right now?**.
5. If your ads are not showing you'll receive an explanation detailing what is causing this (such as low ad rank or limited budget):

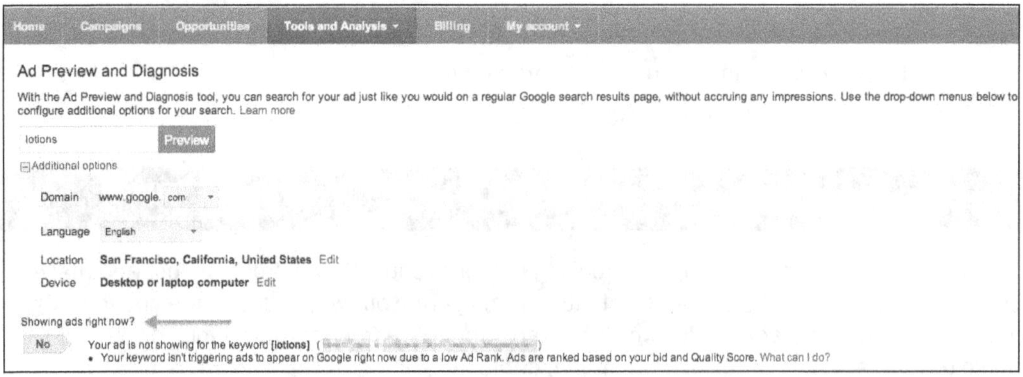

6. Clicking on the **What can I do?** link will take you to a help article with tips on how to resolve your issue.

At the bottom of the **Ad Preview and Diagnosis tool**, you'll see Google's search results for your query. If your ad is currently showing up, you can preview your ad through this tool, rather than searching on `Google.com` and accumulating impressions on your own keywords.

How it works...

Ad Preview and Diagnosis tool is available to all AdWords advertisers to help preview ads and troubleshoot performance issues. It diagnoses your budgets, bids, Quality Scores and other settings to provide a custom analysis of why your ads are not showing. It's also helpful when you'd like to see the ad position your ads are appearing on `Google.com`, or see ads that are appearing in multiple geographies.

See also

- The *Finding out your ad's approval status* recipe

Finding out your ad's approval status

Each ad submitted to AdWords goes through editorial review to ensure that your ads and website comply with Google's advertising policies. Depending on your approval status, your ads might not be showing to all users, so make sure you understand your ad's status. An automated AdWords check makes the ad "eligible" to show to users with safe search turned off. Once the ads have been approved, they can be shown to all users.

How to do it...

To check the status of your ads:

1. Click on the **Campaigns** tab.
2. Click on the **Ads** tab.

3. Check the **Status** column for each ad to see an ad's current approval status:

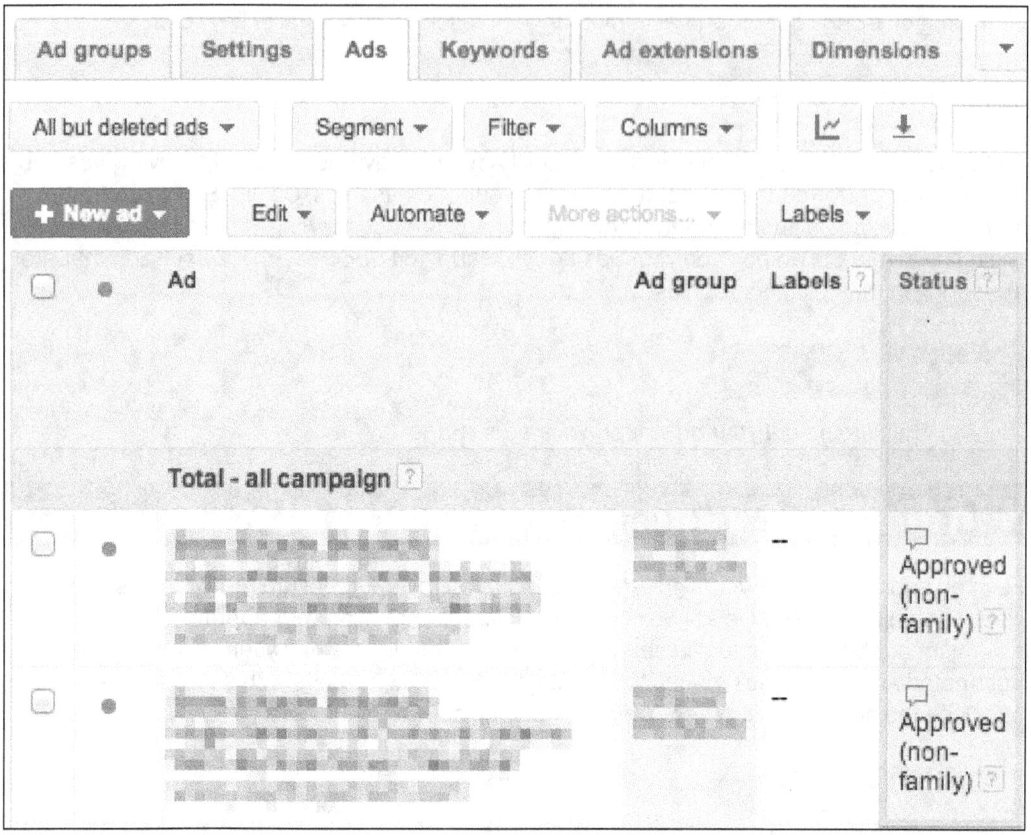

4. If your ad is disapproved, you'll find out why your ad was rejected as you hover over the disapproved status speech bubble.
5. Create a filter if you wish to easily access any disapproved ads or ads that are under review. Go to your **Ads** tab and click on **Create filter** from the **Filter** drop-down menu. Choose **Approval Status** from the available filter options, and select the ad statuses you wish to monitor:

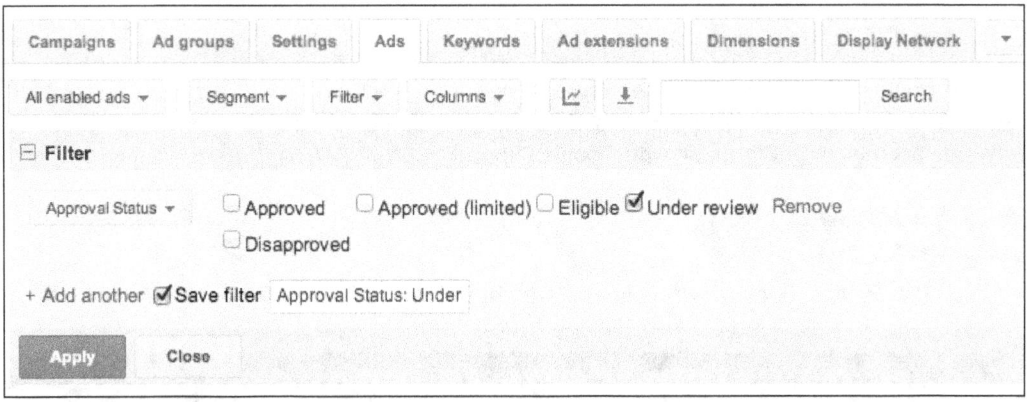

How it works...

Your ad's status determines if your ad is eligible to run and who can see your ads. Ads that have not yet been reviewed may not be showing up. If an ad does not meet the editorial and product requirements, your ads are disapproved and you'll receive an e-mail. However, if your ad has been approved or is still pending, you will not receive an e-mail and you'll need to check your account to understand the status of your ads.

Possible approval statuses include:

- **Under review**: Your ad is in queue to be reviewed and is not currently running.
- **Eligible**: Your ad has still not been reviewed but it's eligible to show on Google.
- **Approved**: Your ad passed the editorial review and is eligible to run.
- **Approved (limited)**: Your ad was approved but there are limitations on where or when it can show. This is a common approval status for groups of restricted products like alcohol or trademarks.
- **Approved (non-family)**: Your ads and website content have adult themes and will not appear to users who have activated safe search filters.
- **Approved (adult)**: Your ads have nudity and other non-family safe content and will only appear to select users searching for adult content. Your ads may not be eligible to show up in all countries.
- **Disapproved**: Your ads violated advertising policies and are currently not running.
- **Site suspended**: Your website does not comply with AdWords policies and none of your ads pointing to the suspended website are currently running.

There's more...

If you submitted your ad and it's been under review for more than three days, you can contact AdWords to expedite the review process. Click on the **Help** link at the top-right corner of your AdWords account to get in touch with Google support.

See also

- The *Troubleshooting why your ads are not showing up* recipe

Creating custom alerts to monitor performance

If you're worried about missing key AdWords trends or issues related to your account, you can schedule an automated e-mail to be sent to you when certain conditions are met. This feature can help you stay on track with important developments and can help you quickly fix problems before they become major issues.

Getting ready

Decide what you'd like to monitor. Here are some ideas on e-mail alerts you can set up for potentially troublesome issues:

- Campaigns or ad groups receive no impressions
- Keyword CTR falls below a certain threshold
- Keywords are not triggering ads or are not eligible to run
- Keywords have below first page bids
- Keywords have low Quality Scores
- Ads are under review or disapproved
- You are losing impression share

How to do it...

To set up e-mail alerts, follow these instructions:

1. Click on the **Campaigns** tab.
2. Select the tab related to the alert you wish to receive. For example, if you'd like to receive an alert about keywords, click on the **Keywords** tab. You can also go into a specific campaign or ad group first.
3. From the **Automate** drown-down menu, choose **Send email when...**.

4. Choose what this rule should apply to. For example, all enabled keywords.
5. Select your **Requirements** or conditions that should be met. For example, your condition could be a status alert for **Keywords not triggering ads: critical issues**:

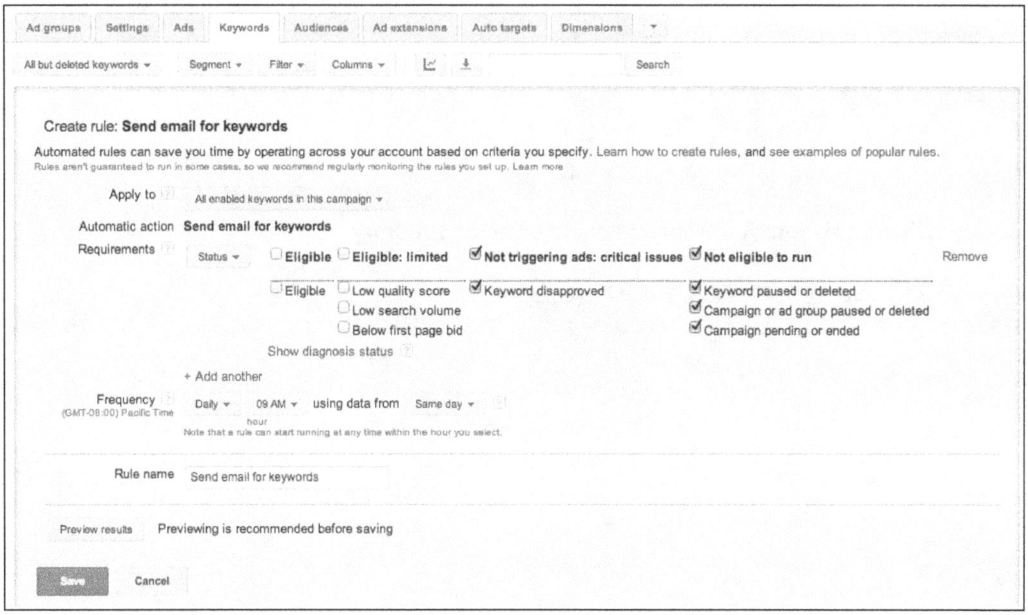

6. Choose your **Frequency**, or how often your rule will run. Create multiple instances of the same rule if you wish to run a rule multiple times a day.
7. Name your rule and preview your results.
8. Click on **Save**.

How it works...

Automated rules allow you to monitor performance trends and receive e-mail alerts when certain conditions are met. You can create multiple e-mail alerts and pause or edit your requirements at any time. To access and edit your rules, go to **Bulk operations** in your AdWords account and choose **Automated rules**.

See also

- The *Automating actions based on rules and goals* recipe

Reviewing past changes and revisions

Change history in AdWords allows you to access past revisions made within your AdWords account. This tool can help you track edits made by multiple users, as well as help diagnose changes to traffic patterns or performance.

How to do it...

To access your change history, follow these steps:

1. Go to **Tools and Analysis** and choose **Change history**:

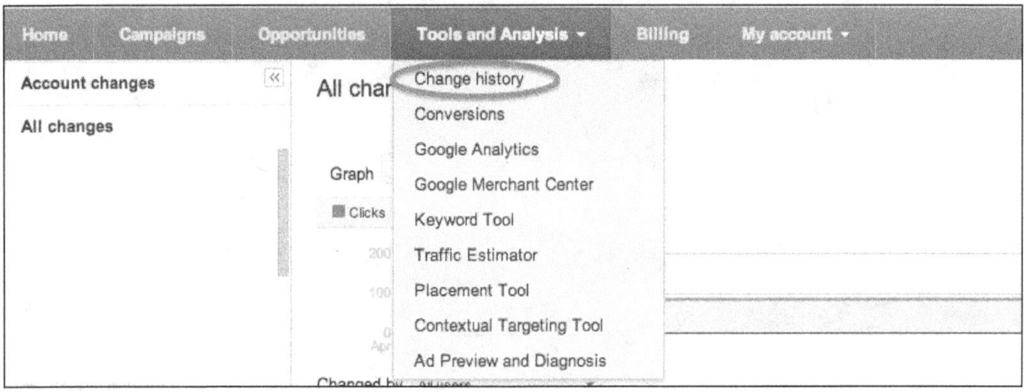

2. Adjust your date range to reflect your desired dates with the same date selector you use for all other tasks in AdWords.
3. You have the option to view a graph with traffic and conversion patterns, so you can zero in on specific dates that show spikes or significant dips.
4. Under **Changed by**, you can view only the changes made by specific users:

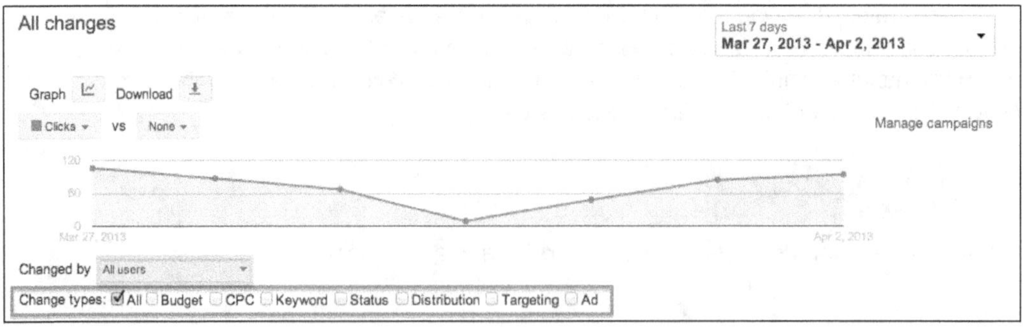

5. Under **Change types**, you can select what changes you would like to focus on. The options include:
    - **All**
    - **Budget**
    - **CPC**
    - **Keyword**
    - **Status**
    - **Distribution**
    - **Targeting**
    - **Ad**
6. When you click on **Show details** next to a specific change, you can see additional information, such as what new text ad was created.
7. If you hover over a specific campaign or ad group until you see a pencil icon, clicking on it will take you directly into that campaign or ad group, so you can make any other necessary changes.
8. Click on **Download** to export the changes to one of the following formats:
    - CSV for Excel
    - CSV
    - TSV
    - XML
    - GZipped CSV

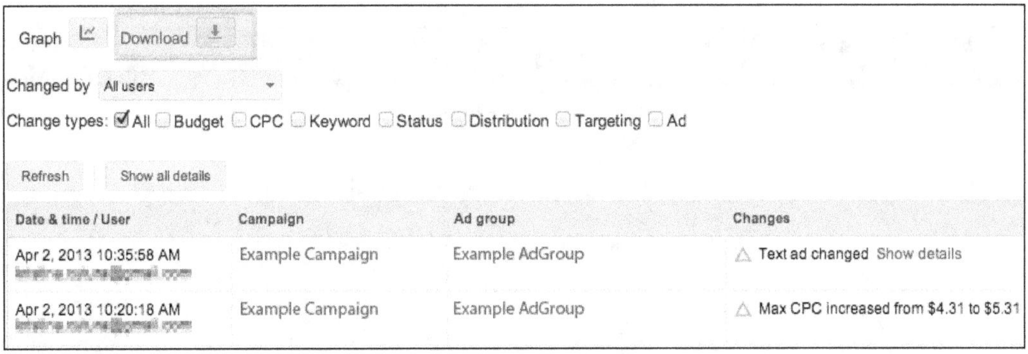

How it works...

Change history is an AdWords tool that allows you to access changes made by various users. You can see all changes made in the last two years or select specific dates of interest. A graph helps you pinpoint traffic patterns, and a download button allows you to export all changes.

See also

- The *Running and scheduling reports* recipe in *Chapter 9, Reporting and Analysis*

Viewing or hiding paused or deleted items

The AdWords campaign management page can be customized so that you are only looking at data of interest to you. One of the more basic features is viewing or hiding paused or deleted items. For example, if you have a lot of campaigns you have been testing, you may choose to hide deleted or paused campaigns so that you can focus on just the campaigns you are currently running.

Getting ready

Before you can use this feature, you will need to have a few campaigns, keywords, or ads in your account. Some of them should be active while others can be paused or deleted.

How to do it..

To hide paused or deleted items, follow these steps:

1. Click on the **Campaigns** tab.
2. Navigate to your sub-tab of interest. For example, click on **Campaigns**.
3. Select **All enabled** to only see active campaigns and hide paused or deleted campaigns:

To view paused or deleted items:

1. Click on the **Campaigns** tab.
2. Navigate to your sub-tab of interest. For example, click on **Keywords**.
3. Select **All** to see active as well as previously deleted keywords:

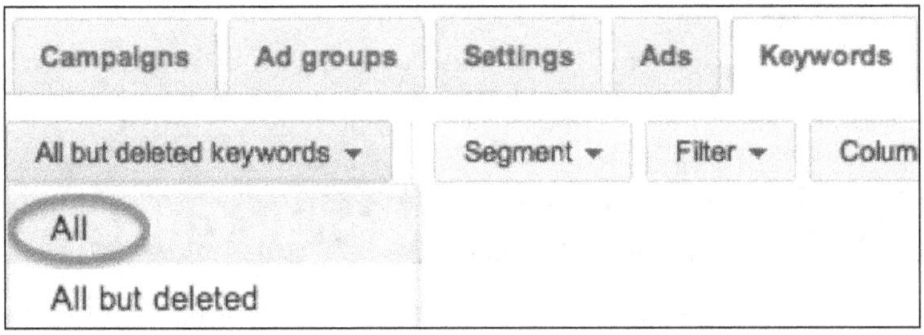

How it works...

AdWords hides campaigns, ad groups, keywords and ads that you may not want to review at this time. However, this information will still remain in your account should you want to reference it at a later date.

In sub-tabs **Campaigns** and **Ad Groups**, choose from one of the three options:

- **All**
- **All enabled**
- **All but deleted**

In all other sub-tabs, choose from the following two options:

- **All**
- **All but deleted**

Here is an explanation of what the settings mean:

- **All**: Lets you view all currently active and previously paused or deleted items.
- **All enabled**: Lets you view currently active items only. Any paused or deleted items will not show.
- **All but deleted**: Lets you view currently active and paused items only. Any deleted items will not show.

There's more...

There is no way to permanently delete data from your account and have it disappear completely from the interface. Deleted campaigns, ad groups, keywords, and ads will continue to show up in the interface if you select to view all data.

See also

- The *Reviewing past changes and revisions* recipe

Getting started with AdWords Editor

AdWords Editor is a free Google tool that helps you manage and update your campaigns. It's ideal for advertisers who need to make bulk changes to keywords or ads. This can be done through AdWords Editor in just minutes. You can work offline and sync your changes to AdWords, making daily management and updates much more efficient than working through the AdWords online interface.

Getting ready

You'll need your AdWords account and username in order to download your account to AdWords Editor.

How to do it...

To download your account to AdWords Editor:

1. In your browser, go to `http://www.google.com/intl/en/adwordseditor/`
2. Specify if you use Windows or a Mac, though the correct option should be automatically checked for you.

3. Click on **Download AdWords Editor** and follow the prompts to install the tool.

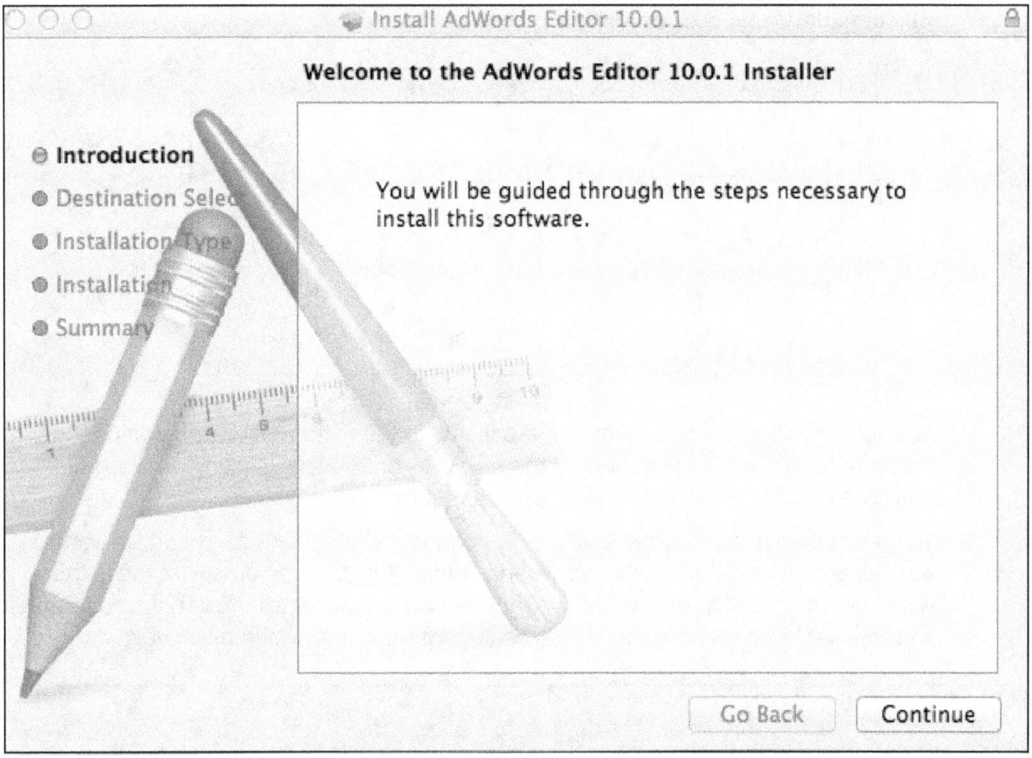

4. Once AdWords Editor has been downloaded, you'll need to open your AdWords account. The prompt to do so should appear automatically after you download AdWords Editor.
5. Click on **Add account**.
6. Enter your AdWords e-mail address and password. Check **Remember this password** if you want to save it.

7. Click on **Next** and choose which parts of the account you want to download. You can choose all campaigns or select specific campaigns. Generally, you'll want to choose **All campaigns** and click on **OK**:

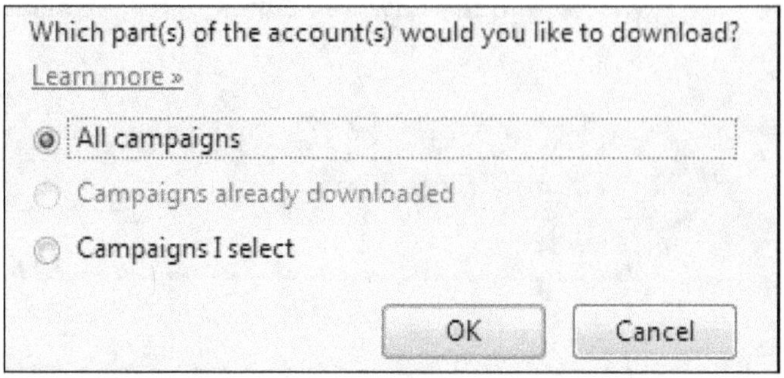

8. After downloading your account, get familiar with the various view and edit options. Your campaigns will be listed out in the tree view on the left. Clicking on a specific campaign will show you the individual ad groups.
9. The tabs in the middle of the AdWords Editor application allow you to edit keywords, ads, ad groups, targeting, extensions, and campaigns. Clicking on any of these tabs will show additional available options for that category, such as the various ad formats you can add or edit. For example, you can update text ads or add new image ads.

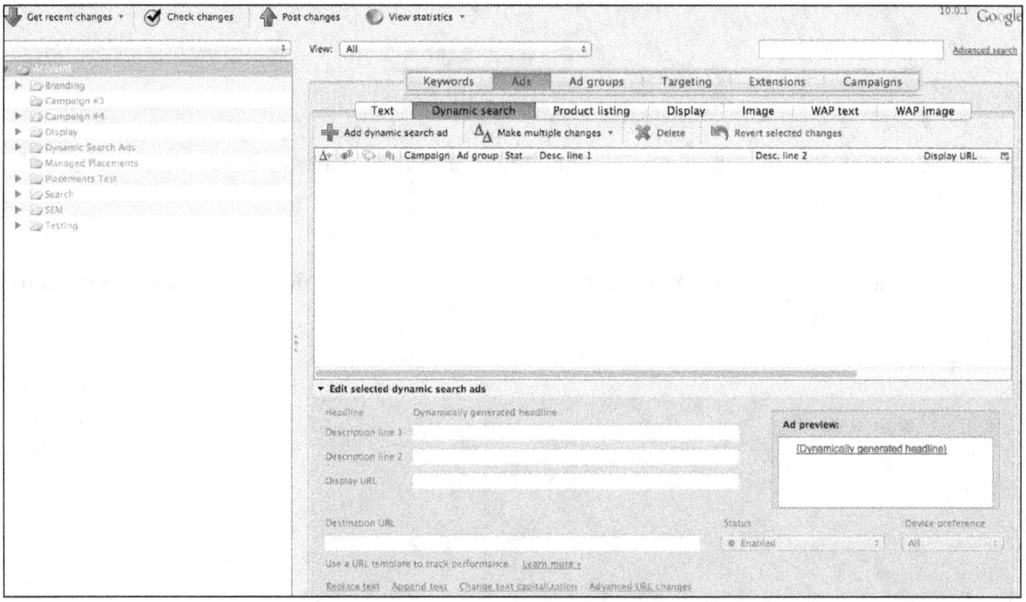

10. The changes you make in AdWords Editor will be saved but not posted to your account until you choose to post changes.

How it works...

AdWords Editor is a Google application that allows you to make changes to your AdWords account offline. The changes you make in AdWords Editor are saved but are not live until you choose to publish them to your account. The tool allows you to collaborate with others and share proposed edits. You can export your entire account or specific campaigns, as well as import files (such as new keywords) into your account.

There's more...

Before working on your account in AdWords Editor, or posting any changes to AdWords, make sure you click on **Get recent changes** to have the latest version of your account downloaded to your AdWords Editor application:

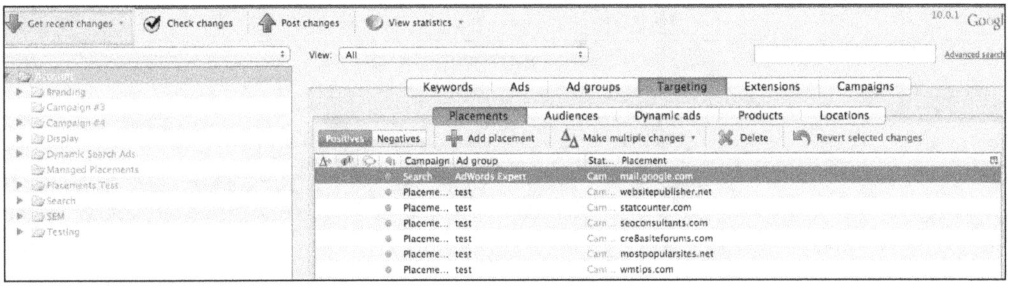

See also

- The *Planning account structure* recipe in *Chapter 3, Structuring Your Account*
- The *Reviewing past changes and revisions* recipe

Making changes to campaign settings via AdWords Editor

If you need to make changes to campaign settings, like adjusting budgets or location targeting across multiple campaigns, you can do so easily and quickly through AdWords Editor.

Getting ready

Download AdWords Editor and sync your account to the application. Next, decide what changes you would like to implement across your campaigns and which campaigns you'll need to edit.

How to do it...

To adjust campaign settings through AdWords Editor:

1. Open up AdWords Editor.
2. Click on **Get recent changes** to ensure you are editing the current version of your account.
3. Click on the **Campaigns** tab.
4. Select the campaigns you wish to edit.
5. Click to expand the **Edit select campaigns** panel.
6. Here you can adjust campaign settings for multiple campaigns you select at once in bulk. For example, you can change all selected campaigns' ad rotation to optimize for conversions or adjust mobile bids across multiple campaigns.

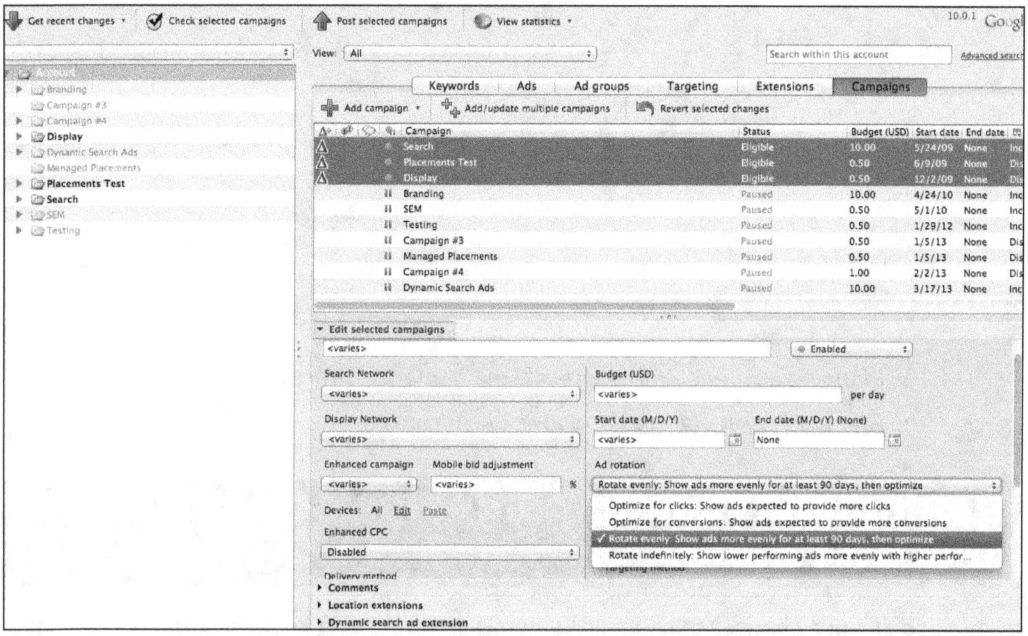

7. The campaigns you edit will be highlighted in bold in the tree view on the left of your AdWords Editor application. They'll also display a triangle icon in your **Campaigns** tab.
8. Click on **Post selected campaigns** when you are ready to make the changes live.

How it works...

AdWords Editor allows you to adjust campaign settings offline and later post your changes to your account. You can edit multiple campaigns at once and make bulk changes in a more scalable way than going through the AdWords interface. Examples of changes you can make include:

- Pause or enable multiple campaigns at once
- Change campaign budgets
- Adjust mobile bids
- Enable or disable Enhanced CPC
- Change delivery method, which dictates if ads are shown evenly throughout the day or as quickly as possible
- Adjust campaign start and end dates
- Edit network targeting
- Change ad rotation
- Edit location or language targeting

See also

- The *Getting started with AdWords Editor* recipe

Reviewing account statistics through AdWords Editor

AdWords Editor allows users to view AdWords account statistics, such as ad position and costs, within the application so you can make changes based on the latest data. Perhaps you are considering making a change to bids or budgets, but want to first reference the latest performance? Rather than switching back and forth between the AdWords user interface and AdWords Editor, you can download data to AdWords Editor and see everything you need on one screen.

How to do it...

To view account statistics in AdWords Editor:

1. Open up AdWords Editor.
2. Click on **Get recent changes**.
3. Click on **View statistics** at the top of your AdWords Editor application.

4. Choose if you'd like to download statistics for your entire account or for selected campaigns or ad groups.
5. Select one of the pre-set date range options or enter a custom date range:

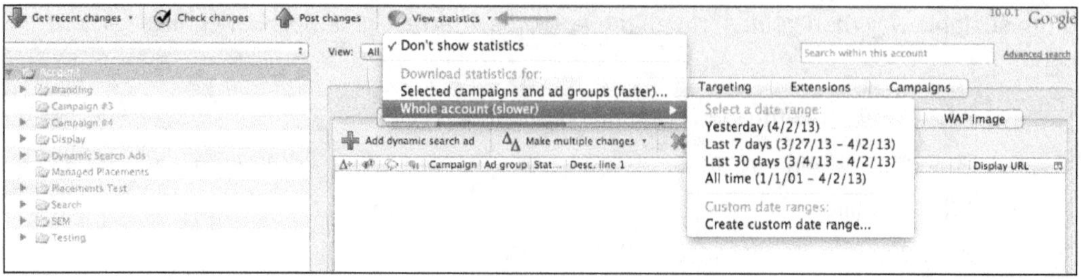

6. Once AdWords Editor has finished downloading the data, you'll see your statistics in the various tabs.
7. Customize your column views so you are seeing the data you need, such as conversions:

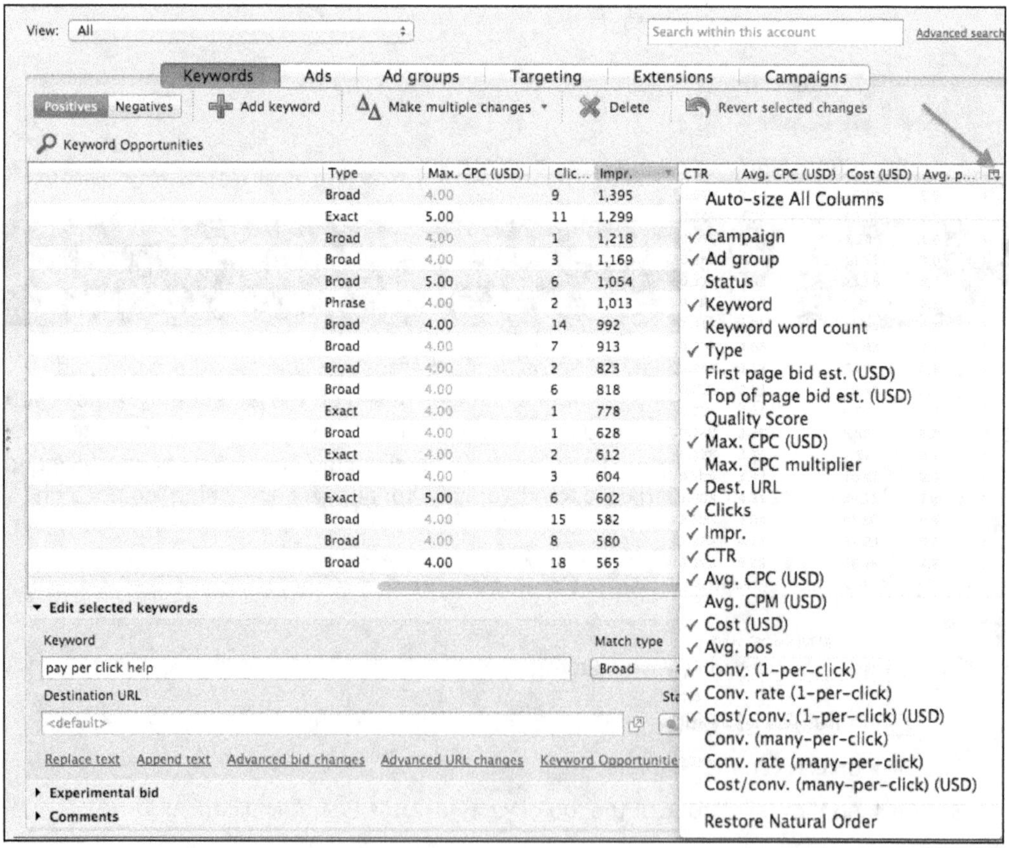

8. You can sort your statistics by various column headers, such as impressions and CTR. Sorting can help you prioritize where to make changes by identifying low CTR keywords, for example.
9. Make changes based on your data, such as bid and budget adjustments, and post to AdWords.

How it works...

The view statistics feature in AdWords Editor downloads performance data for selected campaigns and ad groups or for your entire account. You can customize columns to see statistics you care about and sort the data by various performance metrics, such as CTR or average position.

See also

- The *Getting started with AdWords Editor* recipe

Copying campaigns or ad groups with AdWords Editor

Do you need to create mirror versions of your campaigns to target different locations? Or perhaps you want to copy entire ad groups and simply replace certain phrases to create new, unique ad groups? You can do all of that easily through AdWords Editor.

Getting ready

Decide which campaigns or ad groups you'll need to copy. Next, figure out what you'll need to adjust once you copy a campaign or an ad group.

For example, if you are copying a campaign, you'll likely want to adjust a copied campaign's target locations and budget.

How to do it...

To copy campaigns or ad groups in AdWords Editor:

1. Open up AdWords Editor.
2. Click on **Get recent changes**.
3. Click on the **Campaigns** tab. If you are planning to copy ad groups, click on the **Ad groups** tab.

4. Select the campaigns or ad groups you wish to copy.
5. Go to **Edit** and click on **Copy**, and then **Paste**. You can also use keyboard shortcuts.

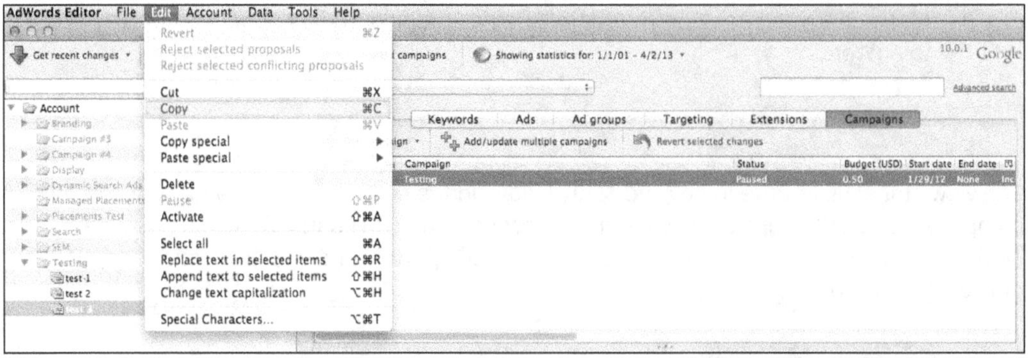

6. Next, you'll want to rename your copied campaigns or ad groups and make any other necessary adjustments. For example, if you copied an ad group, you might want to replace keyword phrases or text in the copied ad groups. Go to **Edit** and click on **Replace text in selected items** or use keyboard shortcuts:

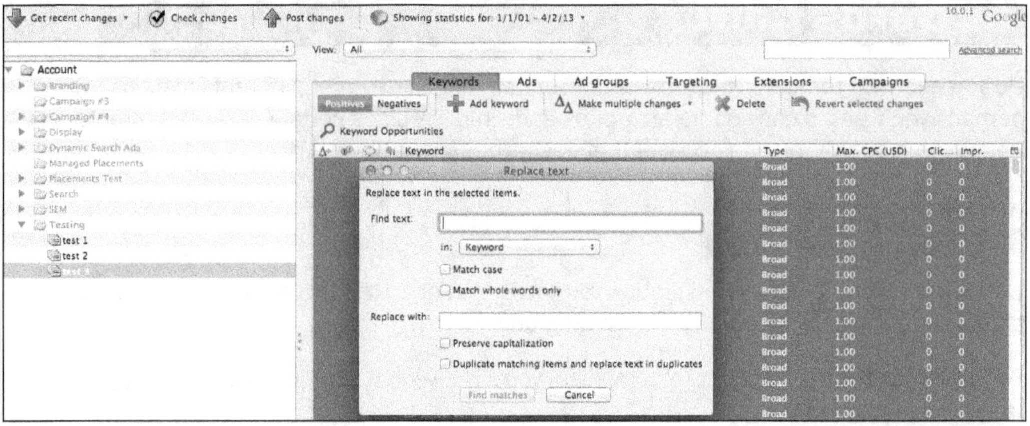

7. When you are confident that the changes are ready to go live, click on **Post changes**.

How it works...

The copy and paste features in AdWords Editor help you expand your account in a scalable way. The various elements of campaigns or ad groups being copied are duplicated in the application and can be posted directly to your AdWords account. Keep an eye on Quality Scores when copy-pasting a large amount of campaigns or ad groups.

See also

- The *Getting started with AdWords Editor* recipe

Adding keywords in bulk using AdWords Editor

If you have dozens, hundreds, or thousands of keywords that you need to add to your account, AdWords Editor can be a great time saver. You can import your keywords from a spreadsheet into the application, or copy and paste keyword lists you are working on into select campaigns and ad groups.

Getting ready

Prepare your new keywords and figure out which campaigns and ad groups they should be added to. You have the following options:

- Create an AdWords Editor-friendly CSV file and import it to AdWords Editor. The easiest way to get started would be to export your current campaigns and then add any new keywords you wish to create to the exported spreadsheet. In AdWords Editor, go to **File**, choose **Export spreadsheet (CSV)** and select what you would like to export. Click on **Save** to keep a copy of your file and choose where on your computer you'd like to save it. Your new keywords should have campaign and ad group names filled in so Editor knows where those keywords should go. Make sure you include keyword match types as well as unique bids, if necessary.

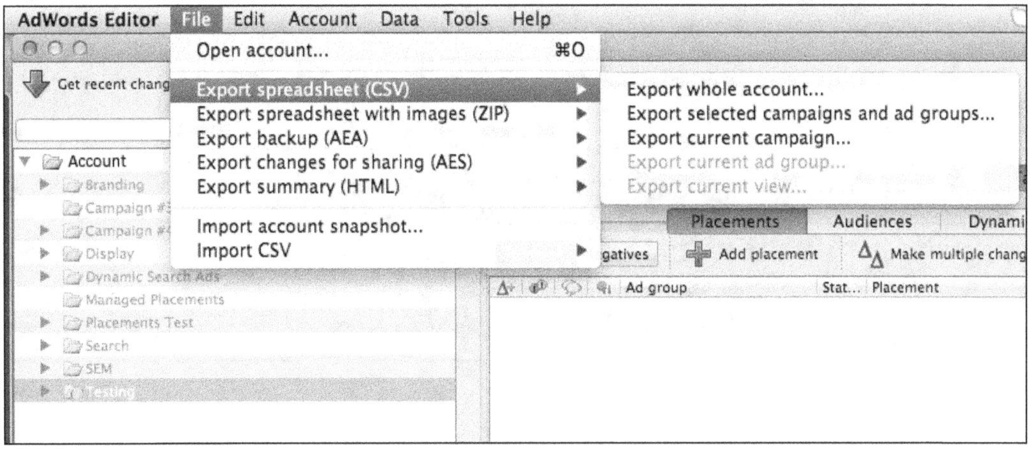

- The other option is to copy and paste keywords you're working on directly into select campaigns and ad groups. You do not need to create custom columns for your campaigns and ad groups, and you can choose keyword match types after you add your keywords to AdWords Editor.

How to do it...

To add keywords via AdWords Editor, follow these steps:

1. Open up AdWords Editor.
2. Click on **Get recent changes**.
3. If you have an AdWords Editor-ready CSV file to import, go to **File**, choose **Import CSV**, and choose if you would like to paste text or import an actual file. Move through the prompts to confirm and review your changes:

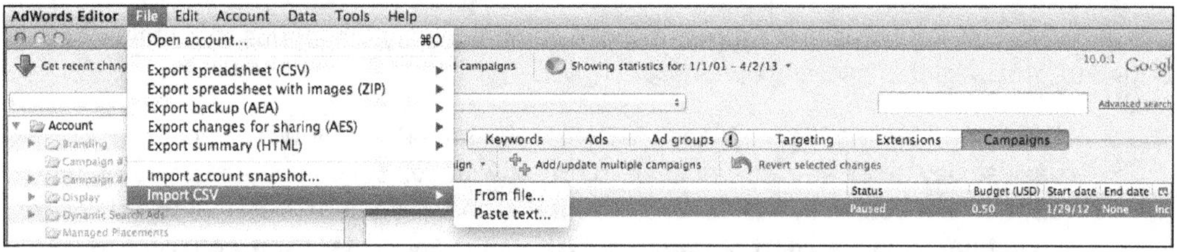

4. AdWords Editor will summarize the changes you are about to make for you, including how many keywords you'll be adding and any other edits.
5. The new additions will be highlighted in green and you'll be able to keep or reject the changes:

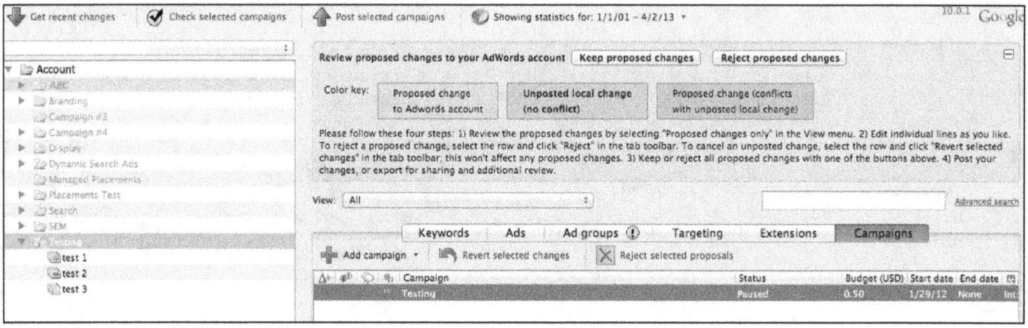

6. If you do not have a properly formatted CSV file, you can still add new keywords through a simple copy and paste. Click on the **Keywords** tab. You can either add a single keyword by clicking on **+ Add keyword**, or you can add multiple keywords by choosing **Make multiple changes**:

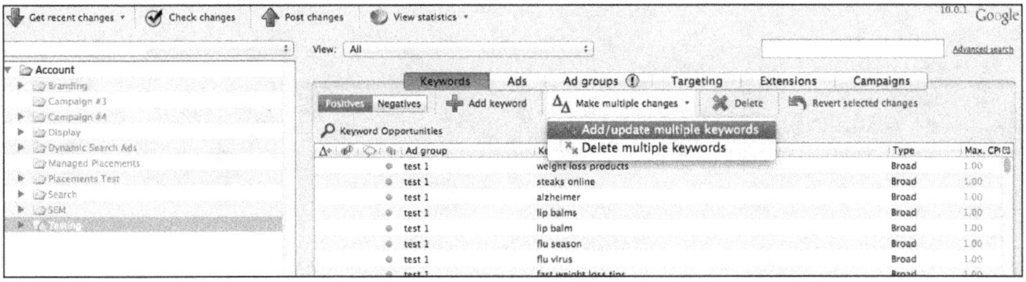

7. Select the campaigns and ad groups your keywords should be added to. Type or paste your keywords into the keyword box. You can also set match types, maximum CPCs, and unique destination URLs, as well as a keyword's status. Once your keywords have been entered in, click on **Process** and then on **Finish**.

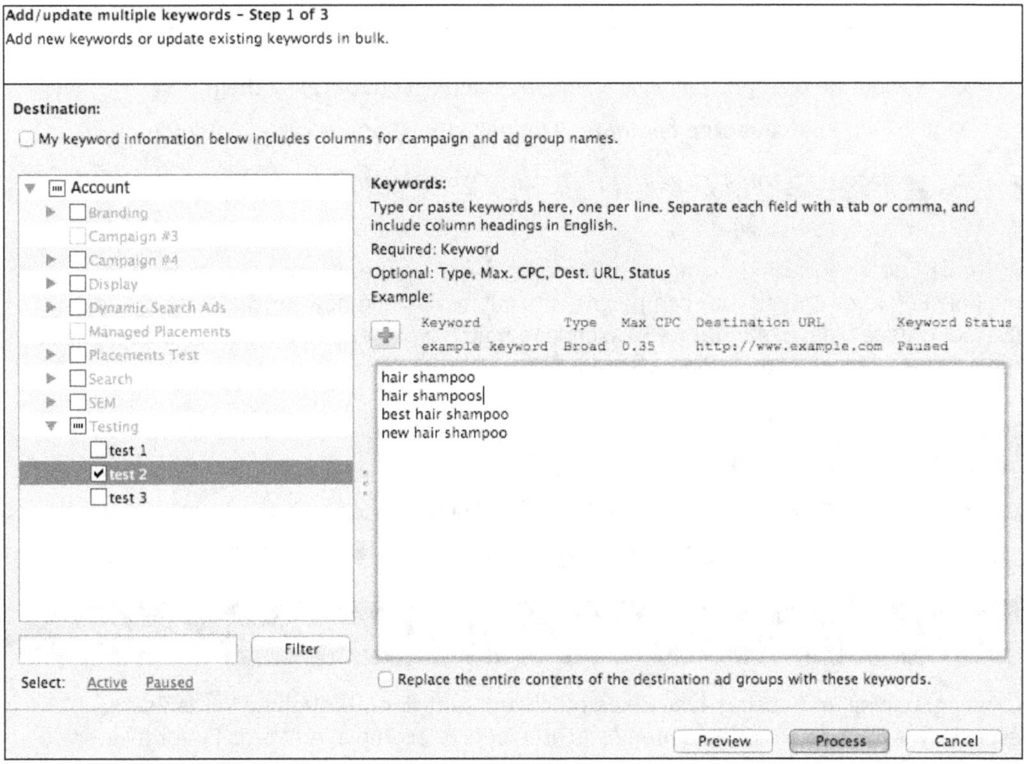

8. If you do not set specific match types, you can change them in the **Keywords** tab after you import the new terms:

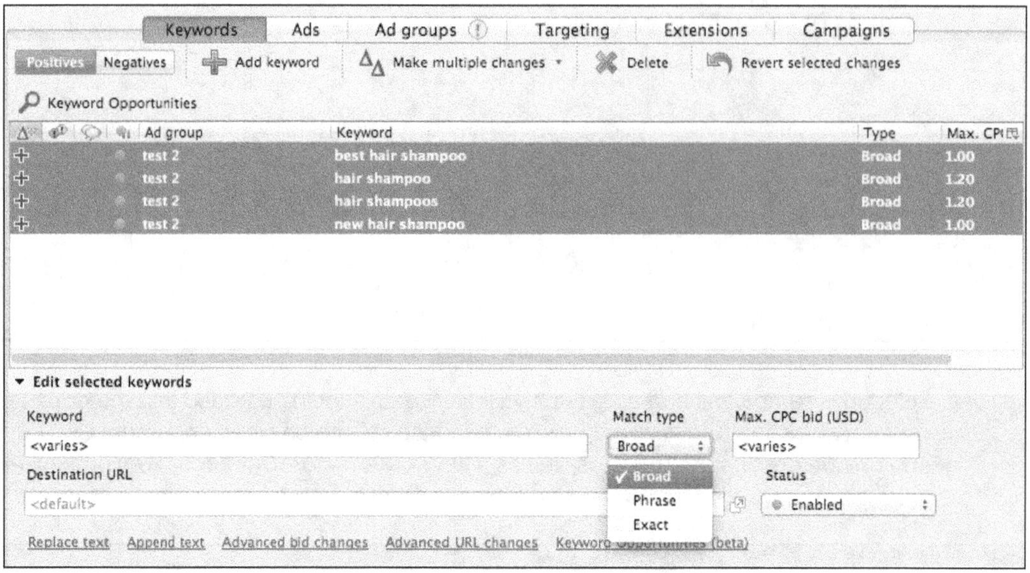

9. Review the changes highlighted in green and accept or reject them.
10. Click on **Post selected campaigns** to make the changes live in AdWords.

How it works...

AdWords Editor allows you to import keyword lists from a spreadsheet to add or update multiple keywords across your campaigns. You can review the new keywords before they go live, set unique bids, destination URLs, choose match types and keyword statuses, and post the new keywords to your AdWords account.

See also

- The *Getting started with AdWords Editor* recipe
- The *Copying campaigns or ad groups with AdWords Editor* recipe

Updating ads in bulk using AdWords Editor

Creating, editing, or pausing ads can be much more efficient through AdWords Editor, especially if you need to update many ads at once. For example, AdWords Editor allows you to update destination URLs across all of your campaigns and ad groups at once, without the need to click into individual campaigns and ad groups in your AdWords online interface.

Getting ready

Decide which campaigns and ad groups will need to be updated. If you would like to add new ads, prepare the new ad copy elements, and plan out where they should go.

You can add, edit, pause, or delete ads either manually or by importing a CSV spreadsheet. If you would like to use the spreadsheet option, download your current ads first. Go to **File**, choose **Export spreadsheet (CSV)**, and choose which parts of your account you'd like to work on. Click on **Save** to keep a copy of your CSV file. Make sure to preserve all of the exported columns as you work on your ads, so that the revised file remains compatible with AdWords Editor.

How to do it...

To update ads in bulk through AdWords Editor, follow these steps:

1. Open up AdWords Editor.
2. Click on **Get recent changes**.
3. Click on the **Ads** tab. Then, click on **+ Add text ad** to add a single ad to a specific campaign or ad group:

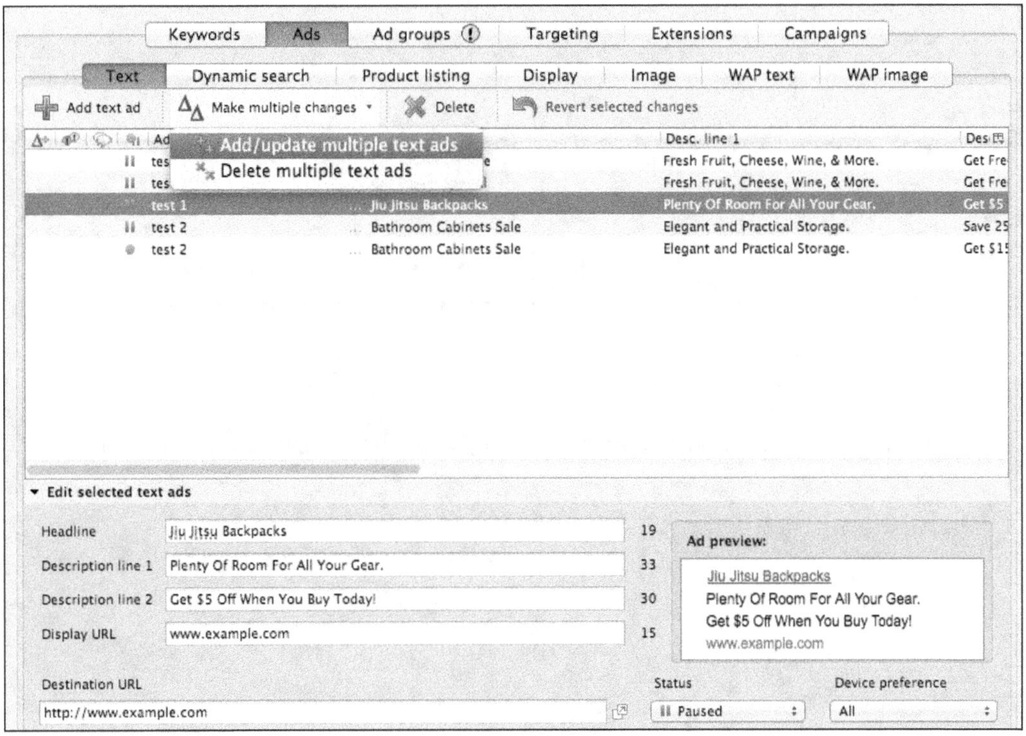

4. Click on **Make multiple changes** and choose **Add/update multiple text ads** to create ads in multiple campaign and ad groups. Write your headline, description line 1 and 2, and set a display and destination URL.
5. If you would like your new ads to replace your current ads, check the **Replace the entire contents of the destination ad groups with these text ads** checkbox:

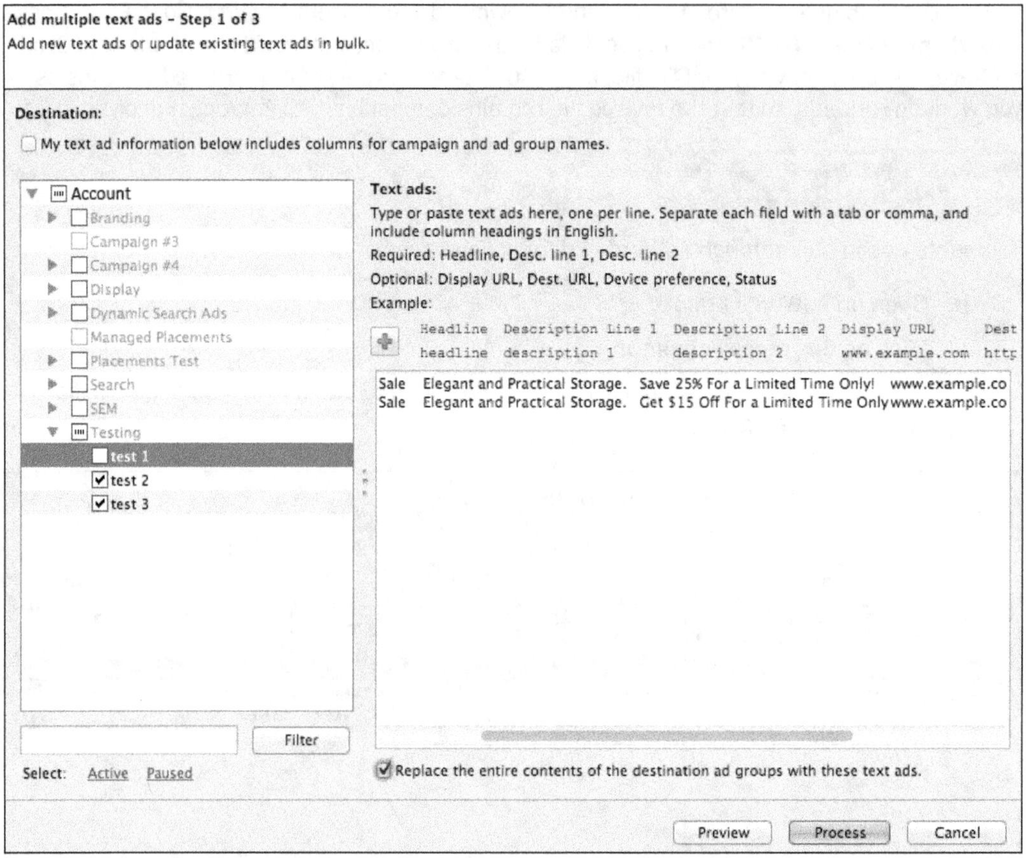

6. Click on **Process**, then on **Finish**, and review your new ads before posting them.

7. If you would like to update all ads containing specific URLs or phrases, use the search feature at the top-right corner of the tool above your **Ads** tab to filter out your desired parameters. Then, highlight the ads you want to update and make the necessary change, such as replacing text in the selected items:

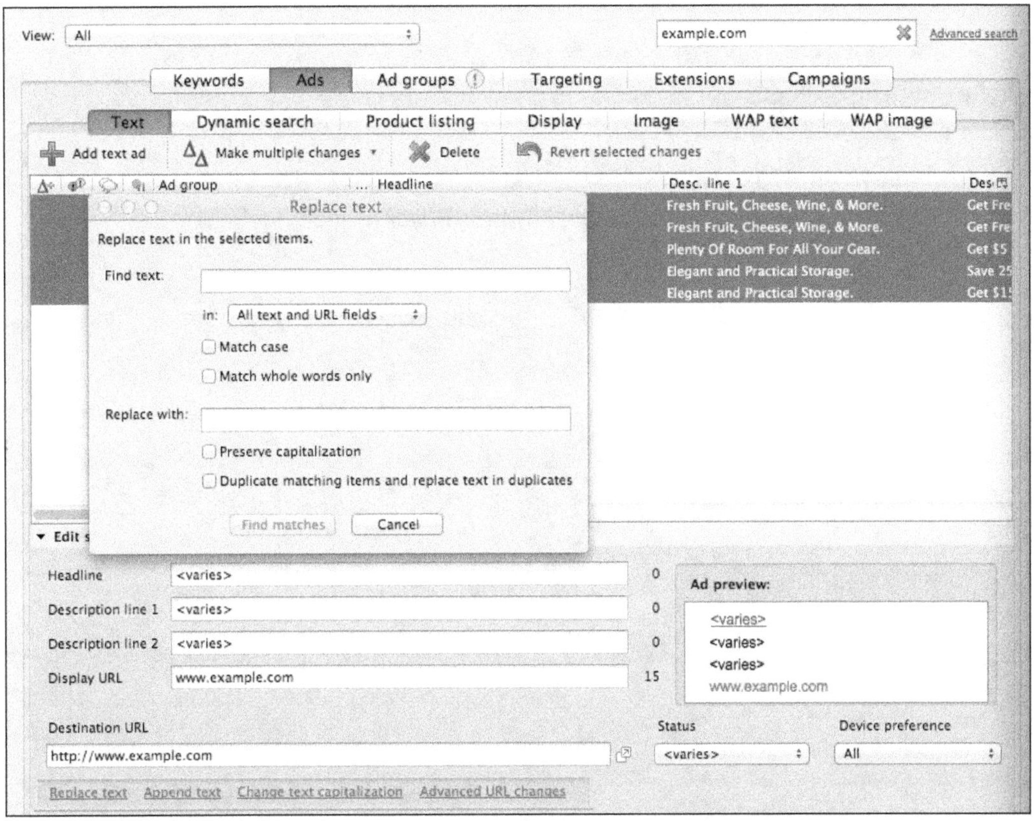

8. If you have an AdWords Editor-friendly CSV spreadsheet, where you made all of your desired edits, go to **File**, choose **Import CSV**, select **From file** and find your spreadsheet on your computer. Follow through the prompts to import and review your edits or additions.
9. Click on **Post changes** to make the new ads live in your AdWords account.

How it works...

AdWords Editor helps you add, edit, pause, or delete multiple ads across your campaigns. You can replace or append text, change text capitalization or edit URLs in bulk. The edits you make are saved offline, and you can choose to sync them and post to your account when they are ready to go live.

See also

- The *Getting started with AdWords Editor* recipe
- The *Adding keywords in bulk using AdWords Editor* recipe

Index

Symbols

A

B

N

O

P

Q

R

Thank you for buying
Advertising on Google:
The High Performance Cookbook

About Packt Publishing

Packt, pronounced 'packed', published its first book "*Mastering phpMyAdmin for Effective MySQL Management*" in April 2004 and subsequently continued to specialize in publishing highly focused books on specific technologies and solutions.

Our books and publications share the experiences of your fellow IT professionals in adapting and customizing today's systems, applications, and frameworks. Our solution-based books give you the knowledge and power to customize the software and technologies you're using to get the job done. Packt books are more specific and less general than the IT books you have seen in the past. Our unique business model allows us to bring you more focused information, giving you more of what you need to know, and less of what you don't.

Packt is a modern, yet unique publishing company, which focuses on producing quality, cutting-edge books for communities of developers, administrators, and newbies alike. For more information, please visit our website: `www.PacktPub.com`.

About Packt Enterprise

In 2010, Packt launched two new brands, Packt Enterprise and Packt Open Source, in order to continue its focus on specialization. This book is part of the Packt Enterprise brand, home to books published on enterprise software – software created by major vendors, including (but not limited to) IBM, Microsoft and Oracle, often for use in other corporations. Its titles will offer information relevant to a range of users of this software, including administrators, developers, architects, and end users.

Writing for Packt

We welcome all inquiries from people who are interested in authoring. Book proposals should be sent to `author@packtpub.com`. If your book idea is still at an early stage and you would like to discuss it first before writing a formal book proposal, contact us; one of our commissioning editors will get in touch with you.

We're not just looking for published authors; if you have strong technical skills but no writing experience, our experienced editors can help you develop a writing career, or simply get some additional reward for your expertise.

Google Visualization API Essentials

ISBN: 978-1-84969-436-0 Paperback: 252 pages

Make sense of your data: make it visual with the Google Visualization API

1. Wrangle all sorts of data into a visual format, without being an expert programmer
2. Visualize new or existing spreadsheet data through charts, graphs, and maps
3. Full of diagrams, core concept explanations, best practice tips, and links to working book examples

---

Instant Google Map Maker Starter [Instant]

ISBN: 978-1-84969-528-2 Paperback: 50 pages

Learn what you can do with Google Map Maker and get started with building your fi rst map

1. Learn something new in an Instant! A short, fast, focused guide delivering immediate results.
2. Understand the basics of Google map maker
3. Add places of interest such as your hotels, cinemas, schools, and more
4. Edit and update details for existing places

Please check **www.PacktPub.com** for information on our titles

[PACKT] enterprise
professional expertise distilled
PUBLISHING

Instant Google Drive Starter [Instant]

ISBN: 978-1-78216-048-9 Paperback: 82 pages

Use Google Drive to safely store and access your fi les online in the cloud using your web browser, phone, or tablet

1. Learn something new in an Instant! A short, fast, focused guide delivering immediate results.
2. Use Google Drive to safely store, organize, and access your files from anywhere with your computer, phone, or tablet
3. Upload files and folders from your hard drive into Google Drive

---

Google SketchUp for Game Design: Beginner's Guide

ISBN: 978-1-84969-134-5 Paperback: 270 pages

Create 3D game worlds complete with textures, levels, and props

1. Learn how to create realistic game worlds with Google's easy 3D modeling tool
2. Populate your games with realistic terrain, buildings, vehicles and objects
3. Import to game engines such as Unity 3D and create a first person 3D game simulation
4. Learn the skills you need to sell low polygon 3D objects in game asset stores

Please check **www.PacktPub.com** for information on our titles

www.ingramcontent.com/pod-product-compliance
Lightning Source LLC
LaVergne TN
LVHW080018210926
848481LV00011B/3050
* 9 7 8 1 8 4 9 6 8 5 8 4 9 *